THE STORY OF NORTH DEVON BOXING
Volume..Two

Part 1

Scrap-book

Some Of The Illustrations, Photographs And Press-Cuttings On The Following Pages Are Not Of The Best Quality. They Came To Me In A Very Rough State But Were Very Important To The Owners And To 'The Story of North Devon Boxing.' To Have Discarded Them Would Have Been A Tragedy And Would Probably Have Involved Me In A Few Bare Knuckle Street Fights!

Everything Is In Black And White As Mixing Colour Would Have Made The Asking Price Prohibitive.

Dick Brownson
NORTH DEVON

First published 2017
DICK BROWNSON
TORRIDON HOUSE
CHUBB ROAD
BIDEFORD
EX39 4HF
DEVON
U.K.
Telephone..
01237 700901
email..
brownson7@aol.com

ISBN: 978-0-9954686-9-6

THE STORY OF NORTH DEVON BOXING
Volume...2

DICK BROWNSON

Typeset, printed and bound by
DB Associates
PO BOX 55
BIDEFORD
EX39 3WB
DEVON
U.K.

NIKKI BROWNSON   CARL HAWKINS
SHADOWSMEDIA   HAWK MEDIA
Their expert advice with the technical problems
of compiling this book was invaluable.

My thanks to all the boxers and officials of NORTH DEVON CLUBS
who helped me during my extensive research for this book.

A big thank-you to the NORTH DEVON JOURNAL
and the
NORTH DEVON GAZETTE
for use of their reports on NORTH DEVON BOXING.

ACKNOWLEDGEMENTS

A local boxing historian is on the hunt for great tales from North Devon's past.

Dick Brownson is finishing off **his research for upcoming book** '*The Story of North Devon Boxing - Volume Two*', after the success of his first book.

Dick is keen for boxers past and present to get in touch with their photos, programmes, tickets, pamphlets and newspaper cuttings

Since the 1950s, there have been several clubs in North Devon: Barnstaple, Bideford, Combe Martin, Ilfracombe, Lynton and Lynmouth and South Molton, and Tiverton members have been actively involved in the local scene, too.

FINAL CALL
Local newspapers featured the above requests.

God Luck Dick

Carmen Basilio

DID IT NOT SEEM REAL?

BOXING GYM TALK

I have used the descriptive term TRAINER throughout this book and not the
modern word COACH. My old trainer heard this word used to describe his job
in the early 1950's and the result was a bout of hysterics from him.
'Another***Yankee word left here, coach is a posh name for a*** bus!'
That was the first time I heard the word COACH described in that way,
many times since.
Nevertheless, I'll stick with TRAINER!
PS...The British Boxing Board of Control Ltd., founded in 1929, STILL issue a
TRAINER licence.

BOXER SCRAP-BOOKS.

**These should always be compiled by a PROUD MOTHER or
SISTER ! They carefully cut out the newspaper reports on
the family member, adding the date and source. This is, sad to
say, a rare occurrence but I have included almost all
NEWSPAPER CUTTINGS that came in as they are of such
great interest and historical value to the boxing enthusiast.
Some are difficult to read but persevere, the content is well
worth the effort.**

PHOTOGRAPHS

A few group photos. have been duplicated in this book. This was
necessary because the only known image of a particular BOXER
was in that group and he has been identified.

Part 1

CONTENTS

FOLLOW UP FROM VOLUME...1

BARNSTAPLE ABC

Please read...
For DICK BROWNSON..DB
For the NORTH DEVON JOURNAL..NDJ
For the NORTH DEVON GAZETTE..NDG

INTRODUCTION

I was told by a writer friend that people rarely read an introduction so if I intended to do one, keep it brief. Now you have this book in front of you I hope you will spare a few minutes to read this.

For the past six years the North Devon Journal (NDJ) and North Devon Gazette (NDG) have run requests from me for photographs..newspaper cuttings..programmes..posters or anything of interest from boxers and officials of all the NORTH DEVON BOXING CLUBS. Apart from attending boxing tournaments, I also visited all the clubs mentioned in this book, some many times, asking for anything about their club and past and present members. Some responded magnificently, others proved hard work.

So if you, a relative or friend are not mentioned in this book it was not through lack of effort on my part.

Volume..1 took much longer to research and write due mainly to the fact that over ninety per cent of all people featured in it were dead. With Volume..2 it was the opposite state of affairs and I could talk to a great many boxers and officials about their careers and memories of bygone days.

In the early days after the 1939-45 War local newspapers rarely contained many photographic images. If your picture appeared in a newspaper it was an event that generally resulted in a family reunion! I never remember seeing a camera in any gym and only occasionally at a boxing show. Now with Social Media Sites people are familiar with mass personal exposure but all that can vanish with the press of a button.

If Volume..2 resembles a massive scrap-book I am happy to rest with that description, at least it will not disappear into orbit when the covers are closed!

All captions are my work and a particular comment or personal opinion is noted by my initials, DB.

Should any error in spelling personal names occur I profoundly regret this as I have paid special attention to this area of writing.

In group photographs where doubt existed on identification, I have left it blank.

Volume..2 covers the period from 1950 to June 2016.

The responsibility for all the content of this book is mine alone.

Dick Brownson,
Bideford,
North Devon.

THE STORY OF NORTH DEVON BOXING
Volume..1

FOLLOW-UP

A BIG THANKYOU to the following people for their interest in VOLUME..1 and their contribution to this FOLLOW-UP.

JUDITH CASEY

BARBARA SENIK

SAMMY WREY

JILL GREEN

PETRA HICKS

FRIENDS OF LOU ASHMAN

JOHN WHITLOCK

TONY REED

PHIL COX

JILL and BILLY CAMPBELL

VERONICA and DAVID POWE

BOB SYMONDS

...and to the many who made telephone calls and left interesting information, also those who posted items to me, all anonymous.

Left: MICKEY
KIELY'S BOXING
'BOOTH.'
Photo courtesy of
the University of
Sheffield

Below: BERNARD McKEOWEN'S BOOTH. Wrestling was now an added feature.
This photograph was taken not long before it finally closed for good.

Photo courtesy of the University of Sheffield

THE BARNSTAPLE AMATEUR BOXING CLUB

AMATEUR BOXING TOURNAMENT
(Under A.B.A. Rules)

In aid of

The Royal Society for the Prevention of Cruelty to Animals

at the

PANNIER MARKET, BARNSTAPLE

on

Monday, December 10th, at 7-30 p.m.

The Trophies will be presented by

LADY WREY

OFFICIALS

Officials appointed by Devon, Dorset and Cornwall A.B.A.

Timekeeper : Mr. J. Easton (Barnstaple)

M.C.: Capt. Leeming, R.E.M.E.

Hon. Medical Officer : Dr. R. M. J. Harper, M.A., M.D.

PROGRAMME 3d.

WALTER 'TINY' GREEN with an unidentified boxer who fought in 1951 on one of the AMATEUR TOURNAMENTS in BARNSTAPLE PANNIER MARKET.

VOLUME....1

Three Rounds Contest

LEN HARVEY v. OTTO SENIK

Apollo   Bideford

OTTO SENIK

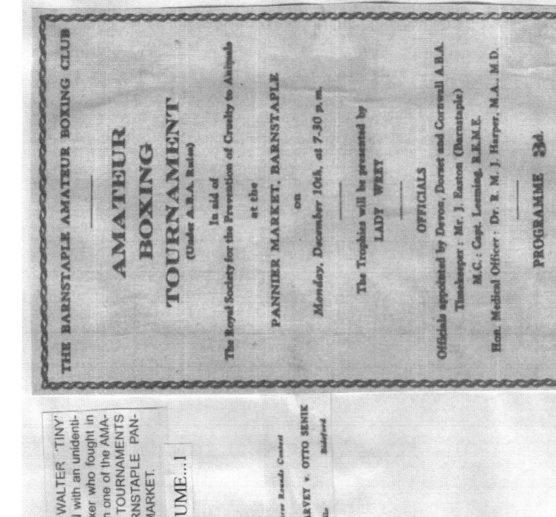

Mystery boxer identified.

12

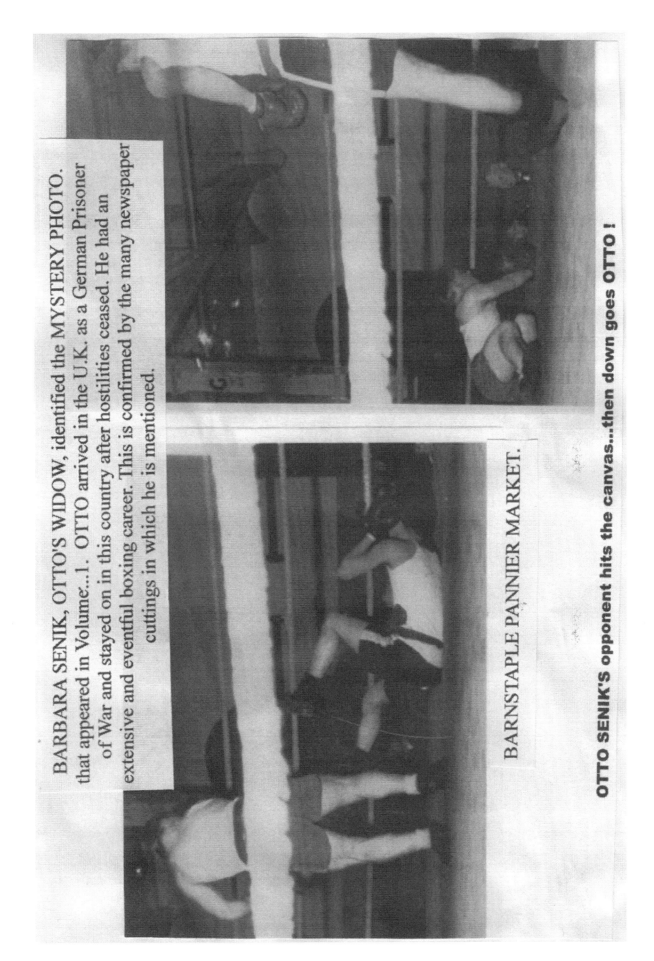

BARBARA SENIK, OTTO'S WIDOW, identified the MYSTERY PHOTO. that appeared in Volume...1. OTTO arrived in the U.K. as a German Prisoner of War and stayed on in this country after hostilities ceased. He had an extensive and eventful boxing career. This is confirmed by the many newspaper cuttings in which he is mentioned.

BARNSTAPLE PANNIER MARKET.

OTTO SENIK'S opponent hits the canvas...then down goes OTTO !

JOHN WILLIAMS of APPLEDORE...
still looking formidable !

JOHN WILLIAMS

JOHN WILLIAMS of APPLEDORE
chats to friend,
John Henry 'SONNY' WHITLOCK,
perhaps about his exploits in the
BOXING RING, LONG LONG AGO.

TOM, JOE and FRED POW

The TOM POW MEMORIAL PLATE donated to the CLUB by JILL CAMPBELL, TOM'S DAUGHTER.

THEIR FIGHTING DAYS OVER...
TOM POW, JOE POW, FRED POW.

FRED POWE'S B.B.B.of C. licence.

The format has hardly changed in over 80 years.

JILL CAMPBELL presenting Trophies at a
BIDEFORD COLLEGE SHOW

Always there when needed...

BILLY CAMPBELL does the job!

VERONICA POWE
presents
TROPHIES at a BIDEFORD COLLEGE SHOW.

DAVID POWE presents Trophies at a BIDEFORD COLLEGE SHOW.
The present generation of the POWE FAMILY continue to be ardent
supporters of LOCAL BOXING

Legendry boxer JIMMY JURY, DB, Boxing historian BOB SYMONDS.

JIMMY JURY, BOB SYMONDS, HAL BAGWELL.

JIMMY and HAL ham it up for the camera. Years before in was a much more SERIOUS BUSINESS in the RING.

NORTH DEVON ADVERTISER

SHOVE-HAPENNY FINALS

Second prize winner Angelo Valsechhi and singles champion Tom Stribling (right) receive their trophies from Jimmy Jury.

Jimy Jury, the well known Barnstaple boxer of the 1930's and 40's presented the trophies to the winners of the Barnataple Shove ha-penny Summer league at the finals and presentation night held recently at the Royal Exchange. The Stags Head team were the League winners, with The Royal Exchange in second position. Winner of the singles competition was Tom Stribling, representing the Royal Exchange, with Angelo of the Horse and Groom second.

JIMMY presents Prizes at the ROYAL EXCHANGE PUB, BARNSTAPLE.

EXPRESS & ECHO, Saturday, November 13, 1993

EDDIE COX

Return match ends drought

TONIGHT'S return of professional boxing to the area ends a break of some 30 or 40 years.

But the North, Mid and East Devon areas were not always such a boxing desert. In fact there used to be so much going on round here that much of it was not reported in the press, *writes KEITH TAYLOR.*

Professional fighting was at its peak in the 1920s and 30s and there were several local boxers whose reputation spread throughout the South West and even further afield. But World War II effectively ended their careers and, although it carried on after the war it was never as successful again.

One man who knew many of the old fighters, although not old enough to have seen them in action, is Dick Brownson, North Devon's "Mr Boxing".

Dick, currently a promoter, manager, trainer and regional board of control representative, used to run the Royal Exchange pub in Barnstaple. The pub was a mecca for boxers in North Devon, previously a hotbed of the sport.

"There were several Exeter fighters who rampaged through the South West between the wars," he said. "It was a very different sport in those days with much less control. Most of the boxers did no training. Fighting was their training. A lot of them would fight once a week, some even more.

"With the lack of press communications and coverage, a man could get away with fighting at, say, the Foresters Hall in Barnstaple and then having a bout in somewhere like Truro five days later, quite possibly against the same opponent if they were big names in the sport. It was not reported other than possibly in the local paper and nobody would be any the wiser.

"But don't think it wasn't hard. Those men were very competitive."

The big names in the Exeter area in those days were Kid Noble, son of famous pre World War I fighter Billy Noble, Bill Denning, Fred Rowland, who was heavyweight champ of the West of England in 1930, Tommy Webb and Eddie Cox, who was followed into the ring by his son Phil, who became a mainstay of the Exeter Amateur Club, and a third generation in Chris.

EXETER GREAT: The late Eddie Cox

King of ring had to watch out for mum

The secret life of Les

Seconds out! And Exeter's West of England Champion, Jack Cox (on the right) takes on the great Phil Scott in an exhibition bout at the County Ground Stadium, Exeter, during the 1920s.

THEY may seem fearless in the ring, but when it comes to facing a mother's anger, professional boxers can be less than braze — at least that was the case for one of Exeter's fighting stars of the 1930s.

For Les Martyn, now retired and living in Herbert Road, Exeter, had to appear under the name "Young Smith" because his mother disapproved of the sport.

He used to have to explain his cuts and bruises as the results of accidents at the building site where he was working; and although his mother eventually discovered the secret, the name "Young Smith" had already become too well known to change.

Now in his retirement, after working in the building trade and later the funeral business, Les has a fascinating collection of posters and other memorabilia from the years when prize fighting was one of Britain's leading spectator sports.

And with unemployment as high as it was, people without work formed a large part of the audience at tournaments. In fact, an event on October 24, 1932, was one of several promoted by the Exeter Branch of the Devon Unemployed Association, which — the programme tells us — any unemployed or employed person could join for the price of one penny per week.

The programme also shows that the master of ceremonies for the evening was Jack Cox, who died only recently, and is still well-remembered by boxing enthusiasts as the West of England light-heavyweight champion during the late 1920s.

Les's collections includes many items relating to Cox, with the man's name emblazoned across the top of several tournament posters from events in Exeter, Brixham, and other parts of the country, during the 1920s.

Les himself also features on a number of the posters as Young Smith, often with a high billing, such as when he was pitted against his long-time friend and rival, the late Kid Noble.

And, although Young Smith and friends are not seen in the ring any more, with Les's fascinating collection of memorabilia, it is easy to imagine those between-the-wars years when boxing was one of Devon's best-loved sports.

Drinks in — for some of Exeter's greatest fighters: Front row (left to right) — Arthur Brown, Kid Noble, Bill Denning, and Young Smith; at rear — Eddie Cox and Jack Cox.

These boxers often fought on NORTH DEVON PROMOTIONS.

PHIL COX, with his SON, CHRISTOPHER and BROTHER, CHRIS.
All three had eventful and successful
AMATEUR and PROFESSIONAL BOXING CAREERS.

BOXING NEWS

MAY 17, 1968

Cox Gets Another Chance

PHIL COX, the 24-year-old Exeter heavyweight, knocked up his first and second knuckles of his right hand, in outpointing **Paul Cassidy**, Bournemouth, at the Bedfordshire Sporting Club show, and disappointingly had to turn down a fight for **Mickey Duff**, at the Anglo-American Sporting Club, at the Hilton Hotel, against **Joe Bugner.**

Phil now gets his chance against Bugner at York Hall, Bethnal Green, next Tuesday.

The Exonian fighter will be moving to London shortly and signing up with one of the top London managers and training at the British Boxing Board of Control gymnasium, at the " Noble Art," Haverstock Hill, where he hopes to get really fit.

AMATEUR BOXING ASSOCIATION CHAMPIONSHIPS 1963

Organised by the Amateur Boxing Association

FRIDAY · APRIL 26th 1963

Semi-Finals from 4.0 p.m.
FINALS from 8.0 p.m. (approx)

OFFICIAL
PROGRAMME
ONE
SHILLING

EMPIRE POOL & SPORTS ARENA

WEMBLEY

CHRIS COX lost on POINTS to MURPHY,
a hotly disputed decision.
JIMMY ISAAC lost on POINTS to PACKER.
TONY BROGAN lost on POINTS to DAVIES.

AMATEUR BOXING ASSOCIATION

Semi-finals and Finals

(from 4.0 p.m.)   (at 8.0 p.m. approx.)

3 ROUNDS OF 3 MINS. EACH

Semi-final Winners

Silver Cup at full A.B.A. Value
for winners and runners-up.
Final Winners

FLYWEIGHT (8 st.) Holder: M. I. Pye
1. M. LAUD (St. Ives and District A.B.C.) Huntingdonshire
2. K. TATE (Rothwell Colliery A.B.C.) North Eastern Counties
3. B. FOXWELL (Rootes A.B.C.) Midland Counties
4. L/Cpl. F. REA (Army B.A.)
} Final Bout 1

BANTAMWEIGHT (8 st. 7 lb.) Holder: P. Benneyworth
5. B. PACKER (Dartford A.B.C.) Southern Counties
6. J. JONES (Plean A.B.C.) Scotland
7. J. ISAAC (Barnstaple A.B.C.) Devon, Dorset & Cornwall
8. Pte. J. MORRISON (Army B.A.)
} Final Bout 2

FEATHERWEIGHT (9 st.) Holder: W. T. Wilson
9. W. T. WILSON (Barking A.B.C.) London
10. E. ARMSTRONG (Ayr Y.M.C.A.) Scotland
11. A. J. RILEY (Rootes A.B.C.) Midland Counties
12. M/E. M. FRAMPTON (Royal Navy B.A.)
} Final Bout 3

LIGHTWEIGHT (9 st. 7 lb.) Holder: B. Whelan
13. B. ANDERSON (Middle Row, A.B.C.) London
14. W. BRESLIN (Litherland A.B.C.) North Western Counties
15. K. COOPER (Kyrle Hall A.B.C.) Midland Counties
16. Pte. B. O'SULLIVAN (Army B.A.)
} Final Bout 4

LIGHT-WELTER (10 st.) Holder: L/Cpl. B. Brazier
17. L. D. O'CONNELL (Fitzroy Lodge A.B.C.) London
18. R. McTAGGART (Kelvin A.B.C.) Scotland
19. L. McATEER (Buckley A.B.C.) Wales
20. L/Cpl. B. BRAZIER (Army B.A.)
} Final Bout 5

WELTER (10 st. 8 lb.) Holder: J. Pritchett
21. R. CHARLES (West Ham A.B.C.) London
22. J. MALCOLM (Sparta A.B.C.) Scotland
23. J. PRITCHETT (Bingham & Dist. A.B.C.) Midland Counties
24. R/O. 2 A. E. PHEBY (Royal Navy B.A.)
} Final Bout 6

LIGHT-MIDDLE (11 st. 2 lb.) Holder: Vacant
25. S. PEARSON (Cowes Medina A.B.C.) Southern Counties
26. A. WYPER (Witchknowe A.B.C.) Scotland
27. E. AVOTH (Victoria Park A.B.C.) Wales
28. Cook A. HAMILTON (Royal Navy B.A.)
} Final Bout 7

MIDDLE (11 st. 11 lb.) Holder: A. I. Matthews
29. E. J. LONGHURST (Dartford A.B.C.) Southern Counties
30. A. J. MATTHEWS (Litherland A.B.C.) N. W. Counties
31. L. SAMUELS (Wolverhampton A.B.C.) Midland Counties
32. Pte. E. LOFTHOUSE (Army B.A.)
} Final Bout 8

LIGHT-HEAVY (12 st. 10 lb.) Holder: Vacant
33. D. POLLARD (Fitzroy Lodge A.B.C.) London
34. B. MURPHY (Chorley Boys' Club) North Western Counties
35. C. S. COX (Exeter A.B.C.) Devon, Dorset & Cornwall
36. L/Cpl. T. MENZIES (Army B.A.)
} Final Bout 9

HEAVY (any weight) Holder: L/Pat R. Dryden
37. J. TAYLOR (Polytechnic A.B.C.) London
38. R. DAVIES (Droylsden A.B.C.) North Western Counties
39. A. BROGAN (Bideford A.B.C.) Devon, Dorset & Cornwall
40. Cpl. R. D. SANDERS (Royal Navy B.A.)
} Final Bout 10

Even allowing for the disappointing results, it was a
GREAT ACHIEVEMENT in the days when ALL GREAT BRITAIN
entered BOXERS for the NATIONAL CHAMPIONSHIPS.

MERVYN 'MEL' GREEN

Tributes for Mel who 'wrote his own rule book'

BY MARK JENKIN
mjenkin@northdevonjournal.co.uk

FRIENDS and family paid tribute to Mervyn "Mel" Green, a respected North Devon sportsman and entrepreneur who died aged 79.

As a young man growing up in Barnstaple he was well known as a talented footballer and amateur boxer.

Mel later showed his foresight as a businessman in the 1970s when he founded the first cosmetic surgery clinic in Europe.

Working with a colleague, he patented a water-saving valve for toilets known as Decim8 and last year became a published author.

Mel's wife, Jill, described her husband as a "true entrepreneur" who had made the journey from "rags to riches".

"He could speak comfortably to the man washing the windows of your house as well as sitting down with men for boardroom meetings," she said. "He had that connection through all levels."

Born on December 20, 1934 in Barnstaple, Mervyn was one of 10 children.

At Barnstaple Secondary School, he set a record for scoring 120 goals in a football season.

The Green family founded Barnstaple Boxing Club and Mel gained a reputation as a talented amateur, along with his brothers, including Walter "Tiny" Green, who became professional.

As a footballer, he represented Barnstaple and Ilfracombe Town. After having a trial with Tottenham Hotspur, he later signed with Derby County as a professional.

Having served an apprenticeship at Vanstones in Barnstaple he qualified as a carpenter and joiner.

When Mel married his first wife, Nora, the couple moved to her home town of Derby and had three children, Kevin, Rachel and Deborah.

After serving two years' national service in the RAF, mainly at RAF Stafford, he then qualified as an architect and draughtsman.

Mel turned his attention to various business ventures, making money in construction and real estate and, after his marriage to Nora ended, spotting potential in cosmetic surgery.

Based in Nottingham, Mel's Sherwood Court clinic became the industry's European centre of excellence with stars such as John Wayne and David Niven among its clients.

He appeared on national television and radio lobbying for properly recognised qualifications for those practising cosmetic surgery.

Mel assisted the Margaret Thatcher government in implementing changes to the 1984 Nursing Homes Act.

In 1984, he met Jill and within two years they were married. The couple started life together with Jill's son and daughter Christian and Anneliese, in Derby.

Mel and Jill were drawn together by their love of music and he admired singers like Frank Sinatra, Danny Kaye and Gene Kelly.

In 1995, they moved to Instow and became involved in local amateur dramatics. They made a film together called The Passion and worked with a touring German film company covering the works of Rosamunde Pilcher.

Mel became chairman of the Musical Comedy Society and worked with Barnstaple Young Generation.

After years working on his book, Mel fulfilled another ambition when his novel A Bad Penny was published by Amazon for Kindle in May.

Since undergoing spinal surgery in 2008, Mel had not enjoyed good health. He passed away on February 18.

A service to celebrate his life was held at North Devon Crematorium on March 7 when mourners sang Mel's favourite songs, including The Ugly Duckling by Danny Kaye and My Way by Frank Sinatra.

"Everybody came out smiling instead of weeping and wailing," said Jill.

"He wrote his own rule book, did Melly – and lived by it."

● To find out more about A Bad Penny or investing in Decim8, Jill can be contacted by email, msgreen@decim8.co.uk.

■ MEL GREEN: A full and varied life.

JILL and MERVYN 'MEL' GREEN
at a BIDEFORD ABC SHOW.

Always staunch supporters.
JILL presents Trophies.

WALTER 'TINY' GREEN
A
LEGEND

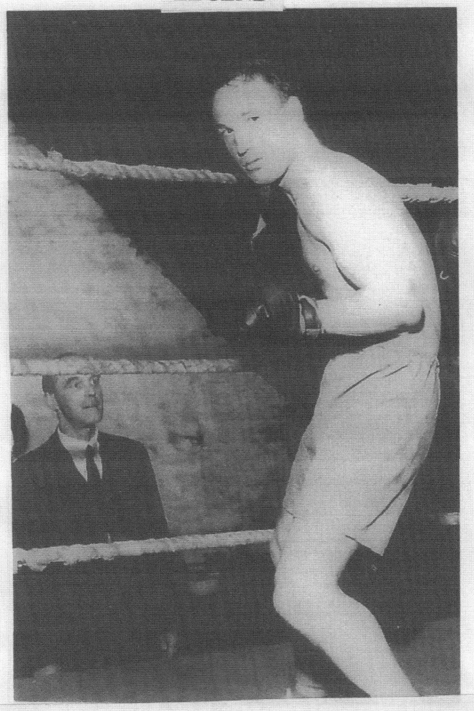

WALTER 'TINY' GREEN was such an important figure in NORTH DEVON BOXING and the formation of BARNSTAPLE ABC, his contribution, and that of his family, can never be over-stated.

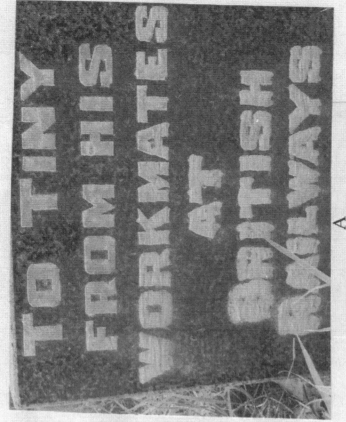

A
FLOWER VASE HOLDER
from his workmates at
BRITISH RAILWAYS.

TREASURED
MEMORIES
OF
A
DARLING HUSBAND & FATHER
WALTER THOMAS GREEN,
DIED APRIL 6TH 1970,
AGED 50.

SAFE IN THE ARMS OF JESUS.
UNTIL WE MEET AGAIN.

EDITH GREEN
WIFE OF WALTER
DIED 7 FEB 2005
AGE 81

The
GRAVE of LOCAL BOXING LEGEND,
WALTER 'TINY' GREEN
in
BEAR STREET CHURCHYARD,
BARNSTAPLE.

REG and FRANK REED

TONY REED, son of boxer REG REED with DB in the COACHING INN, SOUTH MOLTON.

PROFESSIONAL BOXER REUNION.

DAI MORGAN, REG REED, FREDDIE COURTNEY,
FRANK REED, BERT GRIFFITHS, EDDIE GILL.
Bert Griffiths aka Bert Monk was a MANAGER and PROMOTER.

REG REED, brother to boxer FRANK REED from SOUTH MOLTON.

Whatever happened to all the other boxers from SOUTH MOLTON?
In the 1920's and 30's there were some good ones and they boxed
regularly on NORTH DEVON SHOWS.

Licence No. 20054.
Valid up to and including
the....................................
Sig,.....................................

LOU ASHMAN

LOU had around a dozen bouts as a PROFESSIONAL in the 1930's and 1940's but also boxed under different names (most boxers at less than CHAMPIONSHIP LEVEL have done so, no fight...no money!) Promoters turned a 'blind eye' to this practice, they needed bouts for their show.
I've traced some more fights for him as MAXIE ASHMAN and also MAX ASH, suffice it to say he had an eventful boxing career.
Settling in NORTH DEVON his main interest became MOTOR CYCLES, which is much more clearly documented!

LOU ASHMAN and his father H.C.ASHMAN.

ALL research material was donated by
FRIENDS of LOU ASHMAN.

LOU ASHMAN

LOU with a YOUNG HOPEFUL?

MAXIE ASHMAN

LOU, KEN AYRES, PHILIP PETHERICK.

LOU ASHMAN

LOU on a TRIUMPH 500cc during MOTORCYCLE TRIALS.

LOU, second from the right in a FORMIDABLE LINE-UP!

HENRY CLIFFORD ASHMAN

I received a large number of telephone calls about
LOU ASHMAN
after the publication of Volume..1. He was a very popular man.
One caller informed me that his father had survived the sinking of
the LUSITANIA in May 1915 and had helped in the rescue of
survivors. Although HENRY CLIFFORD ASHMAN
was not a native of NORTH DEVON or a BOXER his life and
account of the LUSITANIA tragedy intrigued me and is worth
telling.
BRIEFLY, THIS IS HIS STORY.

RMS LUSITANIA

LUSITANIA

*Cunard S.S. Co.; 1907; J. Brown & Co.; 30,396 tons; 762·2×
87·8×56·6; 68,000 i.h.p.; 25·85 knots; turbine engines.*

On the outbreak of the First World War the *Lusitania* continued to
maintain the service between Liverpool and New York, without
incident until the spring of 1915, completing five round trips in all.
On May 1st of that year there appeared in the New York newspapers
an ominous advertisement, couched in the form of an official state-
ment. It was remarked upon at the time that this advertisement was
inserted at very short notice, for the *Lusitania* was scheduled to sail
from New York on the same morning.

The advertisement ran as follows:—

'Travellers intending to embark for an Atlantic voyage are
reminded that a state of war exists between Germany and her
allies and Great Britain and her allies; that the zone of war
includes the water adjacent to the British Isles, that in accord-
ance with the formal notice given by the Imperial German
Government, vessels flying the flag of Great Britain or any of
her allies are liable to destruction in those waters; and that
travellers sailing in the war-zone in ships of Great Britain
and/or any of her Allies do so at their own risk.'

IMPERIAL GERMAN EMBASSY
WASHINGTON, D.C.,
April 22nd, 1915

Despite this warning, the total number on board when the ship
left New York was 1,959, of whom 1,257 were passengers and 702
crew, the commander being Capt. W. J. Turner. The voyage across
the Atlantic was uneventful but on approaching the Irish coast the
captain was warned by wireless of the presence of German submarines. For some time the entrance to St. George's Channel had
been a cause of much anxiety to the British Admiralty, for the
patrols available were weak and scattered. In the week of the
Lusitania's crossing one ship was attacked and three others sunk in
this area, and reports of submarines lying off the coast were too
frequent and too detailed to permit of the danger being taken
lightly. Instructions wirelessed to ship-masters were to avoid
headlands and steer a mid-channel course. The first warning reached
the *Lusitania* on the 5th and she was again warned on the 6th and
7th. On approaching St. George's Channel double look-outs were
posted and speed reduced to 18 knots so that the vessel should not
arrive at the Mersey Bar before the tide permitted her to cross. At

12.40 p.m. on the 7th she altered course and closed Brow Head in
order to fix her position. Soon afterwards another warning was
received stating that submarines had been sighted 20 miles off
Coningbeg. Captain Turner thereupon decided to keep inshore until
a last warning, reporting that submarines had been sighted south of
Cape Clear, 30 miles astern, caused him to believe that the danger
was now past and he returned to his former course.

At 2.15 p.m., when the *Lusitania* was about ten miles south of the
Old Head of Kinsale, she was struck by a torpedo between the
third and fourth funnels. A second and less violent explosion,
which may have occurred in the boiler room, came shortly after.
The turbines stopped immediately and the ship continued under
way until she sank, which together with an increasing list to star-
board considerably hindered the launching of the boats. At
2.26 p.m. the *Lusitania* foundered, having remained afloat for less
than 15 minutes from the time of being torpedoed.

Of those on board no fewer than 1,198 were drowned, including
291 women, 94 children and 124 American citizens. Altogether
761 persons, including Capt. Turner were saved, either by the ship's
boats or by the trawler *Bluebell*, which arrived in time to rescue
many from the water.

The submarine which fired the torpedo was the *U-20*, commanded
by Capt.-Lt. Schwieger, who entered in his log that he discharged
one torpedo. This record must be set against that of several
witnesses on the *Lusitania* who asserted that two torpedoes were
fired, and it can only be assumed that the second explosion occurred
within the ship.

The reactions throughout the world on receipt of the news of the
torpedoing of the *Lusitania* were profoundly damaging to the
German cause, and it did much to alienate the sympathy of neutral
nations, as well as to arouse a resentment in the United States
which undoubtedly influenced that nation to enter the war on the
side of the Allies at a later date.

THE SHEPTON MALLET JOURNAL

FRIDAY, MAY 14, 1915.

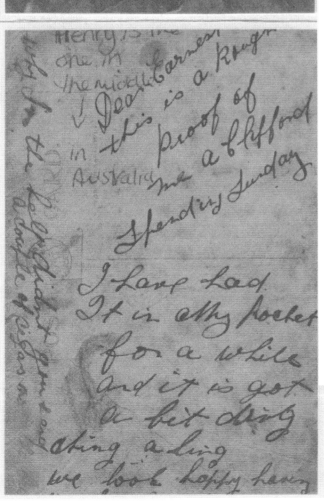

SHEPTONIAN'S ESCAPE.
VALUE OF BEING A SWIMMER.
INSTRUCTIONS NEEDED IN THE USE OF LIFEBELTS.

Mr. Henry G. Ashman, of the Beacon farm, Shepton Mallet, had a surprise, welcome in a double sense, in a telegram he received from his son Clifford, stating that he was a survivor of the Lusitania. He knew that his son was contemplating a return home to England to assist him on his farm, in the absence of his brother at the front with the North Somerset Yeomanry, but he had no idea that he had started, or what boat he was travelling by. Sunday afternoon Mr. Ashman, jun., arrived in Shepton Mallet by the first train from Bristol, between three and four o'clock, and made his way up the familiar road to the old home on Mendip, only too glad to reach its shelter again after a varied and widely travelled experience, of which the most exciting incident came at the close of the voyage across the Atlantic. Mr. Clifford Ashman has tried farming in the West, and other occupations, before settling down as a copper miner at Butte City, Montana. Here he has held various positions, above and under ground. When he left, he was in charge of the magazine and explosives above and under ground, handing them out to the men charging with firing the shots, and supervising and assisting where necessary. He "figured out" that he would start about the 15th April, but had no knowledge how the boats were running. His enquires led him to believe that it might be possible to catch the Lusitania, and he travelled to New York by the Northern Pacific Railway to Chicago, and thence by the Lake Erie Railway. When he reached New York, he found he had about a couple of days to spare, which he spent in the city, and then took his berth aboard the Lusitania. He had cut the time finely, and feared he had missed the boat, but found when on board that she was due to leave a couple of hours later. She ran down the river all right, and outside handed mails to a British vessel they met there, and the only one (except an auxiliary cruiser), that he saw till after the explosions and wreck of the liner. There was little incident crossing the Atlantic, except that the voyage was a particularly pleasant one. Everyone had noticed the warning of the Germans, and he was informed that a number of registered letters which were being delivered to passengers, were warnings and advice to them to change their vessel, and go by another route. Many of these were torn up, it is stated, and thrown away. They sailed at 10 a.m. on May 1st, and were clear of the dock by noon. Then they were stopped by a British cruiser, and the ship's papers examined, and afterwards proceeded on the voyage.

HENRY CLIFFORD ASHMAN

Mr. Ashman did not actually see the ship go down, though he found that it had done so from the suction of the water, which he was able to avoid. He saw a number of boats which went down with the ship return to the surface. Many of those were upside down, but a few were right way up. They appeared to have been cut loose. He made for one that had righted, and was the first to clamber into her, and was then able to assist others in. Some of these were smothered with soot and dirt from the funnels of the vessel, but Mr. Ashman escaped this. They tried to get one or two ladies close by who were floating on the water, and in this they succeeded. There were some who could swim a little, but not more, apparently, than about one in four or five. One woman whom they were able to rescue had a couple of little kids with her, he said. A third child had been drowned. The people in the boat who could swim did not hesitate to plunge in again to rescue others, and in this way several lives were saved. Others who appeared to be too dangerous in gripping at their rescuers, were saved by passing out oars for them to grasp. Two, or three oars were in some cases lashed together to reach them. Three boats got together and lashed up and assisted in the work of rescue, and remained in company, in that way. Some of the poor fellows were in a terrible plight from injuries received. Many clung to the bottoms of the upturned boats, and a few were rescued from these. One young fellow who could swim a little had his legs torn about, and skinned, and others had had injuries through coming in contact with the wreckage, or in their removal from the ship. Several of those on board were young men coming over to England to visit friends, and with the intention of joining the army.

Mr. Ashman's party were on the boat for some hours. "I figure they picked us up about six o'clock," he said, "and we got into Queenstown somewhere between ten and eleven. The telegram I sent home at once, as soon as I got ashore. It is timed as sent out at 1.20, but I handed it in very much before that, I am sure." Amongst the persons pulled out of the water was a lady, quite dead. She was evidently a saloon passenger, as she had a large number of very valuable rings on her finger, and her clothing was of the very best. Several of the boats seemed to have capsized. Amongst the men in one of the three boats was a doctor, and his services were very valuable in saving some of the lives of those who were almost gone, "He knew how to pump the water out of him, and the air in."

On the 9th they ran into a belt of fog, and slowed down. After that, though the fog was lifting, and they could see land, though not very plainly, he made up his mind to go below to his berth, and lie down and have a read. He threw himself down in an old pair of trousers and shirt, and was comfortably employed when the explosion occurred. Finding their vessel starting to list he went up to the upper decks, and heard that she had been torpedoed. He had a look round and helped in whatever way he could for a time. He saw the first boat lowered. Something went wrong, and it was, split into matchwood. The stewards were busy with the passengers, providing them with lifebelts, and fixing them on, but many did not know the way the belts should be fixed, and passengers put them on upside down, and in such ways that later he saw many floating in the water feet upwards. They had had apparently no instructions in the use of the belts, though there were ample provided. Those who were in the saloons had a worse chance than those ... who were below ... sleeping places, chiefly, whilst others (and especially the first and second class passengers), were evidently of opinion that the ship would not sink. The vessel, however, settled down rapidly, and as soon as he found the list become more pronounced, Mr. Ashman jumped overboard, and swam for all he was worth to get clear of the vessel before the mast and funnels could strike him. He just succeeded in doing this. The time he struck the water, as shown by his watch, which he had set to ship's time, was 2.32. Whilst he was on board everybody seemed to be trying to do their best for the time, with one or two exceptions. One man appeared to be demented on the time, for he was rushing round with five lifebelts, with neither of which he would part. He may have been looking for relatives whom he could not find in the confusion which prevailed. There were a very great number of women and children. "One woman in our bunch had six," he remarked. He did not see any of these arrive at Queenstown. A few were still in their berths through sickness, but nearly everybody was able to be about the decks at the time the ship was destroyed.

Two men rescued were in a very bad state— one had his clothes torn off him; and was badly cut and scraped. They were, however, holding a woman up between them by the hair of her head the best they could, as they clung to some wreckage. They had had a terrible time. The woman proved to be dead. This party was seen about half an hour before the boat, Indian Empire, came and picked them up. One torpedo boat destroyer came out to their aid, but that was the first war vessel Mr. Ashman had seen this side of the Atlantic. Other vessels were in the distance, but he could not see what they were. The most of the vessels that came to the assistance of the Lusitania were trawlers.

Mr. Ashman landed in very scanty attire, but the Cunard company had orders given that their passengers were to be supplied at any place where they could get clothes, and he obtained sufficient to travel in. The people again and again showed them every kindness. No man could possibly wish for more kindness than they shown them than they received everywhere in Ireland. He was taken to Rosslare, and across to Fishguard, and reached Bristol via Cardiff, arriving home as stated soon after three o'clock Sunday afternoon. Amongst his fellow-travellers was a gentleman, who was coming over with his wife and three children, only one of whom was saved. Another party was a gentleman, his wife and brother-in-law, all of whom were saved.

There was one remarkable incident on the boat. A lady asked them to sing something to keep their spirits up, and a clergyman on board started one or two hymns. They also sang "Tipperary," and then went back to a hymn, but this was too much, and the singing had to be stopped on account of some of the women being in such an excited state. They also cheered and shouted, "Are we down," &c.—"No!!" and other like cries. The weather, at the time of the disaster, he says, was beautiful. It had cleared up wonderfully, and the sea was calm and almost motionless, which gave many of the people a better chance of rescue, and also aided those who could swim but a little. He had never in his experience of a good many voyages, long and short, known such beautiful weather at sea as it was in the afternoon, but all the morning it had been very foggy.

SAMMY WREY

SAMMY WREY in his ARMY DAYS.
He had a SPARRING SESSION with RANDOLPH TURPIN
when the CHAMPION BOXER toured GERMANY.

BACK in CIVVY STREET!

TOMMY LANGFORD, DB, SAMMY WREY.
The FUTURE LOOKS BRIGHT for TOMMY.
We are all shouting for him!

DB with former boxer, SAMMY WREY giving a look-over
to some of the research for Volume..2

SAMMY WREY with DB at a BOXING SHOW.

SAMMY is always ready to help out at BOXING SHOWS.
This was BEN OWEN'S last fight for BIDEFORD ABC
before joining the PROFESSIONAL RANKS.

REX CASEY

REX 'STRANGLER' CASEY in his heyday.

The Strangler kicks-in with punchy show

A Devon man whose strength and vice-like grip have earned him the name "The Strangler" all over the world, will soon put his skills to the test in his home town.

Rex Casey, boxer, wrestler, ex-mercenary, chef, and soldier of fortune, has turned promoter.

And he is staging one of the most spectacular Superfight occasions Barnstaple has ever seen.

Not only will he step into the ring at Queen's Hall, but so will other stars of the fight world, including Steven Cusak, of Barnstaple, Steve Dexter, a Royal Marine commando, and Plymouth's Derrek McManus.

The big fight is destined to be a Professional Kick-Boxing match between Peter Sullivan, a former pro-boxer, and John Smith, a Fifth Dan karate black belt, the former British champion.

The occasion is not the first in Barnstaple that Rex "Strangler" Casey has staged.

"I put on the first boxing tournament in Barnstaple 25 years ago," said Rex, who admits to being between 45 and 50.

But he doesn't look it. Daily workouts with light weights, a rowing machine, and the occasional jog, have kept him in trim despite the rigours of wrestling anywhere from Hong-Kong to Houston, and fighting as a mercenary in Vietnam or Africa.

"I don't do as much as I used to. I wasn't going to fight because I'd thought of giving it up. But there still seems to be some interest in me," said Rex, who was born in Paignton and brought up in Totnes.

In his time he has boxed for the Navy, for Devonport, and has been billed as representing England in countless bouts in the Far East, Australia, New Zealand and the United States.

He has fought in a promotion with Randolph Turpin, tried his hand at Cumberland and Westmorland wrestling, and is also skilled in the martial arts.

"Kick-boxing is amazing. It's going to prove very popular," he said.

Rex first came to Barnstaple after leaving the Navy, when he rolled up with a boxing booth on a travelling fair. Ever since then he has had very close connections with the town, and is well known by the locals.

"Quite often people come up to me and remember when I used to fight at Queen's Hall more than 20 years ago," he added.

Since then he has travelled across all five continents fighting in one way or another, and using his hands often in more delicate ways, as a chef.

"I used to do a lot of cooking. . . but not so much now, it's too much like hard work," he joked.

His latest venture, promoting Superfight Nights is partly in conjunction with Mr. John Smith of Plymouth, who is also taking part in the big event on May 6 at Queen's Hall.

REX CASEY

REX CASEY holding RAY PENFOLD JUNIOR at
'YOUNG RAY'S CHRISTENING.

RAY JUNIOR...some YEARS LATER!

At an EX-BOXERS REUNION, PHIL COX next to him.

REX CASEY

JUDITH CASEY with JANE BROWNSON in the ROYAL EXCHANGE PUB, BARNSTAPLE. JANE checks the camera, before an
EX-BOXERS REUNION.

The bar packed with EX-BOXERS so into the old 'lounge bar' for a rest.

We all seem to be having a good time!
The ROYAL EXCHANGE PUB, BARNSTAPLE.

F.W. 'FLIPPER' STACEY.

Captioned in Volume..1 as 'TWO of the SULLIVAN BROTHERS SPARRING.' The BOXER on the RIGHT is in fact ERNEST STACY, JUDITH CASEY'S father. ERNEST was the son of the respected BARNSTAPLE BUSINESSMAN, F.W. 'FLIPPER' STACEY, proprietor of the QUEEN'S HOTEL.

REX and DB, a drink and a laugh about the 'OLD TIMES.'

An Iconic Photograph

JUDITH CASEY with close friends, legendary BOXING BOOTH FAIR-GROUND SHOWMEN, BERNARD McKEOWEN and MICKEY KIELY. Her HUS-BAND REX WORKED for THEM BOTH, as a BOXER and WRESTLER.

JUDITH entertains the FAMOUS FAIRGROUND DUO prior to the start of an EX- BOXER REUNION at the ROYAL EXCHANGE PUB, BARNSTAPLE.

SADNESS: *Fairground family mourns loss of businessman*

Tributes to boxing booth showman

Evening Herald, Thursday, June 22, 2000

■ by LOUISE YEARLING

A TRAVELLING showman from Plymouth who toured the country with his boxing booth has died at the age of 79.

Mickey Kiely's West of England Boxing Academy was recognised at fairgrounds across Britain.

He was the son of the fairground showman and a clairvoyant.

When his family stopped touring the country in the winter, he would go to the gym to train as a boxer.

From an early age he was determined to have his own boxing show, a wish he fulfilled when he married Phyllis Whitelegg, daughter of Tommy Whitelegg – a prominent showman in the West of England.

Ambitious

Mr Kiely's brother Jimmy said: "He was a person who enjoyed life and loved to be in the public eye. He wanted to see people enjoying themselves, which is why he took to the fairgrounds."

Mr Kiely's family settled in Plymouth just before the outbreak of the Second World War when he joined the Merchant Navy.

He returned to the city in the 1940s and, in partnership with his late brother Pat, opened two shoe repair shops.

With Phyllis by his side, they ran a shooting gallery at The Olympia in Union Street, an undercover funfair known as the "snake pit", which was owned by the Whitelegg family.

He would stand on the stairs of the booth with boxers on either side and challenge people to step forward and fight for a chance to win money.

Eventually, Mr Kiely left the partnership and bought his own boxing and wrestling show in the late 1950s.

Mr Kiely was a member of the Showmen's Guild of Great Britain and the British Boxing Board of Control.

Over the years, he had many quality fighters working for him including Rinty Monaghan, the former World Flyweight Champion.

He organised the first open air boxing show in Plymouth at the former Pennycross Sports Stadium and attracted professional boxers from across the country.

He was also president of the Devonport Boxing Club.

By the 1950s, Mr Kiely had launched the boxing booth which toured with the Whitelegg fair.

and, up until his death was president of the Mayflower Boxing Club. The great grandfather, who has four children, retired about 10 years ago and spent his time taking a bouncy castle to fetes in Plymouth.

He died on Friday of a heart attack. His brother Johnny said: "It was unbelievable how he was recognised.

"If he walked through town he would be stopped about 20 times by people saying hello. He left a mark wherever he went."

MICKEY KIELY

SHOWMAN: Mickey Kiely

'TEN BELLS' for a GREAT SHOWMAN!

WELL-KNOWN ATTRACTION: The West of England Boxing Academy

Photo. taken during a Get-To-Gether of
EX-BOXERS and LEGENDS from the BOXING WORLD
at the
ROYAL EXCHANGE PUB, BARNSTAPLE, early 1980's.

MICKEY KIELY'S BOXING BOOTH.

Standing, REX CASEY, DB. Seated left to right, FREDDIE COURTNEY, FREDDIE FEWINGS, RON TAYLOR, ESTHER McKEOWEN, BERNARD McKEOWEN, MICKEY KIELY.

51

REG HICKS

BOXING NEWS

World's Premier Fight Weekly

Glovely memories

I ENJOYED Dick Brownson's novel, *A Distant Friendly Party*, about a pro boxing gym in the 1950s, reviewed recently in the *Gazette*.

A great read that brought back memories for me as I was involved in boxing in those days and knew Dick quite well.

There has always been a strong affinity between boxing and villainy, and some people find both "trades" glamorous.

Ronnie and Reggie Kray were both ex-boxers and always invited us to the local café after training for a free meal when they visited the gym.

We had lots of invitations to parties and weddings, and it was at a reception that the story of Ronnie and his comment about the "lovely tulip buttonholes" came out; no one would tell him they were carnations!

Afterwards Dick owned nightclubs and was always seen with Terry Downes, the former middleweight champion.

We met again years later, when he was landlord of the Royal Exchange pub in Barnstaple, and I had many a yarn about the old times with him and Reg Hicks, another ex-boxer. Dick had remained close to boxing and still is today.

The fight game and the underworld have always gone hand in hand ... or should I say glove in glove!

Joe Adam
Barnstaple

NORTH DEVON
Gazette

Opinion

REG HICKS

REG with mother, EMILY.

Mr Reg Hicks, a well known man from the Woodhay area, died recently after a short illness, he was 63.

Although he finally lived in Devon, Mr Hicks was brought up locally and will be remembered by most for his love of sport, particularly boxing. Indeed, he would often take on all comers at the fairground in Newbury.

After completing his National Service in the Navy, Mr Hicks moved to London where he pursued his love of weightlifting. In 1961 he won the title of Body Builder for London and the Home Counties, along with many other contests. Latterly he was a long distance lorry driver.

He leaves a wife, Barbara, five daughter and three grandchildren.

REG was 'HARD MAN' from hard old times!

The
GRAVE of OLD PAL REG HICKS
in
BEAR STREET CHURCHYARD, BARNSTAPLE.

DAUGHTER,

PETRA HICKS with DB.

Foresters' Hall, Barnstaple

MONDAY, MARCH 31st, 1930,
at 8 p.m.

OFFICIAL PROGRAMME of

BOXING

PROCEEDS IN AID OF

YE BARUM LODGE R.A.O.B. (G.L.E.) RESTORATION FUND

OFFICIALS:

REFEREE   Bro. LEN D. HOOPER, R.N. (Rtd.)

TIMEKEEPER   Bro. JACK BELL, R.N. (Rtd.)

M.C.   Bro. BERT GRIFFITHS

DOCTOR IN ATTENDANCE   Dr. K. G. W. SAUNDERS,

WHIP   Bro. BERT GILBERT

ASSISTANT WHIP   Bro. JACK EASTON

SECONDS   Bros. J. LEWIS, W. BARROW and W. GILBERT W. SYMONS.

PRICE: TWO PENCE.

Charles Cann, Printer, Green-Lane, Barnstaple.

A LATE ARRIVAL programme.

OFFICIAL PROGRAMME.

Important Ten (2-Min.) Rounds Welterweight Contest

BERT TUBBS (Barnstaple)

v.

BILLY MOORE (Barnstaple)

Six (2-Min.) Rounds Contests.

TOM HARRIS v. JOE SULLIVAN
(Barnstaple)   (Barnstaple)

JIMMY JOY v. FRED TUCKER
(Bideford)   (Ilfracombe)

FRED BROOKS v. BERT BARTLETT
(Ilfracombe)   (Barnstaple)

Bruce PARKHOUSE v Arthur MERRETT
(Barnstaple)   (Barnstaple)

FRED ISAAC v. JACK CLEMENCE
(Barnstaple)   (Ilfracombe)

PLEASE NOTE.—The way to watch boxing is in silence. You can raise the roof between the rounds.

Note. The whole of the proceeds of this tournament are in aid of the Ye Barum Lodge R.A.O.B. (G.L.E.) Restoration Fund.

SOME GREAT OLD-TIME BOXERS ON THIS BILL.

A Great and Attractive Fifteen (2-Min.) Rounds Middleweight Contest.

BILLY NOBLE (Kemp's Hill, S. Wales)

Considered to be the best middleweight in Wales, and is open to meet any middleweight in Wales. Has defeated Billy Green, Micky Watts, Fred George, Dick Harry, Griff James, Alf Brooks, Jerry Maloney, Alex Foster, Billy Delaney, Boy Wills, Jack Morris, Red Pullen, Dicky Brown, Jack Josephs, Tod Nicholls, Shoeingsmith Fred Davies, Jack Marshall, and others. Has taken part in well over 100 contests.

v.

SONNY DOKE (Battersea, London)

Fought over 150 fights and won most of them against the best middleweights in the country. Has fought such men as Joe Bloomfield, Martin Jordan, Dixie Brown, Fred George, Battling Sullivan, Charlie McDonald, Lauri Raten, Joe Lowther, Dudley Kid Harris, Rocky Knight, Eddie Success, Seaman Hardy, Sid Chilton, Norman Morris, Billy Adair, and a host of others.

Special Six (2-Min.) Rounds Bantamweight Contest £5 a-side (real money) and the Promoter's Purse.

VIC MANSFIELD (Ilfracombe)

v.

REGGIE REED (Southmolton)

This contest will decide who is the best bantam in North Devon.

A MARVELLOUS PHOTOGRAPH that exactly depicts the times!

MOUNTBATTEN HALL, FREMINGTON

What a crowd and over 100 turned away!
Even a FEW LADIES in the audience.

Results

LIVELY CONTESTS AT FREMINGTON
North Devon Journal Herald Dec. 1948

Well over 100 people were turned away from Mountbatten Hall, Fremington, on Friday night when they were unable to get into the hall to watch two hours of amateur boxing. The contests, under A.B.A. rules, were held in aid of the Fremington Boys' Clubs, and the whole seating capacity was filled long before the first bout commenced.

The most exciting match of the evening was a David-and-Goliath affair. B. Shaddick, a youngster from the Bickington Boys' Club, was matched with E. Powe (Barnstaple) in a cruiserweight contest. In the second round Powe took three counts and in the third round was down for two counts of eight before he retired. Shaddick punched with devastating speed and power.

The sensation of the night was provided by Rifleman Koorlander (Fremington). After the first round of his bout with Gunner Jarvis (Fremington) he went back to his corner, and did not seem to be suffering from the punishment he had received. No sooner had he sat down when he slumped unconscious to the canvas. His seconds managed to revive him, but before the second round began Koorlander again became unconscious and had to be carried from the ring. Fortunately no serious harm was caused and he was able to get into the ring at the close of the evening to receive his medal.

Bantamweight.—J. Hill (Fremington) k.o. Sapper Haslett (C.O.X.E.), second round. Flyweight.—P. Fewings (Barnstaple) beat C. Cornish (Bickington) on points. Welterweight.—A. Turner (Barnstaple) k.o. Pte. Brennan (C.O.X.E.) first round. Lightweight.—Winsor (Bickington Boys' Club) beat Sapper Jones (C.O.X.E.) on points. Featherweight.—F. Fewings (Barnstaple) beat L. Moody (Bickington Boys' Club). Retired second round.

Welterweight. — Gunner Jarvis (Fremington) beat Rifleman Koorlander (Fremington). Retired after first round. Cruiserweight.—B. Shaddick (Bickington Boys' Club) beat E. Powe (Barnstaple). Retired third round. Lightweight.—A-C. Bartlett (R.A.F. Chivenor) beat Sapper Puttnam (C.O.X.E.). Referee stopped the bout in the last round. L-Cpl. Brogden (C.O.X.E.) beat R. Jennings (Fremington) on points. A-C. Duncan (R.A.F. Chivenor) beat J. Taylor (Salem Club, Barnstaple) on points.

Cup for most meritorious winner.—P. Fewings. Cup for most meritorious loser.—Sapper Puttnam.

H. Lawrence (Crewkerne), a sparring partner to Freddie Mills, was to fight J. Pearce (Barnstaple) in an exhibition bout, but he had to decline because of an injury. In his place Flight-Sergt. J. Pearce (R.A.F. Chivenor) gave an exhibition with J. Pearce, of Barnstaple.

The cups and medals were presented by Mrs. Barclay Black, and the officials were: Judges, Capt. A. C. Snow, J.P., and Capt. Cairns, R.A. Referee, Mr. W. Fewings; timekeeper, Mr. Jack Easton; M.C. R.-S.-M. W. Riley; whip, N. Thompson; 2nd seconds, Clr.-Sgt. Crocker, R.M., and Mr. J. J. Downes.

Little Jennifer Stacey presented sprays to Mrs. Barclay Black and Mrs. L. F. Durnford-Slater, and Mr. R. H. Stacey auctioned various articles.

LIVELY BOXING

Mountbatten Hall, Fremington, was filled to capacity last night for the amateur boxing tournament staged to aid the funds of Fremington Boys' Club. The sponsors were Capt. A.C. Snow and Mrs W. T. King.

Almost without exception, contests were very fiercely but sportingly fought, and a thriller was the cruiserweight bout in which B. Shaddick (Bickington) bt. E. Powe (Barnstaple), a S.W. area champion. Exchanges were fast and ferocious. Powe, the older man, after taking a number of long counts, had to acknowledge defeat in the final round.

A big disappointment was that H. Lawrence (Crewkerne), a sparring partner of Freddie Mills, was unable to box owing to injury. He hopes to be able to take part in a future tournament.

Flight-Sergt. J. Pearce (R.A.F. Chivenor) was a capable deputy for Lawrence in a four-rounds light heavyweight exhibition bout with the polished J. Pearce, of Barnstaple, the South-West area champion.

CUPS FOR TWO

The silver challenge cup subscribed for by residents of Fremington parish for the most meritorious winner went to P. Fewings (Barnstaple). Another silver cup, donated by Major and Mrs. Barclay Black, for the best loser was won by Sapper Puttnam (C.O.X.E.).

FRIDAY, 10th DECEMBER, 1948

10 Grand AMATEUR BOUTS

MOUNTBATTEN HALL, FREMINGTON

(SCHOOL OF COMBINED OPERATIONS)

GRAND EXHIBITION OF

BOXING

By kind permission of Brig. L. E. C. M. PEROWNE. O.B.E.
Proceeds in aid of Fremington Boys Club
Sponsored by Capt. A. C. SNOW, J.P. and Mrs. W. T. KING

FRIDAY, 10th DECEMBER, 1948

10 Grand AMATEUR BOUTS
(HELD UNDER A.B.A. RULES)

Doors Open 7 p.m.   **Commence 7.30**

Grand Cruiserweight Contest

E. Powe (Barnstaple)   v.   **L.A.C. Patterson** (R.A.F. Chivenor)
(S. W. AREA CHAMPION)

Featherweight
F. Fewings (Barnstaple)   v.   A.C. Renshaw (R.A.F. Chivenor)
(A.S.A.A. CHAMPION)

Welterweight
A. Turner (Barnstaple)   v.   A.C. Early (R.A.F. Chivenor)

Lightweight
Pte. Mason (Fremington)   v.   Sapper Jones (C.O.X.E.)

Great Light Heavyweight Exhibition
6 - 2 min. Rounds

H. LAWRENCE   v.   J. PEARCE
(LAWRENCE)   (BARNSTAPLE)
(Freddie Mills Sparring Partner)   (S. W. Area Champion)

	LIGHTWEIGHT	
Sapper TUTTMAN (C.O.X.E.)	v.	A.C. BARTLETT (R.A.F. Chivenor)
P. FEWINGS (Barnstaple)	FLYWEIGHT v.	R. SMALE (Barnstaple)
R. JENNINGS (Fremington)	WELTERWEIGHT v.	L.Cpl. BROGDEN (C.O.X.E.)
J. HILL (Fremington)	BANTAMWEIGHT v.	Sapper HASLETT (C.O.X.E.)
Gunner JARVIS (Fremington)	WELTERWEIGHT v.	Sapper POWER (C.O.X.E.)

A Magnificent Silver Challenge Cup, subscribed to by the Residents of Fremington Village will be presented at the conclusion of the evening to the most meritorious winner. The Cup to be named the "Fremington Challenge Cup."
Also a suitably engraved Cup will be presented to the best loser of the evening kindly donated by Major and Mrs. Barclay Black.
Major & Mrs. Barclay Black have kindly consented to present the Prizes at the conclusion of the evening.

ADMISSION 10/6 (Ringside), 5/- & 2/6
SERVICEMEN IN UNIFORM 1/-
Tickets can be obtained at Three Tuns, Barnstaple, New Inn, Fremington, Marine Hotel, Instow, New Inn, Bideford or at the Door.
AUGMENTED BUS SERVICE

The BOXING PROGRAMME lists
BARNSTAPLE BOXERS who ALL
had PROFESSIONAL BOUTS previously.

A GREAT STORY and quite a line-up of PROMINENT LOCAL BOXERS on the BILL.

In January 1950 I along with Nick Linden who lived down West Lane and Bill Short who hailed from Petrockstowe were buying fish and chips from Bill Clement's mobile fish and chip van, he told us a boxing match in aid of The Beaford British Legion was being arranged between the Bideford boxing club and the Bideford army cadets and they were also looking for local talent to take part, jokingly, or so we thought. Bill Clements asked us if we would volunteer to take part, we said yes we would, thinking nothing more would come of it. about a week or so later we were surprised to see a large poster in the van with our three names on it listed as 'local talent', so this meant we were now fully committed. Both Nick and I were not entirely new to boxing having often sparred together in Nick's living room in West Lane with the furniture pushed to one side.

The boxing match was to take place at 7.30 on March 1st 1950 at the Victory Hall, Beaford. Nick had been matched with Bill Short and I was to fight a member of the army cadets named Otto Senik who lived at Weare Giffard.

We cycled to Beaford that evening arriving at the victory hall and sat anxiously in the changing room waiting for the other competitors to turn up. when they eventually arrived we found them a friendly bunch of lads and sat for a while chatting to them. Surprisingly no one had thought to set up a proper boxing ring in the hall so members of the audience were obliged to form a square holding the rope in their hands. fortunately there was a selection of boxing gloves provided by the two clubs otherwise it might have turned out to been a complete 'slaughter of the innocents'.

Otto and I were first on the bill and after three rounds our match was declared a draw by the referee whereupon we both got changed and decamped to the local pub missing the rest of the evenings entertainment. Nick and Bill's match was also declared a draw.

Nick who sadly is no longer with us went on to win boxing medals both in the Royal Artillery and the Metropolitan Police.

Bill Baker.

BEAFORD BOXING STORY

For LEN WREY read SAMMY WREY.

BRITISH LEGION, BEAFORD.

- A -
BOXING
TOURNAMENT
will be held in the
VICTORY HALL
On Wednesday, March 1st, 1950.

Bideford Army Cadets V. Bideford Boxing Club and Local Talent.

Bill Baker, Dolton	v.	Otto Senik, B.A.C.
Bill Short, Little Torrington	v.	Mich Lendon, Dolton.
Cadet Coombes, B.A.C.	v.	Gerald Lee, B.B.C.
Cadet Hew "	v.	Garfield Watkins, B.B.C.
L/C. Short "	v.	Len Wrey, B.B.C.
Bob Wrey "	v.	Len Tythcott, "
Cpl. Sprey "	v.	George Clifford "
Raymond Scoynes "	v.	D. Coombes "
Arthur Cole	v.	Arthur Wright

Judges - Messrs. C. Bright and W. Skinner.
Referee - To be nominated by the Bideford Boxing Club.
M.C. - Mr. H. Cole.   Medical Officer - Dr. Maitland Jones.
Seconds - Messrs. V. Folland and F. Squires.   Timekeeper - Mr. F. Briggs.

Prices: Reserved Seats 3/- and 2/6, Unreserved 2/-
Doors open 7 p.m.   -   Commence 7.30 p.m. sharp.
Bookings taken by Post up to February 28th, to A. Headford, Hon. Sec., Beaford, N.D.

BILLY BROWN, second from the right, back row.
What a FANTASTIC SHIELD!

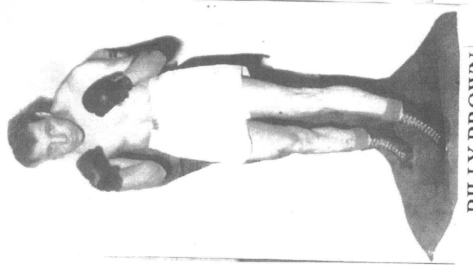

BILLY BROWN

DB

BILLY BROWN

We meet again, the early days a distant memory.

BOOK SIGNING at WALTER HENRY'S BOOKSHOP, BIDEFORD.

DB and Publisher EDWARD GASKELL.

TONY BOTTRILL, DB.

GREAT SUPPORTERS!
BILLY and JILL CAMPBELL, DB.

DAVE SHORT, ROGER BROWNSON, DB.

TERRY DOWNES,
Former WORLD MIDDLEWEIGHT BOXING CHAMPION,
MICHAEL GRIFFITHS, DB.

...at the ROYAL EXCHANGE PUB, BARNSTAPLE.

TERRY DOWNES and DB in 1972.

DB, MICHAEL STACK, PETER HEATH.

TERRY DOWNES, LES ALLEN, DB...enjoy a drink!

HAPPY BIRTHDAY, TERRY DOWNES

TWO LEGENDS: Downes [*right*], pictured alongside the great Robinson in the lead-up to their contest

We revisit the career of Britain's oldest surviving former world champion, who turns 80 this week

Alex Daley
@thealexdaley

Historian & author

ALTHOUGH he first boxed as a London schoolboy, the swarming, non-stop style of Terry Downes was fashioned in the tough rings of 1950s America.

But it was tragedy that brought Terry, a Paddington native, to the States when he was 16. His elder sister, a dancer, lost her right arm in a coach accident on a US tour and the family flew out there to support her. The Downeses decided to stay in America and Terry continued to box via the Baltimore YMCA, with whom he won the State Novice championships.

At 17, he joined the US Marines. The regime was severe (two members of his draft committed suicide during basic training), but Downes had an outlet to further his boxing career. Despite being British, he won Marine and Inter-Services titles, and was even shortlisted for America's 1956 Olympic trials until they realised he was a Brit.

Straight after leaving the Marines, having served for three years, Terry worked London. To stay sharp, he joined Bermondsey's Fisher ABC and had a few more amateur bouts. Although he had planned to return to America to become a pro, he was persuaded by Britain's top promoter, Jack Solomons, to turn pro here instead. On Solomons' advice, Terry signed with Jarvis Astaire, who later brought in Sam Burns as co-manager.

Turning over in April 1957, Downes handily won his first two paid fights – a first-round KO of Peter Longo and a third-round stoppage of Jimmy Lynas – but disaster struck when he met an unknown Nigerian named Dick Tiger in fight number three. This Shoreditch Town Hall eight-rounder was stopped in the sixth in Tiger's favour after Downes had been floored repeatedly. Their joint purse for that small hall classic was just £185, yet five years later both were world champions. Asked in his dressing room by reporters who his next opponent would be, Terry quipped: "The geezer who made that match!"

Undeterred, 16 months later Terry stopped Phil Edwards (Cardiff) to win the vacant British middleweight title in his 20th pro outing. In September 1959, he lost his title in bizarre fashion to Scot southpaw John McCormack, who was floored eight times – mainly from body blows – before the referee disqualified Downes for allegedly hitting low. But Terry regained the title two months later, stopping McCormack in eight in a return.

In July 1960, Downes successfully defended against Edwards to win a Lonsdale Belt outright, and that October beat future world champion Joey Giardello. In Boston, Terry challenged another American, Paul Pender, for the world middleweight crown in January 1961, but was stopped on cuts in the seventh. In the July rematch at Wembley's Empire Pool, Downes won the title, Pender retiring after the ninth.

But Terry's reign was short-lived, as Pender regained the crown with a 15-round points win in Boston in April 1962. In November '64, Downes got another tilt at world honours when he challenged Willie Pastrano for the light-heavy belt in Manchester. Going into the 11th Downes was ahead, but Pastrano floored him twice in that round, causing the stoppage. It was Downes' final fight.

The most notable scalp on Terry's record – on paper at least – is that of the great Sugar Ray Robinson. But Downes refuses to take credit for beating the 41-year-old version of Robinson. "I didn't beat Sugar Ray," he once said. "I beat his ghost."

BOXING NEWS. MAY 12 - 2016

DB, JANE BROWNSON, RON TAYLOR, TERRY DOWNES,
former WORLD MIDDLEWEIGHT BOXING CHAMPION.
The ROYAL EXCHANGE PUB, BARNSTAPLE, 1979.

Book Signing 27th December 2014. Royal Exchange Pub, Barnstaple
THE STORY OF NORTH DEVON BOXING by Dick Brownson

MICHAEL 'MITCH' WARBURTON, ROY SAVAGE, DB,
JOHN GREENWOOD, JIMMY ISAAC.

BARNSTAPLE ABC

Extract from a 'NORTH DEVON DIARY'
dated JANUARY 19th 1950, NDJ.

Club Without Sub

A SOCIETY without a subscription is the recently-formed Barnstaple Amateur Boxing Club, which will soon be presenting its first public programme. Any young man or boy can join; there is nothing to pay at all. The club was started last summer, when a few individuals decided that the time was ripe for a revival of amateur boxing in North Devon. The present membership is eighty, out of which two-thirds are regularly in the ring. Earl Fortescue is the president, Mr. G. P. Walker the secretary, and Mr. R. E. House the treasurer. The chairman is Mr. William Child.

BARNSTAPLE ABC,
formed during the summer of 1949.

BOXERS UNKNOWN.

Stand back!! The Mayor of Barnstaple (Alderman A.C.Blackmore) motions the man who is still on his feet to a neutral corner during a visit to Barnstaple Amateur Boxing Club's gymnasium this week when he stood in on a practice bout. See a North Devon Diary

The FIRST OFFICIAL BOXING PROMOTION by BARNSTAPLE ABC.
JANUARY 30th 1950, FORESTERS' HALL BARNSTAPLE.
BARNSTAPLE ABC versus BIDEFORD ABC.

THE BARNSTAPLE AMATEUR BOXING CLUB

In June, 1949, the Club was formed with the object of teaching the youth of Barnstaple and District, The Noble Art of Self Defence. Any boy or young man, providing he is willing to learn, may receive tuition under the expert guidance of ex-amateur champions. *He will have nothing to pay in the way of subscriptions, etc. All services are given without any charge whatever.*

Boxing is essentially an English Sport. A good boxer is one to be admired. He must possess moral and physical courage. He must acquire skill, physical fitness, self-reliance, and he must be a good sportsman.

He requires moral courage to eschew the many pleasures permissable to the non-boxer, otherwise his physique would suffer; physically imperfect, he could not hope to endure the strain of fistic combat.

He must have physical courage to absorb the punishment expected in the ring.

Upon his skill depends his ability to defend himself and to attack his opponent.

He must be self-reliant. The ring is a lonely place where he cannot expect any help. Solely upon his own efforts he stands or falls.

Above all, he must be a good sportsman; able to say—win or lose—to an opponent, "Thanks, a good show! When shall we have a return bout?"

In short—a boxer is, first and foremost, a sportsman.

Should you, gentle reader, feel that boxing is a sport worthy of your support, and, should you feel generously inclined—The Hon. Treasurer, Mr. R. E. House, Lloyds Bank, Barnstaple, is ever willing to acknowledge, with gratitude, any subscription you can afford to help maintain The BARNSTAPLE A.B.C. in training the youth of the District to become boxers, and, consequently, Englishmen.

THE BARNSTAPLE AMATEUR BOXING CLUB

AMATEUR
BOXING TOURNAMENT

(Under A.B.A. Rules)

BARNSTAPLE A.B.C. V BIDEFORD A.B.C.

at the

FORESTERS' HALL, BARNSTAPLE

on

Monday, January 30th, at 7-30 p.m.

The President of the Barnstaple A.B.C.,
The EARL FORTESCUE, C.B., M.C., O.B.E.,
will present the Trophies assisted by
His Worship the Mayor of Barnstaple,
Alderman A. C. BLACKMORE, J.P.

OFFICIALS:

Referee: R.S.M. Riley, Coldstream Guards.

Judges: Commander H. Hayes, D.S.O., R.N.
Lt. Commander G. S. B. St. G. Beal, R.N.

Timekeeper: Flt./Lt. M. Gidman, R.A.F.

M.C.: Councillor A. M. Carpenter.

Hon. Medical Officer: Dr. R. Harper, M.D.

PROGRAMME 6D.

BOUT 8

Bout of 3 Rounds of 2 minutes each

KEN SMITH (116 pounds)

v.

JACK KEEN (124 pounds)

BOUT 9

SPECIAL LIGHT HEAVY-WEI

of 4 Rounds of 3 mi

JIM PEARCE (166 pou...)

v.

ALBERT BENNETT (168 po...)

BOUT 10

Bout of 3 Rounds of 2 minutes each

MERVYN GREEN (106 pounds)

v.

BOB WREY (108 pounds)

BOUT 11

Bout of 3 Rounds of 2 minutes each.

BILL GABRIEL (135 pounds)

v.

PETER WREY (136 pounds)

BOUT 12

SPECIAL MIDDLE-WEIGHT CONTEST

of 4 Rounds of 3 minutes

WALTER CASINELLI *v.* CYRIL HEARN

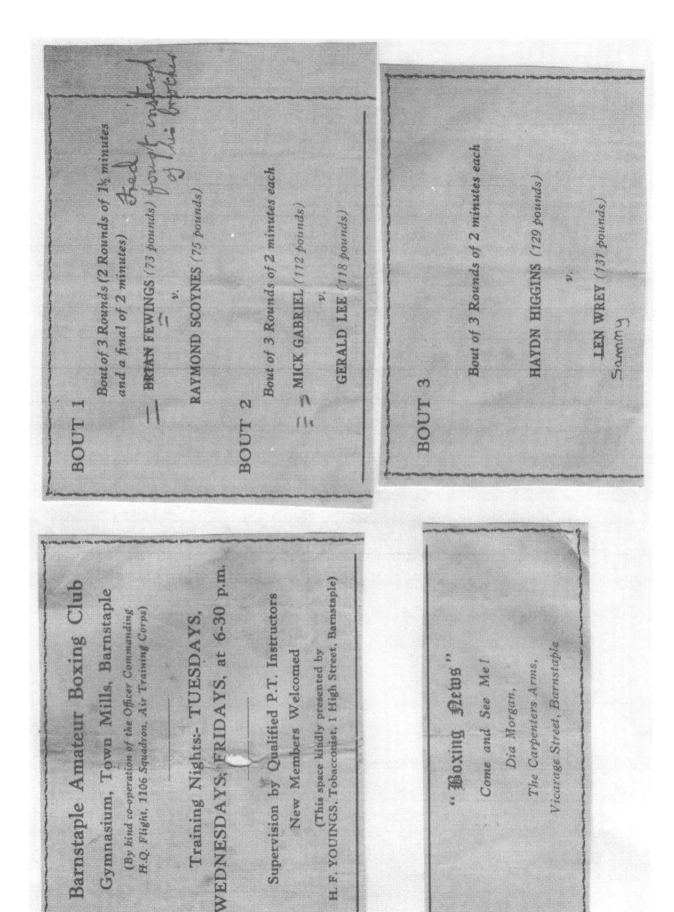

BOUT 1

Bout of 3 Rounds (2 Rounds of 1½ minutes and a final of 2 minutes) *Fred fought instead of his brother*

BRIAN FEWINGS (73 pounds)

v.

RAYMOND SCOYNES (75 pounds)

BOUT 2

Bout of 3 Rounds of 2 minutes each

MICK GABRIEL (112 pounds)

v.

GERALD LEE (118 pounds)

BOUT 3

Bout of 3 Rounds of 2 minutes each

HAYDN HIGGINS (129 pounds)

v.

LEN WREY (131 pounds)
Sammy

Barnstaple Amateur Boxing Club

Gymnasium, Town Mills, Barnstaple

(By kind co-operation of the Officer Commanding
H.Q. Flight, 1106 Squadron, Air Training Corps)

Training Nights:- TUESDAYS,
WEDNESDAYS, FRIDAYS, at 6-30 p.m.

Supervision by Qualified P.T. Instructors
New Members Welcomed

(This space kindly presented by
H. F. YOUINGS, Tobacconist, 1 High Street, Barnstaple)

"*Boxing News*"

Come and See Me!

Dia Morgan,
The Carpenters Arms,
Vicarage Street, Barnstaple

BOUT 4

Bout of 3 Rounds of 2 minutes each

RAYMOND JEWELL (144 pounds)

v.

TERRY TYTHCOTT (147 pounds)

BOUT 5

Bout of 3 Rounds of 2 minutes each.

GEORGE LEY (159 pounds)

v.

ARTHUR COLE (157 pounds)

CHALLENGE BOUT

OTTO SENIK of Bideford A.B.C., challenges any Amateur Boxer up to the middle-weight limit over amateur championship distance—3 Rounds of 3 minutes. Barnstaple accepts the challenge and nominates MICHAEL CHILD

BOUT 6

MICHAEL CHILD (149 pounds) v. OTTO SENIK (145 pounds)

BOUT 7

Bout of 3 Rounds of 2 minutes each

SIDNEY SMITH (122 pounds) v. LEWIS ELLIS (128 pounds)

INTERVAL OF 15 MINUTES

THANKS

The Committee and Members of the Barnstaple Amateur Boxing Club wish to express their thanks to the following Donors of Cups:—

Garnish and Winkles

A. E. Dart and Sons

Hill and Sons, Jewellers

H. Chapman and Sons

H. Samuel and Son, Ltd.

A. Foulkes, Esq.

J. Reed, Outfitter

Messrs. Boots

and any donors of prizes given too late for acknowledgment in this programme.

The Committee also thank Bernard Smith, for ring lighting and amplifying, and all who have assisted in any way to make the Show a success.

BOUT 13

Bout of 3 Rounds of 2 minutes each

FREDDY PILE (142 pounds)

v.

REG. ANSTIS (145 pounds)

OTTO – DARK SHORTS.

Boxing

GERMAN WAS DEFEATED

Amateur Bouts in Barnstaple

OTTO SENIK, a German member of Bideford A.B.C., who challenged any amateur boxer up to the middle-weight limit over amateur-championship distance, was beaten by Michael Child in a Barnstaple-v.-Bideford boxing tournament in The Foresters' Hall, Barnstaple, on Monday.

The referee (R.-S.-M. Riley, Coldstream Guards) stopped the contest in the third and last round. It was Barnstaple's sixth successive win of the evening, altogether the home club won ten of the thirteen bouts.

From the start of the Child-Senik fight the Barnstaple man looked the more finished boxer, though he had a cut over his left eye at the end of the first round and was knocked down once in the second. Child (146lbs.) connected with a number of clean rights, though he relied mainly on his left, to whose constant attack Senik (146lbs.) could find no answer. For most of the third round Child pentied Senik in a corner, the German retaliating with one wild swing that missed completely just before the contest was stopped in Child's favour.

Walter Cassinelli (160lbs.) the Ilfracombe Town and former Barnstaple Town and Braunton footballer, was seen in a new role. He opposed George Gifford (161lbs.) in a four-round middle-weight match, the Bideford man defeating him on points.

The fight was spoiled by too many clinches. Cassinelli scored in the first round with terrific rights to the body, but Gifford, who was in fine condition, was not perturbed and managed to evade similar punches in the second round. At first the Bidefordian found Cassinelli an elusive target. His opponent, however, had sapped his own strength by his early dash, and in the third and fourth rounds tired rapidly.

GIFFORD'S TURN

Gifford dictated the course of events in the last round, and it was his turn to land some heavy rights to the body.

Other three-round bouts resulted (Barnstaple names first): Brian Fewings (79lbs.) beat Raymond Symes (75lbs.) on points; Mick Gabriel (112) beat Gerald Lee (118), the referee stopping the contest in the second round; Haydn Higgins (120) beat Len Wrey (131) on points; Raymond Jewell (144) beat Terry Tythcott (147), who retired after the first round; George Ley (139) beat Arthur Cole (137) on points; Sidney Smith (122) beat Lewis Ellis (128) on a knock-out in the third round.

Ken Smith (116) lost to Jack Keen (124) on points; Jim Pearce (170) lost to Albert Bennett (168) on points; Mervyn Green (106) beat Bob Wrey (108), the referee stopping the contest in the second round; Bill Gabriel (135) beat Garfield Watkins (133) on a knock-out in the third round; Freddy Fewings (131) beat Reg Anstis (145) on points.

The prizes were distributed by The Earl Fortescue, who was escorted by the Mayor of Barnstaple (Ald. A. C. Blackmore).

The officials were: Judges: Commander H. Hayes R.N. and Lieut.-Commander O. S. R. St. G. Beal, R.N.; time-keeper Flt.-Lt. M. Gifford, R.A.F., M.C. Councillor A. M. Carpenter, and Hon. Medical Officer, Dr. R. Harper.

The Barnstaple Club accepted Bideford's challenge for a return tournament at Bideford.

WILLIAM 'BUNGY' FEWINGS in the RING, at left!

BARNSTAPLE V BIDEFORD BOXING MATCH, FORESTER'S HALL. BARNSTAPLE. OTTO SENIK grabs the headlines, but is stopped in the third round. He certainly was a busy boxer and popular with the press and boxing crowd.

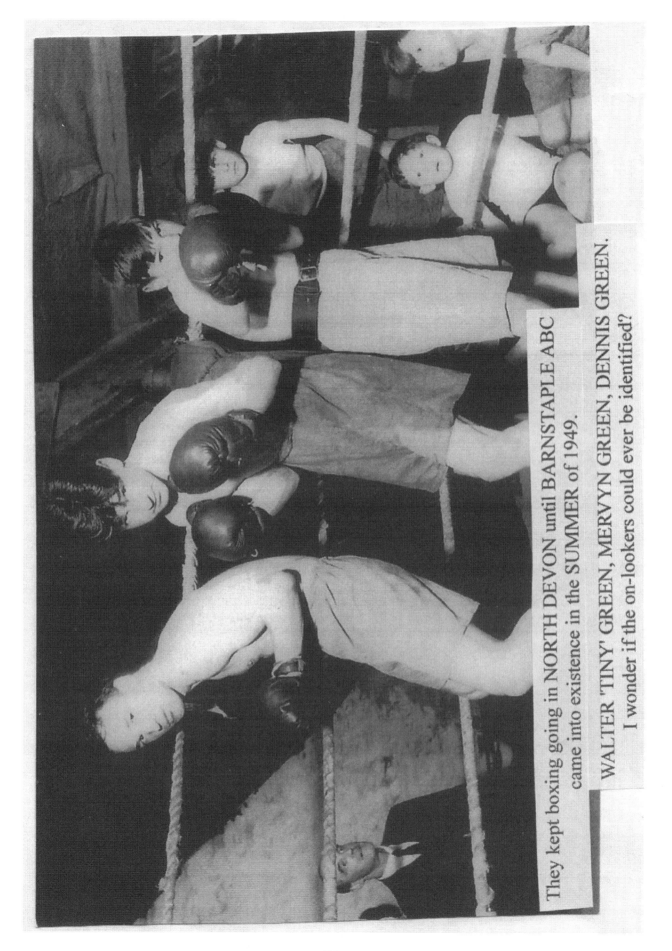

They kept boxing going in NORTH DEVON until BARNSTAPLE ABC came into existence in the SUMMER of 1949.

WALTER 'TINY' GREEN, MERVYN GREEN, DENNIS GREEN.
I wonder if the on-lookers could ever be identified?

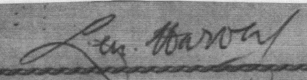

THE BARNSTAPLE AMATEUR BOXING CLUB

AMATEUR
BOXING
TOURNAMENT
(Under A.B.A. Rules)

IN AID OF BARNSTAPLE OLD PEOPLES' HOSTEL

at the

PANNIER MARKET, BARNSTAPLE

on

Monday, January 22nd., at 7-30 p.m.

The President of the Barnstaple A.B.C.
The EARL FORTESCUE, C.B., O.B.E., M.C., J.P.
will present the Trophies assisted by
His Worship the Mayor of Barnstaple,
Alderman A. C. BLACKMORE, J.P.

OFFICIALS

Referee and Judges appointed by Devon A.B.A.

Timekeeper : F./Lt. M. Gidman, R.A.F.

M.C.: Councillor A. M. Carpenter

Hon. Medical Officer : Dr. R. M. J. Harper, M.A., M.D.

PROGRAMME 6d.

'BUNGY' FEWINGS with some EARLY MEMBERS
of the newly formed
BARNSTAPLE AMATEUR BOXING CLUB?
Origin of photo. unknown.

BOUT 1

Three Rounds Tissue-paperweight Contest

BOY DOBER v. BOY COOKE

Barum   Barum

BOUT 2

Three Rounds Contest

RAYMOND SCOYNES v. JOEY OVEY

Bideford   Barum

BOUT 3

Three Rounds Contest

B. WREY v. M. GABRIEL

Bideford   Barum

BOUT 4

Three Rounds Contest

O. BENNETT v. RAYMOND JEWELL

Tiverton   Barum

BOUT 5

Three Rounds Contest

L. SAFFER v. BRIAN SCOYNES

Tiverton   Bideford

BOUT 6

Three Rounds Contest

S. SNOW v. L.A.C. STEVENSON

Tiverton   R.A.F. & Barum

BOUT 7

Four Rounds Heavyweight Contest

L.A.C. PATTERSON v. NORMAN SHADDICK

R.A.F. & Barum   Barum

BOUT 8

Three Rounds Contest

P. MAUNDER v. CHARLIE CORNISH

Tiverton   Barum

BOUT 9

Three Rounds Contest

LEWIS ELLIS v. SIDNEY SMITH

Bideford   Barum

BOUT 10

Four Rounds Middleweight Contest

ARTHUR COLE v. MICHAEL CHILD

Bideford   Barum

BOUT 11

Four Rounds Contest

D. JOHNS v. DEREK WINDSOR

Exeter   Barum

BOUT 12

Three Rounds Contest

ALAN BIRKS v. STANLEY BRIGHT

Exeter   Barum

BOUT 13

Four Rounds Contest

L. HUTCHINGS v. HADYN HIGGINS

Exeter   Barum

BOUT 14

Four Rounds Contest

JIM OFFIELD v. GEORGE LEY

Barum   Barum

BOUT 15

Three Rounds Contest

SAMMY

LEN WREY v. OTTO SENIK

Bideford   Barum

THREE VERY IMPORTANT BOXING PROMOTIONS undertaken by
BARNSTAPLE ABC in the PANNIER MARKET.
WHAT A 'MIXTURE' of LICENSED PROFESSIONAL BOXERS in the RING
with definite 'AMATEURS!'

THE BARNSTAPLE AMATEUR BOXING CLUB

AMATEUR BOXING TOURNAMENT

(Under A.B.A. Rules)

IN AID OF BARNSTAPLE OLD PEOPLES' HOSTEL FUND

at the

PANNIER MARKET, BARNSTAPLE

on

Monday, October 29th, at 7-30 p.m.

The President of the Barnstaple A.B.C.

THE EARL FORTESCUE, K.G., C.B., O.B.E., M.C., J.P.

will present the Trophies

OFFICIALS

Referee and Judges appointed by Devon A.B.A.

Timekeeper : Mr. J. Easton

M.C.: Alderman A. C. Blackmore, J.P.

Hon. Medical Officer : Dr. R. M. J. Harper, M.A., M.D.

PROGRAMME 3d.

BOUT 1

Three Rounds Contest

DENNIS GREEN
BARNSTAPLE

v.

L. SAFFER
TIVERTON

BOUT 2

Three Rounds Contest

JOEY OVEY
BARNSTAPLE

v.

M. BIBBY
EXETER

BOUT 3

Three Rounds Contest

MERVYN GREEN
BARNSTAPLE

v.

DENNIS HEARD
BIDEFORD

BOUT 4

Three Rounds Contest

A.C. PERKINS
BARNSTAPLE

v.

GNR. THOMAS
R.A., CLEAVE

BOUT 5

Three Rounds Contest

STANLEY BISHOP
BARNSTAPLE

v.

LEWIS ELLIS
BIDEFORD

BOUT 6

Three Rounds Contest

STAN IVY
BIDEFORD

v.

A. BIRKS
EXETER

BOUT 7

Three Rounds Contest

L.A.C. ADCOCK
BARNSTAPLE

v.

CFN. MILES
R.E.M.E., CLEAVE

BOUT 8.

Three Rounds Contest

L.A.C. CHAPPELL
BARNSTAPLE

v.

R. MAUNDER
TIVERTON

BOUT 9

Three Rounds Contest

C. MOORE
TIVERTON

v.

D. DREW
EXETER

BOUT 10

Three Rounds Contest

BDR. BUTLER
R.A., CLEAVE

v.

L. KING
TIVERTON

BOUT 11

Three Rounds Contest

A. COLE
BIDEFORD

v.

D. MITCHELL
EXETER

BOUT 12

Three Rounds Contest

D. JOHNS
EXETER

v.

GNR. LUKE
R.A., CLEAVE

BOUT 13

Three Rounds Contest

L.A.C. WALLACE
BARNSTAPLE

v.

L. HUTCHINGS
EXETER

BOUT 14

Three Rounds Contest

L.A.C. PATTERSON
BARNSTAPLE

v.

GNR. LEMMON
R.A., CLEAVE

THE BARNSTAPLE AMATEUR BOXING CLUB

AMATEUR BOXING TOURNAMENT

(Under A.B.A. Rules)

In aid of

The Royal Society for the Prevention of Cruelty to Animals

at the

PANNIER MARKET, BARNSTAPLE

on

Monday, December 10th, at 7-30 p.m.

The Trophies will be presented by

LADY WREY

OFFICIALS

Officials appointed by Devon, Dorset and Cornwall A.B.A.

Timekeeper : Mr. J. Easton (Barnstaple)

M.C. : Capt. Leeming, R.E.M.E.

Hon. Medical Officer : Dr. R. M. J. Harper, M.A., M.D.

PROGRAMME 3d.

BOUT 1

Three Rounds Contest

BIMBO PAYNE v. ANDY GREEN

Barnstaple   *Barnstaple*

BOUT 2

Three Rounds Contest

K. BROAD v. JOEY OVEY

Exeter   *Barnstaple*

BOUT 3

Three Rounds Contest

B. G. DREW v. D. KAY

Exeter   *Apollo*

BOUT 4

Three Rounds Contest

B. STOCKER v. R. DAVEY

Apollo   *Apollo*

BOUT 5

Three Rounds Contest

R. THOMPSON v. D. JOHNS

Apollo   *Exeter*

BOUT 6

Three Rounds Contest

LEN HARVEY v. OTTO SENIK

Apollo   *Bideford*

BOUT 7

Three Rounds Contest

C. F. JARVIS v. STANLEY BISHOP

Exeter   *Barnstaple*

BOUT 8

Three Rounds Contest

R. MAUNDER v. C. CORNISH

Tiverton   *Barnstaple*

BOUT 9

Three Rounds Contest

B. POPE v. MERVYN GREEN

Tiverton   *Barnstaple*

BOUT 10

Three Rounds Contest

C. HEARN v. MICHAEL CHILD

Bideford   *Barnstaple*

BOUT 11

Three Rounds Contest

C. MITCHELL v. V. ADCOCK

Exeter   *Barnstaple*

BOUT 12

Three Rounds Contest

W. WYATT v. L. STEVENSON

Apollo   *Barnstaple*

BOUT 13

Three Rounds Contest

A. BOLT v. SIDNEY SMITH

Tiverton   *Barnstaple*

BOUT 14

Three Rounds Contest

T. HOGAN v. M. BIRGIN

Barnstaple   *Barnstaple*

All seemed quiet then until the
FREDDIE MILLS 'PROFESSIONAL' PROMOTION on SEPTEMBER 8th
1952 for the LYNMOUTH DISTRESS FUND.

Terry Allen v. Tiny Green

LONDON   BARNSTAPLE

FREDDIE MILLS PROMOTION for LYNMOUTH DISTRESS FUND Sept. 8th 1952.

KING'S ARMS HOTEL

(NEXT TO MARKET)

HIGH STREET, BARNSTAPLE.

(Proprietor: A. STAPLETON)

A TRUMAN HOUSE.

All Sportsmen, Catered For.

BED & BREAKFAST.   FULL HOTEL ACCOMMODATION

Free Charge to all Patrons.

An Attractive 8 Round Featherweight Contest:

TINY GREEN v. **DICKIE ROBERTS**

(Barnstaple)   (Prague)

The undefeated local lad.   Undefeated at his weight.

A Special 6 Round Contest:

YOUNG TURNER v. **YOUNG LAMEY**

(Barnstaple)   (Bideford)

Watch this lad's ring appearance.   A lad that is doing well.

MARKET HALL, BARNSTAPLE

FREDDIE MILLS PERSONAL PROMOTION

BOXING

Under B.B.B. of C.

Monday, September 8th

IN AID OF

Lynmouth Distress Fund

OFFICIALS—

Referee: DICK BURT, Plymouth, B.B.B. of C.

Timekeeper: JACK EASTON, Barnstaple.

M.C.: CYRIL BLACKMORE, Barnstaple, B.B.B. of C.

Inspector: JIMMY HOLDER, Weston, B.B.B. of C.

Doctor in Attendance: Dr. R. HARPER.

This is the last time I found evidence of boxers who had fought on many PROFESSIONAL BOXING SHOWS getting into the ring against apparent 'AMATEURS.' After this BOXING became more REGULATED and the AMATEUR BOXING ASSOCIATION exercised more control. DB.

The next fully PROFESSIONAL BOXING PROMOTION, LICENSED by the BRITISH BOXING BOARD of CONTROL LTD., held in NORTH DEVON was not until the 13th NOVEMBER 1995.

PROFESSIONAL BOXING
DINNER & CABARET

ON

13th November 1995

AT THE

BARNSTAPLE HOTEL
BRAUNTON ROAD
BARNSTAPLE

From the early 1900's until the 1950's was an eventful period for NORTH DEVON BOXING but sadly the harsh times and life-style in and out of the RING took its toll on many of the FIGHTERS.

SECRETARIES' ADDRESS DIRECTORY

Association Internationale de Boxe Amateur (AIBA): Lt.-Col. R. H. Russell, 8, New Square, Lincoln's Inn, London WC2. (Holborn 8131.)

Amateur Boxing Association (ABA): J. O. McIntosh, ABA, 69 Victoria Street, London, SW1. (Abbey 3295.)

Scottish ABA: A. F. Jamieson, 32, Knollpark Drive, Clarkston, Renfrewshire. (Giffnock 3684.)

Irish ABA: C. Gallacher, National Boxing Stadium, South Circular Road, Dublin. (Dublin 53371-2.)

Imperial Services Boxing Association: Lt/Cdr. R. S. Attwater, RN Boxing Association, Flathouse Road, Portsmouth.

Royal Navy Boxing Association: Same as for Imperial Services BA.

Army Boxing Association: Lt-Col. R. W. Littlehales, Army BA, c/o. ASCB, War Office, London, S.W.1. (Grosvenor 8040; ext. 45).

Royal Air Force Boxing Association: W/Cdr. L. W. V. Jennens, RAF Station, Watton, Norfolk. Tournaments secretary: F/Lt. H. E. Robinson, RAF Station, Uxbridge, Middlesex (Uxbridge 1240; ext. 205).

London ABA: F. J. Warren, London ABA, 69, Victoria Street, London, SW.1. (Abbey 6458.)

Schools ABA: A. J. P. Martin, 49, Fallowfield Crescent, Hove, 4, Sussex. (Hove 7612.)

London Schools ABA: R. A. N. Jones, Adelaide Road, Hampstead, London, NW3. (Primrose 5935.)

National Association of Boys' Clubs: Capt. S. Cole, 17, Bedford Square, London, WC1. (Museum 5357).

London Federation of Boys' Clubs: P. F. N. Warner, 222, Blackfriars Road, Southwark, London, SE1. (Waterloo 5541-2.)

Sea Cadet Corps BA: E. M. Riley, Grand Buildings, Trafalgar Square, London. (Trafalgar 6722-6.)

Army Cadet Force BA: Major A. C. Munro, 16, Buckingham Palace Road, London, SW.1. (Victoria 1727.)

Air Training Corps BA: W/Cdr. E. H. Rundle, RAF White Waltham, near Maidenhead. (Maidenhead 2300; ext. 232.)

National Coal Board ABA: H. Slade, Room 121, National Coal Board, Hobart House, London, S.W.1. (Victoria 6644; ext. 77.)

Railway Executive ABA: O. I. S. Whitaker, 222, Marylebone Road, London, N.W.1. (Paddington 1601; ext. 232.)

Police Athletic Association: A. F. Plume, City Police Office, Norwich. (Norwich 21212-9.)

Universities Athletic Union: K. S. Duncan, 71, St. George's Square, London, SW.1. (Victoria 8933.)

Referees' and Judges' Association: J. Titmus, 73, Niton Street, Fulham, London, SW.6. (Fulham 5879.)

Honorary Instructors' Association: S. C. Waite, 50, Village Way, Rayners Lane, Pinner, Middlesex.

There was so many BRITISH NATIONAL AMATEUR TITLES to be fought for in the 1940's and 50's.
The number of AMATEUR BOXERS campaigning in 1952 was published and given as approximately 45.000.
The count in 2016 is less than 3000!

NORMAN SHADDICK.

JIMMY ISAAC, NORMAN SHADDICK, DB. STUDY OLD FIGHT
PROGRAMMES.

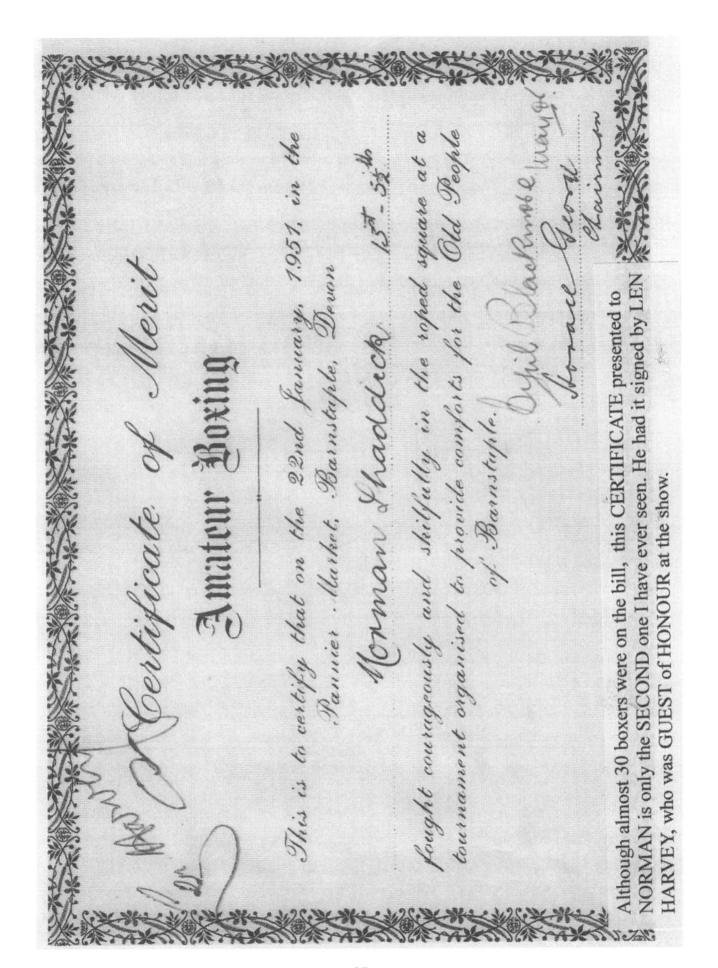

Certificate of Merit

Amateur Boxing

This is to certify that on the 22nd January, 1951, in the Pannier Market, Barnstaple, Devon

Norman Shaddick

13st - 5½lb

fought courageously and skilfully in the roped square at a tournament organised to provide comforts for the Old People of Barnstaple.

Cyril Blackmore, Mayor

Thomas Geon, Chairman

Although almost 30 boxers were on the bill, this CERTIFICATE presented to NORMAN is only the SECOND one I have ever seen. He had it signed by LEN HARVEY, who was GUEST of HONOUR at the show.

There was no easy passage to a WESTERN COUNTIES ABA TITLE in those far off boxing days of the EARLY 1950's. It was not unusual to box 3 or 4 times the SAME DAY !

WESTERN COUNTIES CHAMPION.

BIDEFORD AND DISTRICT AMATEUR BOXING CLUB

AMATEUR
BOXING TOURNAMENT

(Under A.B.A. Rules)

AT THE

PANNIER MARKET, BIDEFORD

THURSDAY, OCTOBER 4th at 7-30 p.m.

Trophies Presented by

THE EARL FORTESCUE, K.G., C.B., O.B.E., M.C.

Officials appointed by Devon, Dorset and Cornwall Boxing Association.
Referee, Judges and other Officials announced before Tournament.
Hon. Medical Officer: Dr. W. Ruddock, M.B. B.Ch., Bideford.
Timekeeper: Mr. G. Eastman, Barum.

Ladies and Gentlemen,

The Bideford and District Amateur Boxing Club has been revived and it is hoped that it will find popular support in the district.

We hope to provide facilities for the Youth of the area to enjoy Boxing and P.T. under competent instructors, and that perhaps we may even find a boy who will become an Amateur Champion. It is our desire also to take Amateurs to Contests in Devon, Dorset and Cornwall and build up a respected Club with high quality Amateurs and Management; may we therefore ask your support in future Tournaments.

His Worship the Mayor of Bideford (Councillor W. H. Copp, J.P.) will introduce the Tournament.

We shall be glad to receive criticisms on Management or Organisation, and such comments should be sent to:

G. POLLEY, Hon. Sec.,
B, Kenwith Terrace, Bideford.

UNCLE, PRINTERS, BIDEFORD

BOROUGH OF BIDEFORD

FESTIVAL OF BRITAIN
1951

BOXING

Souvenir Programme

PRICE 6d.

7.25 p.m.   THE KING

JUNIOR CONTEST
L. SAFFER v DENNIS GREEN
TIVERTON   BARUM

SEVEN STONE TWO CONTEST
RAYMOND SCOYNES v JOEY OVEY
BIDEFORD   BARUM

JUNIOR CONTEST
G. SAFFER v ANDY GREEN
TIVERTON   BARUM

LIGHT WELTER-WEIGHT CONTEST
L. KING v SAPPER ANDERSON
TIVERTON   A.W.X.E., FREMINGTON

FEATHER-WEIGHT CONTEST
DENNIS HEARD v MERVYN GREEN
KILKHAMPTON   BARUM

MIDDLE-WEIGHT CONTEST
ALAN BIRKS v Will Box Opponent selected by Devon A.B.A.
EXETER

HEAVY-WEIGHT CONTEST
NORMAN
PATTERSON v SHADDICK
L.A.C.   BARUM
R.A.F. and BARUM

MIDDLE-WEIGHT CONTEST
D. MAUNDER v STANLEY BRIGHT
TIVERTON   BARUM

LIGHT WELTER-WEIGHT CONTEST
L. HUTCHINGS v L.A.C. WALLACE
EXETER   R.A.F. and BARUM

LIGHT MIDDLE-WEIGHT CONTEST
STAN IVY v MICHAEL CHILD
BIDEFORD   BARUM

WELTER-WEIGHT CONTEST
C. MOORE v D. M. DREW
TIVERTON   EXETER

WELTER-WEIGHT CONTEST
D. MITCHELL v L.A.C. ADCOCK
EXETER   R.A.F. and BARUM

FEATHER-WEIGHT CONTEST
LEWIS ELLIS v STAN BISHOP
BIDEFORD   BARUM

FEATHER-WEIGHT CONTEST
B. WREY v MICHAEL GABRIEL
BIDEFORD   BARUM

Programme indicates PATTERSON versus SHADDICK as the MAIN EVENT.
Some well known local boxers on this bill.

LIVELY CONTESTS AT FREMINGTON

NORTH DEVON JOURNAL HERALD Dec 14 1945

Well over 100 people were turned away from Mountbatten Hall, Fremington, on Friday night when they were unable to get into the hall to watch two hours of amateur boxing. The contests, under A.B.A. rules, were held in aid of the Fremington Boys' Clubs, and the whole seating capacity was filled long before the first bout commenced.

The most exciting match of the evening was a David-and-Goliath affair. B. Shaddick, a youngster from the Bickington Boys' Club, was matched with E. Powe (Barnstaple) in a cruiserweight contest. In the second round Powe took three counts and in the third round was down for two counts of eight before he retired. Shaddick punched with devastating speed and power.

The sensation of the night was provided by Rifleman Koorlander (Fremington). After the first round of his bout with Gunner Jarvis (Fremington) he went back to his corner, and did not seem to be suffering from the punishment he had received. No sooner had he sat down when he slumped unconscious to the canvas. His seconds managed to revive him, but before the second round began Koorlander again became unconscious and had to be carried from the ring. Fortunately no serious harm was caused and he was able to get into the ring at the close of the evening to receive his medal.

Results

Bantamweight.—J. Hill (Fremington) k.o. Sapper Haslett (C.O.X.E.), second round. Flyweight.—P. Fewings (Barnstaple) beat O. Cornish (Bickington) on points. Welterweight.—A. Turner (Barnstaple) k.o. Pte. Brennan (C.O.X.E.), first round. Lightweight.—Winsor (Bickington Boys' Club) beat Sapper Jones (C.O.X.E.) on points. Featherweight.—F. Fewings (Barnstaple) beat L. Moody (Bickington Boys' Club). Retired second round.

Welterweight. — Gunner Jarvis (Fremington) beat Rifleman Koorlander (Fremington). Retired after first round. Cruiserweight.—B. Shaddick (Bickington Boys' Club) beat E. Powe (Barnstaple). Retired third round. Lightweight.—A.-C. Bartlett (R.A.F., Chivenor) beat Sapper Puttnam (C.O.X.E.). Referee stopped the bout in the last round. L.-Cpl. Brogden (C.O.X.E.) beat R. Jennings (Fremington) on points. A.-C. Duncan (R.A.F., Chivenor) beat J. Taylor (Salem Club, Barnstaple) on points.

Cup for most meritorious winner. —P. Fewings. Cup for most meritorious loser.—Sapper Puttnam.

H. Lawrence (Crewkerne), a sparring partner to Freddie Mills, was to fight J. Pearce (Barnstaple) in an exhibition bout, but he had to decline because of an injury. In his place Flight-Sergt. J. Pearce (R.A.F. Chivenor) gave an exhibition with J. Pearce, of Barnstaple.

The cups and medals were presented by Mrs. Barclay Black, and the officials were: Judges, Capt. A. C. Snow, J.P., and Capt. Cairns, R.A. Referee, Mr. W. Fewings; timekeeper, Mr. Jack Easton; M.C., R.-S.-M. W. Riley; whlp, N. Thompson; and seconds, Clr.-Sgt. Crocker, R.M., and Mr. J. J. Downes.

Little Jennifer Stacey presented sprays to Mrs. Barclay Black, and Mrs. L. P. Durnford-Slater, and Mr. R. H. Stacey auctioned various articles.

Harvey helps mayor complete 'hat-trick'

THIRD CHAMPION INTRODUCED

THE Mayor of Barnstaple (Alderman Cyril Blackmore), who on previous occasions had introduced Tommy Farr and Bruce Woodcock to Barnstaple audiences, completed his "hat-trick" on Monday when he introduced Len Harvey from the ring at an amateur boxing tournament in the Pannier Market.

The former British and Empire champion was kept busy between rounds by hordes of autograph-hunters.

The boxing programme he saw provided plenty of variety, with the ratio of lively bouts to unexciting ones disappointingly low before the interval; however, some bright matches in the second half made amends.

Unfortunately, what could have been one of the most attractive matches of the evening, a four-round middleweight contest between Arthur Cole (Bideford) and C. McHugh, was spoilt by the boxers' repeatedly going into clinches. McHugh seemed to be the principal offender, and one felt that the booing that greeted the points decision in Cole's favour was directed not so much at the winner as at the general standard of the match.

ONE KNOCK-OUT

Only three contests failed to go the scheduled distance. Alan Birks (Exeter) knocked out Stanley Bright (Barnstaple) in the second round of their three-round match, and L.A.C. Towler gained the decision when P. Raymond retired with an injured hand at the end of the second round of a four-round bout. Towler was later awarded a cup for the best senior.

A three-round match between L. Hutchings (Exeter) and Sidney Smith (Barnstaple) was stopped in Hutchings' favour in the second round.

The disadvantage of conceding several inches in both height and reach proved too much for Otto Senik (Barnstaple), who lost on points to D. J. Mitchell. Senik showed that the obstacle of his opponent's long left was by no means insuperable, but, plugging away with his left in all three rounds, Mitchell built up an adequate points lead.

There was plenty of life, with spells of flurried in-fighting, in a four-round heavyweight contest between Norman Shaddick (Barnstaple) and L.A.C. Patterson (R.A.F. and Barnstaple). Shaddick won on points, Patterson taking a brief count in the last round.

GAMEST LOSER

A cup for the gamest loser went to O. Bennett (Tiverton), who, although his face was covered in blood during the last two rounds of a three-round bout with Raymond Jewell (Barnstaple), fought back pluckily against a hard-hitting opponent.

The winner of a cup for the best junior was Raymond Scoynes, whose style and cool temperament could have been copied profitably by some of the older boxers. He defeated L. Saffer (Tiverton) on points.

Other results: Boy Cooke (Barnstaple) bt. Boy Dober (Barnstaple) on points; M. Gabriel (Barnstaple) bt. B. Wrey (Bideford) on points; L.A.C. Stevenson (R.A.F. and Barnstaple) bt. K. Williams on points; Charlie Cornish (Barnstaple) bt P. Maunder (Tiverton) on points; D. Johns (Exeter) bt. Derek Windsor (Barnstaple) on points; George Ley (Barnstaple) bt. Jim Offield (Barnstaple) on points.

The tournament was organized by the Barnstaple Amateur Boxing Club in aid of the Barnstaple Old People's Hostel.

Cups and certificates were distributed by the Mayoress.

YOUNG BOXERS ARE CONGRATULATED

Fremington decision

Two young boxers from the Fremington area will shortly receive messages of congratulation on their achievements from Fremington Parish Council.

They are Norman Shaddick, of Bickington, who has won the West of England heavyweight boxing championship of the Amateur Boxing Association, and David Davis, of Belmont College, who has reached the final of the intermediate class of the English schoolboys' championship. Davis will fight in the final at Harringay on Monday.

When it was decided to send these messages at a meeting of the Council on Monday, Mr. R. H. Stacey said it seemed that fighting was the only thing in which the parish excelled, and Mr. F. George said he hoped that Dr. Edith Summerskill would put forward no objections.

THIRD CHAMPION INTRODUCED

THE Mayor of Barnstaple (Alderman Cyril Blackmore), who on previous occasions had introduced Tommy Farr and Bruce Woodcock to Barnstaple audiences, completed his "hat-trick" on Monday when he introduced Len Harvey from the ring at an amateur boxing tournament in the Pannier Market.

The former British and Empire champion was kept busy between rounds by hordes of autograph-hunters.

The boxing programme he saw provided plenty of variety, with the ratio of lively bouts to unexciting ones disappointingly low before the interval; however, some bright matches in the second half made amends.

Unfortunately, what could have been one of the most attractive matches of the evening, a four-round middleweight contest between Arthur Cole (Bideford) and C. McHugh, was spoilt by the boxers' repeatedly going into clinches. McHugh seemed to be the principal offender, and one felt that the booing that greeted the points decision in Cole's favour was directed not so much at the winner as at the general standard of the match.

22-1-1951

ONE KNOCK-OUT

Only three contests failed to go the scheduled distance. Alan Birks (Exeter) knocked out Stanley Bright (Barnstaple) in the second round of their three-round match, and L.A.C. Towler gained the decision when P. Raymond retired with an injured hand at the end of the second round of a four-round bout. Towler was later awarded a cup for the best senior.

A three-round match between L. Hutchings (Exeter) and Sidney Smith (Barnstaple) was stopped in Hutchings' favour in the second round.

The disadvantage of conceding several inches in both height and reach proved too much for Otto Senik (Barnstaple), who lost on points to D. J. Mitchell. Senik showed that the obstacle of his opponent's long left was by no means insuperable, but, plugging away with his left in all three rounds, Mitchell built up an adequate points lead.

There was plenty of life, with spells of flurried in-fighting, in a four-round heavyweight contest between Norman Shaddick (Barnstaple) and L.A.C. Patterson (R.A.F. and Barnstaple). Shaddick won on points, Patterson taking a brief count in the last round.

GAMEST LOSER

A cup for the gamest loser went to O. Bennett (Tiverton), who, although his face was covered in blood during the last two rounds of a three-round bout with Raymond Jewell (Barnstaple), fought back pluckily against a hard-hitting opponent.

The winner of a cup for the best junior was Raymond Scoynes, whose style and cool temperament could have been copied profitably by some of the older boxers. He defeated L. Saffer (Tiverton) on points.

Other results: Boy Cooke (Barnstaple) bt. Boy Dober (Barnstaple) on points; M. Gabriel (Barnstaple) bt. B. Wrey (Bideford) on points; L.A.C. Stevenson (R.A.F. and Barnstaple) bt. K. Williams on points; Charlie Cornish (Barnstaple) bt P. Maunder (Tiverton) on points; D. Johns (Exeter) bt. Derek Windsor (Barnstaple) on points; George Ley (Barnstaple) bt. Jim Offield (Barnstaple) on points.

The tournament was organized by the Barnstaple Amateur Boxing Club in aid of the Barnstaple Old People's Hostel.

ACTION PACKED BOXING

CHILD BEATS COLE

Barnstaple and Bideford really came to grips on Monday when Michael Child, of Barnstaple, and Arthur Cole, of Bideford, provided a thrill-packed quarter-of-an-hour in a contest that was the high-light of a boxing tournament presented by the Barnstaple Amateur Boxing Club. Child was the winner.

There was action throughout the four-round bout, but Cole found no answer to Child's strong two-handed rushes.

There was no doubt of Child's superiority in every round, but what his opponent lacked in skill he certainly made up in pluck.

One of the best action fights was between Stan Bright (Barnstaple) and Birks (Exeter). Birks won on points. Bright was knocked down in the second round.

Otto Senik, of Barnstaple fought gamely against Mitchell, of Exeter, but lost the decision on points. There could be little doubt that Mitchell had built up a points advantage with his repeated and accurate straight lefts.

There was an exciting contest between Adcott (R.A.F. and Barnstaple) and Hutchings, of Exeter. Both boys gave and received hard knocks, but Hutchings hit the harder.

Norman Shaddick (Barnstaple) had a "rare go" with L.A.C. Patterson, of the R.A.F., before losing the decision on points. The bout was surprisingly 'open' for heavyweights and the final round was a terrific tussle between two evenly-matched opponents.

Both boxers went out of the ring in the early seconds of a bout between Desmond Sanders, of Torrington, and L.A.C. Cooper, of the R.A.F. Sanders landed on his head, but they both came back to provide a spirited contest which Cooper won on points.

Other results were: E. Drew (Exeter) outpointed L. Saffer (Tiverton). Joey Ovey (Barnstaple) outpointed M. Saffer (Tiverton); Dennis Green (Barnstaple) outpointed Raymond Scoynes (Bideford). M. Furze (Exeter) outpointed Brian Scoynes (Bideford). B. Wrey (Bideford) outpointed Michael Gabriel (Barnstaple). Mervyn Green (Barnstaple) beat Tele Purdy (Combined Ops. and Barnstaple), referee stopped bout in first round. J. Johns (Exeter) outpointed A. Furze (Exeter). D. Drew (Exeter) outpointed P. Maunder (Tiverton). D. Johns (Exeter) outpointed Brogan (R.A.F.)

BICKINGTON'S VICTORY OVER BARNSTAPLE

The Tomlin Hall, Bickington, was the scene of a well-staged boxing competition on Tuesday evening when Bickington Youth Club, winning six of the eight bouts and drawing one, beat Salem Youth Club, Barnstaple.

The boys, who were aged between 16 and 18, were trained by Messrs. H. Thompson and Taylor. The outstanding contest was the one between Shaddick (Bickington) and Taylor (Barnstaple), which was won by the Bickington youth.

The officials were: chairman of judges, Mr. F. Downling, M.C.; Mr. C. Pennell; timekeeper, Mr. R. Lee; and medical officer, Dr. R. King.—There were two exhibition bouts and the proceeds were in aid of the Bickington Club.

and trailer with inefficient brakes,
Mr. ... Oerton pleaded guilty on his
being ... and summonsed ...

Beaten on points

M. Shaddick, the Barnstaple heavyweight, was beaten on points by W. Halsey (Midland Counties) in the Amateur Boxing Association senior zone championships at Avonmouth on Saturday.

LIVELY BOXING

Mountbatten Hall, Fremington, was filled to capacity last night for the amateur boxing tournament staged to aid the funds of Fremington Boys' Club. The sponsors were Capt. A. C. Snow and Mrs. W. T. King.

Almost without exception, contests were very fiercely but sportingly fought, and a thriller was the cruiserweight bout in which B. Shaddick (Bickington) bt E. Powe (Barnstaple), a S.W. area champion. Exchanges were fast and ferocious. Powe, the older man, after taking a number of long counts, had to acknowledge defeat in the final round.

A big disappointment was that H. Lawrence (Crewkerne), a sparring partner of Freddie Mills, was unable to box owing to injury. He hopes to be able to take part in a future tournament.

Flight-Sergt. J. Pearce (R.A.F. Chivenor) was a capable deputy for Lawrence in a four-rounds light heavyweight exhibition bout with the polished J. Pearce, of Barnstaple, the South-West area champion.

CUPS FOR TWO

The silver challenge cup subscribed for by residents of Fremington parish for the most meritorious winner went to P. Fewings (Barnstaple). Another silver cup, donated by Major and Mrs. Barclay Black, for the best loser was won by Sapper Putnam (C.O.X.E.).

Judges were Capt. A. C. Snow and Capt. Cairns, with Mr. W. Fewings as referee. Mr. Jack Easton was timekeeper, and R.S.M. W. Riley the M.C.

Mr. R. H. Stacey swelled the funds by conducting an auction during the interval. The prizes were presented by Mrs. Barclay Black.

Results:—

Bantamweight: J. Hill (Fremington) knocked out Pte. Haslett (C.O.X.E.) in second round. Flyweight: P. Fewings (Barnstaple) beat Young Cornish (Bickington). Welterweight: A. Turner (Barnstaple) knocked out Pte. Brennan (C.O.X.E.), first round. Lightweight: Winsor (Bickington) beat Pte. Jones (C.O.X.E.). Featherweight: P. Fewings (Barnstaple) beat L. Moody (Bickington), who retired second round. Welterweight: Gunner Jervis (School of Combined Operations) beat Rifleman Koorlander (Fremington), retired second round. Cruiserweight: B. Shaddick (Bickington) beat E. Powe (Barnstaple), retired third round. Lightweight: A. C. Bartlett (R.A.F. Chivenor) beat Sapper Putnam (C.O.X.E.), the referee stopping the fight in the third round. Welterweight: L-Cpl. Brogden (C.O.X.E.) beat R. Jennings (Fremington). Featherweight: A. C. Duncan (R.A.F. Chivenor) beat J. Taylor (Barnstaple).

Pyrrhus III., 8, 1200 ......

THREE DEVON BOXERS GAIN WEST COUNTIES TITLES

EXCELLENT boxing was seen at the Torquay Town Hall on Saturday, when the new holders of the Western Counties titles were decided. Torquay Apollo Sports Club were the organisers.

The champions of Devon, Dorset, and Cornwall faced the champions of Gloucester, Somerset, and Wilts in six title bouts, and each won three contests.

C. Davies (Torquay Apollo, welterweight), P. Bourne (Exmouth, light-middle), and Brian Pollard (Exmouth, middle) won titles for Devon.

The new title-holders will box the Midland counties champions at Bristol on March 31.

L. Goodman (Virginia House, Plymouth), bantam-weight champion of Devon, Dorset, and Cornwall, was over-weight and his opponent, S. A. Meek (Cinderford B.C.) was declared the winner of the Western Counties' title.

J. D. Johns (Exeter B.C.), featherweight champion of Devon, Dorset, and Cornwall, was also over-weight and K. Faull (Cinderford B.C.) added the Western County title to his record.

Both Goodman and Johns beat the championship rivals in special supporting bouts on points.

L. Hutchings (Exeter), who recently won the Devon, Dorset, and Cornwall lightweight title, was unable to compete as he had injured his fingers in an accident.

C. Hariatt (Poole), who took his place, was beaten on points by Ivor George (Olympia B.C.).

THE RESULTS

Western Counties' championships.—Lightweight—Ivor George (Olympia B.C.) bt C. Hariatt (Poole B.C.). Light-welter — W. Ashman (Bedminster B.C.) bt J. E. Cope (Kingsbridge), third round. Welter—C. Davies (Torquay Apollo) bt T. A. le Cheminant (Salisbury B.C.). Light-middle—P. Bourne (Exmouth) bt J. Plenty (Bedminster B.C.). Middle—B. Pollard (Exmouth) bt N. Rogers (National Smelting B.C.). Light-heavy—E. James (Swindon B.C.) bt A. Stanley (Poole).

W. Wyatt (Torquay Apollo, flyweight) and K. Shaddick (Barnstaple, heavy-weight) are Western Counties champions on walk-overs.

Other contests.—Middle-weight—J. Mudge (Apollo) k.o. E. Quick (National Smelting B.C.), third round. Light—T. Towler (R.A.F. and Apollo) k.o. J. Dixon (National Smelting B.C.), first round. Welter—K. Ernst (R.A.F. and Exeter) outpointed P. King (Army and Apollo). Feather—R. Thompson (Apollo) bt L. Honeybon (Weymouth), on points. Bantam — L. Goodman (Virginia House) bt S. A. Meek (Cinderford B.C.), on points. Feather—J. D. Johns (Exeter) bt K. Faull (Cinderford B.C.).

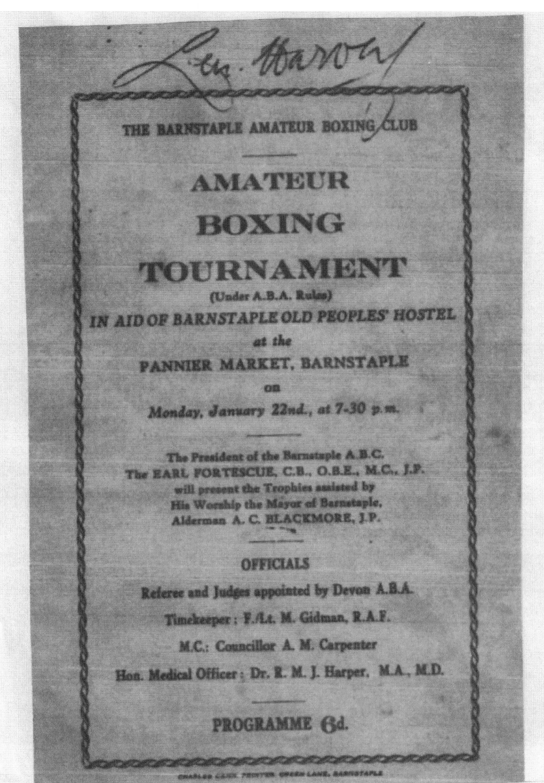

THE BARNSTAPLE AMATEUR BOXING CLUB

AMATEUR
BOXING
TOURNAMENT

(Under A.B.A. Rules)

IN AID OF BARNSTAPLE OLD PEOPLES' HOSTEL

at the

PANNIER MARKET, BARNSTAPLE

on

Monday, January 22nd., at 7.30 p.m.

The President of the Barnstaple A.B.C.
The EARL FORTESCUE, C.B., O.B.E., M.C., J.P.
will present the Trophies assisted by
His Worship the Mayor of Barnstaple,
Alderman A. C. BLACKMORE, J.P.

OFFICIALS

Referee and Judges appointed by Devon A.B.A.

Timekeeper : F./Lt. M. Gidman, R.A.F.

M.C.: Councillor A. M. Carpenter

Hon. Medical Officer : Dr. R. M. J. Harper, M.A., M.D.

PROGRAMME 6d.

CHARLES CASE, PRINTER, GREEN LANE, BARNSTAPLE

The BARNSTAPLE ABA show on JANUARY 22nd 1951 in the BARNSTAPLE PANNIER MARKET saw NORMAN in ACTION. He won on POINTS. Known as 'BRUISER,' his fighting style would have proved successful if he had decided to turn PROFESSIONAL. Looking at his 'AMATEUR' record, it is full of bouts with boxers who had great experience in the paid ranks.

BOUT 1

Three Rounds Tissue-paperweight Contest

BOY DOBER v. BOY COOKE *won*

Barum   *Barum* *Pts*

BOUT 2

Beat Junior

Three Rounds Contest

RAYMOND SCOYNES v. JOEY OVEY

Bideford   *Barum*

BOUT 3

Three Rounds Contest

B. WREY v. M. GABRIEL *won Pts*

Bideford   *Barum*

BOUT 4

Three Rounds Contest

O. BENNETT v. RAYMOND JEWELL

Tiverton   *Barum* ...

BOUT 5

Three Rounds Contest

L. SAFFER v. BRIAN SCOYNES

Tiverton   *Bideford*

BOUT 6

Three Rounds Contest

S. SNOW v. L.A.C. STEVENSON

Tiverton   *R.A.F. & Barum*

BOUT 7

Four Rounds Heavyweight Contest *won*

L.A.C. PATTERSON v. NORMAN SHADDICK

R.A.F. & Barum   *Barum* *Pts*

BOUT 8

Three Rounds Contest *won Pts*

P. MAUNDER v. CHARLIE CORNISH

Tiverton   *Barum*

BOUT 9

Three Rounds Contest

LEWIS ELLIS v. SIDNEY SMITH

Bideford   *Barum*

BOUT 10

Four Rounds Middleweight Contest

ARTHUR COLE v. MICHAEL CHILD

Bideford   *Barum* ...

BOUT 11

won Pts *Four Rounds Contest*

D. JOHNS v. DEREK WINDSOR

Exeter   *Barum*

BOUT 12

wre Ko *Three Rounds Contest*

ALAN BIRKS v. STANLEY BRIGHT

Exeter   *Barum* ...

BOUT 13

Ko *Four Rounds Contest* *S. Smith*

L. HUTCHINGS v. HADYN HIGGINS

Exeter   *Barum*

BOUT 14

Four Rounds Contest *won Pts*

JIM OFFIELD v. GEORGE LEY

Barum   *Barum*

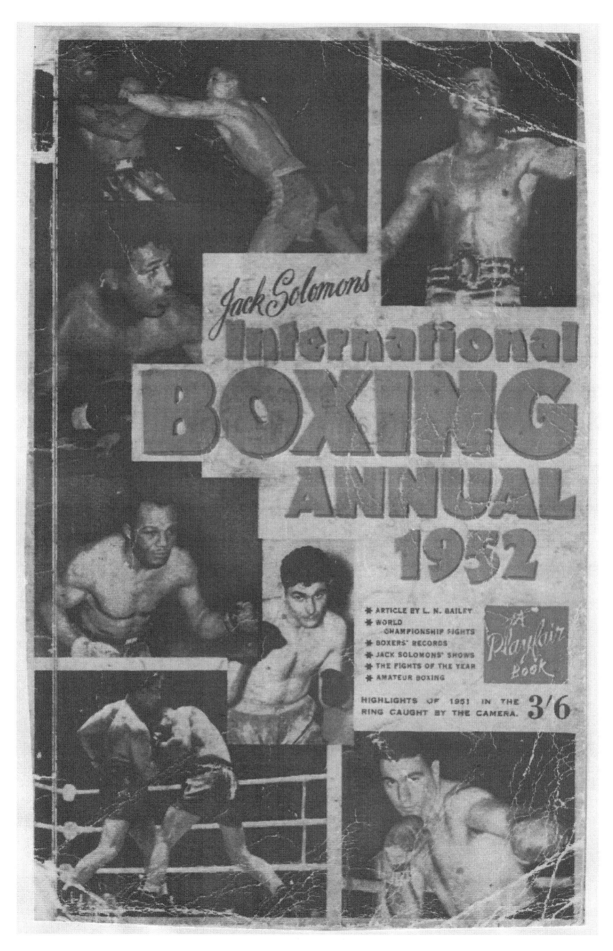

LONDON

Fly—G. JOHN (Slough)
Bantam—A. SILLETT (C.A.V.)
Feather—P. DUFFELL (Southfield School, Oxford)
Light—R. HINSON (W. Ham)
Light-welter—F. WARD (St. Boniface)
Welter—J. MALONEY (Dagenham & District)
Light-middle—A. LAY* (Battersea)
Middle—A. HOWARD* (Crown and Manor)
Light-heavy—G. WALKER* (Thames Refinery)
Heavy—J. CRICKMAR (Stepney Institute)
       * Now professional

NORTH EAST LONDON

Fly—H. GRIVER (New Lansdowne)
Bantam—D. HINSON (W.Ham)
Feather—S. MASTERS (Repton)
Light—R. HINSON (W. Ham)
Light-welter—P. GUTTERIDGE (West Ham)
Welter—J. MALONEY (Dagenham & District)
Light-middle—P. LONGO (Crown and Manor)
Middle—A. HOWARD (Crown and Manor)
Light-heavy—G. WALKER (Thames Refinery)
Heavy—J. CRICKMAR (Stepney Institute)

NORTH WEST LONDON

Fly—D. GLANVILLE (Hoovar)
Bantam—A. MORRIS (Hoover)
Feather—P. DUFFELL (Southfield School, Oxford)
Light—D. HANNELL (Stowe)
Light-welter—R. TARRIER (Polytechnic)
Welter—C. WILLIAMS (Alexandra)
Light-middle—J. BRIARS (Potters Bar)
Middle—F. WOOLLARD (Callowland)
Light-heavy—S. DUNSFORD (Stowe)
Heavy—R. MILES (Stowe)

SOUTH EAST LONDON

Fly—A. SMITH (Redriff Community)
Bantam—R. BOOTMAN (J. and E. Hall)
Feather—B. ROBSON (Croydon)
Light—C. TOUZEL (Ramsgate)
Light-welter—W. PLUMLEY (Fitzroy Lodge)
Welter—W. BECKETT (Camberwell)
Light-middle—D. McCLEAVE (Robert Browning)
Middle—G. RAYMENT (Robert Browning)
Light-heavy—F. HILL (Fitzroy Lodge)
Heavy—T. McNULTY (Eltham)

SOUTH WEST LONDON

Fly—G. JOHN (Slough Centre)
Bantam—A. SILLETT (C.A.V.)
Feather—F. WOODMAN (Earlsfield)

Light—H. DUFFIN (Earlsfield)
Light-welter—F. WARD (St. Boniface)
Welter—B. HEARN (British Lion)
Light-middle—A. LAY (Battersea)
Middle—R. DUNCOMBE (St. Helier, Jersey)
Light-heavy—D. ELMS (Hove)
Heavy—E. HEARN (Battersea)

MIDLAND COUNTIES

Fly—A. JONES (Lucas)
Bantam—T. ICKE (Bournbrook)
Feather—R. JOYCE (Radford)
Light—L. BENNETT (Ludlow)
Light-welter—P. JONES (Sankey)
Welter—R. RICKETTS (Austin)
Light-middle—J. ANDREWS (Morris)
Middle—K. PHILLIPS (Warley)
Light-heavy—D. BRADBURY (Wolverhampton)
Heavy—A. HALSEY (Kyrle Hall)

NORTHERN COUNTIES

Fly—S. HAWKES (Jarrow Community)
Bantam—W. GIBSON (Fishburn)
Feather—R. LONGSTAFF (Darlington R.A.)
Light—C. HARRISON (Steel, Peach and Tozer)
Light-welter—W. CONNER (Lowe House, St. Helens)
Welter—P. KING (St. Augustine's)
Light-middle—W. McHALE (Wombwell)
Middle—G. WILSON (Leeds)
Light-heavy—R. HACKETT (Flying Angel)
Heavy—R. HACKETT (Flying Angel, Salford)

SOUTHERN COUNTIES

Fly—J. LOCKYER (Brighton)
Bantam—D. JAMES (Farnborough)
Feather—K. LAWRENCE (Southampton)
Light—T. BARNES (Brighton)
Light-welter—B. RICH (Hove)
Welter—D. DAVIES (Gosport)
Light-middle—E. BAKER (Chichester)
Middle—W. SPARKMAN (Southampton)
Light-heavy—D. ELMS (Hove)

WESTERN COUNTIES

Fly—W. WYATT (Apollo, Torquay)
Bantam—S. MEEK (Cinderford)
Feather—K. FAULL (Cinderford)
Light—I. GEORGE (Olympia)
Light-welter—W. ASHMAN (Bedminster)
Welter—C. DAVIES (Apollo)
Light-middle—P. BOURNE (Exmouth)
Middle—B. POLLARD (Exmouth)
Light-heavy—E. JAMES (Swindon)
Heavy—N. SHADDICK (Barnstaple)

SCOTTISH WESTERN DISTRICT
(EIGHT WEIGHTS)

Fly—A. MOORE (L.M.S. Rovers)
Bantam—P. McEWAN (Oxford, Glasgow)
Feather—D. McQUEEN (N.B. Loco)
Light—N. MAGUIRE (N.B. Loco)
Welter—D. MALLOY (Scottish National)
Middle—W. ARMSTRONG (N.B. Loco)
Light-heavy—S. DISHER (Meat Trades)
Heavy—Vacant

SCOTTISH EASTERN
(EIGHT WEIGHTS)

Fly—P. JONES (Armadale)
Bantam—R. HUNTER (Sparta)
Feather—D. CARMICHAEL (Leith Victoria)
Light—J. WILSON (Gilmerton)
Welter—J. DRUMMOND (Burntisland)
Middle—J. PRENTICE (Armadale)
Light-heavy—M. BELL (Leith Victoria)
Heavy—M. BELL (Leith Victoria)

SCOTTISH MIDLAND
(EIGHT WEIGHTS)

Fly—R. BLAKELY (Dundee)
Bantam—R. BLAKELY (Dundee)
Feather—P. McINROY (Perth)
Light—W. WRIGHT (Dundee)
Welter—W. ABERNETHY (Montrose)
Middle—T. JOHNSTONE (Dundee)
Light-heavy—P. HARLEY (Lochee)
Heavy—J. STEWART (Montrose)

ALLIED MILITARY CHAMPIONS
(1950 First Year, not boxed in 1951)

Fly—E. DELPLANQUE (Belgium)
Bantam—J. DUMESNIL (France)
Feather—P. LEWIS (Britain)
Light—A. SELBEY (France)
Welter—T. RATCLIFFE (Britain)
Middle—C. LAVNICZACK (France)
Light-heavy—A. PASTOR (Holland)
Heavy—J. ABAD (France)

IMPERIAL SERVICES

Fly—A/B. H. WELIWITIGODA (Navy)
Bantam—A/C. T. NICHOLLS (R.A.F.)
Feather—A/C. P. LEWIS (R.A.F.)
Light—A/C. A. WALLACE (R.A.F.)
Light-welter—L/Cpl. J. DRUMMOND (Army)
Welter—Sig. A. BAIRD (Army)
Light-middle—L/Sgt. D. ROBERTS (Army)
Middle—L/Cpl. E. LUDLAM (Army)

NORMAN SHADDICK.

JIM BARTLETT

BOXING

ROYAL AIR FORCE FAYID

(BY PERMISSION OF GROUP CAPTAIN D.M.T. MACDONALD)

ON

Wednesday 16th May 1951 at 20.00 hours

OFFICIALS

REFEREES :	Major J. A. MANSI.
	Captain J. H. CONNOLLY M.M.
JUDGES :	Squadron Leader L. W. DAVIES
	Flight Lieutenant D. M. BROWN
	Flight Lieutenant G. C. MATHEWS.
TIME KEEPER :	Flying Officer F. J. LAWSON
MASTER OF CEREMONIES :	Warrant Officer W. S. ROWE.
MEDICAL OFFICER :	Flying Officer J. A. S. AMOS.

PROGRAMME 1 P.T.

The Imperial Services Boxing Association Rules

The competition is governed by the above rules, which state that the Referee and Judges must remain outside the ring. Because of this rule it is essential that spectators remain silent while the boxing is in progress in order that the boxers may hear that referee's commands. Spectators are reminded that the intervention of the Referee is only necessary in the event of a foul blow or risk of serious injury and that his first interest is the safety of the boxers. The spectators may show their appreciation between rounds and between fights.

WEIGHTS

		St.	Lbs.
FLY	Under	8	0
BANTAM	"	8	7
FEATHER	"	9	0
LIGHT	"	9	7
LIGHT WELTER	"	10	0
WELTER	"	10	8
LIGHT MIDDLE	"	11	2
MIDDLE	"	11	11
LIGHT HEAVY	"	12	10
HEAVY	"	Catch Weight	

Albertin Press - Ismailia

PROGRAMME

ALL BOUTS WILL CONSIST OF THREE 2 MINUTE ROUNDS

Bout No.	RED CORNER		GREEN CORNER

BANTAM WEIGHT

1. A.C. Moon. (Kabrit) R.A.F. (Egypt) Champion 1951 V Pte Joyce (G.H.Q. M.E.LF.)

LIGHT WEIGHT

2. L.A.C. Bartlett (Fayid) V A.C. O'Reilly (Deversoir) R.A.F. (Egypt) Champion 1951

LIGHT WEIGHT

3. L.A.C. Marshall (Fayid) V Pte Mulholland GHQ MELF.

LIGHT WEIGHT

4. A.C. Sumpter (Fayid) R.A.F. (Egypt) Runner Up 1951 V A.C. O'Brien (Abyad)

NOVICE LIGHT WEIGHT

5. A.C. D'Arcy (107 M.U.) V A.C. O'Flaherty (Abyad)

LIGHT WELTER WEIGHT

6. L.A.C. Notman (Fayid) Inter Service (Egypt) Champion 1951 V A.C. Ferguson (El Hamra) R.A.F. (Egypt) Champion 1951

LIGHT WELTER WEIGHT

7. A.C. Hunter (Abyad) R.A.F. (Egypt) Runner Up 1951 V L.A.C. Trainor (Shallufa)

INTERVAL

Bout No.	RED CORNER		GREEN CORNER

SPECIAL LIGHT WEIGHT

8. Mohamed Atila Champion of Egypt V Mohamad Abdul Samad Champion of Canal Zone Runner Up Egypt

WELTER WEIGHT

9. Cpl. Flannagan (Kabrit) V L/Cpl. Mouer GHQ. MELF. Army Egypt Inter Service Egypt Champion 1951

LIGHT MIDDLE WEIGHT

10. J/T Elkins (Abyad) V A.C. O'Meilia (El Hamra) Welter Weight R.A.F. Egypt 1951 Inter Service Champion 1951

LIGHT MIDDLE WEIGHT

11. L.A.C. Adjetunmobi (Fayid) V Sgt. Downing (Deversoir) R.A.F. (Egypt) Champion 1951

HEAVY WEIGHT

12. W.O. Hiscock (Fayid) R.A.F. Egypt Champion 1950 V S.A.C. Gorge (Shallufa) R.A.F. Egypt Runner Up 1951

MIDDLE WEIGHT

13. A.C. Flynn (Kabrit) R.A.F. Inter Service (Egypt) Champion 1951 V Pte Parkes G.H.Q. M.E.LF. Army (Egypt) Champion 1951

LIGHT HEAVY WEIGHT

14. A.C. Scott (Kabrit) R.A.F. Egypt Champion 1951 V Cpl. Flood (El Firdan) R.A.F. Egypt Runner Up 1951

PRESENTATION OF PRIZES

GOD SAVE THE KING

BOXING

AMATEUR BOXING TOURNAMENT

BIDEFORD AMATEUR BOXING CLUB v. BICKINGTON AMATEUR BOXING CLUB

for the SNOW ANNUAL TROPHY (Donated by the President, Bideford & District Amateur Boxing Club)

PANNIER MARKET, BIDEFORD
THURSDAY, JUNE 9th

COMMENCING 7.30 P.M. SHARP

EACH BOUT TO CONSIST OF THREE TWO MINUTE ROUNDS

BIDEFORD		BICKINGTON	BIDEFORD		BICKINGTON
LEN DIBBLE	V	B. BUTLER	TERRY TYTHCOTT	V	C. BARTLETT
MICK SCHILLERS	V	MICK CHILDS	LEWIS ELLIS	V	S. SMITH
RAYMOND SCOINES	V	M. MILLER	RON ANSTIS	V	S. BISHOP
GARFIELD WATKINS	V	D. WINSOR	CYRIL HEARN	V	J. PEARCE
ARTHUR COLE	V	D. FRENCH	PETER WREY	V	S. BRIGHT
BASIL TUER	V	R. SHADDICK	DEREK BROMELL	V	C. CORNISH
			REG. ANSTIS	V	M. MOLLAND

Cups and trophy to be presented at the conclusion by Mrs. Snow (wife of the President)

OFFICIALS:

Judges: Arthur C. Snow, Major Reynolds, Col. Bullock.
Referee: R.S.M. Riley.
Timekeepers: Reg. Lee, Cliff Branch.
Medical Officer in attendance.

TICKETS AVAILABLE AT CLUB HEADQUARTERS, REAR JOINERS ARMS, MARKET PLACE, BIDEFORD 5.30 to 7 p.m. DAILY OR MESSRS. GALES, MILL STREET, BIDEFORD

PRICES 7/6 5/- 3/6 Reserved. 2/6 Unreserved

JUNE 9th 1949. JIM in ACTION.

101

JIM seated front row, far right.

BARNSTAPLE ABC

Barnstaple Amateur Boxing & Athletic Club

(Affiliated to A.B.A., N.A.B.C., N.D.B.A., B.R.L.)
President : Col. J. N. OLIVER, C.B.E., T.D., J.P.
Chairman : Mr. J. J. F. TALBOT, North Gate Hotel
Treasurer : Mr. J. W. C. SAUNDERS, 7 River View, Landkey Road

Coach :
J. BARTLETT

Trainer :
W. NEALE.

Rolle Street Warehouses
MON. - WED. - FRI. - 7 p.m.

Hon. Secretary :
Mr. J. A. MASON,
9 Ashleigh Road,
Barnstaple

October 2nd /59

AN OPEN LETTER TO JIM BARTLETT - COACH

Jim Bartlett
Coach
Barnstaple A.B.A.C.

Dear Jim,
It has been a great shock to us to learn that
you have been thinking of dropping off of the Clubs training
staff as Coach, as it has been our pleasure to have been
associated with you in that capacity, since our first joining
the Club;- won't you please reconsider this move Jim ?, and
stay with us for at least one evening per week, and be in our
corners when we need you the most.

Perhaps events of the past may have dampened your enthusi-
iasm, and interfered with the interest you have shown in the
past, but as our official Coach, we would like you to know
that we would like to remain your proteges this season; and
the Club Secretary has promised that the right kind of co-op
eration, will be forthcoming from the Club Committee, and
that no kind of interference, (in your duties as Coach, or
your training schedule) will be tolerated.

This plea comes from your junior and senior boxers, trainers
and supporters, please stay with us Jim, we need you.
Sincerely

A PETITION,
SIGNED BY the BOXERS in SUPPORT of JIM BARTLETT.

PAT JONES	D. J. ISAAC	JOHN WEBBER	F. YEO
A. MASON		DREW WILLIAMS	R. J. BURRIDGE	H. YEO
G. HALLET	H. BAGLOLE	GEOFFREY YEO	JOHN W NEALE	CAROL
W. MAYO	A. TYTHCOTT	MALCOLM SMITH	R. TRUTE	
T. DOBER	E. PRISCOTT	PETER DAVEY	R.SLADE	
G. ROODE		GRAHAM BODY	MICHAEL KENWOOD	
SIDNEY PHILLIPS		MICHAEL LEY	MICHAEL ORCHARD	
J,ISAAC				
D.J. HARDING		JIM STAYED ON at BARNSTAPLE ABC.		

Barnstaple Amateur Boxing & Athletic Club

(Affiliated to A.B.A., N.A.B.C., N.D.B.A., B.R.I.)
President: Col. J. N. Oliver, C.B.E., T.D., J.P.
Chairman: Mr. J. J. F. Talbot, North Gate Hotel
Treasurer: Mr. J. W. C. Saunders, 7 River View, Landkey Road

Coach:
J. Bartlett

Trainer:
W. Neale.

Rolle Street Warehouses
MON. - WED. - FRI. - 7 p.m.

Hon. Secretary:
Mr. J. A. Mason,
9 Ashleigh Road,
Barnstaple

October 7th /59

Jim Bartlett Esq.
87 Gould Road
Forches Estate
Barnstaple

Dear Jim,

At a committee meeting last night, I was directed
by our committee to send you a sincere letter of appreciation
for services rendered, and it was hoped by everyone that you
would continue to act as you have done in the past.

Incidents of the past are sometimes hard to forget Jim,
but many of the past mistakes, and blunders, were made by members
no longer with the Club, and it was hoped that the Executive and
Working sides of our committee would continue forward with the
same objective in mind,— to build a first Class Club that produc-
es first class boxers;— may I say on behalf of every committee
member, thank you Jim

Yours Sincerely

J. A. Mason Hon Sec
Barnstaple A.B.A.C.

This letter, dated October 2nd 1959,

clearly indicates how popular JIM was.

NORTH DEVON AMATEUR BOXING LEGEND, JIMMY ISAAC with JIM BARTLETT,
who was a COACH at BARNSTAPLE BOXING CLUB in the early 1950s. JIM
BARTLETT BOXED on BOTH SHOWS, 1948 and 1949 while serving in the ROYAL
AIR FORCE at CHIVENOR.

104

A Boxer's Farewell

Fast and fit, fit and fast,

I'll keep going to the last.

Fit and fast, fast and fit,

You will never see me quit.

Old and slow, slow and old,

I move in and try to hold.

Slow and old, old and slow,

Just waiting for the knock-out blow.

Jim Bartlett

EDDIE PRISCOTT

..always 'billed' as PRESCOTT.
He still looks fit enough to do a few rounds!

NORTH DEVON JOURNAL-HERALD, OCTOBER 15, 1959

Disqualification and cut eye mars boxing

THE two most popular bouts of the evening at Barnstaple Boxing Club's first tournament of the season on Friday, were spoilt by a cut eye and a disqualification.

Eddie Prescott, who met Dick Damarell, a former Junior A.B.A. Champion, from Docklands Plymouth, was disqualified, and Graham Hallett lost his fight with Ray Waters, also of Docklands, when the referee stopped the contest because the Barnstaple boy had a cut eye.

Nineteen-year-old Graham, who in his second season as a senior is considered a possible future A.B.A. welterweight champion, was stopped in the second of a four round contest when he received a cut under his left eye.

It was the fifth time Hallett has met Waters. Now after his victory on Friday, Waters has three wins to his credit while Hallett has got the decision twice.

Eddie Prescott was disqualified just before the end of the last round of his contest with Damarell for "persistent ducking."

Prescott was warned twice about ducking and when he did it again in the fourth round, the referee immediately stopped the bout.

After his fight Prescott said he could not help ducking. He was fighting with a burnt foot, after an accident at his place of work, and when he had to take his weight on his right foot, it was painful enough to make him duck and ease the weight.

NORTH VERSUS SOUTH

The tournament on Friday was between boxers from North and South Devon.

The three North Devon boys to win their contests were Roger Burridge, Jimmy Isaac and Pat Jones, all of the Barnstaple A.B.A.C.

Roger Burridge won his junior fight against Dave Jackson, of Torbay A.B.C. Jackson's brother, Keith, had previously beaten Gordon Roode in a very close contest.

Roode, who is 16 years old, was taking part in his 17th fight. He has won ten of them and the crowd thought he should have won his contest against Jackson.

He fought hard all the way and although he was out-reached his punch was harder. Jackson beat Roode about a year ago with a knock-out in the second round, but Gordon has improved his style on last season and with more experience should be one of Barnstaple's foremost boxers.

Fourteen-year-old Jimmy Isaac met T. Wood, of Virginia House, for the fourth time, and by outpointing him, he brought off his first victory against him.

In spite of the torchlight procession through Barnstaple, cele-

OVER 800 AT BIDEFORD BOXING SHOW

A WHIRLWIND bout in a Bideford boxing tournament at the Pannier Market last night ended in a disqualification.

He was Barnstaple's Eddie Prescott, who met Bideford's Graham Fishleigh in the intermediate class at 11 stone—a "local derby" match, which was one of the main attractions of the evening.

Right from the start they let loose at each other with practically every punch in the book.

This was the way it was at the start of the second round, with both men hammering it out quite evenly. Then the trouble started.

The referee, Mr. C. Parsons, warned Prescott about using his head. Seconds later the same happened again, and the referee gave him a final warning. But again Prescott went in with his head, and he was disqualified. In his favour it must be pointed out that his head never got close to Fishleigh in attack, only in defence when things were getting pretty hot about his ears.

The decision of a technical knockout against Army representative Sgt. Chalmers, who was getting slightly the worse of the next bout against F. Tooley (Teignmouth), was another unpopular finish.

RULED OUT

Chalmers went down in the third round, and was as fresh as a daisy as he waited to rise. He appeared to do so on nine, but the referee ruled him out.

By far the most curious display was produced by P. Hine, the South-West Army champion, and E. Daniels (Dockland Settlement). This was a beefy battle in which both men took some wicked punishment about the face. In the second round Daniels got a nasty cut under the right eye, and after that it was a blood bath. The bout was stopped in the third round, when Hine was floored by a right to the neck and jaw.

The light welter contest between Graham Hallett (Barnstaple) and A/C Keedle (R.A.F., Chivenor) was also of great local interest. Hallett did a lot of manoeuvring from a crouching position during the first two rounds, but caused the southpaw Airman—upright and unruffled —no worry.

But three times in the third round Keedle went crashing to the canvas. The third and last time was when Hallett found his solar with a right. He failed to rise.

There was a crowd of over 800.

TOE TO TOE. Eddie Prescott, the Barnstaple Boxing Club welterweight slogs it out, toe to toe with Dick Damarell, a former Junior A.B.A. Champion, from Docklands, Plymouth. The two boxers met in a tournament arranged by the Barnstaple Club, when a North Devon team met 15 fighters from South Devon clubs. Damarell went on to win the contest in the fourth round, when Prescott was disqualified for ducking.

EDDIE moved to BIDEFORD ABC towards the end of his boxing career and featured in some memorable bouts for that club.

Boxing audience excited as Ted Prescott is disqualified

HOGAN STOPS HIS OPPONENT

BARNSTAPLE boxing fans were excited at the Queen's Hall on Thursday, when a local boy was disqualified in the last round of his fight. Edward Prescott was making a come-back after twice being on the canvas in his light middle-weight bout with B. Turner, of Exeter, when the referee stopped the fight and awarded the decision to Turner.

They were fighting in the first boxing tournament to be organised by the new Barnstaple District Combined Cadet Units Amateur Boxing Club.

Prescott opened strongly, and had the large crowd on its feet when he drew blood from the Exeter boy's nose early in the first round, but although he attacked repeatedly, he was unable to land any really telling blows on his opponent.

After being on the receiving end throughout the first round, Turner, using his longer reach to advantage, slowly took the initiative in the second, and after landing some solid blows, put Prescott down for a count of eight.

The Exeter boy then bore into the flagging Prescott and sent him reeling on to the canvas again early in the third round, but he could not land the deciding blow, and Prescott made a great recovery to put Turner down for a short count.

A slugging match ended, but, with both boxers noticeably tired, few damaging blows were landed by either before the referee ended the contest.

The best display of the evening came from quicksilver Jimmy Hogan, of Barnstaple, who, boxing immaculately, pummelled C. Newberry, of Tiverton, into a second round standstill.

The Tiverton boy was never in there with a chance and neatly side-stepping and ducking Newberry's blows Hogan was able to pick his own spot to land telling punches.

The biggest surprise of the evening was the points defeat of Micky Isaacs, of Barnstaple. Only a fortnight before, Micky had scored a sensational second round knock-out over Godfrey, National A.C.F. champion. After being evenly matched with W. Drew, from Exmouth, for two rounds, he was pressed in the last round.

After a lively opening, the all-Barnstaple fight between Johnny Rowe and Bill Young, ended disappointingly when the referee stopped the fight at the end of the first round, because Rowe had a cut lip.

Results: P. Clancey (Exmouth) beat J. Norton (Exeter) on points. Light welter-weight: A. Hancocks (Farringdon School) beat Cadet Sgt. Stanbury (Bude) on points. T. Crees (Exmouth) beat Main (Tiverton) on points. Light middle-weight: B. Turner (Exeter) beat E. Prescott (Barnstaple), Prescott disqualified. W. Drew (Exmouth) beat M. Isaacs (Barnstaple) on points. Feather-weight: M. Hogan (Barnstaple) beat C. Newberry (Tiverton), referee stopped the fight in the second round.

B. Woodward (Exmouth) beat Gould on points. Light welter-weight: R. McArthur (Farringdon School) beat H. Found (Barnstaple) on points. R. Rowe (Barnstaple) beat C. Jacobs (Exeter) on points. Light welter-weight: B. Young (Barnstaple) beat J. Rowe (Barnstaple), referee stopped fight. K. Jacobs (Exmouth) beat T. Lee (Exeter) on points.

EDDIE PRESCOTT WINS THIS TIME AT BARNSTAPLE

OVER 800 spectators at the Pannier Market, Barnstaple, saw the two North Devon light-middleweight rivals — Graham Fishleigh (Bideford) and Eddie Prescott (Barnstaple), settle their account on Saturday. All must have voted it the best contest of the evening (writes our Boxing Correspondent).

At Bideford in April their first clash ended unsatisfactorily. Prescott being disqualified in the second round for continual use of his head and at a time when the younger Fishleigh seemed to be well on top.

A different-tactics Prescott fought the return bout. By superior boxing he foiled Fishleigh's attempts at a quick knock-out in the first round. It seemed his plan was to dictate the fight with snappy lefts and hard counter-punches. The second round was even, with the Bideford man getting home more often with blows to the head.

The third round, however, decided the issue. Throwing caution aside, Fishleigh ran into a perfect left hook, which sent him to his knees. He was up in a flash, but the blow had unsettled him and while he seemed to finish the stronger of the two, Prescott was deservedly a points' winner.

BOUSTEAD UNLUCKY

Gerald Boustead (Audley Park, Torquay), former six counties' featherweight champion, resuming after a long lay off, was unlucky not to get the verdict over L/Corpl. Guy, the Army representative and former Golden Gloves team captain. Boustead baffled Guy with his raking left in the first two rounds, and only in the last round could the soldier get to close quarters and win on points.

Eric Daniel, the Dockland Settlement, Devonport, light-middleweight, although losing on points to C. Bellingham, the Welsh A.B.A. champion, nearly upset the form book when, after taking a count of eight in the second round, he put the Welshman down for eight in the next. Bellingham got the points' verdict on his boxing skill.

The tournament, which was staged by the Barnstaple Boxing Club provided excellent boxing by the various champions on view. The event was in aid of the Barnstaple Youth Centre.

THE RESULTS

Bantam-weight: C. Boyey (Audley Park, Torquay) outpointed D. James (Wales).

Lightweight: D. Jones (British Railways) outpointed W. May (Price's Club, Plymouth).

Light-welter-weight: G. Guy (R.E.M.E.) outpointed G. Boustead (Audley Park, Torquay); G. Hallett (Barnstaple) outpointed B. Slade (Yeovil); R. Bell (British Railways) outpointed D. Deldridge (Wales); A. Consotis (British Railways) outpointed N. Gilfeather (R.E.M.E.).

Welter-weight: J. Phillips (Ammanford) beat R. Damarell (Dockland Settlement), r.s.f. second round (cut eye).

Light-middle-weight: E. Prescott (Barnstaple) outpointed G. Fishleigh (Bideford).

Middle-weight: C. Bellingham (Wales) outpointed E. Daniel (Dockland Settlement).

Juniors: T. Wood (Price's Club) outpointed R. Burridge (Barnstaple); P. Jones (Barnstaple) outpointed G. Turner (Dockland Settlement); J. Lucky (Barnstaple) k.o. R. Hodge (Dockland Settlement); J. Isaacs (Barnstaple) outpointed R. Arnott (Price's); G. Roode (Barnstaple) outpointed G. Finlay (Price's); J. Cudmore (Bideford) outpointed C.

EDDIE PRESCOTT

PRESCOTT WINS BOUT BY A KNOCK-OUT

SOUTHPAW Eddie Prescott, of Barnstaple Amateur Boxing Club, sent F. Roberts, of Exeter, out for the count at Tiverton on Friday.

The fight was part of a programme promoted by the Tiverton Amateur Boxing Club—and it ended in the first round.

Prescott's left cross did the damage. Roberts—also a southpaw—was given no chance to show his mettle because within seconds he had been sounded by his opponent.

Prescott moved in for a second time and hammered a little harder Then came the third encounter, and down went Roberts.

This was Barnstaple's only success. Young Jimmy Isaac was outpointed by W. Wood, of Plymouth, who had the advantage of two or three years more experience coupled with the fact that Isaac was giving away four-and-a-half pounds.

TOO LATE . . .

The Barnstaple boy acquitted himself well and by the third round he had sized up Wood. But by then, it was too late—Wood's points margin from the earlier rounds was enough to give him the fight.

Henry Found, the Bideford boy, lost his second fight on the trot to the same opponent—David Scrace, of Williton A.C. It was a points decision.

Found is now being taken out of the front line for a month or so, to get down to some solid training. Living in Bideford makes it difficult for him to put in his full quota.

He has the makings of a good boxer, but needs a lot of sparring practice.

1958

SOLAR REGION. Albert Ensor, of Barnstaple, is at the receiving end of a solar plexus punch in his bout with Eddie Prescott, of Bideford, in the boxing tournament at Combe Martin. He took further punishment, too, before Prescott finally won on points.

Eddie Prescott, of Bideford, was too good for Nick Ellis, of Dockland Settlement, and appeared to win every round in a convincing points victory.

GREAT CHANCE FOR EDDIE PRESCOTT

BOXERS from the Middle Row Boxing Club, London, visit Torquay on Saturday night when at the Town Hall they clash with a team of Devon amateurs in a tournament staged by the Torbay Boxing Club (writes our Boxing Correspondent).

The Middle Row Club team includes a number of last year's London A.B.A. champions, the outstanding one being Sam Holbrook the English middle-weight international.

I understand Holbrook's opponent will be the sturdy Bideford boxer Eddie Prescott. Win or lose, it will be a great chance for this North Devon boxer if he carries the distance

Boxers of promise

Revealed at Barum tourney

BARNSTAPLE Amateur Boxing Club's first tournament of the season staged before a good crowd at the Queen's Hall, Barnstaple, on Saturday night not only produced plenty of thrills, but brought to light several promising amateur boxers in the town who should go far in Westcountry A.B.A. championships this season.

Particularly impressive was Harry Carr's point victory over D. Mudge (Audley Park, Torquay), present holder of the six county's amateur middleweight title. Although Mudge moving right away in this light-heavyweight class, it did not minimise the powerful - punching Barnstaple boy's victory. In fact in the second round he had Mudge in trouble following an all-out attack to head and body.

C. Prescott, the Barnstaple welterweight, nearly upset the form book in an all-out battle with Brian Turner (Exmouth), the three-county's light-middleweight champion.

Prescott clearly won the first two rounds with his superior boxing and looked all set for victory in the last session, when Turner waded into him and with powerful rights dropped the Barnstaple boy twice for counts of 8, before the referee stepped in and stopped the bout in Turner's favour. Up until then it was touch and go for the Exmouth man.

Terry Nicholas, the Exmouth welterweight figured in the fastest cleverest bout of the evening to lose on points to A. McGinnes (Price's Club, Plymouth), recent conqueror of Mike O'Connor (Sidmouth), the national A.B.A. light-welterweight semi-finalist.

OVER 800 AT BIDEFORD BOXING SHOW

A WHIRLWIND bout in a Bideford boxing tournament at the Pannier Market last night ended in a disqualification.

He was Barnstaple's Eddie Prescott, who met Bideford's Graham Fishleigh in the intermediate class at 11 stone—a "local derby" match, which was one of the main attractions of the evening.

Right from the start they let loose at each other with practically every punch in the book.

This was the way it was at the start of the second round, with both men hammering it out quite evenly. Then the trouble started.

The referee, Mr. C. Parsons, warned Prescott about using his head. Seconds later the same happened again, and the referee gave him a final warning. But again Prescott went in with his head, and he was disqualified. In his favour it must be pointed out that his head never got close to Fishleigh in attack, only in defence when things were getting pretty hot about his ears.

Bideford boxers' chance to-morrow

Three members of the Bideford Boxing Club are among the 27 Devon contestants who will take part in the Devon, Dorset and Cornwall championships at Den Pavilion, Teignmouth, to-morrow (Saturday), the first step towards honours in this year's A.B.A. championships.

Graham Fishleigh must be rated as one of the best prospects in the five-strong light-middleweight contingent, and Eddie Prescott is one of the strongest punchers in the middleweight division.

Among the four Devon heavyweights is Ron Sherbourne, of Bideford, who could well be matched against his old rival, Charlie Norman, of Barnstaple.

Winners will go forward to the Western Counties championships at Wells on March 19th.

Eddie Prescott breaks a boxing jinx and sleeps tight

SOUTHPAW DEFEATS YOUNG

By PETER BROCK

LIGHT middleweight Eddie Prescott, of Barnstaple Boxing Club went to bed a happy man on Tuesday—he had broken a jinx by beating Brian Turner, of Exmouth, on points.

Their fight was one of the best in a programme organised by the Barnstaple club in the Queen's Hall.

As Prescott left his stool for the last round, he knew it was then or never. Turner had already beaten him three times in a row and was looking tough enough to notch a fourth win.

But at last Prescott found the Exmouth boy's weak point and hammered at its for all he was worth. Gamely Turner struggled through to the end without going down.

In the second round, I thought I was seeing the same old story, as Prescott stopped a Turner hook and sank to one knee to take a breather —and a count of seven. It was then that the comeback was staged.

Tiverton hero halted by Eddie Prescott

SURPRISE flashed into the eyes of Jack Broomfield, of Tiverton, on Thursday. He was on the end of a knock-out jab from Barnstaple boxer Eddie Prescott (writes Peter Brock).

This happened in the last round of their light-middleweight bout in the Heathcoat Hall, Tiverton. Immediately afterwards Broomfield sank to the canvas for the count of nine and, although he staggered through to the end of the fight, Prescott was a good points winner.

When the boxers entered the ring it looked as though Prescott was in for a stormy passage because Broomfield—a local knock-out hero—was bigger and broader than the Barnstaple boy.

But Prescott has made remarkable progress since his first fights. Gone was his wild swinging and "I-must-sink-him-with-this-one" tactics. In short, Broomfield faced a cool, competent boxer.

Another good Barnstaple win came from welterweight Billy Young who never looked in trouble against local boy Les Garland. Boxing confidently, Young won on points.

But that is where the Barnstaple winning ended. Gordon Hooge lost his junior bout on points to Richard Gratie, of Tiverton, and Graham Hallett was on the wrong end of a points decision in his welterweight scrap with John Westcott, another Tiverton fighter.

Young Hooge started strongly enough but faded in the final round and his opponent stepped in to forge his way to victory.

Even though Hallett was under a height and reach handicap, he should never have allowed himself to be flustered by his opponent's wild punching.

In several series of flurried pummelling by both fighters, Westcott came out on top and though Hallett was not lacking in grit he was unable to pull a winning punch from the bag.

PRESCOTT WINS BOUT BY A KNOCK-OUT

SOUTHPAW Eddie Prescott, of Barnstaple Amateur Boxing Club, sent F. Roberts, of Exeter, out for the count at Tiverton on Friday.

The fight was part of a programme promoted by the Tiverton Amateur Boxing Club—and it ended in the first round.

Prescott's left cross did the damage. Roberts—also a southpaw—was given no chance to show his mettle because within seconds he had been sounded by his opponent.

Prescott moved in for a second time and hammered a little harder. Then came the third encounter, and down went Roberts.

This was Barnstaple's only success. Young Jimmy Isaac was outpointed by W. Wood, of Plymouth, who had the advantage of two or three years more experience coupled with the fact that Isaac was giving away four-and-a-half pounds.

TOO LATE . . .

The Barnstaple boy acquitted himself well and by the third round he had sized up Wood. But by then, it was too late—Wood's points margin from the earlier rounds was enough to give him the fight.

Henry Found, the Bideford boy, lost his second fight on the trot to the same opponent—David Serace, of Williton A.C. It was a points decision.

Found is now being taken out of the front line for a month or so, to get down to some solid training. Living in Bideford makes it difficult for him to put in his full quota.

He has the makings of a good boxer, but needs a lot of sparring practice.

Boxing Notes

Now that Eddie Prescott, formerly of Barnstaple, has joined Graham Fishleigh at the Bideford Amateur Boxing Club, the club possesses two of the finest light-middleweights in Devon. But local enthusiasts will not have a chance of seeing either in action again until late in April.

Although Bideford Pannier Market is suitable for boxing tournaments for much of the year, lack of heating facilities do not make it the best of places for this kind of entertainment in the winter. It is for that reason that the club will not put on another show till the end of April.

However, club activities have by no means stopped, especially where the juniors are concerned. The Club is putting on two tournaments for the juniors at the Athletic Club H.Q., one being on February 13th, when youngsters from Barnstaple, Torbay and Northbrook (Exeter) will provide the opposition.

Both Prescott and Fishleigh will be entering for the A.B.A. championships this year. It would be a pity if they had to meet each other, and it is to be hoped there will be a difference in their weights by that time.

One thing the club badly needs is its own gymnasium. Secretary Mr. P. Plant is searching for new premises, and meanwhile the club continues training at the Grammar School gym and at the Athletic Club.

NEARLY A SURPRISE

C. E. Prescott, the Barnstaple welterweight, nearly brought off a surprise during a gruelling contest with Brian Turner (Exmouth), the Three Counties light middleweight champion.

Prescott, a clever boxer and fighter, had the Exmouth man in trouble in the second round and was well ahead on points. Then came a dramatic last round turn when Turner sent Prescott to the canvas twice for counts of eight. The Barnstaple man rose each time full of fight and it came somewhat as a surprise to the large crowd when referee B. Treeby stopped the bout in Turner's favour.

111

ALEX MASON came to BARNSTAPLE from CANADA after a severe
industrial accident made living conditions there difficult.
His time as BOXING TRAINER at BARNSTAPLE ABC produced

CHAMPIONS as is evident by the great many PHOTOS. and
NEWSPAPER CUTTINGS in which he is mentioned. He eventually
settled in AUSTRALIA where he continued to train BOXERS to
CHAMPIONSHIP level.

Looking Back

By Alex Mason

I found new beginnings in my life in Barnstable, Gerry Gist, the other bartender put me in touch with the former boxing club secretary, of some 20 years previous.

This led to my being told of the old boxing ring in the top story of the old Flour Mill in Barnstable.

It was an old direlect building of five stories, so one day I made my way there to where the old ring lay, festooned in cob webs and encrusted with rust, the ropes and canvas had rotted away.

It took me a few afternoons to take the ring apart, then with a group of my junior boxers we lowered the ring down the five stories, piece by piece, we had to remove planks on each floor to accomplish that feat.

One parent then took the ring to a vacant lot, where I used up my free time from the pub, to remove the rust and put on a couple of coats of paint, new ropes were acquired from the fishermen while an old boxing fan donated a new canvas.

Then I set about to organize a junior boxing tournament at the old Forrester's Hall, it took me eight hours to assemble the ring with boxers coming from Exeter and South Devon to take part.

Of course our lads were all rookies but they did very well with Jimmy Isaac showing himself to be a future champion

Then I found a new home for our club, in the old direlect Ice Factory on the outskirts of town, through the goodwill of the local people windows were replaced and repairs made, the biggest item was in our installing a new stairway to the second floor.

We spent a weekend then sweeping the floor and erecting the ring, then in bold white letters I printed on the wall "THE HOME OF FUTURE CHAMPIONS"

That challenge was accepted by both the juniors and the seniors for in just six years, they had won over 60 local and area championships, as well as four national titles.

OFF TO MOSCOW. Jimmy Isaac says goodbye to his trainer Alex Mason at Barnstaple Junction Station before he leaves for London to join the rest of the English boxing team that flies to Russia today.

JIMMY ISAAC FLIES TO MOSCOW TODAY

BARNSTAPLE boxing star, Jimmy Isaac, flies out to Moscow today to fight with the English boxing team, against Russia.

Jimmy left Barnstaple on Tuesday to spend two days in London for training prior to his trip to Russia.

During his eight days behind the Iron Curtain he will fight twice.

Jimmy, who lives at 38, Ashleigh Road, Barnstaple, will be fighting in the bantamweight class. This is his second fight for England. In his first international, against the Hungarians, he was narrowly defeated on points.

GOOD LUCK CHARMS

At the Barnstaple Youth Centre on Tuesday Jimmy was presented with two lucky horse-shoes given by the boys and girls of the club. The two lucky horse-shoes were engraved with his name.

The horse-shoes were presented to Jimmy by the chairman of the club, Mr. R. W. Sim.

He trains at the youth club under the guidance of his father, Mr. J. Isaac.

114

PROUD TRAINER, ALEX MASON SEES OFF BOXER JIMMY ISAAC at
BARNSTAPLE RAILWAY STATION.

ALEX MASON A.A.U.
CDN - - Welter Champion

COMBE'S YOUNG BOXERS WILL BE IN ACTION

BOXING coach Alex Mason is planning to hold a series of amateur tournaments in Ilfracombe during the winter months.

Mr. Mason, who was Canadian welterweight champion in 1949, was in charge of boxing until recently at Barnstaple Sports Centre.

But he has been living in Ilfracombe for some time, and so he is concentrating on coaching youngsters in the seaside town.

The Ilfracombe Sports Club, which

ALEX MASON

is sponsored by the local youth committee, has Ilfracombe Town football secretary Mr. Reg Boyen as its chairman.

Its young boxers—over 20 of them—meet twice a week in their Cow Lane gymnasium, and it is here that Mr. Mason teaches them the noble art of self-defence.

During the past winter their performances suggested that this coaching was paying dividends, and Mr. Mason is convinced that many of them will make the grade.

He was responsible for coaching the 19-year-old Barnstaple boxer, Jimmy Isaac, who won a junior A.B.A. title from the age of 11.

"The Ilfracombe youngsters have a long way to go before they are Jimmy Isaacs," "but nobody could beat them for keenness."

Boxers from other clubs in North Devon will take part in tournaments at Ilfracombe, and invitations may later be extended to South Devon boxers.

*Boxing Exhibitions at Fete in Ilfacombe
-1967 (I was a special constable at the time)* ALEX MASON.

RETIREMENT IN AUSTRALIA

Kalamunda boxer wins gold in NSW

Kalamunda boxer Clint Hindmarsh has won gold in Sydney at the Australian National Championships.

The WA Golden Gloves champion defeated NT champion Jason Garling, when the referee stopped the bout in Clint's favour in the second round.

The following day he repeated the effort by beating Shane Hamilton, Queensland's champion, with the referee stopping the contest in Clint's favour in the third round.

Clint will box as a senior next year, and his goal is to win a place on the Australian Olympic Team for 1996.

According to coach Alex Mason, the way Clint is training and competing he could be the first Australian to win a gold medal in boxing at the Olympic Games.

STILL TRAINING CHAMPIONS!

JIMMY ISAAC
BARNSTAPLE ABC.

WALTER ISAAC

The Devonshire Regiment

ARMY DAYS
WALTER seated, second left, front row.

WALTER, standing far left, back row.   The DATE on the RUGBY BALL is 1936.

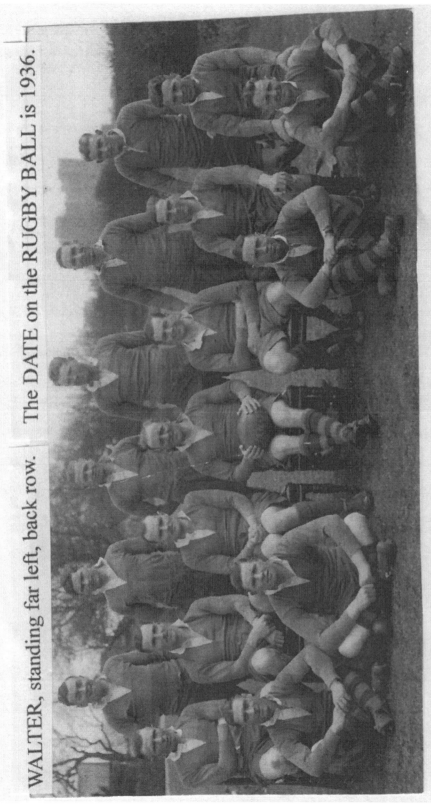

WALTER boxed on PROFESSIONAL SHOWS in the early 1930's and was quite a sportsman after joining the DEVONSHIRE REGIMENT, active in both boxing and rugby. The REGIMENT was stationed in MALTA throughout the terrible blitz and it was there that WALTER met his future wife PAULINE. After leaving the ARMY and settling back in BARNSTAPLE with PAULINE, he resumed his sporting activities and introduced a very young JIMMY to boxing. He continued to train him and kept a watchful eye on his progress when he joined the local boxing club. He was an inspiration and confident to JIMMY throughout his illustrious career.

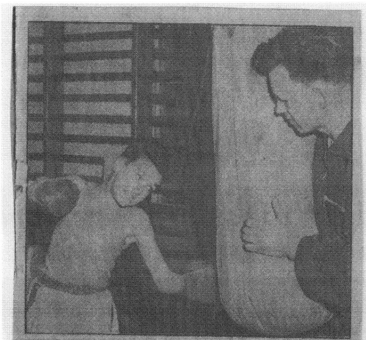

YOUNG CHAMPION. Jimmy Isaac, of Barnstaple A.B.C., has a work out on a punch bag to celebrate his schoolboy championship victory in Plymouth on Saturday. Coach Alex Mason keeps a close watch on this hard-hitting youngster's style . . . . experts say that Isaac is bound for the Albert Hall, London—and the National Schoolboy Championships.

DAVID DOES A JIMMY ISAAC

EIGHT-YEAR-OLD David Bayliss stole the show at an inter-club boxing tournament at Barnstaple Youth Centre on Saturday.

David, a Blue Coat School pupil, who lives at 9, Corporation Street, Barnstaple, was boxing in his first tournament.

He was fighting eight-year-old Eddie Cockran, from Ilfracombe, whom he beat on points.

DAVID BAYLISS

David opened up his attack as soon as the bell went for round one, and he soon had Eddie cornered

It was obvious after the end of the second round that David was going to win the bout as he had Eddie almost on the floor with a left of which even Barnstaple international Jimmy Isaac would have been proud.

David has been attending the Youth Centre for the past six months, and he has been boxing for three.

The five clubs taking part—Barnstaple, Bideford, Appledore, Ilfracombe, and Exeter—were fighting for the Ken Winkle Cup. The trophy went to Barnstaple.

Jimmy Isaac, who is at Wembley tomorrow for the A.B.A. semi-finals, gave a three-round exhibition bout with Sid Phillips.

THE RESULTS

R. Kenwood (Barnstaple) beat G. Gardner (Appledore), stopped in first round; M. Dorey (Appledore) beat W. Keeton (Ilfracombe), stopped in first round; J. Smale (Appledore) beat R. Ellis (Bideford), on points.

D. Bayliss (Barnstaple) beat E. Cockran (Ilfracombe) on points; A. Alcock (Ilfracombe) beat K. Ward (Exeter) on points; R. Kenwood (Barnstaple) beat E. Byrne (Exeter) on points; P. Mallott (Barnstaple) beat C. Alcock (Ilfracombe) on points; K. Smale (Appledore) beat E. Ellis (Bideford) on points; M. Clements (Bideford) beat D. Barrett (Appledore) on points.

J. Popplewill (Barnstaple) beat J. Mead Larkin (Ilfracombe) on points; P. Ballard (Barnstaple) beat S. Brown (Bideford) on points; V. Horsley (Exeter) beat P. Evans (Bideford) on points; R. Gillard (Exeter) beat E. Evans (Bideford) on points; R. Bright (Bideford) beat Barnshaw (Exeter) on points.

NORTH DEVON HAS YOUNG BOXING CHAMPIONS

Jimmy Hogan wins in Coventry

NORTH Devon has two schoolboy boxing champions— Jimmy Isaac, of Barnstaple Grammar School and Barnstaple A.B.C., and M. Shahmanesh, of Grenville College, Bideford. They brought their titles home from Plymouth on Saturday.

They fought—or rather Isaac's did —in the Devon Schools championships. Shahmanesh (10 stone 2lbs.) gained his title by a walk-over. Isaac's was in the 5 stone 4 lbs. division.

In the semi-finals he comfortably outpointed Hughes, of Torquay, and in the finals, his scientific punching gave him a unanimous decision over Harris, of Plymouth. Jimmy's next step is to enter for the Devon, Dorset, and Cornwall Championships at Exmouth next month.

The other local boxers who fought—Sid Phillips, of Barnstaple, and G. Cross, of Grenville College— lost. Cross's fight was stopped in the first round, and Phillips was on the wrong end of a narrow points decision.

At the other end of the country— Coventry to be exact—Jimmy Hogan, of Barnstaple A.B.C., was punching his way to a technical knock-out victory over F. Lydon, of the Coventry Irish Club.

This was the first time that Lydon—a former junior A.B.A. champion—had ever been off his feet inside a boxing ring.

Hogan was a member of the Devon team in an inter-county challenge tournament. The team brought back seven wins from 13 bouts.

Barnstaple might be the venue for a return engagement with the Midland Club.

NOT THIS TIME. Bobby Woods, of Pines A.B.C., Plymouth (black trunks), wards off a left from Jimmy Isaac, of Barnstaple, during the Bideford boxing tournament. Woods won on points.

JIMMY ISAAC BARNSTAPLE ABC.

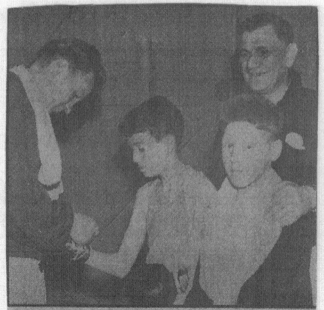

Preparing for their bout in the Bideford Youth Amateur Boxing Tournament at Bideford Pannier Market, J. Isaacs, of Barnstaple, receives attention to his glove from coach Alex Mason before being outpointed in a junior bout with W. Wood, of Price's Club, Plymouth. Both boys are three counties school champions at their respective weights.

Fourteen-year-old Jimmy Isaac met T. Wood, of Virginia House, for the fourth time, and by outpointing him, he brought off his first victory against him.

JIMMY ISAAC and Geoff Yeo in training at the Barnstaple Youth Centre. Both boxers, who have been trained by Wilf Cooper, are taking part in the A.B.A. championships. Jimmy will be in the A.B.A. semifinals at Wembley Stadium on Friday and Geoff in the junior quarter finals, at Chichester on May 8.

GRAHAM HALLET slams a left into a medicine ball held by TRAINER ALEX MASON. A young JIMMY ISAAC in HOOPED shirt. On his left SID PHILLIPS.

Barnstaple Amateur Boxing & Athletic Club

(Affiliated to A.B.A. and N.A.B.C.)

President : Col. J. N. OLIVER, C.B.E., T.D., J.P.
Chairman : Chief Inspector J. BICKNELL, Lyndend, Lynhurst Avenue, Barnstaple
Vice-Chairman : R. BREND, Dunhaved, Victoria Road, Barnstaple
Treasurer : J. W. SAUNDERS, 7 River View, Landkey Road, Barnstaple

Training Quarters :
Rolle Street, Warehouses
MON. - WED. - FRI. - 7 p.m.

Coach : J. BARTLETT

Trainers : W. NEALE and J. HOGAN

Hon. Secretary :
J. A. MASON,
9 Ashleigh Road,
Barnstaple
_____
(Former Canadian Amateur Champion)

15-3-60

Master James Isaac
Ashleigh Crescent
Barnstaple

Dear Jim,

      I am very happy to inform you that at
a meeting yesterday evening, I was directed by my
committee to tender an official letter of appreciation, for your very fine efforts at Birmingham on
March 5th, when you won the School-Boys Quarter-
finals.

      Please take our very best wishes with you to
Coventry, on the 19th of this month, and we know
that win or lose you will do your best, and be a
credit not only to this Club, but to your home town
of Barnstaple. - Good luck Jimmy, and may God Bless
you.

      Yours Sincerely

J.A. Mason Hon Sec
Barnstaple A.B.& A.C

Isaac fails narrowly in A.B.A. final

BROGAN ALSO BEATEN

By our Boxing Correspondent

JIMMY ISAAC, the 18-year-old Barnstaple bantam-weight, his first year as a senior, missed the chance of landing British Amateur Boxing title by the narrowest of margins the Empire Pool, Wembley, last night.

Having won his semi-final by knocking out Jimmy Jones, Scottish champion, in the second round, Isaac started off confid of winning the coveted title.

His opponent, Brian Packer, the Dartford southpaw can thank his lucky stars for the second-round incident when Isaac, who was getting on top, ran into a left, which dropped him for a compulsory count of eight.

In the first round both boys boxed at long range, but Packer was looking very apprehensive every time Isaac went into the attack. And the Barnstaple boy took the round.

Then came a dramatic moment early in the second when Isaac, after scoring well with two rights, was caught by the left and took the count of eight. He, however, continued to box coolly and handed out considerable punishment.

The Barnstaple boy boxed magnificently in the last round, landing continually with rights to the chin, but Packer had done sufficient to gain a narrow points verdict.

Last round decides

Tony Brogan, Bideford's heavy-weight hope, lost on points in the semi-final to Ron Davies (Droylesdon, Manchester) in a very scrambling and uninteresting bout.

It was the last round that decided the bout in Davies's favour. He threw in a number of hefty rights to Brogan's chin, which shook the Barnstaple man, and while Brogan came back fighting every time, Davies seemed just to have that little bit extra.

Marine Corporal Bob Sanders (41 Commando, Bickleigh) brought off a brilliant win in his heavyweight semi-final with Joe Taylor (Polytechnic, London).

Sanders clipped his man with a lovely right in the first minute. The Londoner took a compulsory count of eight, and 30 seconds later went down again after receiving another terrific right. The referee then stopped the bout.

Chris Cox, the Exeter light-heavyweight, was not so fortunate in his semi-final with Brian Murphy (Chorley). Cox literally chased Murphy around the ring in the first round. The Chorley man seemed loath to come to grips and Cox the round easily.

In the second round Cox blood from Murphy's nose, but not land a decisive punch. Mu kept back-pedalling, but still s freely with left jabs.

In the last round Murphy sh his real form, scoring continua the body. Cox was ever game kept on trying to land a knoc but Murphy was always well o distance.

Michael Frampton (Royal Plymouth Command) was unluc drop a points verdict to Tony (Rootes, Coventry) in the fe weight semi-final. Frampton si off each round in style, but s up towards the end and al Riley to get home with stiff co punches.

Had Frampton used his right frequently he might have pulle fight out of the fire. As it wa points verdict in Riley's favou a mixed reception.

FINALS

Middle: A. J. Matthews (Lith Liverpool), holder, bt. Pts. E. Lof (Army).

Light-middle: A. Wyper (Witchl Scotland) bt S. Pearson (Cowes Me

Welter: J. Pritchett (Bingham, b w.o. R. Charles (West Ham) scr.

Light-welter: R. Mctaggart (B bt L. O'Connell (Fitzroy Lodge).

Light: Pte. B. O'Sullivan (Arm K. Cooper (Kyrle Hall).

Feather: A. J. Riley (Rootes) P. Wilson (Barking, holder).

Bantam: B. Packer (Dartford) Isaac (Barnstaple).

Fly: M. Laud (St. Ives) bt K (Rothwell Colliery).

Marine Cpl. Bob Sanders Commando, Bickleigh) won heavyweight title, beating Davies (Droylesden) on poir

ISAAC STOPS DUTCH CHAMPION

DEVON, Dorset and Cornwall beat a Dutch team by seven bouts to five in Rotterdam at the Riviera Hall, before a crowd of over 2,000, in a tournament staged by the Rotterdam club.

Bobby Arnold, the Plymouth Mayflower featherweight beat Bram Klopert on a disqualification in the first round for alleged butting, but Arnott was well on top when the closure came.

Jimmy Banks, Torbay lightweight, gave a fine display to outpoint Dutch lightweight Freek Bandell, whilst Arthur Tyrell, the strong Exeter middleweight knocked out Benny Bor, in the second round.

Finest bout of the evening came when Jimmy Isaac, pictured above, the brilliant Barnstaple and England featherweight, classically stopped Peit Kerkhof, last year's Dutch Champion.

He was in devastating form, attacked from the start, and dropped his opponent in the first round, and dropped him again in the second, when the bout was stopped.

Results—Feather: R. Arnott (Plymouth Mayflower) bt A. Kloppert, disq. 1; J. Isaac (Barnstaple) bt P. Kerkhof, stpd. 2. Light: J. Banks (Torbay) outpd. F. Bandel. Light-welter: R. Waters (Mayflower) lost to H. le Cocq, stpd. 3; S. Phillips (Barnstaple) lost to G. Bok, pts. Welter: W. Choules (Exeter) outpd. F. Tilburg. Light-middle: D. Stacey (Torbay) lost to A. Bor, pts.; R. Withers (Truro) outpd. F. Gelens. Middle: A. Tyrrell (Exeter) bt. B. Bor, K.O. 2; M. Laine (Mayflower) outpd. L. Valk. Light-heavy: G. Gunn (Redruth) lost to F. Heerik, pts. Heavy: D. Challice (Torbay) lost to B. Nikkelen-Kupper, pts.

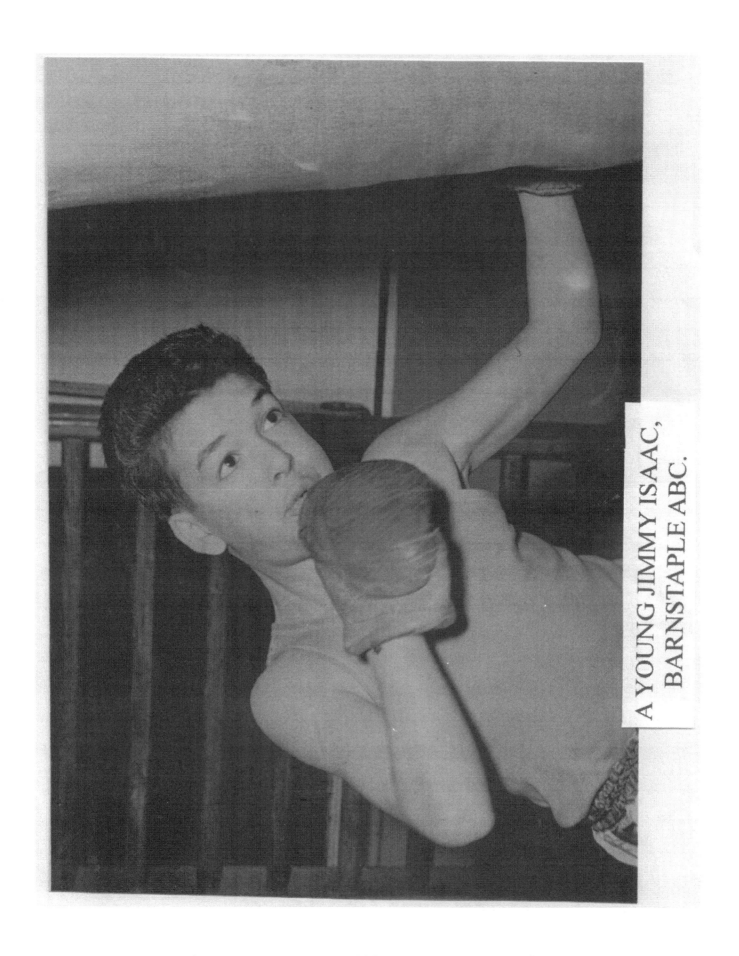

A YOUNG JIMMY ISAAC, BARNSTAPLE ABC.

JIMMY ISAAC

BARNSTAPLE ABC

JIMMY thinks this one out!

TWO BIG DATES: Barnstaple boxers Jimmy Isaac (right) and Geoff Yeo, here seen sparring at the Youth Centre, have two big dates. Tomorrow Jimmy will be in the A.B.A. semi-finals at Wembley, and on May 8 Geoff is in the junior quarter-finals at Chichester. Both of them are being trained by Wilf Cooper.

GEOFF YEO, another BARNSTAPLE ABC BOXER who WON REPRESENTATIVE HONOURS during his career.

BARNSTAPLE ABC

JULY 1965, ABBEYFIELD SCHOOL FETE.
BARNSTAPLE ABC give a BOXING DISPLAY.
On the left, GEOFF YEO...right JIMMY ISAAC.

ONE A.B.A. TITLE CAME TO DEVON

ONLY one Amateur Boxing Association title for Devon this year after last night's finals at the Empire Pool, Wembley.

It went to Cpl. Bob Sanders, of the 41 Commando, Royal Marines, Bickleigh, who got a points verdict against Ron Davies, of Droylesden, Manchester, in the heavyweight section.

Davies earlier had accounted for Bideford's Tony Brogan in a bout which did not reach the expected heights.

It was in the last round that Brogan state was decided. Davies threw a number of hefty rights to the Devon boy's chin, which shook him, but Brogan came back fighting every time. The decision was a close one.

Chris Cox, of Exeter, had the measure of Brian Murphy (Chorley) in the early stages of their light-heavyweight bout.

DREW BLOOD

But Cox failed to land a decisive punch after drawing blood from Murphy's nose. Murphy still managed, however, to score freely with left jabs.

Murphy got right on top in the last round, scoring continually to the body, and, despite the efforts by his opponent to get in a knock-out punch, was always well out of distance.

A second-round compulsory count of eight was the turning point for Barnstaple's 18-year-old bantamweight, Jimmy Isaacs, in his bout with the Dartford southpaw Brian Packer.

Isaacs took the first round, then, after connecting with two rights in the second round, was caught with a left and took an eight count. He continued to box coolly, however, and managed to hand out considerable punishment.

Isaacs put up a great show in the last round, landing repeatedly with rights to the chin. The verdict in Packer's favour was a narrow one.

Jimmy Isaac, of Barnstaple (right), the former A.B.A. feather-weight finalist, who outpointed Danny Polak (Nottingham) in the inter-county team boxing tournament at the Holiday Centre, Westward Ho!, on Saturday, slips a blow to the body and counters with a hard left to his opponent's head.

Jimmy Isaac to box for England in Moscow

BARNSTAPLE MAN'S SECOND CAP

JIMMY ISAAC, the 18-year-old Barnstaple bantamweight, will receive his second international trophy next month—in Moscow.

Isaac has been selected to represent his country against Russia, and leaves Barnstaple on December 3 to begin preparations for the match.

He won his first international "cap" in the Albert Hall Tournament against Hungary. On that occasion he lost narrowly on points, but ringside critics were full of praises for the Barnstaple boy.

Isaac was named as a possible for the Russia trip when first selected for England, and obviously the selectors were waiting to weigh up his form.

A former pupil of Barnstaple Boys' Grammar School, Isaac now works for a local firm of builders. He won a National Association of Boys' Clubs title while a junior, and later became an A.B.A. championship finalist. Three years ago he was selected for an international schoolboys' tournament.

Isaac will spend two days in London before flying to Moscow, where he will stay for eight days.

'Dinner-jacket' boxing at Torquay

Good-class boxing by Imperial Services boxing team was seen at the Palace Hotel, Torquay, last night, when the Services team met a Devon County team in a tournament on the National Sporting Club lines with all patrons wearing dinner jackets.
Results included:—
Light: B. Colter (Mayflower, Plymouth) bt S.A.C. Tarpey (R.A.F.); D. Stacey (Torbay) lost to L.A.C. Dearie (R.A.F. champion) on disqualification 3rd.; D. Thompson (Torbay) lost to Craftsman Brian Manley (R.E.M.E.) on disqualification 1st. Bantam: C. Kane (Fisher Club, London) bt Colin Bovey (Torbay). Junior contests: J. Banks (Torbay) bt Pte. Wardle (Junior Leaders Regt. and Army champion); R. Liddle (Junior Leaders Regt.) bt G. Henry (Royal Signals, Denbury), r.s.f. 2nd.

BARNSTAPLE international amateur boxer, Jimmy Isaac, showed convincing form in winning his first feather-weight fight at the Queen's Hall on Friday.

Isaac, a 19-year-old apprentice electrician, beat 30-year-old Bombardier R. Woodcock, of the Royal Artillery, in a th. round contest on points after some gruelling exchanges.

Isaac, who less than two weeks ago announced that he had changed from bantamweight to featherweight, was one of the seven members of Barnstaple Amateur Boxing Club to fight in a match against the Army's crack 14-man team.

Out of the seven local boxers, three succeeded in winning.

They were Sid Phillips, who scored a knock-out over Driver Michael Rutter, of the Royal Army Service Corps; Johnny Burke, who beat Signalman Arthur Paxton, of the Royal Corps of Signals, on points; and Jimmy Isaac.

The West of England team, including Barnstaple, lost to the Army 9-5.

Isaac's well-known left hook meant business from the start, and this was demonstrated in the second round when Isaac sent the Army champion to the canvas.

Barnstaple's most promising youngster and schoolboy champion, Geoff Yeo, was beaten in the first 20 seconds of round one.

Sid Phillips's win over Mick Rutter proved to be one of the most interesting bouts of the evening.

Just when Phillips seemed certain to lose the match on points, Rutter started to wilt in round three.

Phillips, seizing his chance, piled his opponent with a volley of punches and dropped him with a right to the chin.

Fifteen seconds later Phillips again put the Army man on the canvas, and scored a knock-out.

Burke's comeback

For Barnstaple's Johnny Burke, who beat Signalman Arthur Paxton on points, this was a special victory.

The 25-year-old ex-policeman, who is a newcomer to the local club, had to give up boxing several years ago for health reasons.

Results: Junior: Jnr. Gnr. P. Deans (R.A.) beat G. Yeo (Barnstaple), referee stopped fight. Lightweight: S. Phillips (Barnstaple) knocked out Driver M. Rutter (R.A.S.C.). Welterweight: T. Skinner (Plymouth) beat Pte. P. Lloyd (Parachute Rgt.) on points.

Middleweight: Gdsmn. S. O'Sullivan (Irish Guards) beat J. Newby (Barnstaple and R.A.F.) on points. Welterweight: L/Cpl. A. Tibbs (Queen's Royal Lancers) beat P. Hayfield (Exmouth), referee stopped fight. Light-middleweight: J. B (Barnstaple) beat Sig. A. Pa (R.C.O.S.) on points.

Light-heavyweight: Cpl. R. P ley (R.A.O.C.) beat D. Lewis (chet) on points. Lightweight: Thompson (Torbay) beat Pte Dannaher (R.A.O.C.) on poi Light-welterweight: L./Cpl. Taylor (R.A.O.C.) beat R. Burr (Barnstaple) on points. Lig middleweight: Pte. G. Win (Parachute Rgt.) beat G. Ro (Barnstaple) on points.

Welterweight: L./Cpl. K. Jac (R.A.S.C.) beat W. Choules (Exet on points. Light-welterweight: B. Bebbington (Parachute Ra knocked out G. Gould (Exete Featherweight: J. Isaac (Ba staple and England) beat Bdr. Woodcock (R.A.) on points. Ligh heavyweight: L./Cpl. B. Wh (R.A.O.C.) beat A. Tyrell (Exete referee stopped fight in the thi round.

ER SHOCK

JIMMY ISAAC OUT-GENERALS POLAK

IN AN inter-County boxing match at the Civic Hall, Totnes, the visitors Nottinghamshire, beat Devon ABA by five bouts to three.

Jimmy Isaac, the former ABA finalist from Barnstaple proved that he is well back on the road to recovery from a bad back, by gaining an impressive points victory over Danny Polak, Park Farm Notts.

Isaacs showed all his old confidence and punching ability. After a troublesome first round, he got the measure of his opponent and twice staggered him with rights to the jaw. Another hard right dropped the Notts boxer for a no count, and although Polak fought back hard he was outgeneralled by the brilliant N. Devon boxer.

Dave Short, the Barnstaple light heavy, caught a sucker punch in the first round against Dave Charlton, Mansfield. He appeared to be getting on top when he ran into a terrific right, which dropped him for the full count.

The brilliant Torbay light welterweight Jimmy Banks, gave a fine exhibition of boxing and power punching to stop Marine Tom Burton, Plymouth Mayflower, in a special contest. Burton was dropped in the first round, suffered a cut under the left eye, and when he was again knocked down in the second, the bout was stopped.

RESULTS (Notts first):
Feather, D. Polak (Park Farm) outpd by J. Isaac (Barnstaple); Light, T. Williams (Ruddington) outpd by T. Morgan (Plymouth Mayflower); Welter, D. Melkevik (Bingham) outpd by D. Stacey (Torbay); J. McKay (Park Farm) outpd R. Ellis (Bideford); R. Littleton (Bestwood) outpd P. Edwards (Kingsbridge); Light-middle, M. McPlibin (Ruddington) outpd K. Brooking (Torbay); Light-heavy, H. Reid (Phoenix) stpd D. Challice (Torbay) 1; D. Charlton (Mansfield) stpd D. Short (Barnstaple) 1.

Special Contests: Light-welter, J. Banks (Torbay) stpd Mne T. Burton (Mayflower) 2; Middle, M. Phillips (Mayflower) outpd M. Cox (Torbay); Junior, R. Attrill (Mayflower) outpd R. Hill (Bingham); M. Mimmack (Bestwood) outpd C. Robbins (Bestwood).

BOXING NEWS

BARNSTAPLE BOXERS SUFFER DEFEAT

Barnstaple Amateur Boxing Club suffered two defeats in the Tecalemet boxing show at Plymouth on Saturday. Sidney Phillips lost to Ken May on points while May's brother Billy, beat Jimmy Hogan, also on points.

At Exmouth on Monday Graham Hallett knocked out Lomax of Exeter in the second round while Gordon Rood beat Goulde of Exmouth on points.

Jimmy Isaac won his bout with Evans of Weymouth although Burridge lost to Tucker of Exeter and Billy Chugg lost to Jackson of Audley Park.

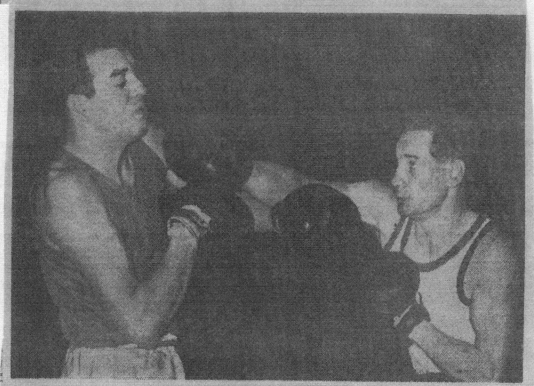

OFF TARGET: Barnstaple and England boxer Jimmy Isaac wards off a straight right delivered by his Army opponent, Bdr. R. Woodcock, of the Royal Artillery. Jimmy won this his first bout as a featherweight on points.

ISAAC'S FIRST VICTORY IN FEATHERWEIGHT CLASS

'BARUM FIGHTERS FOR COVENTRY

Two men and two boys will leave North Devon this week in an effort to put Barnstaple well and truly on the amateur boxing map.

Welterweights Jimmy Hogan and Eddie Prescott are travelling with coach Alex Mason to Coventry as part of a Westcountry boxing team.

Assistant coach, Jim Bartlett, will take Jimmy Isaac and Sid Phillips down to Plymouth to compete in the Devon Schoolboy Championships.

Now a "feather"

ISAAC GOES UP A WEIGHT

BARNSTAPLE boxing international, Jimmy Isaac, makes his debut as a featherweight at the West of England v. the Army match in Barnstaple next Friday.

Nineteen-year-old Isaac, who has fought many times for England as a bantamweight, will be matched against one of the army champions.

At least three other internationals will be on the fight programme: flyweight, Colin Bovey, of Torbay and England; Tony Brogan, the Bideford boy who boxes for Ireland.

The third man is a newcomer to Barnstaple, army middleweight Spr. Bill Sutherley, a Scottish international.

Spr. Sutherley's opponent will be another serviceman, John Newby, from R.A.F., Chivenor, who is a member of the official Air Force team. Newby now trains with the Barnstaple club.

Barnstaple's newest fighter, light middleweight John Burke, is recovering from a severe cold but is almost certain to be fit for the tournament.

FREMINGTON H.Q.

Ex-policeman Burke was East Lancashire and Cheshire welterweight champion in 1959/60, and the following year he was a finalist in the European police championships, only to be beaten by the master Italian boxer, Andreas Pascall.

The full army team of 22 boxers will arrive in North Devon two days before the tournament.

And on the day before the contest the Mayor of Barnstaple, Mr. S. Williams, will hold an official reception for the army team.

A former Mayor of Barnstaple, Michael Huxtable, who is pr' of the Barnstaple Boxing C' agreed to present the prizes tournament.

PANNIER MARKET, BIDEFORD

THE BIDEFORD & DISTRICT
AMATEUR YOUTH BOXING CLUB
President : Lt. Col. R. D. D. BIRDWOOD, M.C.

Ninth
TOURNAMENT

Wednesday, 28th March, 1962
at 7.30 p.m.

Officials in Charge :

Official in Charge :	J. MANSFIELD
Clerk of Scales :	A. MASON
Referees and Judges :	J. RADFORD B. POLLARD
	A. COLLINGWOOD
Timekeeper :	T. YEO
M.C's :	Mr. F. MAYNE Mr. C. BRIGHT

Tournament Secretary :
Mr. S. FISHLEIGH, Watertown, Landcross, Bideford
Phone Bideford 1059

Club Secretary :
Mr. B. BECKERLEY, 48, Barton Tors, Bideford

PROGRAMME—SIXPENCE

JIMMY ISAAC, BARNSTAPLE ABC.
HIS FIRST SENIOR BOUT
on a
BIDEFORD PANNIER MARKET SHOW.

PROGRAMME

OPEN CLASS

Bout

1

Lightweight   3 x 2 min. Rounds

D. THOMPSON   v.   B. COTTAR
Torbay A.B.C.   Mayflower A.B.C.
Three Counties Featherweight   Three Counties Lightweight
Champion 1962   Champion 1962

2

Bantamweight   3 x 3 min. Rounds

J. ISAAC   v.   R. BROAD
Barnstaple A.B.C.   Mayflower A.B.C.
Junior A.B.A. Champ. 1961   Six Counties Champion 1962

3

Light Heavyweight   3 x 3 min. Rounds

A. BROGAN   v.   M. COLEMAN
Bideford A.B.C.   Virginia House
Three Counties Champion   Western Counties Contender

SPECIAL CONTEST

4

Middleweight   3 x 3 min. Rounds

G. FISHLEIGH   v.   A. ENSOR
Bideford A.B.C.   Barnstaple
Three Counties Finalist

INTERMEDIATE CLASS

5

Heavyweight   3 x 3 min. Rounds

J. MASON   v.   A. MURRAY
Exeter A.B.C.   Virginia House & R.A. Regt.

6

Welterweight   3 x 2 min. Rounds

D. STACEY   v.   A. SKINNER
Torbay A.B.C.   Virginia House A.B.C.

7

Middleweight   3 x 2 min. Rounds

E. PRISCOTT   v.   C. TURNER
Bideford A.B.C.   Exmouth A.B.C.

NOVICE CLASS

Bout

8

Bantamweight   3 x 2 min. Rounds

R. BURRIDGE   v.   T. STONEMAN
Barnstaple A.B.C.   Torbay A.B.C.

9

Middleweight   3 x 2 min. Rounds

S. CRANER   v.   D. JARVIS
Appledore A.B.C.   Kingsbridge A.B.C.

10

Bantamweight   3 x 2 min. Rounds

T. SPILLER   v.   B. WILSHIRE
Bideford A.B.C.   Northbrook School

11

Light Welterweight   3 x 2 min. Rounds

B. DALTON   v.   A. THORNE
Dockland A.B.C.   Northbrook School

JUNIOR CLASS

2 x 2 min. and 1 x 1½ min. Rounds

12

C. MARREN   v.   D. JACKSON
Virginia House A.B.C.   Torbay A.B.C.

13

R. BARTER   v.   R. BONNER
Appledore A.B.C.   Northbrook School

14

G. REEVES   v.   D. SAUNDERS
Exeter A.B.C.   Northbrook School

15

R. DRAYTON   v.   M. ELLIS
Bideford A.B.C.   Barnstaple A.B.C.

NO DECISION CONTEST

S. BROWN   v.   A. DRAYTON
Bideford A.B.C.   Bideford A.B.C.

RESERVES

G. KROLL (Exeter), D. WILLIAMS (Barnstaple),
A. McDONALD (Barnstaple).

There will be an Interval for Refreshments obtainable in this Hall

135

Jimmy Isaac Shines In 6—4 Win Over Germans

ON the Torbay dinner jacket show at the Palace Hotel, Torquay, West country boxers won six of the ten contests against the touring German team Sudbaden, who, however, proved a very capable side.

Jimmy Isaac, Barnstaple, twice former ABA feather finalist, showed impressive form when he stopped Elbert Dehn, the German retiring in the second round from body punishment.

Teignmouth bantamweight Graham Tooley, after three clever rounds, outpointed Roland Schaller. Tooley suffered a bad cut eye in the last round, but weathered the storm and nearly dropped the German in the closing seconds.

Bobbie Mudge, the Torbay feather and son of Trainer Johnny Mudge, scored a fine victory in stopping Hubert Wenk in the second round, and Jimmy Banks, the Torbay light-welter, gave his usual immaculate performance of combination punching to outbox Josef Radle over three fast and gruelling rounds, with the visitor always looking dangerous.

RESULTS: Bantam, G. Tooley (Teignmouth) outpd R. Schaller (Sudbaden); Feather, R. Mudge (Torbay) bt H. Wenk (Sudbaden) rtd 2; J. Isaac (Barnstaple) stpd E. Dehn (Sudbaden) 2; Light, W. Spittler (Sudbaden) ko'd Cpl T. Smith (Army) 1; Light-welter, J. Banks (Torbay) outpd J. Radle (Sudbaden); B. Sus (Sudbaden) outpd L/Cpl P. Overall (RCT, Yeovil); Welter, L/Cpl D. Gibbons (RCT) outpd S. Bdimer (Sudbaden); Light-middle, K. Broking (Torbay) stpd K. Schroeder (Sudbaden) 2; Middle, H. Fortschegger (Sudbaden) outpd Cpl M. Hinchcliffe (RCT); Lightheavy, M. Metzger (Sudbaden) outpd F. Tooley (Teignmouth).

* * *

JIMMY ISAAC

... BUT, 24 HOURS LATER. THE VISITORS GET REVENGE

AFTER being beaten at Torquay the night before, the German team Sudbaden gained their revenge over a combined West country and Welsh team by six bouts to three at the City Hall, Truro.

Young Ashley Mugford, The Redruth welterweight, turned in a fine performance to outpoint the Sudbaden champion in one of the hard punching bouts of the evening.

Terry Godolphin, the Camborne lightweight, put up a very game show in losing on points to Werner Spittler, another Sudbaden champion, who had a big advantage in height and weight.

George Gunn, the Camborne light heavy did not produce his usual fireworks being outpointed by one of the best Germans.

Jimmy Banks, the brilliant Torbay light-welter, was up against a tough handful in Bruno Sus, a former West German Junior champion, and it was not until the last round that the Torbay boy got on top and carried the decision.

BOXING NEWS
NOVEMBER 17, 1967

ISAACS'S CHANCE OF NATIONAL HONOURS

MORE than 50 Plymouth, Devon, and Cornwall Schoolboy boxing champions clash at Honicknowle Secondary Modern School, Plymouth, tomorrow to decide who shall go forward to the Western Counties stage of the National Schoolboy boxing championships.

One of the key bouts will see Bobby Wood (Valletort, Plymouth) who last year reached the finals of the National titles, opposed to Jimmy Isaacs, of Barnstaple.

Both boys are old rivals, having hopes on Roger may early. Wood two years ago fought his way to the national finals. He may have two bouts tomorrow for there are two other boys at his weight—D. Melhuish (Ford, Plymouth) and L. Cudmore (Barnstaple).

Kenneth Graham, from Grenville College, Bideford, who already holds a Welsh Schools title, has a bye through to the Western Counties championships which are being staged at Teesdemit Hall, Marsh Mills, Plymouth, on February 20.

Other prominent Devon boys competing are David Jackson (Audley Park, Torquay) who meets R. Arnold (Tamar Secondary, Plymouth) and Graham Tooley (Teignmouth) who boxes R. Smith (Burleigh, Plymouth).

Treherras Secondary Modern, Newquay has once again a good entry for the championships, including D. Jermyn, A. Yeo, H. Jose, and P. Perry.

Last junior boxing tournament

Barnstaple A.B.C. held their final tournament—a junior event—of the season on Saturday.

The A.B.A. official in charge, Mr. Ken Woodyatt, described it as one of the best tournaments he had ever attended.

Results: S. Bates (Sidmouth) beat G. Hopkins (Exeter), r.s.f. first round; D. Kersey (Bideford) beat J. Cochrane (Capstone Hill), on points; R. Smith (Barnstaple) beat G. Spencer (Sidmouth), on points; T. Williams (Barnstaple) beat P. Wakefield (Exmouth), on points; C. Lewis (Barnstaple) beat M. Williams (Exmouth), r.s.f. in first round; S. Mackay (Exmouth) beat P. Jenkins (Barnstaple), on points; M. Griffiths (Barnstaple) beat A. Dunn (Bideford), on points.

M. Davey (Sidmouth) beat C. Summerwill (Capstone Hill), on points; N. Westlake (Teignmouth) beat C. Blackmore (Capstone Hill), on points; J. Hunkin (Teignmouth) beat D. Barrow (Barnstaple), on points; S. Willis (Teignmouth) beat P. Marriott (Capstone Hill), on points; P. Pile (Teignmouth) beat A. Shaddick (Bideford), on points; S. Westlake (Teignmouth) beat J. Dowling (Exmouth), on points; R. Cochrane (Capstone Hill) beat C. Redfern (Teignmouth), on points.

NARROW DEFEAT FOR BARUM BOXER

The three counties junior boxing champion, M. Bayliss, of Barnstaple, was beaten in the six counties championship at Truro on Saturday by MacAfferty, of Cheltenham.

It was a close points decision after Bayliss had been on top in the early part of the fight.

BARNSTAPLE ABC

ISAAC STOPS DUTCH CHAMPION

Sanders.   Brogan.   Isaac.   Cox.

FIVE WESTCOUNTRY BOXERS BATTLE FOR A.B.A. TITLES

SANDERS LOOKS BIG HOPE

By our Boxing Correspondent

THERE will be a minor Westcountry invasion at the Empire Pool, Wembley, tonight, when three Devon boxers and two Service men with close county links compete in the annual A.B.A. championships.

Devon has never yet produced a British amateur champion, and the fact that this year there is such a big representation has made boxing history in the county, which in the past has had to be content with only occasional finalists.

The five who do battle tonight are Tony Brogan (Bideford) and Marine Corpl. Bob Sanders (41 Commando, Bickleigh), in the heavy-weight division: light-heavy-weight Chris Cox (Exeter), Jimmy Isaac, the Barnstaple bantam-weight, and L. E. M. Michael Frampton (Plymouth Command), in the feather-weight class.

I rank Sanders, 27-year-old, as the best man with a chance of winning a title. The Marine, who has long associations with Devon, and is still a member of Dockland Settlement, Devonport, has a vast amount of experience coupled with excellent boxing skill, which is enhanced with a long and devastating left.

He should prove too experienced for Brogan if they should meet, good as the Bideford man is. The other two men he may have to contend with are Ron Davies (Manchester), whom he has beaten before, and Joe Taylor (London Polytechnic).

DEVON, Dorset and Cornwall beat a Dutch team by seven bouts to five in Rotterdam at the Riviera Hall, before a crowd of over 2,000, in a tournament staged by the Rotterdam club.

Bobby Arnold, the Plymouth Mayflower featherweight beat Bram Klopert on a disqualification in the first round for alleged butting, but Arnott was well on top when the closure came.

Jimmy Banks, Torbay light-weight, gave a fine display to out-point Dutch lightweight Freek Bandell, whilst Arthur Tyrell, the strong Exeter middleweight knocked out Benny Bor, in the second round.

Finest bout of the evening came when Jimmy Isaac, pictured above, the brilliant Barnstaple and England featherweight, classically stopped Peit Kerkhof, last year's Dutch Champion.

He was in devastating form, attacked from the start, and dropped his opponent in the first round, and dropped him again in the second, when the bout was stopped.

Results—Feather: .R. Arnott (Plymouth Mayflower) bt A. Kloppert, disq. 1; J. Isaac (Barnstaple) bt P. Kerkhof, stpd. 2. Light: J. Banks (Torbay) outpd. F. Bandel. Light-welter: R. Waters (Mayflower) lost to H. le Cocq, stpd. 3; S. Phillips (Barnstaple) lost to G. Bok, pts. Welter: W. Choules (Exeter) outpd. P. Tilburg. Light-middle: D. Stacey (Torbay) lost to A. Bor, pts.; R. Withers (Truro) outpd. F. Gelens. Middle: A. Tyrrell (Exeter) bt. B. Bor, K.O. 2; M. Laine (Mayflower) outpd. L. Valk. Light-heavy: G. Gunn (Redruth) lost to F. Heerik, pts. Heavy: D. Challice (Torbay) lost to B. Nikkelen-Kupper, pts.

Awkward

I do not underrate the ability of Brogan to spring a surprise. He has not been boxing long, but on the road to Wembley he has claimed as his victims some of the best men in the game. A south-paw, he is a particularly awkward customer.

Twenty-one-year-old Chris Cox will of course be relying on his formidable knock-out punch to carry him through but the big bogy for him could be Dennis Pollard, the policeman who is already an England international.

Brilliant Jimmy Isaac, boxing for the first time as a senior will not find the occasion too big for him for he has boxed before huge crowds in winning two national junior titles.

The fact that Peter Bennyworth, twice A.B.A. champion, was beaten in the qualifying London championships would seem to leave the road open for 18-year-old Isaac, but he will probably have to meet the man who beat the ex-champion—the Dartford southpaw Brian Packer, a boy with a big reputation.

For Frampton, aged 18, to win a Navy and I.S.B.A. title in his first year of senior boxing is no mean achievement, and if he

JIMMY ISAAC
BARNSTAPLE ABC.

TO RUSSIA WITH GLOVES —Barnstaple's Jimmy Isaac packs his suitcase in readiness for his journey as a member of the England boxing team. Jimmy today left Barnstaple on the first stage of his trip to Russia.

BARNSTAPLE ABC

JIMMY takes a punch from eventual points winner, KEN BUCHANAN.
BRITISH ABA FEATHERWEIGHT FINAL 1965.
BUCHANAN immediately joined the PROFESSIONAL RANKS and went on to WIN a WORLD TITLE at LIGHTWEIGHT.

JIMMY ISAAC

BOB SIMS presents JIMMY with a PAIR of ENGRAVED SILVER CUFF
LINKS…'GOOD LUCK.'
JIMMY'S MOTHER, PAULINE, front row, far left.
At left in centre is KEN WINKLES, on his left, ALEX MASON.
BARNSTAPLE ABC boxers look-on.

YOUNG BOXER TAKES LETTER FROM DUKE TO MAYOR

JIMMY ISAAC TAKES THE DUKE'S LETTER

The 16-year-old Barnstaple boxer, Jimmy Isaac, presented a personal letter from the Duke of Gloucester to the Mayor of Barnstaple, Mr. Stanley Woolaway, on Monday.

The letter was in reply to one written by Mr. Woolaway to the Duke.

Mr. Woolaway sent his letter via the young boxer, who was Barnstaple Sports Centre's official representative at the opening of National Boys' Club Week.

The centre won the right to be represented at the ceremony by selling the second highest number of competition tickets in the county during last year's Boys' Club Week.

The Duke is president of the National Association of Boys' Clubs, in which capacity he attended the opening.

Jimmy Isaac handed him the Mayor's greeting personally, and was handed back a reply.

After the Duke's message was passed over on Monday, the Mayor opened it and read out the greeting it contained.

It wished the Barnstaple Sports Centre "every success."

Duke thanks Mayor

JIMMY ISAAC, the boxing champion of Barnstaple Sports Centre, was one of Devon's two representatives at a London ceremony to herald the opening of the National Association of Boys' Clubs Week.

Part of Jimmy's task was to take a letter of greetings from the Mayor of Barnstaple, Mr. Stanley Woolaway, to the N.A.B.C. President, The Duke of Gloucester, at St. James's Palace.

Last night 16-year-old Jimmy handed over a letter replying to the Mayor at Barnstaple.

The Duke expressed thanks to Mr. Woolaway for his interest in boys' clubs, and for the support he has given to such clubs in Barnstaple.

A Barnstaple boy was chosen because of the number of tickets sold by the Sports Centre in a competition last year Barnstaple sold the second highest number of tickets in the county.

Less than 48 hours before meeting the Mayor, Jimmy Isaac was boxing for the West of England against South London in a tournament at Weymouth. Captain of the West of England team, Jimmy, won on a points decision.

The Barnstaple Boxing Club had two other members in action at Weymouth. Roger Burridge won his bout, but Geoffrey Yeo lost his on points

BARNSTAPLE ABC

POST OFFICE

TELEGRAM

Charges to pay

___ s. ___ d.

RECEIVED

At _____ m

From _____

By _____

No. _____

OFFICE STAMP

At _____ m

To _____

By _____

Prefix. Time handed in. Office of Origin and Service Instructions. Words.

V110 1.57 PAIGNTON EX 15

J ISAAC KINGS HALL BELLEVUE MANCHESTER =

DEVON ABA WISH YOU GOOD LUCK TONIGHT =

BRIAN POLLARD +

ABA + MRO 32

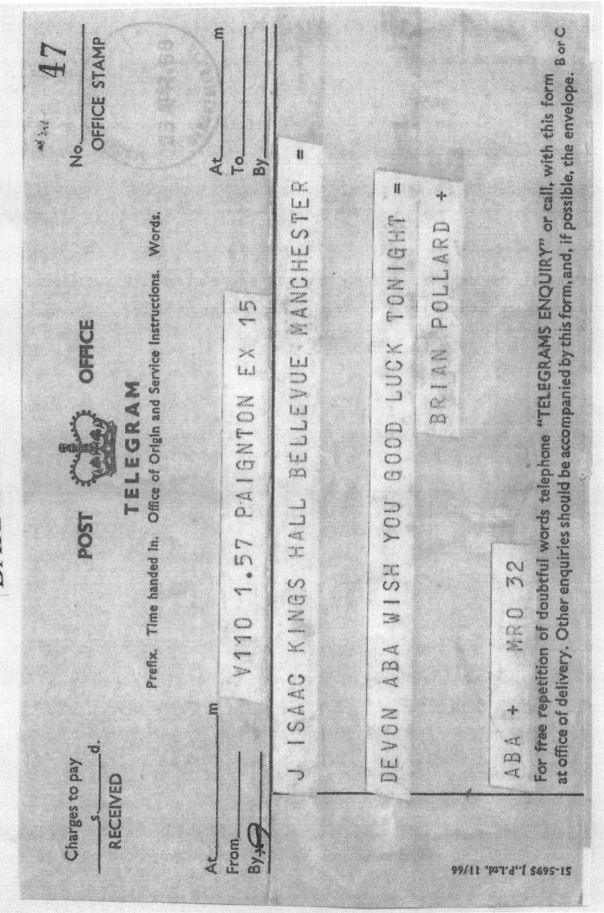

BARNSTAPLE ABC

Charges to pay
______s.______d.
RECEIVED
203

POST OFFICE
TELEGRAM

Prefix. Time handed in. Office of Origin and Service Instructions. Words.

No.______
OFFICE STAMP

At______m
From______
By______

L246 5.56 LONDON T S/W 28

At______m
To______
By______

J ISAACS 38 ASHLEIGH CRESCENT BARNSTAPLE =

CAN YOU REPRESENT ABA
AGAINST RUMANIA MONDAY EVENING 21ST
NOVEMBER AT WOLVERHAMPTON PLEASE PHONE MR BONE
LONDONFREMANTLE 4411 =
LOVETT AMATEUR BOXING ASSOCIATION +

~~38 21ST 4411 , TS T GMS LN~~

...all, with this form
If possible, the envelope.

B or C

51-2505 J.,P.Ltd.

BEFORE!

BARNSTAPLE ABC

AFTER!

TWO PHOTOS. Obviously taken during the same TRAINING SESSION.
JIMMY ISAAC front row left, ROGER BURRIDGE front row right.
BILL MAYO standing, back row third from the right.
SID PHILLIPS standing on his right.

145

BARNSTAPLE ABC

JIMMY watched over by TRAINER JIM BARTLETT helps support the impressive ALEX MASON TROPHY.

146

BARNSTAPLE TOWN MAYOR, MICHAEL HUXTABLE presents JIMMY with a TRAVELLING BAG. Far right, TRAINER ALEX MASON.

BARNSTAPLE ABC

JIMMY in ACTION! The REFEREE is BRIAN POLLARD:

ENGLAND versus HUNGARY.

The ENGLAND TEAM LINE UP. JIMMY ISAAC second from the right.

But Army outgun West boxers

BARNSTAPLE international amateur boxer, Jimmy Isaac, showed convincing form in winning his first featherweight fight at the Queen's Hall on Friday.

Isaac, a 19-year-old apprentice electrician, beat 30-year-old Bombardier R. Woodcock, of the Royal Artillery, in a three round contest on points after some gruelling exchanges.

Isaac, who less than two weeks ago announced that he had changed from bantamweight to featherweight, was one of the seven members of Barnstaple Amateur Boxing Club to fight in a match against the Army's crack 14-man team.

Out of the seven local boxers, three succeeded in winning.

They were Sid Phillips, who scored a knock-out over Driver Michael Rutter, of the Royal Army Service Corps; Johnny Burke, who beat Signalman Arthur Paxton, of the Royal Corps of Signals, on points; and Jimmy Isaac.

The West of England team, including Barnstaple, lost to the Army 9—5.

Isaac's well-known left hook meant business from the start, and this was demonstrated in the second round when Isaac sent the Army champion to the canvas.

Barnstaple's most promising youngster and schoolboy champion, Geoff Yeo, was beaten in the first 20 seconds of round one.

Sid Phillips's win over Mick Rutter proved to be one of the most interesting bouts of the evening.

Just when Phillips seemed certain to lose the match on points, Rutter started to wilt in round three.

Phillips, seizing his chance, plied his opponent with a volley of punches and dropped him with a right to the chin.

Fifteen seconds later Phillips again put the Army man on the canvas, and scored a knock-out.

Burke's comeback

For Barnstaple's Johnny Burke, who beat Signalman Arthur Paxton on points, this was a special victory.

The 25-year-old ex-policeman, who is a newcomer to the local club, had to give up boxing several years ago for health reasons.

Results. Junior: Jnr. Gnr. F. Deans (R.A.) beat G. Yeo (Barnstaple), referee stopped fight. Lightweight: S. Phillips (Barnstaple) knocked out Driver M. Rutter (R.A.S.C.). Welterweight: T. Skinner (Plymouth) beat Pte. P. Lloyd (Parachute Rgt.) on points.

Middleweight: Gdsmn. S. O'Sullivan (Irish Guards) beat J. Newby (Barnstaple and R.A.F.) on points. Welterweight: L./Cpl. A. Tibbs (Queen's Royal Lancers) beat P. Hayfield (Exmouth), referee stopped fight. Light-middleweight: J. Burke (Barnstaple) beat Sig. A. Paxton (R.C.O.S.) on points.

Light-heavyweight: Cpl. R. Priestley (R.A.O.C.) beat D. Lewis (Watchet) on points. Lightweight: D. Thompson (Torbay) beat Pte. J. Dannaher (R.A.O.C.) on points. Light-welterweight: L./Cpl. P. Taylor (R.A.O.C.) beat R. Burridge (Barnstaple) on points. Light-middleweight: Pte. G. Winton (Parachute Rgt.) beat G. Roode (Barnstaple) on points.

Welterweight: L./Cpl. K. Jacobs (R.A.S.C.) beat W. Choules (Exeter) on points. Light-welterweight: Pte. B. Bebbington (Parachute Rgt.) knocked out G. Gould (Exeter). Featherweight: J. Isaac (Barnstaple and England) beat Bdr. R. Woodcock (R.A.) on points. Light-heavyweight: L./Cpl. B. White (R.A.O.C.) beat A. Tyrell (Exeter), referee stopped fight in the third round.

HARD PUNCHERS

Nine of the West's hardest punchers are entered for the light-middleweight title, and my vote must go to the tough George Hall (Plymouth Mayflower).

Exeter's big hope is, of course, Arthur Tyrrell, who has several times reached the A.B.A. semi-finals. Among an entry of nine in the light-heavyweight class his chief obstacle could be Derek Gatehouse (Gillingham).

I forecast the following winners in the other weights. Bantam—Dave Tall (Plymouth Mayflower). Light—Bobby Arnott (Mayflower). Welter — Ashley Mugford (Mayflower and Redruth) or Dave Stacey (Torbay). Heavy — Chris Athanasiades (Torbay).

LONG LAY-OFF SHOULD NOT UPSET ISAAC

By JACK TRANTER

FIFTY-FIVE Westcountry boxers will line up at the St. George's Hall, Exeter, on Saturday for the annual Devon, Dorset, and Cornwall A.B.A. championships — first hurdle on the way to Wembley for those lucky to reach the national finals.

This season it will be a battle between young and tough boxers and seasoned men, who have in past years gone a long way in the competition.

So big is the entry that many preliminary and semi-final bouts will have to take place in the afternoon, to be followed at night by the finals.

Devon has the biggest entry with 34 entrants, while Cornwall will have 12.

After a 12-month lay-off, Jimmy Isaac, twice a national finalist, will once again be staking a claim in the featherweight division and, despite the fact that this will be his first ring appearance for such a long time, the opposition at this stage should be too young and inexperienced to eliminate the Barnstaple man.

Jimmy Banks (Torbay), last season's light-

Isaac

welterweight finalist and now a member of Britain's Olympic squad, looks a cert in this division, providing the young, hard-punching Ron Coote (Falmouth) does not spring a surprise.

Big challenge in the middle-weight class is being made by Danny Manley (Barnstaple), fresh from winning a Devon novices' title last Friday, but I do not think he is experienced enough for such men as Pat Williams (Helston), a last season's national quarter-finalist, and Leo Toms (Poole), former national junior A.B.A. champion.

Isaac and Bayliss bid for Six Counties titles

Two Barnstaple boxers — featherweight Jimmy Isaac and light-welterweight M. Bayliss — won Three Counties titles at the Devon, Dorset and Cornwall championships on Saturday.

Although Isaac succeeded convincingly against W. Crouch (Gillingham) and R. Richards (Plymouth), he looked rather "ring rusty" after his long lay-off.

Bayliss, who is only 17 and in his first year as a senior, gave a competent performance in outpointing P. Head (Devonport) in a hard bout, and later he had a points decision against P. Denley (Teignmouth).

Two other North Devon boxers — Bob Ellis (Bideford) and Dave Manley (Barnstaple) — also did well in their fights although no titles came their way.

In a light-middleweight contest, Ellis beat P. Sanderson (Stadium Club), who was disqualified for low hitting, but he received his dismissal from the championships at the hands of R. Barlow (Virginia House, Plymouth), last year's champion.

Barlow, incidentally, later received a trophy for the best boxer of the day.

Manley, in his middleweight bout, stopped last year's champion, P. Williams (Helston), in less than a minute.

Williams failed to beat the count after being put down twice with hard left hooks to the body.

But in the final Manley lost on points to L. Toms (Poole), a former schoolboy champion.

Isaac and Bayliss now go forward to the Six Counties championships at Salisbury on Saturday week.

Isaac and Bayliss reach national quarter-finals

Two Barnstaple boxers—featherweight Jimmy Isaac and light welterweight Mike Bayliss — have qualified for the A.B.A. quarter-finals at Birmingham on April 11.

They surmounted another hurdle in the national championships at Salisbury on Saturday when they took part in Western Counties finals.

Isaac, who beat M. Bryson (Bath) on points, gave evidence that he is returning to international form.

Bayliss had a walk-over as L. White (Poole) failed to pass the doctor.

● DEVON ABA team secretary Stan Fishleigh, pictured above centre, invites inquiries from any ABA honorary secretary interested in matches. Comprising this Devon County team of last season are (back row): M. Baylis (Barnstaple); R. Denley (Teignmouth); T. Pincombe (Capstone Hill); T. Morgan (Mayflower); D. Clarbull (Exmouth); Mr Fishleigh; M. Phillips (Mayflower); D. Stacey (Torbay); K. Brooking (Torbay); A. Tyrell (Exeter); D. Chambers (Mayflower) and F. Tooley (Teignmouth). Front row: D. Manley (Barnstaple); G. Clatworthy (Teignmouth); Fred Tooley's young son; T. Tooley (Teignmouth) and R. Ellis (Bideford). Devon ABA are at home to Wales, Western Division, on November 2 at Bideford.

BILLY WELLS

HEAVYWEIGHT

Over 12st 10lb

Billy Wells (Lynn)
Frank Carpenter (Rootes)
Dan McAlinden (Edgewick)
George Harris
(RN & Battersea)
Richard Dunn (Halifax Star)
Dave Hawkes (Border)
Jack Cotes (Huthwaite)
John McKinty (Army)
Les Stevens (Reading)
Dave Pellegrinetti (Army)
Alan Burton (Caius)
Frank Heaney (Chiswick)
Bill Aird (Golden Gloves)
Bill Ives (Colverstone)
Willie Gilfillan (Sparta)

CRUISERWEIGHT

12st 10lb

Max Smith (Royal Marines)
Willie Stack (Leamington)
Pat Long (Edgewick)
Barry Francis (Lynn)
Tommy Wright (Mold)
Dave Wallington (Keystone)
Bill Peters (North Shields)
Keith Stephens
(Brookdale Park)
Keith Drewett (Earlsfield)
Johnny Banham
(Met. Police & Battersea)
Jackie Woods (5/6 Staffs)
Sammy Frankham (Reading)
Mick Molyneaux
(Liverpool-Scottish)
Bill Bruce (Army)
George Francis (Battersea)

MIDDLEWEIGHT

11st 11lb

Chris Finnegan (Hayes)
Barney Burns (Small Heath)
Frank Isaacs (Middle Row)
Scott Barbour (Larkhall)
Bill Sutherley (Army)
Bobby Barrett (Border)
Johnny Frankham (Reading)
Brian Deans (St Oswald's)
Tony Soul (Southend)
Seymour Ellwood (Lynn)

BROUGHTON'S ☆ AMATEUR ☆ RATINGS

LIGHT-MIDDLEWEIGHT

11st 2lb

1 Eric Blake (Battersea)
2 Tom Imrie (Buccleuch)
3 Eammon McCusker (Ban-bridge)
4 Alan Edwards (Worcester)
5 Bob Murphy (BDS)
6 Jim Smith (St Francis)
7 Peter Lloyd (Army)
8 John Green (Wilton Works)
9 Brian Glossop (Llangefni)
10 Mike McCluskie (Croeserw)
11 Daryl Hallett (RAF)
Freddie Knowles (Fitzroy Lodge)
13 Terry McCarthy (Crumlin)
14 Tommy Gray (Willaston)
15 Michael Beeney (Lynn)

WELTERWEIGHT

10st 8lb

1 Alan Tottoh (BDS)
Frank Young (Dominic Savio)
3 Brian Whelan (Chiswick)
4 Terry Henderson
(Robert Browning)
5 Tommy Joyce (Tom Hill YC)
6 Dave Simmonds
(Cinderford & Gloucester)
7 Geoff Cutts (Army)
8 Frank McCabe (Lancaster)
9 Dave Proud (S. Norwood)
Tony Petch (Fitzroy Lodge)
11 Ken Beedie (Brechin)
12 Ken Hookins

LIGHT-WELTERWEIGHT

10 stone

1 Jim McCourt (Immaculata)
2 Terry Waller (Lynn)
Jim Watt (Cardowan)
4 Colin Booth (Army)
5 Ron Thurston (Raven)
6 Frank Downes (Crumlin)
7 Les Pearson
(Rothwell Colliery)
8 Terry Sellars (Somercotes)
9 Jimmy Banks (Torbay)
10 Dennis Delbridge (Porthcawl)
Fred Applegate (BDS)
12 Vince Halpin (Langley Park)
13 Willie Burns (St Francis)
14 Dave Davies (Bangor)
15 John Rodgers (Lisburn)
Jimmy Fairweather
(Battersea)
Sam Dougherty (Army)

LIGHTWEIGHT

9st 7lb

1 John Stracey (Repton)
2 Martin Quinn (St John Bosco)
3 Bobby Fisher (Hartcliffe)
4 Maldwyn Evans (Porthcawl)
5 Mickey Oates (West Ham)
6 Howard Hayes (Plant Works, Doncaster)
7 Larry Spriggs (Battersea)
8 Graham Moughton (Barking)
Willie Pringle (Golden Gloves)
10 Walter Breslin (Mayfair)
11 Sean Graham (Middle Row)
12 Peter Harrison (Glasgow

ALAN TOTTOH

FEATHERWEIGHT

9 stone

1 Johnny Cheshire (Repton)
2 Alan Richardson (White Rose)
3 Eddie Treacy (Arbour Hill)
4 Bobby Mallon (Kelvin)
5 Pat Devanney (Crumlin)
6 Gilbert Gunn (RAF)
7 Jimmy Isaacs (Barnstaple)
Eddie Pritchard (Llangefni)
9 Joe Murphy (Kelvin)
10 Hugh McAvoy (St. Matthew's)
11 Paul Carson (St. John Bosco)
12 Harry Dunne (Kensington)
13 Ron Russell (Glasgow Corp. Transport)
14 Danny Polak (Park Farm)
15 Terry Chapman (Sir Phillip Game)

BANTAMWEIGHT

8st 7lb

1 Mickey Carter (Fisher)
2 Leslie Pickett (Merthyr)
Frank Taberner (Blackpool)
4 Mick Dowling (Arbour Hill)
5 John Mitchell (Eastbank)
6 Terry Beardsmore (Stoke-on-Trent)
7 Mick Anthony (Repton)
8 Gerry Jordan (St John Bosco)
9 Pat McAuley (Holy Family)
10 Mick Piner (Hayes)
11 Ray Daniells (Portsea)
12 Dennis Rusby (R. Browning)
13 Mick Cullen (Wexford)
14 Joe Farrell (Dalmarnock)
15 Bob Galloway (Poplar)
Errol McBean (RAF)

FLYWEIGHT

8st and under

1 Brendan McCarthy (Arbour Hill)
2 Johnny McGonigle (Army)
3 Maurice Steves (Wandsworth)
Alex McHugh (Kelvin)
5 Steve Curtis (Roath Youth)
6 Peter Wakefield (St. Patrick's)
7 Ron Isaacs (Barnstaple)
8 Terry Wenton (Golden Gloves)
9 Steve Whyte (Rolls Royce)
10 Neil McLaughlin (St. Eugene's)
11 Harry Cunningham (St. Matthew's)

A GREAT ACHIEVEMENT!
JIMMY and RONNIE in the BRITISH AMATEUR RATINGS.
AUGUST 2nd 1968.

FLYWEIGHT

8st and under

1 Brendan McCarthy (Arbour Hill)
2 Johnny McGonigle (Army)
3 Maurice Steves (Wandsworth)
4 Alex McHugh (Kelvin)
5 Steve Curtis (Roath Youth)
6 Peter Wakefield (St. Patrick's)
7 Ron Isaacs (Barnstaple)
8 Terry Wenton (Golden Gloves)
9 Steve Whyte (Rolls Royce)
10 Neil McLaughlin (St. Eugene's)
11 Harry Cunningham (St. Matthew's)
12 Bobby Flower (Battersea)
13 Mick Abrams (Battersea)
14 Mick Craven (Splott YMCA)
15 Paul Lefley (New Enterprise)

FEATHERWEIGHT

9 stone

1 Johnny Cheshire (Repton)
2 Alan Richardson (White Rose)
3 Eddie Treacy (Arbour Hill)
4 Bobby Mallon (Kelvin)
5 Pat Devanney (Crumlin)
6 Gilbert Gunn (RAF)
7 Jimmy Isaacs (Barnstaple)
8 Eddie Pritchard (Llangefni)
9 Joe Murphy (Kelvin)
10 Hugh McAvoy (St. Matthew's)
11 Paul Carson (St. John Bosco)
12 Harry Dunne (Kensington)
13 Ron Russell (Glasgow Corp. Transport)
14 Danny Polak (Park Farm)
15 Terry Chapman (Sir Phillip Game)

153

Brogan unlucky to lose title fight

JIMMY ISAAC ALSO FAILS

BOTH of North Devon's national title aspirants —Barnstaple's Jimmy Isaac and Torbay and Bideford's Tony Brogan—found nothing but disappointment at the end of the long trail to Wembley when they lost their boxing finals at the Empire Pool.

But there were many in the crowd who were convinced that Irish international Brogan should have been awarded the A.B.A. title in his heavyweight bout with London's representative, W. Wells.

He dropped Wells for a count of eight in the first round, when he piled up the points in a display of cool but aggressive boxing.

He held his own in the second round against Wells, who is a Fleet Street newspaper electrician, but in the third his opponent scored heavily.

Even then, Brogan seemed a narrow winner, and the decision

TONY BROGAN

was greeted with surprised disbelief by a section of the crowd.

But in the semi-final, Brogan had been a little lucky to win against A.B. Chris Field (H.M.S. Ark Royal), who dealt out a lot of punishment in the second round.

Isaac outboxed

Making his second appearance at Wembley, Isaac was outboxed in the featherweight event by brilliant Ken Buchanan (Spartan Club, Edinburgh) after showing promise early in the bout.

But then Buchanan began to take the fight to his opponent, whose movements were often those of a tired man, and his clever boxing enabled him to take the first and second rounds.

Isaac gave everything he had in the third round, and it was now Buchanan's turn to look jaded, but despite a supreme effort he was unable to turn the bout in his favour.

In the semi-final, clever boxing had enabled Isaac to win the first two rounds against former A.B.A. flyweight champion, 21-year-old M. Pye, of the Harris Lebus A.B.C., London.

Although Isaac slackened a little in the third round to reserve some of his energy for the final, he was a comfortable and popular winner.

THREE WESTCOUNTRY BOXERS THROUGH TO A.B.A. FINALS

COX, ISAAC AND BROGAN

THREE Westcountry boxers reached the Wembley finals of the A.B.A. championships with fine victories in the quarter-finals at Coventry last night.

Chris Cox (Exeter) was put on the canvas by his Welsh opponent, J. Cassidy (Buckley A.B.C., North Wales), in the light-heavy-weight, but he fought back superbly to fell the Welshman with a short right to the body.

Cassidy staggered to his feet at the count of nine, but he was so obviously groggy that the referee stopped the fight in Cox's favour after 1min. 56sec. of the first round.

DISQUALIFIED

Bantam-weight Jimmy Isaac (Barnstaple) followed this up by pasting southpaw I. Frost (Pontypridd) all over the ring with solid right hands until Frost was disqualified in the third and last round for persistent holding.

Wales won their first bout when E. Avoth (Victoria Park A.B.C., Cardiff) outpointed the Negro, Johnny Elliot, of Birmingham, father of five children, in the light-middle-weight.

Elliot, last year's losing finalist, came within an ace of winning this bout, but his fight-back after being knocked down was not enough.

Tony Brogan (Barnstaple) made it a hat-trick for the Westcountry by outpointing John Simisker (Wales) after a gruelling heavy-weight bout.

Bantam—J. Isaac (Barnstaple) bt I. Frost (Pontypridd), disqualified third round.

Light-middle—E. Avoth (Victoria Park, Cardiff) outpointed J. Elliot (Wednesfield).

Middle—L. Samuels (Wolverhampton) outpointed C. J. Waters (Richmond A.B.C., Cardiff).

Light-heavy—C. Cox (Exeter) bt J. Cassidy (Buckley, North Wales), stopped first round.

Heavy—T. Brogan (Barnstaple) outpointed J. Simisker (Wales).

ISAAC TO BOX IN MOSCOW

Moscow will be the destination of an 18-year-old Barnstaple boxer, Jimmy Isaac, next month, when he is to represent England against Russia.

The Barum bantamweight gained his first international honour when he recently boxed in London against Hungary.

Although he narrowly lost his bout, the selectors were greatly

JIMMY ISAAC

impressed by his performance, and the invitation to join the Moscow-bound party followed.

While a junior, Isaac won the National Association of Boys' Clubs title, and subsequently he was an A.B.A. championship finalist.

After leaving Barnstaple on December 3, he will train hard in London for two days before flying to Moscow, where he will spend eight days.

ISAAC TO BOX FOR ENGLAND

BARNSTAPLE bantam-weight boxer Jimmy Isaac has been chosen to represent England in an international match at Manchester on November 11.

Isaac learnt last week that he was on the short list for this match against Hungary, and now he has been informed that he is definitely a member of the England team.

A good performance against his Hungarian opponent could win 18-year-old Jimmy a trip to Russia later this year.

He has been named as one of the boxers from which the touring group will be chosen, and obviously the selectors are waiting to see how he shows up in Manchester.

FIGHTS TONIGHT

On Monday Isaac travelled to Worcester to meet a German boxer

JIMMY ISAAC

in a special tournament, and won on points. He hopes to keep up this form when he meets international bantam-weight M. Pye in a London tournament this evening.

More Barnstaple boxing news today: there will be a tournament between Devon boxers and the Birmingham club at the Queen's Hall, Barnstaple, on Saturday, November 2.

Isaacs' Triumph

DEVON ABA defeated the Oxon., Berks. and South Bucks. ABA at Oxford by six bouts to five, and prominent among the winners, were the Isaac brothers from Barnstaple.

Ron Isaac scored a narrow points win in three action packed rounds against Ray Flowers (Battersea). Isaac was the heavier and more accurate puncher but had to survive a nasty period in the last round.

Jimmy Isaac was much too strong for Frank Read, Reading, and dropped him for a count of eight in the first round. He again dropped the Reading boxer and the referee stepped in to stop the bout.

Results (Oxon. names first):

Senior: Fly: R. Flowers (Battersea) lost on pts. to R. Isaac (Barnstaple); feather: F. Read (Reading) lost to J. Isaac (Barnstaple) stpd 1; light: G. Frankish (Rootes and YMCA) outpd R. Mudge (Torbay); light-welter: R. Passmore (High Wycombe) lost to J. Banks (Torbay) stpd 1; welter: G. Daniels (Reading) bt R. Ellis (Bideford) stpd 3; light-middle: C. Prince (Oxford) outpd K. Brooking (Torbay); Middle: S. Hitchens (Reading) bt D. Chambers (Plymouth Mayflower) stpd 1; light-heavy: R. Nugent (Reading) outpd D. Challice (Torbay).

Junior: T. Smith (Balliol Boys) lost on pts. to J. Hunting (Teignmouth); S. Lapper (Morris Motors) lost to R. Attrill (Mayflower) rtd 1; R. Jefferies (Oxford YMCA) lost to C. Ebdon (Teignmouth) rtd

Isaac Beats Champ

JIMMY ISAAC, Barnstaple, brilliant young bantam, gained a convincing victory over Ron Coutts, Western Counties champion, at Barnstaple on Thursday.

In a rather scrambly bout, with Coutts moving forward to get in close, Isaac brought a right uppercut in to play that effectively stopped the Bristol boxer often in his tracks.

Tommy Westlake, Royal Engineers and Patchway heavyweight, nearly brought off a surprise victory over Tony Brogan, Bideford, in the first round, when the Bideford light-heavy was caught with some strong two-handed punches when he elected to trade punches with the strong Army boxer.

Brogan's superior boxing, however, came into play in the second round, and the third stanza saw him well on top, dropping the Patchway boxer for four counts.

T. Tooley (Teignmouth) outpd R. Burridge (Barnstaple); B. Tait (Plymouth Mayflower) outpd R. Burge (Appledore); S. Phillips (Barnstaple) outpd R. Thompson (Devonport); B. Salter (Torbay) outpd P. Burns (Patchway, Bristol); B. Cotter (Plymouth Mayflower) outpd D. Thompson (Torbay); F. Tooley (Teignmouth) outpd D. Stacey (Torbay); A. Ensor (Barnstaple) outpd T. Prescott (Bideford); J. Isaac (Barnstaple) outpd R. Coutts (Patchway); K. Wilson (Plymouth Mayflower) outpd P. Crowe (Patchway); T. Stoneman (Torbay) beat M. Wainmaring (Patchway) dis. 2; B. Sleeman (Northbrook, Exeter) outpd D. Harvey (Torbay); A. Brogan (Bideford) outpd T. Westlake (Patchway). Junior: K. McDowell (Devonport) outpd A. McDonald (Barnstaple); F. Williams (Barnstaple) outpd K. Brooking (Torbay).

Arthur Tyrrell   Dave Short   Ron Isaac   Harold Clatworthy

GEORGE GUNN GETS HIS CHANCE OF REVENGE

GEORGE GUNN, the popular Cornish light - heavyweight, has a return contest at St. John's Hall, Penzance, on Saturday with Dave Frape (Synwell, Gloucester), the boxer who two years ago was the innocent party in robbing the Camborne man of a six Western Counties' A.B.A. title, writes our Boxing Correspondent.

On that disastrous occasion, Gunn apeared to have dropped the Gloucester boxer for keeps with a right hook, but the referee ruled that he had struck another blow just as the falling Frape reached the canvas.

On Saturday I think Gunn will make amends for his earlier impetuosity. Frape is a durable boxer but he was convincingly outpointed by Dave Short (Barnstaple) in the Western Counties' championships at Westward Ho! last Saturday.

The tournament will be the second this season to be staged by the Penzance Boxing Club in conjunction with the Redruth Club, and Gunn and Frape will be one of the contests in a team match between a combined Devon and Cornish side, and boxers from Gloucestershire and Wiltshire.

Included in the Devon and Cornwall team will be the brilliant young Torbay light-welterweight Jimmy Banks, who lost on points in last Saturday's Western Counties' championship finals; Terry Godolphin (Camborne), three counties' A.B.A. featherweight semi-finalist; Bob Foster (Truro); Boris Jones (St. Austell) and Sid Phillips (Barnstaple).

In the junior match, Cornwall's boxers will include three boys who reached this season's semifinals of the School's national boxing championships — Rodney Walsh (Penzance), Trevor Martyn (Newquay) and Keith Barker (Newquay).

Cornwall's national Sea Cadets' champion, Ron Coote (Falmouth), will also be in action, his opponent being the classy Ken Hawke (Virginia House, Plymouth).

KNOCK-OUT BY BURRIDGE

The junior bouts of the Barnstaple boxing tournament produced a minor sensation. Roger Burridge, of Barnstaple, knocked out his Bideford opponent, Langmead, in the second round.

I have watched many junior and schoolboy bouts and a k.o. is generally the last thing expected by the crowd.

But the storming approach work of Burridge made the local supporters sit up. He immediately drove his opponent to the ropes; not in a schoolboy rush but in the style of a senior boxer.

His whiplash left and heavy right soon had the Bideford youngster in difficulty in the second round. Burridge stepped out of a clinch and delivered an old fashioned one-two.

This contest was one of three arranged between Bideford and Barnstaple for the Alex Mason trophy which goes to the best junior team of the two towns.

Barnstaple won—but by default. There was no third and deciding bout. The Burridge win put Barnstaple on level terms with their neighbours who went ahead with a win by Blackmore over Elliot.

Another junior matching featured the county schoolboy champion, Jimmy Isaac, who fought in Barnstaple colours. His opponent was Jackson, of Audley Park, Torquay. Isaac had just recovered from a hand injury. But Jackson would never have known that from the way he bounced off the canvas on the end of an Isaac left hook.

The Barnstaple lad went on to take the fight on points.

His colleague John Neale lost to an Exmouth southpaw, Clarbull, after turning in a promising display during the first two rounds. He flagged in the third and missed his chances.

BARNSTAPLE BC
Junior

Junior: E. Cochrane (Capstone Hill, Ilfracombe) outpd. S. Bates (Sidmouth); S. Westlake (Teignmouth) outpd K. Binmore (Sidmouth); D. Manley (Barnstaple) bt D. Barratt (Bideford) KO 3; P. Pile (Teignmouth) outpd. A. Shaddick (Bideford); P. Coates (Capstone Hill) outpd A. Lunn (Bideford); S. Willis (Barnstaple) outpd T. Williams (Teignmouth); N. Westlake (Teignmouth) outpd. M. Griffiths (Barnstaple); M. Bayliss (Barnstaple) outpd M. Shaddick (Bideford); R. Kerswell (Barnstaple) outpd. C. Ebdon (Teignmouth); N. Gabriel (Exeter) outpd. C. Lewis (Barnstaple); T. Coates (Capstone Hill) outpd. C. Redfrern (Teignmouth); A. Spry (Bideford) outpd C. Hopkins (Exeter); R. Hopkins (Exeter) outpd. R. Smith (Barnstaple).

March 4th 1968.

BARNSTAPLE BC

Junior: S. Bates (Sidmouth) bt G. Hopkins (Exeter) stpd 1; D. Kersey (Bideford) outpd J. Cochrane (Capstone Hill, Ilfracombe); R. Smith (Barnstaple) outpd G. Spencer (Sidmouth); T. Williams (Barnstaple) outpd P. Wakefield (Exmouth); G. Lewis (Barnstaple) bt M. Williams (Exmouth) stpd 1; S. Mackay (Exmouth) outpd P. Jenkins (Barnstaple); M. Griffiths (Barnstaple) outpd A. Dunn (Bideford); M. Davey (Sidmouth) outpd C. Summerwell (Capstone Hill); M. Westlake (Teignmouth) outpd C. Blackmore (Capstone Hill); J. Hunting (Teignmouth) outpd D. Barrow (Barnstaple); S. Willis (Teignmouth) outpd P. Marriott (Capstone Hill); R. Pile (Teignmouth) outpd S. Shaddick (Bideford); S. Westlake (Teignmouth) outpd J. Dowling (Exmouth); E. Cochrane (Capstone Hill) outpd C. Redforn (Teignmouth).

April 13th 1968.

BOXING NEWS 28-6-1968

Devon Lament The Lack Of Senior Talent

AT the Devon ABA Annual General Meeting held at the Exeter Golf and Country Club, the decline of senior boxers in the County was reported.

It is now difficult to produce a County team of senior open class boxers at all weights to take part in inter-county matches.

Several good juniors, however, are in the transitional stage, and these could ease the situation as they mature.

The Isaac brothers, Jimmy and Ron, of Barnstaple, were congratulated on reaching the ABA semi-finals, whilst Jimmy Banks (Torbay) and Arthur Tyrrell (Exeter) completed a good season for Devon by becoming quarter-finalists.

In the National Schoolboy championships two Devon lads, George Payne (Teignmouth) and Graham Simons (Exeter), won national titles.

Sixteen senior tournaments have been held in the County during the past season, with ten junior shows, but Plymouth made a poor contribution with only one tournament, although there are six affiliated clubs in the town.

Devonport ABC were praised for their contribution to youth boxing, having staged half the total of junior tournaments.

A recommendation that the Devon, Dorset and Cornwall ABA be amalgamated with the Gloucester, Somerset and Wilts ABA to form a Western Counties Provincial Association was agreed, and would be forwarded to the Three Counties ABA for consideration at their AGM.

This would mean that there would be no change in the administration in the present set up, but would give greater representation to the South West Counties on the ABA Council.

This suggestion has been put forward before, but has up to now been unsuccessful.

■ BOXING BROTHERS: The picture, left, shows Jimmy Isaac in action. Above, the brothers all set for a bout.

OFF to a BOXING SHOW.

Left to right...
RON BONE, WALTER ISAAC, WILF COOPER, KEN MANLEY,
RUTH WILLIAMS, JIMMY ISAAC, KEN WILLIAMS, RONNIE ISAAC.

BARNSTAPLE ABC

ROCK PARK CLUB RUGBY TEAM.

TONY NUDDS, HUTCHINSON, BRIAN TUCKER, LES SYMONS, CHARLIE BRACHER, JOHN KELSO, BOB COATES, BARRY TRAWIN.

GRAHAM WARE, RON ISAAC, ROGER STONE, COLIN ROWE, CHRIS BAMENT, DOUG WADDLE, JIMMY ISAAC.

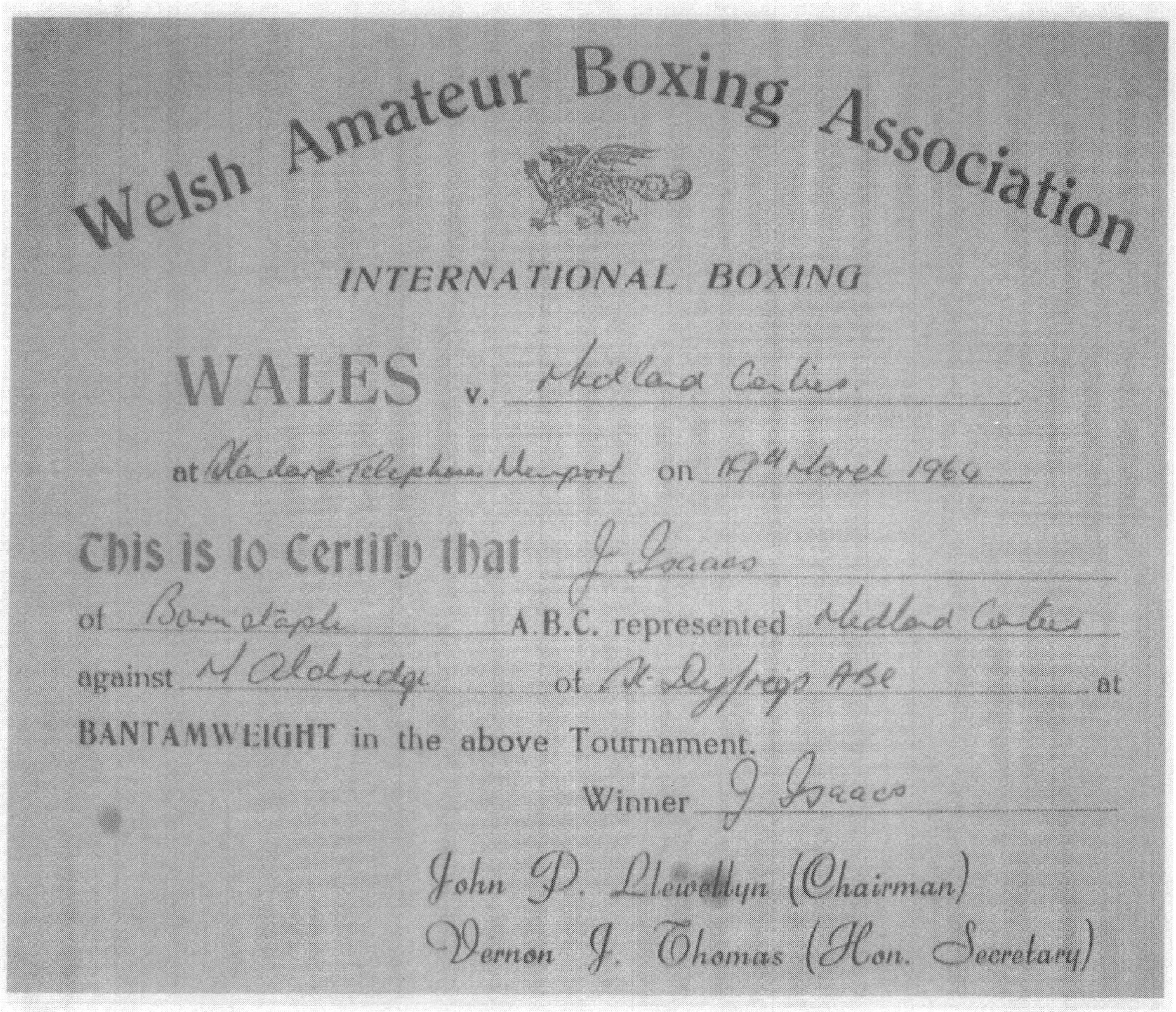

Welsh Amateur Boxing Association

INTERNATIONAL BOXING

WALES v. _Northern Counties_

at _Abertillery/Clydach, Newport_ on _19th March 1960_

This is to Certify that _J. Isaac_

of _Bargoed_ A.B.C. represented _United Counties_

against _N. Aldridge_ of _A. Dyffryn A.B.C._ at

BANTAMWEIGHT in the above Tournament.

Winner _J. Isaac_

John P. Llewellyn (Chairman)

Vernon J. Thomas (Hon. Secretary)

160

ALWAYS a SUPPORTER of LOCAL BOXING,
JIMMY ISAAC presents Trophies at a BOXING SHOW.
A YOUTHFUL TOMMY LANGFORD on his right.

JIMMY with ENGLISH BOXING CHAMPION
ROBBIE SQUIRES.
Looking on is TRAINER and BARNSTAPLE ABC BOSS,
MARK SIMPSON.

Counting the cost of floods

HIGH-LYING Princetown, which always seems to bear the brunt of bad weather in the Westcountry, has been drenched in the period from 9 a.m. Thursday until 9 a.m. yesterday morning with 5.55 inches of rain, as torrential downpours brought floods to low-lying areas.

Next in the wetness league is Bastreet, on the eastern edge of Bodmin Moor, with 4.47 inches in the same period. Okehampton had 3.66 inches and Plymouth 2.6.

Mopping-up operations started yesterday as North Devon counted the cost.

Several villages were still isolated by a few feet of water in the streets while waterworkers continued their unofficial go-slow in defiance of union orders. A detachment of Royal Marines remained on emergency call.

Only one flood-victim was taken to hospital and treated for shock. An elderly lady was evacuated from her home in the Kenwith Valley, Bideford.

Yesterday the fire brigade spent several hours pumping water from two flooded homes in Bishop's Tawton on the outskirts of Barnstaple.

A landslip and a fallen tree also stopped traffic for an hour on the Torrington-Bideford road at Beam.

Three villages — Weare Giffard, a tiny riverside hamlet near Bideford; Taddiport down by the River Torridge at Torrington; and Umberleigh on the River Taw between Barnstaple and Exeter — were still severely flooded.

The train service between Barnstaple and Exeter was cut due to flooding on the line. Alternative bus transport was provided for passengers. The bus also collected mail and newspapers.

The cost of the floods will run into thousands for one family.

The home of John Robinson, Buckingham House, Taddiport, was flooded to a depth of four and a half feet.

Heavy mahogany furniture, including a valuable bookcase and a rare piano, were tossed around inside the Robinsons lounge like matchwood, as the floodwater surged in on Monday evening.

The floor has been badly damaged and walls are crumbling.

It was not until 1.45 p.m. that traffic finally overcame the floodwater on the Bideford side of the village, near Halfpenny Bridge, and vehicles were able to get through to Bideford.

At the village post office, run by Alan Hooper and his wife Gwen at Riversdale, the force of floodwater, more than four feet high, tipped over a freezer and chests of drawers during the night.

A fireman paddles through the flood-water at Bishop's Tawton.

STILL IN THE NEWS!
JIMMY in the DEVON FIRE BRIGADE.

RONNIE and JIMMY ISAAC at a WELSH EX-BOXERS REUNION with NATHAN CLEVERLY.

163

Boxing Tournament

(under A.B.A. Rules)

Presented by Barnstaple Amateur Boxing Club

President: R. M. HUXTABLE

Queen's Hall, Barnstaple
Saturday, 12th February, 1966

commencing at 7.30 p.m.

OFFICIALS

A.B.A. Official in Charge	K. WOODYATT
Clerk of Scales	A. MASON
Referees	MESSRS. J. COOTE AND B. POLLARD
Judges	MESSRS. K. WOODYATT, A. MASON, H. EITELBERG, C. BRIGHT, M. BOWDEN, D. CURRY, A. SEATHERTON, C. RALPH
Hon. Medical Officer DR. G. S. ASTON, M.B., CH.B., M.R.C.S.	
Medical Officer's Assistant	S. FISHLEIGH
Timekeeper	W. HEAD
M.C.	R. HERNAMAN
Recorder	I. BURNELL
Tournament Secretary	W. COOPER
Assistant Tournament Secretary	D. HAYDON

PRICE SIXPENCE

RED CORNER	BLUE CORNER

BOUT 1

JUNIOR   2 x 1½ min. — 1 x 2 min. rounds
Ron Kenwood (Barnstaple) v D. Byrne (Exeter)

BOUT 2

LIGHT MIDDLE   3 x 2 min. rounds
J. Bracher (Barnstaple) v G. Gaston (Exeter)

BOUT 3

WELTER WEIGHT   3 x 2 min. rounds
P. Hayfield (Exmouth) v K. Brooking (Torbay)

BOUT 4

LIGHT MIDDLE   3 x 3 min. rounds
W. Charles (Exeter) v T. Cook (Bristol)

BOUT 5

LIGHT WELTER   3 x 2 min. rounds
B. Hawkins (Barnstaple) v I. Mitchell (Penzance)

BOUT 6

LIGHT WELTER   3 x 2 min. rounds
R. Ellis (Bideford) v V. Denley (Teignmouth)

BOUT 7

LIGHT WEIGHT   3 x 3 min. rounds
D. Horrocks (Penzance) v G. Tooley (Teignmouth)

INTERVAL—15 minutes

RED CORNER	BLUE CORNER

BOUT 8

WELTER WEIGHT   3 x 2 min. rounds
P. Jordan (Exmouth) v A. Rowe (Exeter)

BOUT 9

LIGHT WELTER   3 x 2 min. rounds
G. Yeo (Barnstaple) v A. Richards (Penzance)
A.B.A. Junior Finalist

BOUT 10

MIDDLE WEIGHT   3 x 2 min. rounds
H. Laird (Barnstaple) v J. Sedgemore (Exmouth)

BOUT 11

FEATHER WEIGHT   3 x 3 min. rounds
J. Isaac (Barnstaple) v M. Bryson (Bath)
English International   A.B.A. Quarter Finalist
A.B.A. Junior Champion
and Senior Finalist

BOUT 12

LIGHT HEAVY   3 x 3 min. rounds
D. Lewis (Watchet) v D. Barnes (Penzance)
S.W. England Champion

BOUT 13

HEAVY WEIGHT   3 x 3 min. rounds
A. Thomas (Bristol) v G. Gunn (Redruth)
Western Counties Champion

BOUT 14

LIGHT WEIGHT   3 x 3 min. rounds
J. Banks (Torbay) v R. Fisher (Bristol)
Former Schoolboy Champion

SUBJECT TO ALTERATION

165

Amateur Boxing Association
Founded 1880

Patron:
H. R. H. The Duke of Edinburgh, K.G., K.T.

This is to certify that at the

Junior Championships

held at Royal Albert Hall, London.

on Thursday 23rd March 1961.

J. Isaac

of National Association of Boys' Clubs

was the Winner Class 'A'.

of the 8 stone weight.

_____ President.

_____ Hon. Secretary.

London, 23rd March 1961

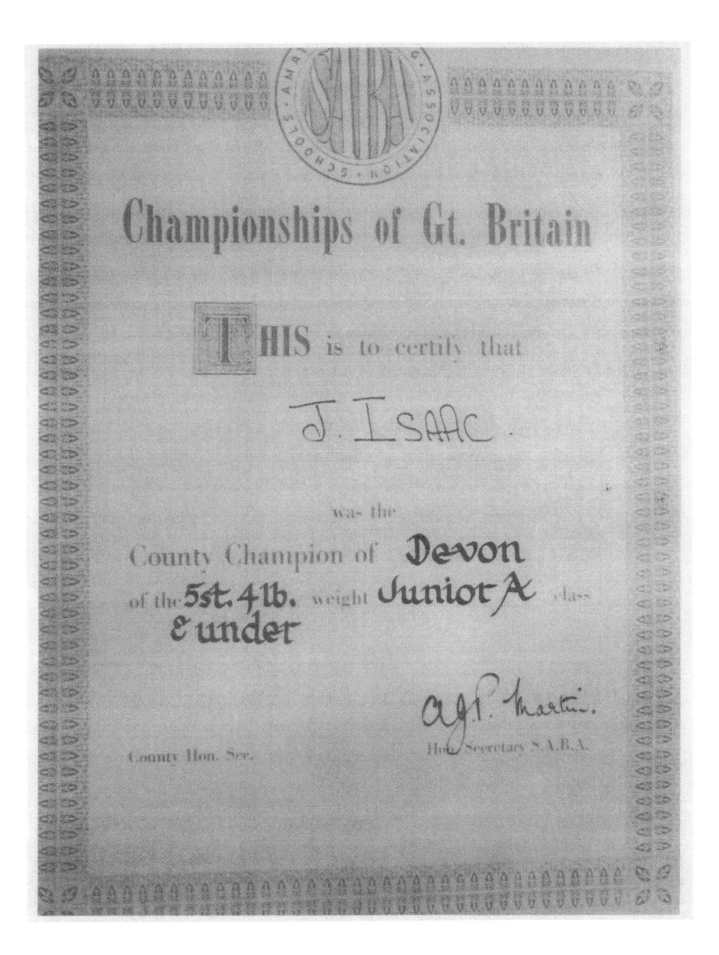

Championships of Gt. Britain

THIS is to certify that

J. Isaac.

was the

County Champion of Devon
of the 5st. 4lb. weight Junior A class
& under

A.J.P. Martin.

County Hon. Sec.   Hon. Secretary S.A.B.A.

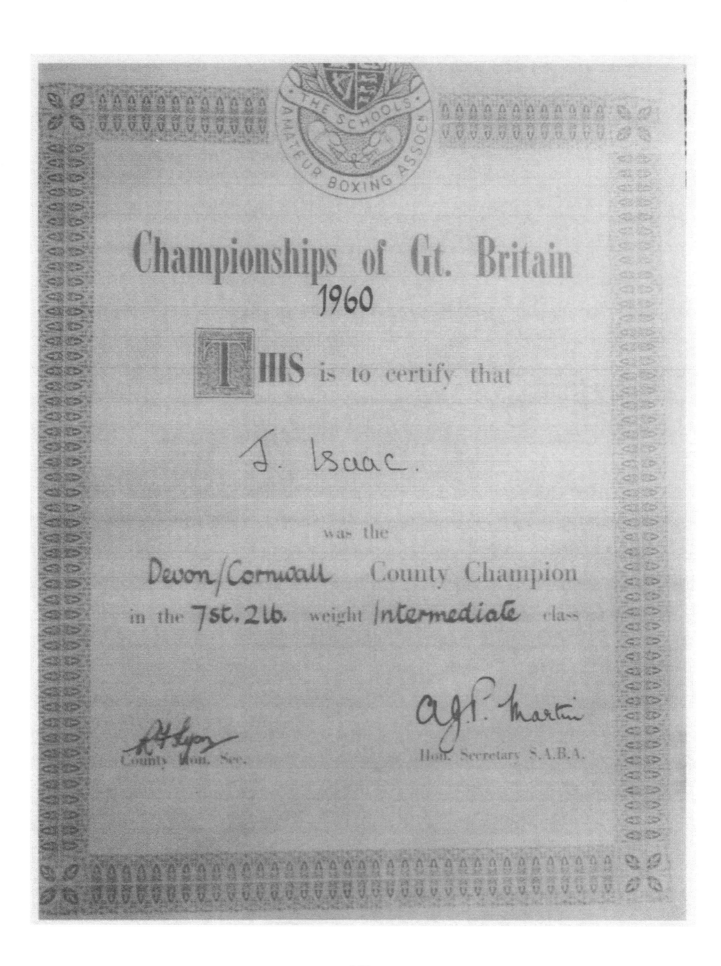

Championships of Gt. Britain
1960

THIS is to certify that

J. Isaac.

was the

Devon/Cornwall County Champion

in the 7st. 2lb. weight Intermediate class

County Hon. Sec.

Hon. Secretary S.A.B.A.

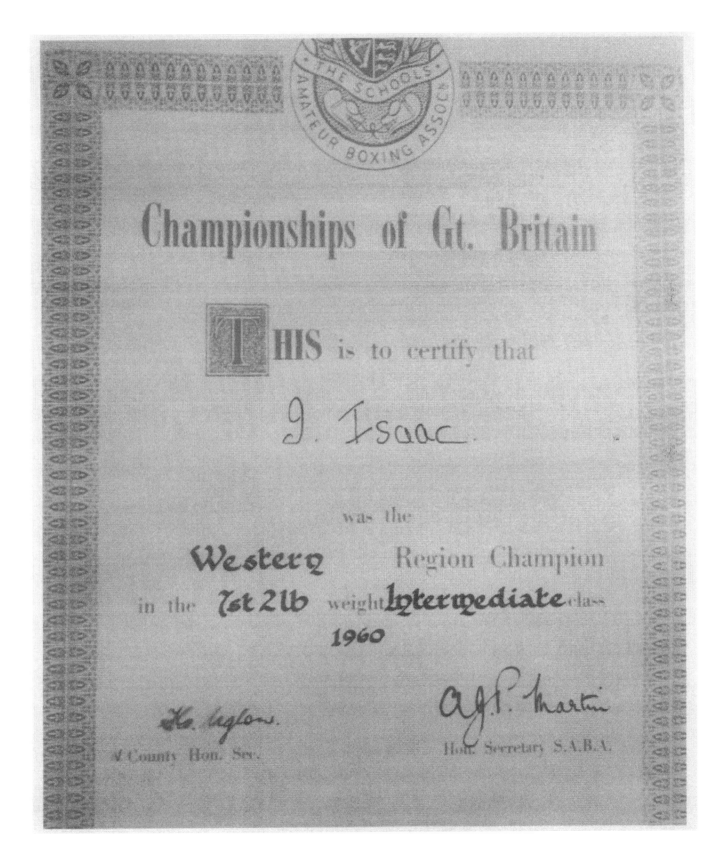

Championships of Gt. Britain

THIS is to certify that

J. Isaac.

was the

Western Region Champion

in the 7st 2lb weight Intermediate class

1960

H. Uglow.

County Hon. Sec.

A.J.P. Martin

Hon. Secretary S.A.B.A.

Schools Amateur Boxing
Championships of Gt. Britain
1960
THIS *is to Certify that*

J.F. ISAAC.   Barnstaple Grammar School,
                Devon.

was a Semi-Finalist

in the 7st. 2lb. weight INTERMEDIATE class

held at the Morris Motors Limited,
Courthouse Green Works, Coventry
on Saturday, March 19th, 1960

Patrick J. Corden
Chairman, S.A.B.A.

A.J.P. Martin
Hon. Secretary, S.A.B.A.

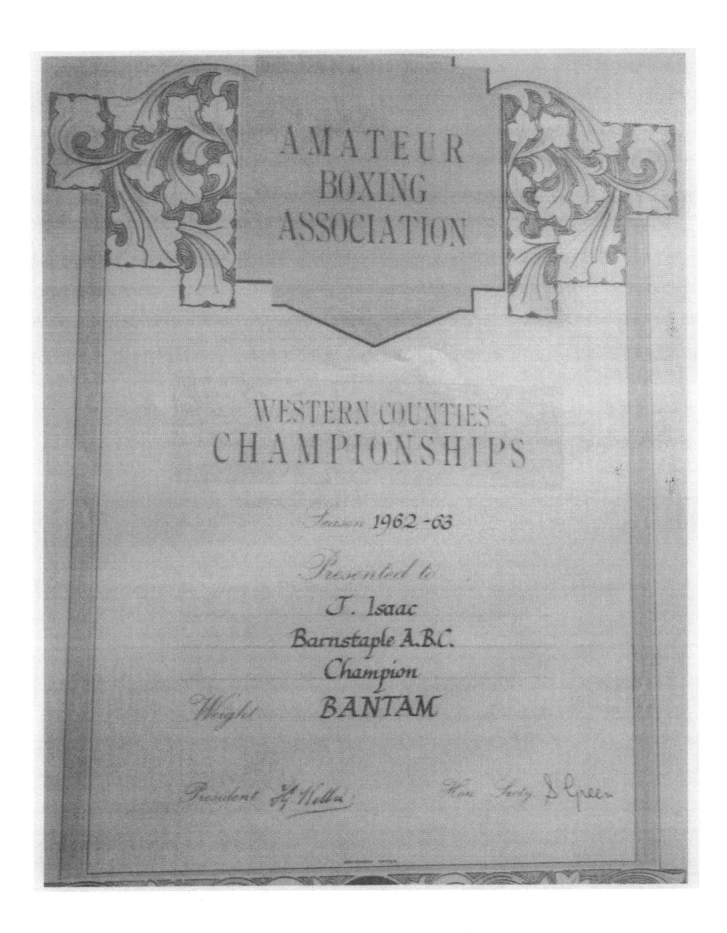

AMATEUR
BOXING
ASSOCIATION

WESTERN COUNTIES
CHAMPIONSHIPS

Season 1962 -63

Presented to

J. Isaac
Barnstaple A.B.C.
Champion

Weight   BANTAM

President   Hon. Secretary

Amateur Boxing Association

Founded 1880

Patron:

H. R. H. The Duke of Edinburgh, K.G., K.T.

This is to certify that at the

Quarter=Finals

of the

Championships

held at *Rootes Ltd*

on *28th March. 1963.*

J. Issaac

of *Barnstaple A.B.C.*

was the *Winner*

of the *Bantam* weight.

President.

Hon. Secretary.

London, *28 March 1963*

Amateur Boxing Association

Founded 1880

Patron:

H. R. H. The Duke of Edinburgh, K.G., K.T.

This is to certify that at the

Championships

held at   The Empire Pool, Wembley.

on   Friday 26th April 1963

J. Asaac

of   Barnstaple A.B.C

was the   Runner up

of the   Bantam   weight.

_____ President.

_____ Hon. Secretary.

London,   26th April 1963.

AMATEUR
BOXING
ASSOCIATION

DEVON, DORSET & CORNWALL
CHAMPIONSHIPS

Season 1963 ~ 1964.

Presented to
J. Isaacs.
Barnstable A.B.C.
Winner.

Weight 8 st. 7 lbs.

President   Hon Secty

J Gardner   S Green

Amateur Boxing Association

Founded 1880

Patron:

H. R. H. The Duke of Edinburgh, K.G., K.T.

This is to certify that at the

Championships

held at ___ Empire Pool and Sports Arena Wembley ___

on ___ Friday 24th April 1964 ___

___ J. Isaac ___

of ___ Barnstaple A.B.C. Devon, Dorset & Cornwall ___

was the ___ Semi-Finalist ___

of the ___ Bantam ___ weight.

_____ President.

W Lovett Hon. Secretary.

London, ___ 24th April 1964 ___

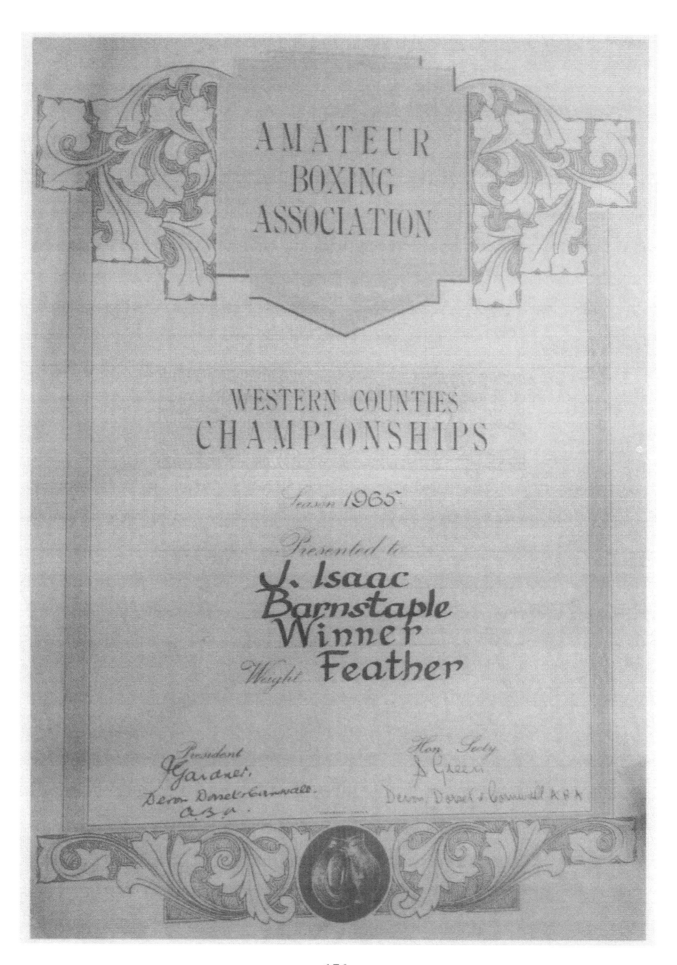

AMATEUR
BOXING
ASSOCIATION

WESTERN COUNTIES
CHAMPIONSHIPS

Season 1965

Presented to

J. Isaac
Barnstaple
Winner
Weight Feather

President
J Gardner.
Devon Dorset & Cornwall.
A.B.A.

Hon Secty
J Green
Devon Dorset & Cornwall A.B.A

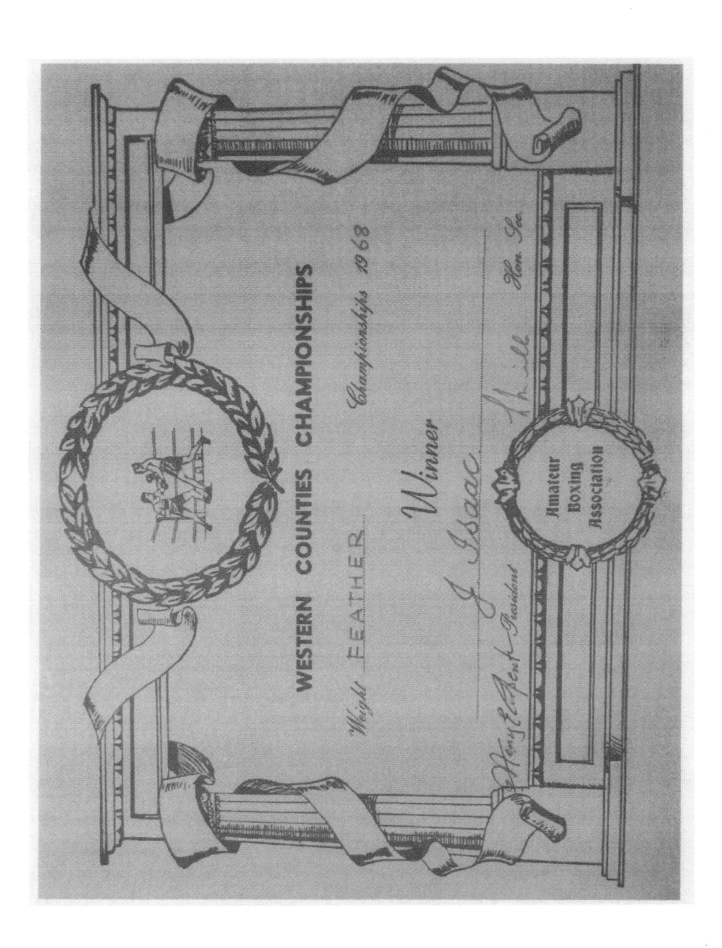

177

AMATEUR
BOXING
ASSOCIATION
CHAMPIONSHIPS
1963

Organised by the Amateur Boxing
Association

FRIDAY · APRIL 26th
1963

Semi-Finals from 4.0 p.m.
FINALS from 8.0 p.m. (approx)

**OFFICIAL
PROGRAMME
ONE
SHILLING**

EMPIRE POOL & SPORTS ARENA
WEMBLEY

AMATEUR BOXING ASSOCIATION

Semi-finals and Finals

(from 4.0 p.m.)   (at 8.0 p.m. approx.)

3 ROUNDS OF 3 MINS. EACH

Silver Cup at full A.B.A. Value
for winners and runners-up.

Semi-final Winners   **Final Winners**

FLYWEIGHT (8 st.) Holder: M. J. Pye
1. M. LAUD (St. Ives and District A.B.C.) Huntingdonshire
2. K. TATE (Rothwell Colliery A.B.C) North Eastern Counties
3. B. FOXWELL (Rootes A.B.C.) Midland Counties
4. L/Cpl. F. REA (Army B.A.)

Final Bout 1

BANTAMWEIGHT (8 st. 7 lb.) Holder: P. Benneyworth
5. B. PACKER (Dartford A.B.C.) Southern Counties
6. J. JONES (Plean A.B.C.) Scotland
7. J. ISAAC (Barnstaple A.B.C.) Devon, Dorset & Cornwall
8. Pte. J. MORRISON (Army B.A.)

Final Bout 2

FEATHERWEIGHT (9 st.) Holder: W. T. Wilson
9. W. T. WILSON (Barking A.B.C.) London
10. E. ARMSTRONG (Ayr Y.M.C.A.) Scotland
11. A. J. RILEY (Rootes A.B.C.) Midland Counties
12. M/E. M. FRAMPTON (Royal Navy B.A.)

Final Bout 3

LIGHTWEIGHT (9 st. 7 lb.) Holder: B. Whelan
13. B. ANDERSON (Middle Row, A.B.C.) London
14. W. BRESLIN (Litherland A.B.C) North Western Counties
15. K. COOPER (Kyrle Hall A.B.C.) Midland Counties
16. Pte. B. O'SULLIVAN (Army B.A.)

Final Bout 4

LIGHT-WELTER (10 st.) Holder: L/Cpl. B. Brazier
17. L. D. O'CONNELL (Fitzroy Lodge A.B.C.) London
18. R. McTAGGART (Kelvin A.B.C.) Scotland
19. L. McATEER (Buckley A.B.C.) Wales
20. L/Cpl. B. BRAZIER (Army B.A.)

Final Bout 5

WELTER (10 st. 8 lb.) Holder: J. Pritchett
21. R. CHARLES (West Ham A.B.C.) London
22. J. MALCOLM (Sparta A.B.C.) Scotland
23. J. PRITCHETT (Bingham & Dist. A.B.C.) Midland Counties
24. R/O. 2 A. E. PHEBY (Royal Navy B.A.)

Final Bout 6

LIGHT-MIDDLE (11 st. 2 lb.) Holder: Vacant
25. S. PEARSON (Cowes Medina A.B.C.) Southern Counties
26. A. WYPER (Witchknowe A.B.C.) Scotland
27. E. AVOTH (Victoria Park A.B.C.) Wales
28. Cook A. HAMILTON (Royal Navy B.A.)

Final Bout 7

MIDDLE (11 st. 11 lb.) Holder: A. J. Matthews
29. E. J. LONGHURST (Dartford A.B.C.) Southern Counties
30. A. J. MATTHEWS (Litherland A.B.C.) N. W. Counties
31. L. SAMUELS (Wolverhampton A.B.C.) Midland Counties
32. Pte. E. LOFTHOUSE (Army B.A.)

Final Bout 8

LIGHT-HEAVY (12 st. 10 lb.) Holder: Vacant
33. D. POLLARD (Fitzroy Lodge A.B.C.) London
34. B. MURPHY (Chorley Boys' Club) North Western Counties
35. C. S. COX (Exeter A.B.C.) Devon, Dorset & Cornwall
36. L/Cpl. T. MENZIES (Army B.A.)

Final Bout 9

HEAVY (any weight) Holder: L/Pat R. Dryden
37. J. TAYLOR (Polytechnic A.B.C.) London
38. R. DAVIES (Droylsden A.B.C.) North Western Counties
39. A. BROGAN (Bideford A.B.C.) Devon, Dorset & Cornwall
40. Cpl. R. D. SANDERS (Royal Navy B.A.)

Final Bout 10

AMATEUR BOXING ASSOCIATION CHAMPIONSHIPS 1964

Organised by the Amateur Boxing Association

FRIDAY · APRIL 24th 1964

Semi-Finals from 4.0 p.m.
FINALS from 8.0 p.m. (approx)

OFFICIAL
PROGRAMME
ONE
SHILLING

EMPIRE POOL & SPORTS ARENA
WEMBLEY

AMATEUR BOXING ASSOCIATION

Semi-finals and Finals

(from 4.0 p.m.)　　　(at 8.0 p.m. approx.)

3 ROUNDS OF 3 MINS. EACH

Silver Cup at full A.B.A. Value for winners and runners-up.

	Semi-final Winners	Final Winners
FLYWEIGHT (8 st.) Holder: Vacant		
1. V. BOWYER (Battersea A.B.C.) London		
2. E. V. PRITCHARD (Menai Bridge A.B.C.) Wales		
3. J. McCLUSKEY (Larkhall A.B.C.) Scotland	Final Bout 1	
4. Pte. P. TEASDALE (Army B.A.)		
BANTAMWEIGHT (8 st. 7 lb.) Holder: B. Packer (Dartford A.B.C.)		
5. B. PACKER (Dartford A.B.C.) Southern Counties		
6. J. ISAAC (Barnstaple A.B.C.) Devon, Dorset & Cornwall		
7. R. MALLON (Glasgow Corporation Youth Clubs) Scotland	Final Bout 2	
8. L/Cpl. F. REA (Army B.A.)		
FEATHERWEIGHT (9 st.) Holder: Vacant		
9. R. SMITH (Fisher A.B.C.) London		
10. K. J. COOPER (Kyrle Hall A.B.C.) Midland Counties		
11. K. BUCHANAN (Sparta A.B.C.) Scotland	Final Bout 3	
12. Marine M. E. FRAMPTON (Royal Navy B.A.)		
LIGHTWEIGHT (9 st. 7 lb.) Holder: Gdsm. B. O'Sullivan (Army B.A.)		
13. A. WHITE (Stock Exchange A.B.C.) London		
14. T. McEVOY (Ladywood A.B.C.) Midland Counties		
15. J. DUNNE (Maple Leaf A.B.C.) North Western Counties	Final Bout 4	
16. Gdsm. B. O'SULLIVAN (Army B.A.)		
LIGHT WELTERWEIGHT (10 st.) Holder: R. McTaggart (Kelvin A.B.C.)		
17. B. ANDERSON (Middle Row A.B.C.) London		
18. R. TAYLOR (Mitchells & Butlers A.B.C.) Midland Counties		
19. R. McTAGGART (Kelvin A.B.C.) Scotland	Final Bout 5	
20. L/Cpl. P. TAYLOR (Army B.A.)		
WELTERWEIGHT (10 st. 8 lb.) Holder: Vacant		
21. A. BROOKS (Fitzroy Lodge A.B.C.) London		
22. M. VARLEY (Clifton A.B.C.) Midland Counties		
23. J. MALCOLM (Sparta A.B.C.) Scotland	Final Bout 6	
24. L.A.C. W. DEARIE (Royal Air Force B.A.)		
LIGHT MIDDLEWEIGHT (11 st. 2 lb.) Holder: Vacant		
25. W. ROBINSON (Stock Exchange A.B.C.) London		
26. P. D. WILLIAMS (Gwent A.B.C.) Wales		
27. P. DWYER (Maple Leaf A.B.C.) North Western Counties	Final Bout 7	
28. Cook A. HAMILTON (Royal Navy B.A.)		
MIDDLEWEIGHT (11 st. 11 lb.) Holder: Vacant		
29. A. MOORE (Arbour Youth A.B.C.) London		
30. E. FIELD (Rothwell Colliery A.B.C.) N. E. Counties		
31. W. J. STACK (Leamington Boys' Club) Midland Counties	Final Bout 8	
32. Spr. W. SUTHERLEY (Army B.A.)		
LIGHT HEAVYWEIGHT (12 st. 10 lb.) Holder: B. Murphy (Chorley Boys' Club)		
33. E. WHISTLER (Hampstead & District A.B.C.) London		
34. F. CARPENTER (Rootes A.B.C.) Midland Counties		
35. J. FISHER (Fauldhouse Miners' Welfare A.B.C.) Scotland	Final Bout 9	
36. L/Sea. B. COLE (Royal Navy B.A.)		
HEAVYWEIGHT (any weight) Holder: Cpl. R. D. Sanders Royal Navy B.A.)		
37. C. WOODHOUSE (Wandsworth A.B.C.) London		
38. C. GIZZI (Prince of Wales A.B.C.) Wales		
39. R. DAVIES (Droylsden A.B.C.) North Western Counties	Final Bout 10	
40. Pte. B. ROBERTSON (Army B.A.)		

7

181

BARNSTAPLE AMATEUR BOXING AND
ATHLETIC CLUB present

A.B.A.
championships
1963

(DEVON, DORSET and CORNWALL ZONE)

QUEEN'S HALL, BARNSTAPLE
SATURDAY, 16th FEBRUARY, 1963
at 7.30 p.m.

A.B.A. Official in Charge B. POLLARD, Esq.
Referees and Judges Messrs. J. RADFORD,
J. COOTE, D. COLLINGWOOD, E. ECKLEY,
R. MOYSE, R. PUNCHARD, J. GARDNER,
B. PRITCHARD.

Clerk of Scales   ...   A. MASON, Esq.
Timekeepers Messrs. T. YEO, K. WINKLE
M.C.   ...   ...   R. HERNAMAN, Esq.
Hon. Medical Officer ...Dr. G. S. ASTON
M.O.A.   ...   ...   M. BOWDEN, Esq.

PRICE 6d.

Saturday, 16th February, 1963

Dear Boxing Supporters and Fans,

The Barnstaple A.B.C. have much pleasure in offering you another "first" this evening, by having the 3 County A.B.A. Championships staged here in our progressive town.

Since the revival of boxing locally in 1956, we are both pleased and proud in having the standards of our young boxers raised to their present level, and we feel confident that the juniors who have, in the past, worked hard in gaining National recognition and honours, will do their best in the senior ranks.

None of this would have been possible without the splendid work of our Supporters Club over the past two years, and I would like to pay tribute to them tonight, thank you one and all.

ALEX MASON (Founder)
Barnstaple A.B.C.

The Barnstaple Youth Centre

108 NEWPORT ROAD

"The Home of Future Champions"

Our Centre is open to past and future members six nights a week.

New members please register now for the many activities (sports or recreational) that we are pleased to offer you at this time.

BOXING — JUDO — FENCING — TABLE TENNIS
WEIGHT TRAINING — ATHLETICS — BILLIARDS
and SOCIAL ACTIVITIES

Joint Leaders : A. MASON and C. DIBBLE

H. J. Sancox, Printer, 29 Holland Street, Barnstaple

ALL CONTESTS 3 ROUNDS OF 3 MINUTES EACH

FLYWEIGHT 8 stone

C. Bovey   Torbay   .... semi-final   FINAL

BANTAMWEIGHT 8 st. 7 lb.

J. Isaac   Barnstaple   ....

T. Stoneman   Torbay   ....

D. A. Tall   Mayflower   ....

FEATHERWEIGHT 9 stone

R. Burridge   Barnstaple   ....

T. Milden   Torbay   ....

R. Tooley   Teignmouth   ....

LIGHTWEIGHT · 9 st. 7 lb.

B. Cotter   Mayflower   ....

B. Dimmick   Devonport   ....

K. Jackson   Torbay   ....

W. G. May   Virginia House ....

S. Philips   Barnstaple   ....

D. Thompson   Torbay   ....

R. Thompson   Devonport   ....

LT. WELTERWEIGHT 10 st.

K. Jackson   Torbay   ....

A. McInnes   Mayflower   ....

WELTERWEIGHT 10 st. 8 lb.   semi-final   FINAL

M. Dixon   Kingsbridge   ....

T. W. Mills   Exeter   ....

D. Stacey   Torbay   ....

R. Skinner   Virginia House ....

J. Tooley   Teignmouth   ....

LT. MIDDLEWEIGHT 11 st. 2 lb.

J. Fennings   Stadium Sports ....

G. Fishleigh   Bideford   ....

K. Jones   Torbay   ....

F. Tooley   Teignmouth   ....

MIDDLEWEIGHT 11 st. 11 lb.

T. E. Brogan   Bideford   ....

J. Dillard   Stadium Sports ....

A. Ensor   Barnstaple   ....

E. W. Lomax   Exmouth   ....

LT. HEAVYWEIGHT 12 st. 10 lb.

A. J. Brogan   Bideford   ....

C. S. Cox   Exeter   ....

D. Challis   Torbay   ....

H. Lightfoot   Devonport   ....

HEAVYWEIGHT 12 st. 10 lb. and over

P. Dimmick   Mayflower   ....

N. L. Diment   Exeter   ....

183

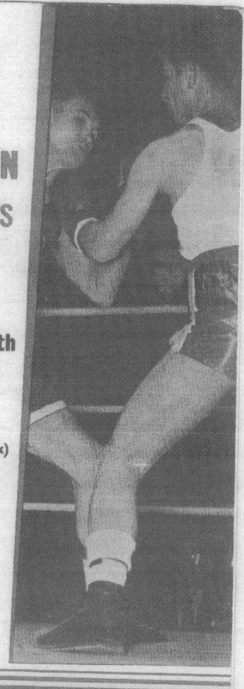

AMATEUR BOXING ASSOCIATION CHAMPIONSHIPS 1965

Organised by the Amateur Boxing Association

FRIDAY · APRIL 30th 1965

Semi-Finals from 4.0 p.m.
FINALS from 8.0 p.m. (approx)

OFFICIAL
PROGRAMME
ONE
SHILLING

EMPIRE POOL & SPORTS ARENA

WEMBLEY

AMATEUR BOXING ASSOCIATION

Semi-finals and Finals

(from 4.0 p.m.) (at 8.0 p.m. approx.)

3 ROUNDS OF 3 MINS. EACH

Silver Cup at full A.B.A. Value
for winners and runners-up

	Semi-final Winners	Final Winners

FLYWEIGHT (8 st.) *Holder: J. McCluskey (Larkhall A.B.C.)*
1. Cpl. G. BLEAKLEY *(Royal Air Force B.A.)*
2. A. A. HUMM *(Harris Lebus A.B.C.)* London
3. C. BOVEY *(Torbay A.B.C.)* Devon, Dorset & Cornwall
4. J. McCLUSKEY *(Larkhall A.B.C.)* Scotland

Final Bout 1

BANTAMWEIGHT (8 st. 7 lb.) *Holder: Vacant*
5. L/Cpl. F. REA *(Army B.A.)*
6. D. MOGFORD *(West Ham Boys' Club)* London
7. T. DWYER *(Roath Youth A.B.C.)* Wales
8. R. MALLON *(Rolls-Royce A.B.C.)* Scotland

Final Bout 2

FEATHERWEIGHT (9 st.) *Holder: Vacant*
9. Jnr. Tech. M. LEWIS *(Royal Air Force B.A.)*
10. M. PYE *(Harris Lebus A.B.C.)* London
11. J. ISAAC *(Barnstaple A.B.C.)* Devon, Dorset & Cornwall
12. K. BUCHANAN *(Sparta A.B.C.)* Scotland

Final Bout 3

LIGHTWEIGHT (9 st. 7 lb.) *Holder: Vacant*
13. S.A.C. G. BYRNE *(Royal Air Force B.A.)*
14. A. WHITE *(Stock Exchange A.B.C.)* London
15. R. GWYNNE *(B.R. Swindon A.B.C.)* Glos., Som. & Wilts.
16. T. JOYCE *(Doncaster Plant Works A.B.C.)* N.E. Counties

Final Bout 4

LIGHT WELTERWEIGHT (10 st.) *Holder: R. Taylor*
(Mitchells & Butlers A.B.C.)
17. Cpl. P. TAYLOR *(Army B.A.)*
18. L. D. O'CONNELL *(Fitzroy Lodge A.B.C.)* London
19. D. P. HUGHES *(Bynea A.B.C.)* Wales
20. R. McTAGGART *(Kelvin A.B.C.)* Scotland

Final Bout 5

WELTERWEIGHT (10 st. 8 lb.) *Holder: M. Varley*
(Clifton A.B.C.)
21. S.A.C. S. CARTHY *(Royal Air Force B.A.)*
22. P. B. HENDERSON *(Robert Browning A.B.C.)* London
23. K. DAVIES *(Llanelly A.B.C.)* Wales
24. A. TOTTOH *(Ardwick Lads' Club)* N.W. Counties

Final Bout 6

LIGHT MIDDLEWEIGHT (11 st. 2 lb.) *Holder:*
W. Robinson (Stock Exchange A.B.C.)
25. Ldg. Cook A. HAMILTON *(Royal Navy B.A.)*
26. R. SMITH *(Hampstead & District A.B.C.)* London
27. A. J. COUCH *(Swansea Youth A.B.C.)* Wales
28. P. DWYER *(Maple Leaf (Bootle) A.B.C.)* N.W. Counties

Final Bout 7

MIDDLEWEIGHT (11 st. 11 lb.) *Holder:*
W. J. Stack (Leamington Boys' Club)
29. L/Cpl. B. WHITE *(Army B.A.)*
30. W. ROBINSON *(Stock Exchange A.B.C.)* London
31. A. BALL *(Bargoed A.B.C.)* Wales
32. J. TURPIN *(Rothwell Colliery A.B.C.)* N.E. Counties

Final Bout 8

LIGHT HEAVYWEIGHT (12 st. 10 lb.) *Holder:*
J. Fisher (Fauldhouse Miners A.B.C.)
33. Sgt. G. FULLER *(Army B.A.)*
34. E. WHISTLER *(Hampstead & District A.B.C.)* London
35. R. JOHN *(Pontypridd Y.M.C.A. A.B.C.)* Wales
36. R. TIGHE *(Hull Boys' Club)* North Eastern Counties

Final Bout 9

HEAVYWEIGHT (any weight) *Holder: C. Woodhouse*
(Wandsworth A.B.C.)
37. A.B. C. FIELD *(Royal Navy B.A.)*
38. W. R. WELLS *(Wandsworth A.B.C.)* London
39. A. BROGAN *(Torbay A.B.C.)* Devon, Dorset & Cornwall
40. B. K. POLLARD *(Lancashire Constabulary S. & S.C.)*
    North Western Counties

Final Bout 10

7

185

SPONSORED BY BIDEFORD AMATEUR BOXING CLUB

Amateur Boxing Association

presents

INTERNATIONAL
BOXING
TOURNAMENT

ENGLAND

versus

POLAND

(Under A.I.B.A. Rules)

Saturday, 21st November, 1964

7.30 p.m.

OFFICIAL PROGRAMME   **ONE SHILLING**

WESTWARD HO ! HOLIDAY CENTRE, N. DEVON

ENGLAND
v.
POLAND

ENGLAND (BLUE CORNER)		POLAND (RED CORNER)
FLYWEIGHT		
1. P. MAGUIRE (Vauxhall Motors A.B.C.)	v.	LEON ZGODA Champion of Slask
BANTAMWEIGHT		
2. L/Cpl. F. REA (Army B.A.)	v.	BRUNON BENDIG Champion of Poland 1964
FEATHERWEIGHT		
3. J. ISAAC (Barnstaple A.B.C.)	v.	JERZY ADAMSKI Champion of Poland 1964
LIGHTWEIGHT		
4. Gdsm. B. O'SULLIVAN (Army B.A.)	v.	JOZEF GRUDZIEN OLYMPIC CHAMPION 1964
L/WELTERWEIGHT		
5. C. HENDERSON (Horden N.C.B. A.B.C.)	v.	RYSZARD RYBSKI Vice-Champion of Poland 1964

Polish Reserves: STANISLAW GALAZKA, Junior Champion of Poland, 1963, STANISLAW GAJEWSKI, Vice-Champion of Poland, 1963

ENGLAND (BLUE CORNER)		POLAND (RED CORNER)
WELTERWEIGHT		
6. P. YOUNG (Hull Boys' Club)	v.	JERZY KULEJ OLYMPIC CHAMPION 1964
L/MIDDLEWEIGHT		
7. P. DWYER (Maple Leaf (Bootle) A.B.C.)	v.	HUBERT KUCZNIERZ Champion of Poland 1963
MIDDLEWEIGHT		
8. W. STACK (Leamington Boys' Club)	v.	LUCJAN SLOWAKIEWICZ Vice-Champion of Poland 1964
L/HEAVYWEIGHT		
9. I. LAWTHER (Vauxhall Motors A.B.C.)	v.	STANISLAW DRAGAN Champion of Krakow 1964
HEAVYWEIGHT		
10. J. HAMER (Halifax Star A.B.C.)	v.	RYSZARD WALICKI Champion of Slask 1964

INTERVAL AS ANNOUNCED

SUPPORTING BOUTS

MIDDLE		
11. J. BURKE (Barnstaple A.B.C.)	v.	L/Sea. GLEESON (Royal Navy) (I.S.B.A. CHAMPION)
12. R. BURRIDGE (Barnstaple A.B.C.)	v.	Mne. BURTON (Royal Marines)
13. G. YEO (Barnstaple A.B.C.)	v.	K. BROOKING (Torbay A.B.C.)
HSAVYWEIGHT		
14. A. BROGAN (Torbay A.B.C.) (IRISH INTERNATIONAL)	v.	A.B. FIELDS (Royal Navy) (I.S.B.A. FINALIST)

Polish champion narrowly beats Jimmy Isaac

WESTWARD HO CONTESTS

BARNSTAPLE featherweight Jimmy Isaac, wearing an England vest for only the third time, lost narrowly on points against the Polish champion on Saturday.

Boxing in the England-Poland international match at Westward Ho on Saturday, Isaac was hurt midway through the third round when the Pole, Jerzy Adamski, champion of his country for the last two years, got home a left hook to the body.

Until then it looked as if Isaac's crisper punching would see him through for his first England win.

But by the interval, the tough-as-nails Poles, performing more like professionals than amateurs, had won all five bouts. And they only lost two of the other five matches.

One was the light middleweight bout in which Merseyside's Pat Dwyer, who proved he could fight and mix it with the best as well as clown a good deal, beat Poland's runner-up, Stanislaw Gajewski.

But, although the top-grade boxing of the international thrilled the capacity crowd, it was the blood and thunder—and good boxing—of the supporting bouts that produced the excitement.

Barnstaple's ex-policeman, John Burke, and Leading Seaman Ken Gleeson, an I.S.B.A. finalist at middleweight, fought a tight, hard-punching battle until the Navy man received a cut over the right eye in the third round.

Roger Burridge, the Barnstaple light welter, who was knocked out at Exmouth a fortnight ago, only just escaped a similar fate in the first round against Marine David Burton. of 43 Commando, Plymouth.

After trading punches, Burridge walked into a loping right which put him down, and although he beat the count the referee decided he was unfit to continue.

Brogan hits hard

Seaman Fields, a 21-year-old I.S.B.A. finalist, soaked up a terrific amount of punishment from Territorial Army heavyweight champion Tony Brogan, a graduate of the host club.

Brogan, with his greater experience, was always in command.

Results: Supporting bouts: Middleweight: J. Burke (Barnstaple) bt L/Seaman Gleeson (Royal Navy), r.s.f. third. Light welter: Marine Burton (Royal Marines) bt R. Burridge (Barnstaple), r.s.f. first. Heavyweight: A. Brogan (Torbay) bt A/B Fields (Royal Navy) on points.

International: Flyweight: Leon Zgoba (Poland) bt C. Bovey (Torbay), r.s.f. third. Bantamweight: Jan Galazka (Poland) bt L/Cpl. F. Rea (Army) on points. Featherweight: Jerzy Adamski (Poland) bt J. Isaac (Barnstaple) on points.

Lightweight: Jozef Grudzien (Poland) k.o. Gdsman. B. O'Sullivan (Army) first round. Light-welterweight: Ryszard Rybski (Poland) bt C. Henderson (Horden N.C.B.) on points. Welterweight: Jerzy Kulej (Poland) bt P. Young (Hull Boys' Club), retired second round.

Light-middleweight: P. Dwyer (Maple Leaf, Bootle) bt Stanislaw Gajewski (Poland) on points. Middleweight: Lucjan Slowakiewicz (Poland) bt W. Stock (Leamington Boys' Club) on points. Light-heavyweight: Zbigniew Pietrykowski (Poland) bt I. Lawther (Vauxhall Motors) on points. Heavyweight: J. Hamer (Halifax Star) bt Ryszard Walicki (Poland) on points.

Journal Leisure

News

Volunteer's charity work recognised

Modest Jim gets 'unsung hero' award

A VOLUNTEER from Barnstaple is among 10 people from the South West being honoured as part of a Government scheme to acknowledge local unsung heroes and heroines.

Jim Isaac, 55, of Sticklepath, is a winner in the Government's regional Active Communities Award.

It recognises four years' hard work with a charity which provides care and support for people with brain injuries.

Mr Isaac became involved with the Headway charity after he went to a volunteer bureau to look for some voluntary work to do.

"I thought about working with children but I found out Headway needed volunteers and I've been there since," he said.

The people I work with are ordinary people who have had various injuries such as being kicked by horses or they may have been involved in road accidents."

He was nominated for the award by co-ordinators from the Headway charity and said the news came as a "complete surprise".

And modest Mr Isaac added: "I don't feel I'm doing anything, but the people around me do and it's nice to be recognised and appreciated. It's lovely news."

Mr Isaac and his wife can look forward to a return trip to London on Wednesday, spending two nights at a top hotel. The couple have a special invitation to attend an event at the Millennium Dome on Thursday and will attend a gala dinner with entertainment.

Mr Isaac said: "We will also have the chance to mingle with celebrities and VIPs. A total of 2,000 people from across the UK will be getting together. My wife and I are looking forward to a lovely time."

Mr Isaac said the Headway charity was looking for new volunteers to help at its drop-in centre at the Castle Centre, Barnstaple, and day centre in Bideford.

He added: "I'm the only one who's been going regularly and we need more people to come along and help. Anyone who comes along does not necessarily have to get involved at the sharp end of the service which can be a bit difficult and traumatic at times.

"They can do administration work or just make the tea during the day. Some people might find it difficult to cope with some of the clients because they have such a wide range of injuries."

Mr Isaac said because the brain was such an important and complex organ, the requirements for head injuries and the needs of Headway clients were extremely diverse.

"Each case is different and the work is very challenging while other clients might just need people to come in and talk to them. The work is a two-way thing and Headway allows the clients' full-time carers to have a break.

"As well as the drop-in group on Mondays and the day centre on Fridays, there are other ongoing events during the week.

"The clients may need help to go to the doctor or other tasks they might not be able to do themselves."

Active Communities Minister Lord Falconer said the South West winners made a remarkable difference to their communities and added: "They are great examples of what can be achieved when people get active and put time and effort into projects which benefit those around them."

Anyone who is interested in becoming a Headway volunteer in North Devon can contact Lorraine Warren on 01271 323088.

HONOURS and RECOGNITION for JIMMY ISAAC.

North Devon Gazette | Wednesday, November 25, 2015

Headway's Jim is shortlisted for national award

BARNSTAPLE: A Barnstaple charity worker, who suffers from daily pain following a spinal cord injury, has been shortlisted for a national award.

Jim Isaac (pictured), 70, founded the North Devon branch of Headway in 1995 to support local families affected by brain injury.

He is one of just three people in the running for the Stephen McAleese Outstanding Contribution to Headway Award, to be presented by Olympian James Cracknell on December 11.

190

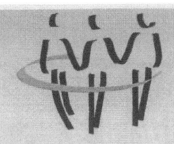

Active Community Awards
Winner 2000
South West

Jim Isaac

In recognition of outstanding contribution
to the community

Active Community Awards and Celebration

2 March 2000

Tony Blair

The Rt Hon Tony Blair MP
Prime Minister

ACTIVE!

JIMMY ISAAC.
Barnstaple A.B.C.

Jimmy Isaac was one of, if not the best Amateur Boxers to come from the County of Devon. Jimmy won many titles throughout his long amateur career. He won a Junior ABA Title, an NABC Junior Title, Devon Dorset and Cornwall, Six County Titles,, ABA Quarter Finals, ABA Semi Finals and twice reached the ABA Final and in one lost on points to the GREAT Ken Buchanan who went on to be the World Lightweight Champion. His career is mapped out over the page and it reads like a list of Who's Who of top class Fighters.

Jimmy also had a six fight International career. He boxed against Russians, Rumanians and Poles and each of them were Reigning Champions of their Country. He always fought his heart out and was able to hold his head up high even when he was beaten. We should all be justly proud of his achievements. Jimmy is also a proud member of the Square Ring EBA and we are just as proud to call him our friend.

Ronnie Isaac, His brother was also a top class Flyweight, even though he took something of a back seat to his more heralded brother. Ronnie reached the ABA Semi Finals and was credited with a win over no less that Mickey Abrams, the three time ABA Light Flyweight Champion.

Thanks Jim & Ron for your outstanding Contribution.

The Square Ring EBA Committee.

Hughes (Devon Schools Final) **1956**	Plymouth	W. Pts
McArthy (Bristol schools)	Bristol	L. Pts
L. Burrows (Barnstaple)	Barnstaple	W. Pts
L. Burrows (Barnstaple)	Barnstaple	W. Pts
Evans (Plymouth)	Plymouth	W. Pts
'Timber' Woods (Plymouth)	Plymouth	L. Pts
'Timber' Woods (Plymouth)		L. Pts
D. Jackson (Torquay)		W. Pts
R. Arnott. (Plymouth)		W. Pts
'Timber' Woods (Plymouth)		W. Pts
'Timber' Woods (Plymouth)		W. Pts
W. Curtis (Swindon)	Plymouth	W. Pts
D W Smith (Birmingham)	Birmingham	W. Pts
V, Bowyer (Croydon)	Coventry	L. Pts
R. Arnott (Plymouth)	Barnstaple	W. Pts
Grieves (Exeter)	Exeter	W. KO 1st
K Graham (Welsh Schools Champ)	Bideford	No Decision
Burton (Exeter)		W. KO 2nd
Frampton (Jun. ISBA champion)	Barnstaple	W. Pts

NABC Championship

J Marsh (Hampshire)	Slough	W. Pts
D Boobyer (Essex)	Slough	W. Pts
D Rooke (London)	London	W. KO 2nd
A McVey (Liverpool) Final	Blackpool Tower	W. Pts

Junior ABA Champs.

A Leitch (Welsh Champ)	Wales	W. Pts
A Craig (ISBA Champ)	Royal Albert Hall	W. KO 2nd
P Dryland (London Champ) Final	Royal Albert Hall	W. Pts
Tucker (Jun.ISBA champ)	Barnstaple	W. KO 2nd
J Burton (Exeter)		W. Pts
M Hanson (London)	Weymouth	W. Pts
Wilshire (Exeter)		W. KO 2nd
T Stoneman (Torquay)		W. KO 1st

NABC Championship

J Russel (Dorset)	Slough	W. KO 1st
G Hosier (Bucks)	Slough	W. Pts
J Dawson (Arbour)	Slough	W. RSF 1st
J Davies (Northumberland) Final	Blackpool Tower	W. RSF 1st

Junior ABA champs

A Duff (Southern Counties)	Cardif	W. RSF 1st
G O' Neil (Wolverhampton)	Royal Albert Hall	L. RSF 1st
R Broad (Plymouth)	Bideford	W RSF 3rd
A Skinner (British Railway Champ)	Exmouth	W. RSF 1st
H Clatworthy (Teignmouth)	Teignmouth	W. Pts
R Couts (Bristol)	Barnstaple	W. Pts
J Coles (Welsh Rep.)	Cardiff	W. Pts
I Frost (Welsh Rep)		W. Pts
G O'Neil (Wolverhampton)	Weymouth	L. Pts
B Foxwell (England Rep. Rootes)	Torquay	W. Pts
M Bowman (Dublin University)	Westward Ho!	W Pts

ABA Championship

D Tall (Mayflower)	3 Counties	Barnstaple	W. KO 1st
M Bryson	6 Counties		W. Pts
M McLoughlin (Midlands champ)	12 Counties		W Pts
I Frost (Welsh champ) Qtr Final			W. Pts
J Jones (Scottish Champ) Semi		Empire Pool, Wembley	W. KO 2nd
B Packer (London) Final		Empire Pool , Wembley	L. Pts

ABA FINAL

C Bovey (Torquay)			W. Pts
T Both (German champ)	Midlands V Germany		W. Pts
M Pye (London, England Inter.)	London		L. Pts

F Cserge (Hungary champ. European silver medallist)		
England v Hungary	Wembley	L. Pts

L/Cpl. Rea (ISBA champ)	W Pts

Iscov (Russia champ)		
England v Russia	Moscow	L.RSB 3rd
Iscov		
England v Russia	Tiblisi	L. Pts

J Murphy (Scotland)		
England v Scotland	Royal Albert Hall	L.Rsb 3rd Cut

ABA Championship

C Bovey(Torquay)	3 Counties		W. Pts
P Barnfield	6 Counties		W. KO 1st
M Mclaughlin (Midlands)	12 Counties		W. Pts
M Aldridge (Welsh champ) Qtr Final			W. Pts
R Mallon (Scot champ) Semi		Wembley	L. Pts

K McDowell (Mayflower)	Plymouth	W. Pts
R Broad (St Ives)	Exeter	W. Pts

Gyula Torok (Olympic champion)		
England v Hungary	Budapest	L. Rsb 1st
L Burgondi (Hungary	Budapest	W. Pts

S Mandera	Wolfenbuttel, Germany	W. Pts
(Brunschwig lightweight champ)		
Ferdi Lehnir	Gifhorn, Germany	W. RSB 3rd
Southern Germany Feather champ)		

BDR. Woodcock(Royal Artillery)	Barnstaple	W. Pts

Lebon (Belgium Champ)	Totquay	W. Pts
C Smith(London)	Bermondsey Baths, London	L. Pts

Jerzy Adamski (Polish champ)	Westward Ho!	L. Pts
England v Poland		

B Pennels (NCB champ)	Devon v South Wales, Plymouth	W. Pts
PVD Kerkoff (5 times Dutch champ)	Teignmouth	W. Pts
Marine Rigg (Champ of Malaya)	Devon v Marines, Exeter	W. RSB 1st

Opponent	Venue	Result
		W. Pts
M Bryson (West of England)		W. RSB 1st
K Cooper (Midlands) 12 Counties		W. RSB 2nd
M Phillips (Wales) Qtr Final	Stoke-on- Trent	W. Pts
M Pye (London) Semi	Wembley	L. Pts
X K Buchanan (Scotland)	Wembley	

ABA FINAL

Opponent	Venue	Result
Piet Kerkoff (Dutch champ)	Rotterdam, Holland	RSB 2nd
SGT. Allen (Army)	Barnstaple	W. Pts
D Wright (Royal Navy)	Exeter	W. Pts
G Shields (Notts. NCB champ)	Westward Ho!	W. Pts
T Dwyer (Welsh champ)	Torquay	L Rsb 1st
T Dwyer (Welsh champ)	Weymouth)	L. Pts
D Cunnick (Truro)	Cambourne	W. RSB 2nd
G Shields (Notts. NCB champ)	Nottingham	W. Pts
M Bryson	Barnstaple	W. Pts

ABA Championship

Opponent	Venue	Result
S McAstocken	3 Counties	Truro	W. RSB 2nd
E Horrocks (Penzance)	3 Counties	Truro	W. RSB 1st
W Crouch (Gillingham)	3 Counties	Truro	W.RSB 1st
R Barker (Truro)	3 Counties	Truro	W. RSB 1st
M Bryson (West of England)		Wells	W. RSB 3rd
K Cooper (Midlands)		Coventry	L. Pts

ONE AFTERNOON

Opponent	Venue	Result
D Polak (Notts) Devon v Notts.	Westward Ho!	W. Pts
L Spriggs (Battersea)	Torquay	L. RSB 1st
G Tooley (Teignmouth)	Barnstaple	L. 1st cut eye
M Micheletti (Jersey) DDC v Jersey	Gillingham	W. Pts
F Read (Oxford) Devon v Oxford	Oxford	W. RSB 1st
D Polack (Notts) Devon v Notts.	Totnes	W. Pts
Charlesworth (Bristol)	Bristol Sporting Club	W. Pts
E Dehn (West Germany)	Torquay	W. RSB 2nd
G Tooley (Teignmouth)	Teignmouth	L. Pts
Sladking (Germany)	Salsgitter, Germany	W. RSB 2nd
J Allen (Battersea)	Exeter	W. Pts

ABA Championship

Opponent	Venue	Result
R Mudge (Torquay) 3 Counties	Gillingham	W. Pts
Gamble (Plymouth) 3 Counties	Gillingham	W. Pts
M Bryson (West of England)	Salisbury	W. Pts
D Polack (Midlands)	Wolverhampton	W. Pts
M Phillips (Wales)		W. Pts
J Cheshire (London) Semi	Belle Vue, Manchester	L. RSB 3rd
S Marchant	Barnstaple	W. Pts

ABA Championships

Opponent	Venue	Result
N Crouch (Gillingham) 3 Counties	Exeter	W. Pts
R Richards (Cornwall) 3 Counties	Exeter	W. Pts
M Bryson (West of England)	Salisbury	W. Pts
D Pollack (Notts) 1970	RETIRED	L. 2nd Cut eye

Twice NABC Champion
Junior ABA Champion
Twice ABA Finalist, Twice semi-finalist
Undefeated West of England champion, winning 6 times

Sydney Leonard Phillips
'Syd'

2nd August 1943 - 24th August 2014

SYD PHILLIPS was a stalwart CLUB BOXER who gained REPRESENTATIVE HONOURS. He was boxing at a time when thousands of AMATEUR BOXERS were active and there was never a easy route to NATIONAL TITLES. Looking at his record and talking to contemporaries of his at BARNSTAPLE ABC, his boxing ability was highly rated and he was liked and respected by everyone.

Almost always 'billed' as SID.

BARNSTAPLE ABC

BARNSTAPLE ABC

A PRESENTATION EVENING.
SYD fourth from the left, on his left,
ROGER BURRIDGE and JIMMY ISAAC.

SYD PHILLIPS

198

BARNSTAPLE ABC

SYD PHILLIPS

TRAINING SESSION. Four North Devon boxers with but a single thought—the A.B.A. championships—do some training at Barnstaple, watched by their coaches. Left to right: Ron Isaac, Sid Phillips, Jimmy Isaac, and Tony Brogan.

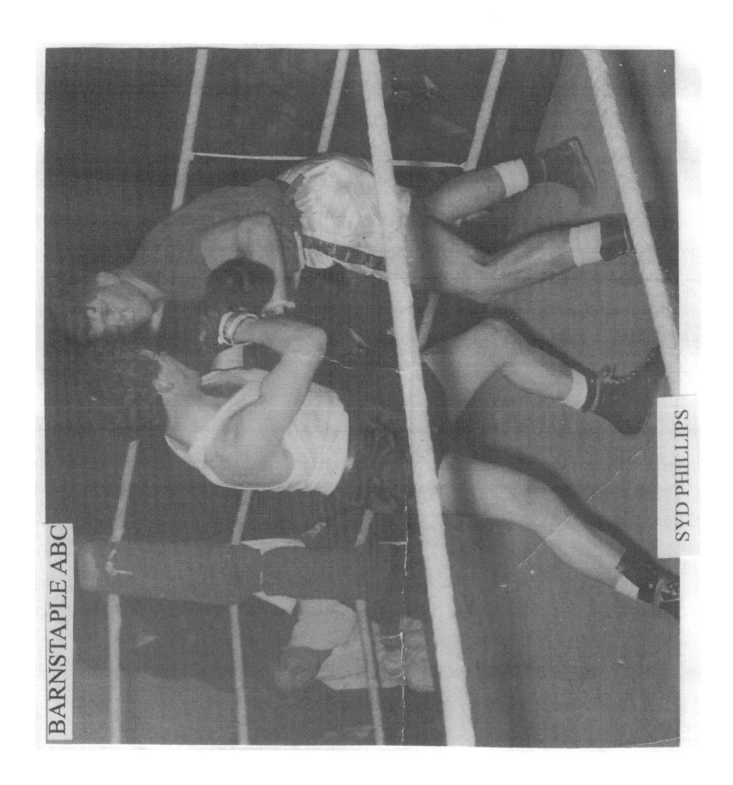

BARNSTAPLE ABC

SYD PHILLIPS

BARNSTAPLE ABC

A STREET SCENE in GERMANY!
TRAINER WILF COOPER and SYD .

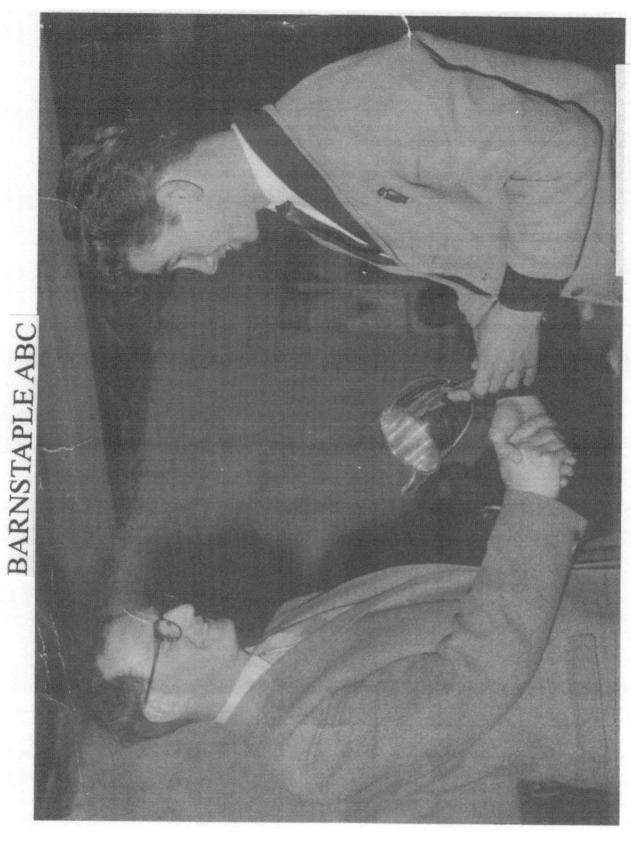

BARNSTAPLE ABC

SYD PHILLIPS

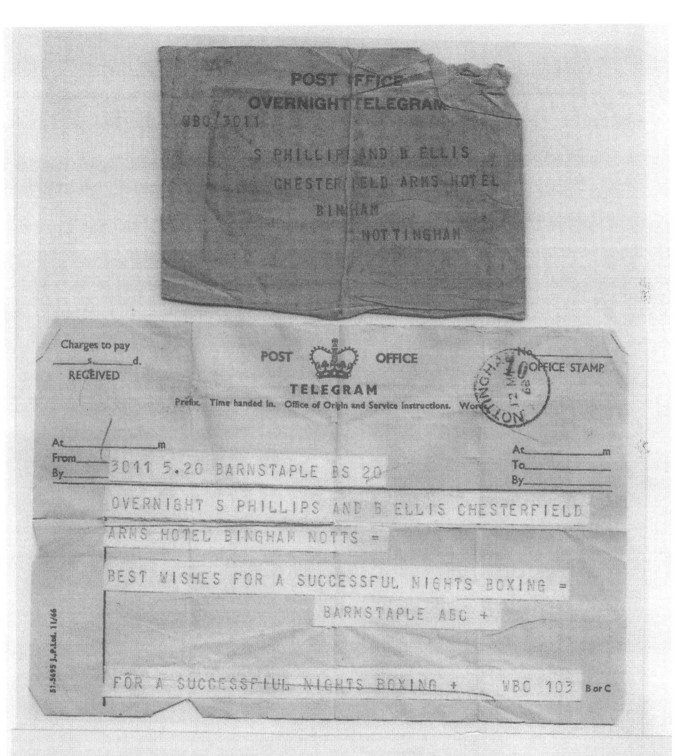

BEST WISHES TELEGRAM to S. PHILLIPS and B. ELLIS from BARNSTAPLE ABC.

BARNSTAPLE
AMATEUR
BOXING
CLUB

RULES & MEMBERSHIP CARD

Name SID PHILLIPS.

Address 18 GREENBANK R.C.

FORCHES BARNSTAPLE

Date	Amount	Signed	Date	Amount	Signed
1967					
SEPT 2ND	7-0	VIM			
9TH	2-0	VIM			
16th	7-0	VIM			
23RD	2-0	VIM			
30	2-0	WRB			
OCT 4	2 0	WRE			
14	2 0	WRB			
21	2 0	WRE.			
28	2-0	WRE			
NOV 4	2-0	WRB			
11	2-0	VM.			
DEC 2nd	2-0				

RULES.

THE TEN COMMANDMENTS OF
THE BARNSTAPLE BOXING CLUB

1. The annual subscription on joining the Club is 10-0d for Seniors, which may be paid in two stages of 5-0d. No member will be allowed to train until the initial 5-0d is paid, a further 5-0d to be paid within 3 months. Members between 16 & 17 years of age will pay an annual subscription of 5-0d, which can be paid in two parts, like the seniors. All Weekly subs to be paid on a Monday night only.

SENIORS 2-0d   Between 16 & 17 1-0d
JUNIORS 1-0d per week.

Any member more than 2 weeks in arrears will not be allowed to train, and temporarily suspended until such payments are made.

SYD PHILLIPS

2. Any loan made to a member to buy personal equipment must be signed for and repaid within two months. A member under 21 must get guardian's signature.

3. All boxers must at all times behave in an orderly way and be a credit to themselves and the Club.

4. Each member must be prepared to accept that the trainers give their time freely and must be obeyed at all times.

5. Misconduct on a club night will mean suspension for a period which the trainers think fit for the particular case.

6. Each member must accept that he must carry on training and boxing to the end of the season.

7. No boxer will participate in competitive boxing unless the trainers think he is fit, and have trained hard at least 3 weeks before a contest.

8. The Club will at all times have first call on your services. Surely it is a credit to box for your Club and not to use the club for personal glory.

9. Each member must be prepared to give 4 nights a week, 3 to training and one to boxing, if required. All boxers must help one another in preparation for contests; by doing this it will create a true club spirit.

10. On tournaments boxers will present themselves with clean towel, shorts, vest and socks, and at all times be a credit to club and trainers. Equipment borrowed must be returned clean the following week.

HIS EARLY MEMBERSHIP CARD.
The RULES are worth taking note of !

TEIGNMOUTH AMATEUR BOXING CLUB

Boxing
Tournament

held under A.B.A. rules

DEVON, DORSET & CORNWALL V ROTTERDAM HOLLAND

London Hotel Ballroom, Teignmouth

Saturday, February 13th, at 7.30 p.m.

206

PROGRAMME

HUIZENAAR BOXING CLUB (Rotterdam) v. DEVON/DORSET/CORNWALL

1. Bantamweight Bout, 3 x 3 min. rounds.

   C. BOVEY v. A. KRIESELS

2. Light-Middleweight Bout, 3 x 3 min. rounds.

   R. SALTIEL v. F. GELENS

3. Lightweight Bout, 3 x 3 min. rounds.

   D. THOMPSON v. P. DOORENBOSCH

4. Light-Middleweight Bout, 3 x 3 min. rounds.

   D. STACEY v. L. VAN DAM VALK

5. Light-Welterweight Bout, 3 x 3 min. rounds.

   S. PHILLIPS v. H. LE COCQ

6. Light-Heavyweight Bout, 3 x 3 min. rounds.

   G. GUNN v. B. NIKKELEN-KUYPER

7. Light-Middleweight Bout, 3 x 3 min. rounds.

   B. WITHERS v. L. BUTTER

8. Middleweight Bout, 3 x 3 min. rounds.

   F. TOOLEY v. T. NETTEN

9. Featherweight Bout, 3 x 3 min. rounds.

   J. ISAAC v. P. VAN DAM KERKHOF

10. Light-Welterweight Bout, 3 x 3 min. rounds.

    R. WATERS v. T. DEKKERS

11. Middleweight Bout, 3 x 3 min. rounds.

    M. LAINE v. F. VAN DAM HEERIK

12. Heavyweight Bout, 3 x 3 min. rounds.

    T. BROGAN v. A. JONGENEEL

Torbay Amateur Boxing Club

President : EDWARD NARRACOTT

Souvenir Programme

PROGRAMME
(Subject to alteration)

Red Corner		Blue Corner
WELTERWEIGHT.		
1. R. CUNNINGHAM (London)	v.	S. PHILLIPS (Barnstaple)
3		West of England Champion
WELTERWEIGHT.		
2. J. FAIRWEATHER (London)	v.	L. GILL (Bristol)
2		West of England Champion
LIGHTWEIGHT.		
3. T. WALLER	v.	J. FISHER (Bristol)
4		West of England Champion
½ TIME.		
S. E. Divisional Champion		
FLYWEIGHT.		
4. G. VANGUYLENBERG	v.	C. BOVEY (Torbay)
6		England International
London Representative		
BANTAMWEIGHT.		
5. J. ALLEN (London)	v.	G. TOOLEY (Teignmouth)
		Devon Novice Champion
S.W. Divisional Champion		

Red Corner		Blue Corner
WELTERWEIGHT.		
6. J. BETTY (London)	v.	K. BROOKING (Torbay)
1		Devon Novice Champion
MIDDLEWEIGHT.		
7. G. FRANCIS (London)	v.	J. BANKS (Torbay)
		West of England Finalist
S.W. Representative		
LIGHTWEIGHT.		
8. W. HAITT (London)	v.	J. ISAAC (Barnstaple)
7		England International
A.B.A. Champion 1966		
FEATHERWEIGHT.		
9. L. SPRIGGS (London)	v.	R. ISAAC (Barnstaple)
8		
S.W. Representative		
FLYWEIGHT.		
10. M. ABRAM (London)	v.	
5		National Boy's Club Champion

209

ROGER BURRIDGE

BARNSTAPLE ABC

ROGER BURRIDGE centre...
flanked by JIMMY ISAAC and SYD PHILLIPS.

PRESENTATION TIME.

Won by ALEX MASON,
boxing in CANADA.

WHAT A MAGNIFICENT
BOXING TROPHY!

BARNSTAPLE ABC

JIM BARTLETT

GRAHAM HALLET

GORDON ROODE

EDDIE PRESCOTT

ROGER BURRIDGE

JIMMY ISAAC

BARNSTAPLE ABC

North Devon Journal   Thursday, April 27, 1989

Sixties Spot

THESE young North Devon boxers made a name for themselves in April 1960 when they won the team championship against South Devon in Exeter for the Alex Mason trophy.

One of the smiles belongs to Jimmy Isaac, then in his mid-teens, who went on to become the region's most celebrated boxer at bantamweight and featherweight.

In 1960 he was already a 12-counties schoolboy champion; later he went on to lose three times in the ABA finals, once on points to none other than Ken Buchanan who later became world featherweight champ.

Now 44, Jimmy is a Barnstaple fireman and still keeps fit, not in the ring but on the roads.

Others in Barnstaple and Bideford who triumphed 29 years ago were G. Yeo, J. Neale, D. Williams, P. Davey, M. Henry, R. Burridge, J. Webber, M. Smith, R. Fishleigh and M. Christie, with R. Slade, M. Orchard, J. Smith, P. Ray, A. Sherborne, J. Spiller and K. Graham the gallant losers.

213

R. BURRIDGE
D.O.B. 20.11.44
BARNSTAPLE A.B.C.
MOB 07811 707 675   01271 - 375290

I HAVE A NAGGING FEELING THAT I FIRST JOINED THE BARNSTAPLE A.B.C. AT THE SECONDARY MODERN SCHOOL/DERBY COLLEGE, ALONG WITH A LOT OF OTHER SCHOOL FRIENDS, BUT MY MOST VIVID MEMORIES LIE WITHIN THE 'OLD ICE FACTORY' UNDER THE DEDICATED GUIDANCE + MENTOR OF ALEX MASON, THEN TO BE JOINED LATER BY 'JIM BARTLETT WHO BETWEEN THEM TRAINED US ALL FOR QUITE A FEW YEARS. WITH NO HEATING, NO SHOWERS, YOU CAN IMAGINE WHAT LUXURIES WE HAD TO ENDURE DURING THE WINTER MONTHS, WE TRAINED HARD.

MY VERY FIRST BOXING EXHIBITION WAS AT THE 'FORRESTERS HALL' IN BARNSTAPLE HIGH ST WHERE I GAINED MY FIRST MEDAL WITH THE INSCRIPTION 'SEA CADET CORPS' AS I WAS ALSO IN THE SEA CADETS, WHETHER THIS WAS A REQUIREMENT TO JOIN THE BOXING CLUB I CANNOT SAY.

MY FIRST PUBLIC BOXING CONTEST WAS AT NORTHBROOK HALL? EXETER WITH ALL BOXERS TRAVELLING IN A HIRED COACH, PROBABLY PUGSLEYS COACHES FROM BEVAN ROAD. I WAS MATCHED WITH A LAD CALLED BRITT STONE FROM TIVERTON, I FELT THAT I WAS BEATEN TO A PULP WITH HIS RELENTLESS SWINGING PUNCHES, YET ALEX MASON ON OUR RETURN JOURNEY SAID THAT I HAD DONE WELL. I HAD THOUGHTS OF AN EARLY RETIREMENT.

I STUCK AT IT AND GAINED EXPERIENCE TRAVELLING OVER N.DEVON TO DIFFERENT VILLAGE LOCATIONS GIVING BOXING EXHIBITIONS AT

VERBATIM from the ORIGINAL.

VILLAGE FETES ORGANISED BY ALEX MASON
THUS PROMOTING BOXING.

MOVING ON MY PERSONAL ACHIEVEMENTS
THAT I REMEMBER WERE,
LONDON, SOUTHERN & MIDLAND COUNTIES N.A.B.C.
TITLE BEFORE LOSING TO DANNY DANAHAR
AT SLOUGH BELIEVED TO BE THE SON OF ARTHUR
DANAHAR FORMER PROFESSIONAL BOXER.

SIX COUNTIES ABA TITLE BEATING RON COUTTS
FROM THE PATCHWAY ABC BRISTOL THEN LOSING TO
TONY RILEY IN THE ZONE CHAMPIONSHIPS AT DEVIZES
WHO WENT ON TO WIN THE FEATHERWEIGHT ABA TITLE
IN 1963 THEN TO TURN PROFESSIONAL.

I THEN MOVED TO MANCHESTER IN 1963 AND JOINED
THE DROYLSDEN ABC UNDER THE GUIDANCE OF
CHARLIE GRICE, WHO WAS AN ACTIVE PROFESSIONAL
BOXER FROM 1962 - 1966. 1 MEMORABLE BOUT
I HAD WAS WITH PAUL PIP TAYLOR, A VERY TALENTED
BOXER WHO WAS AN ARMY & CORPS BOXING CHAMPION
IN THE 1960s.

I ALSO REPRESENTED DEVON ON AT LEAST TWO
OCCASIONS THAT I REMEMBER, ONCE AGAINST A
TEAM FROM THE BELSIZE ABC, LONDON AND THEN
A TEAM FROM THE ARMY AT A TORQUAY VENUE IN
1964, THE WHOLE 3 ROUND BOUT WAS SHOWN LIVE ON
A SATURDAY AFTERNOON ON BBC GRANDSTAND.

I ALSO ONCE CHALLENGED A BOXER AT SAM McKEOWNS
FAIR BOOTH MAKING MYSELF £2 RICHER FOR GOING
THE DISTANCE OF 3 ROUNDS.

I THINK MY LAST CONTEST WAS AS A SUPPORTING BOUT AT WESTWARD HO! DURING AN INTERNATIONAL TOURNAMENT, ENGLAND Vs

I DID NOT DO A LOT OF BOXING AFTER THAT TOURNAMENT, IT WAS LATE 1964 OR EARLY 1965, I MOVED TO LONDON AND WAS NOT ACTIVE WITH BOXING ALTHOUGH I ATTENDED SEVERAL TOURNAMENTS AMATEUR AND PROFESSIONAL AT THE ALBERT HALL, AND OTHER VENUES. AS WELL AS VISITING THE MOST FAMOUS GYM 'THOMAS A BECKET PUB' IN THE OLD KENT ROAD.

SO REALLY MY OWN BOXING CAREER LASTED FOR THE DURATION OF MY TEENAGE YEARS WHICH I ENJOYED AND A GOOD EXPERIENCE TO LOOK BACK UPON.

I THEN UNKNOWINGLY ENGAGED IN PURSUING OTHER INTERESTS.

ROGER, with some of his BOXING AWARDS.

SHOWING the same **DETERMINATION** to tackle this **HILL**
as he did against **OPPONENTS** in the **RING.**

This is to Certify that

R. Burridge

successfully completed

Barnstaple Imperial Wheelers

100 km. Randonnee

in 4 hrs. 12 mins. 5 secs.

March 28th 1982

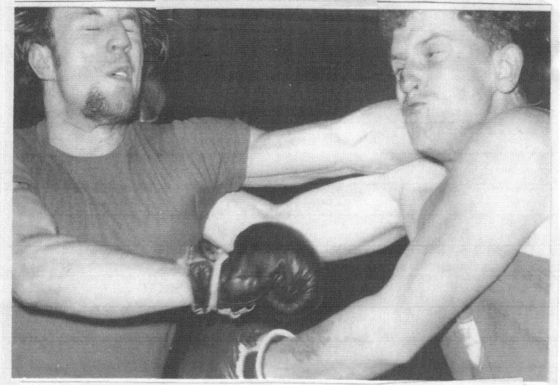

GORDON ROODE on the left, throws a flurry of punches!

GORDON ROODE

BARNSTAPLE ABC

On the right, GORDON ROODE.

BARNSTAPLE ABC

KEN WILLIAMS with JUNIOR BOXERS at DEVONPORT.

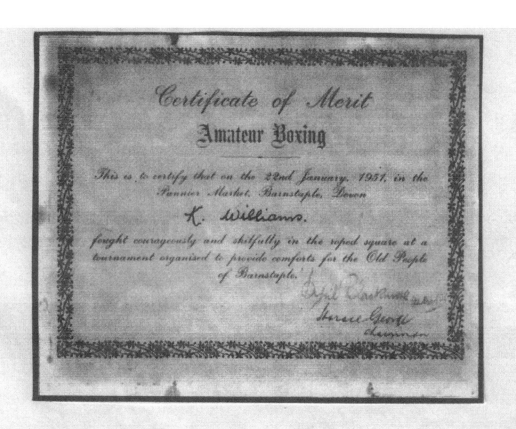

KEN WILLIAMS on the GERMAN BOXING TOUR 1967.
DAVE SHORT, KEN, JIMMY ISAAC.
The CERTIFICATE AWARDED to KEN WILLIAMS for BOXING on the
BARNSTAPLE ABC SHOW at the PANNIER MARKET in JANUARY 1951.
KEN became SECRETARY of BARNSTAPLE ABC.

BARNSTAPLE ABC

KEN'S SON, TIMOTHY WILLIAMS was an active boxer for
BARNSTAPLE ABC.

TIMOTHY on the left in both photos.

JUNIOR BOXERS PRAISED

BARNSTAPLE Boxing Club's final junior tournament of the season drew high praise from experienced A.B.A. official Mr. Ken Woodyatt.

He told the Barnstaple club afterwards that the show was one of the best he had seen.

Results: S. Bates (Sidmouth) bt G. Hopkins (Exeter), r.s.c first round; D. Kersey (Bideford) outpointed J. Cochrane (Capstone Hill); R. Smith (Barnstaple) outpointed G. Spencer (Sidmouth); T. Williams (Barnstaple) outpointed P. Wakefield (Exmouth); G. Lewis (Barnstaple) bt. M. Williams (Exmouth) r.s.c first round; S. Mackay (Exmouth) outpointed P. Jenkins (Barnstaple); M. Griffiths (Barnstaple) outpointed A. Dunn (Bideford); M. Davey (Sidmouth) outpointed C. Summerwell (Capstone Hill).

M. Westlake (Teignmouth) outpointed C. Blackmore (Capstone Hill); J. Hunting (Teignmouth) outpointed D. Barrow (Barnstaple); S. Willis (Teignmouth) outpointed P. Marriett (Capstone Hill); H. Pile (Teignmouth) outpointed S. Shaddick (Bideford); S. Westlake (Teignmouth) outpointed J. Dowling (Exmouth); E. Cochrane (Capstone Hill) outpointed C. Redfern (Teignmouth).

They make great reading!

RESULTS

2-3-69

Senior bouts: Barnstaple B. Cochrane (Teignmouth) b. Davis (Barnstaple); ... Feather—D. Cooley (Teignmouth) b. T. Daws (Barnstaple); Light—G. Gatenby (Teignmouth) bt. D. Prowse (Barnstaple); Welter—R. Denley (Teignmouth) bt. T. Sates (Kingsbridge), r.s.f. first round; D. Carroll (Exmouth) bt. P. Mearns (Kingsbridge); R. Ellis (Bideford) bt. P. Leyton (Teignmouth); Light-heavy—D. Short (Barnstaple) knocked out F. Tooley (Teignmouth), second round. Juniors: A. Cioffi (Devonport) bt S. Willis (Teignmouth); S. Shepherd (Devonport) bt P. Pile (Teignmouth); Nathan (Teignmouth) bt O. Doyle (Kingsbridge); O. Redfern (Teignmouth) bt D. Morgan (Devonport); S. Whitton (Devonport) bt C. Ebden (Teignmouth); N. Westlake (Teignmouth) bt A. Dugn (Bideford); P. Wakefield (Exmouth) bt T. Williams (Barnstaple); G. Payne (Teignmouth).

Boxing results at Ilfracombe

20-3-69

Boxers from North Devon, Cornwall, Torquay, and Plymouth took part in a tournament staged by the Capstone Hill (Ilfracombe) Boxing Club at the Holiday Inn, Ilfracombe, on Saturday. Results:

Seniors—D. Scott (Torbay) beat P. Kersey (Bideford); A. Kirkham (Torquay) bt B. Gregory (Ilfracombe); R. Ellis (Bideford) beat R. Barlow (Virginia House, Plymouth); A. Jury (Bideford) bt D. Dodge (Virginia House); D. Walker (Virginia House) bt J. Pincombe (Ilfracombe).

Juniors—G. Lane (Barnstaple) bt D. Brooking (Torquay); T. Williams (Barnstaple) bt C. Summerwill (Ilfracombe); T. Coates (Ilfracombe) bt A. Spry (Bideford); R. Kennell (Barnstaple) bt P. Coats (Ilfracombe); J. Cochrane (Ilfracombe) bt I. Jones (Camborne), r.s.b. second round; M. Shaddick (Bideford) bt T. Dumbrick (Torquay); M. Baylass (Barnstaple) bt P. Hardwick (Ilfracombe); D. T. Mealey (Barnstaple) bt D. Barrett (Bideford); A. Quick (Virginia House) bt J. McNeill (Ilfracombe); P. Jenkins (Barnstaple) bt P. Marriott (Ilfracombe).

SOUTH DEVON BOXERS TOP THE NORTH

20-3-69

SOUTH DEVON beat North Devon by six bouts to four in a 10-bout junior boxing contest for the Alex Mason trophy at the Holiday Inn, Ilfracombe, on Saturday night.

The South Devon team was slightly more experienced, although the North Devon team, which included Exeter, made them go all the way. The outstanding young boxer, with a style of his own, was 12-year-old Colin Ebden, Teignmouth.

South Devon received the Alex Mason trophy presented by the donor for annual junior boxing from Mr. Ian Pollard, chairman of the Ilfracombe Urban Council, who also presented prizes to the contestants.

Results: T. Williams (Barnstaple) beat S. Willis (Teignmouth), E. Cochrane (Ilfracombe) beat H. Roberts (Devonport), C. Blackmore (Ilfracombe) beat R. Bigland (Devonport), P. Hopkins (Exeter) beat A. Shepherd (Devonport), J. Hunting (Teignmouth) beat E. Barron (Barnstaple), C. Ebden (Teignmouth) beat P. Coates (Ilfracombe), S. Whitting (Devonport) beat R. Kennell (Barnstaple), P. Pale (Teignmouth) beat A. Shaddick (Bideford), N. Westlake (Teignmouth) beat M. Griffiths (Barnstaple), W. Kelly (Sidmouth) beat P. Hardwick (Ilfracombe), r.s.b. second round.

YOUNG WILLIAMS LOSES, BUT HE STILL IMPRESSES

By JACK TRANTER

ALTHOUGH beaten by six bouts to three in their return clash with Devonport Boxing Club Juniors at the Johnston Memorial Hall, Devonport, on Saturday, the combined North Devon boxers gave commendable performances in every bout, many of which were closely contested.

Despite the fact that he was one of the losers, 11-year-old Timothy Williams, son of Mr. Kenneth Williams, secretary of the Barnstaple club, gave an impressive display of left-hand boxing and counter-punching against the classy Alex Cioffi (Devonport), and there were many in the crowd who thought the Barnstaple boy had just pipped Cioffi at the post.

Williams has only been boxing a year, but he gives great promise of making a name for himself in the junior ranks this season.

One of North Devon's best victories was gained by Peter Hardwick (Ilfracombe), who, giving height and reach away, scored a points win over the more experienced Brian Jefferis (Devonport).

VALIANT ATTEMPT

It was Hardwick's south paw style that had the Devonport boxer continually baffled, but, apart from that, he did not produce the same fire and spirit shown by the Ilfracombe boy.

Peter Coates, of Ilfracombe, made a valiant attempt to avenge the defeat inflicted on him recently by Stephen Whitting (Devonport), but once again Whitting, who is a Plymouth Schools' champion, dictated the bout and ran out a comfortable points winner.

North Devon's other winner was Ernest Cockrane (Ilfracombe), who tamed the all-action Harry Roberts (Devonport) with his cool boxing, coupled with a hard and well-directed left.

One of the outstanding boxers of the evening, George Payne (Teignmouth), national schoolboy finalist, outpointed Paul Jefferis (Devonport) for the third time in a special contest.

Once again these old rivals provided a sparkling boxing exhibition, but, as in past encounters the Teignmouth boy was quicker to the punch and added up the stronger of the two.

RESULTS

Team bouts: A. Cioffi (Devonport) ...

Barnstaple boxing

Results in the junior boxing tournament staged by Barnstaple Boxing Club at the Y.M.C.A. Youth Club, Barnstaple, on Saturday, were:—

S. Dyke (Sidmouth) beat G. Hopkins (Exeter), r.s.b. first round; D. Kersey (Bideford) beat O. Cochrane (Capstone Hill, Ilfracombe); R. Smith (Barnstaple) beat G. Spencer (Sidmouth); T. Williams (Barnstaple) beat P. Wakefield (Exmouth); O. Lewis (Barnstaple) beat M. Williams (Exmouth), r.s.b. first round; S. Mackay (Exmouth) beat P. Jenkins (Barnstaple); M. Griffiths (Barnstaple) beat A. Dunn (Bideford); M. Davey (Sidmouth) beat M. Summerwill (Capstone Hill); N. Westlake (Teignmouth) beat C. Blackmore (Capstone Hill); J. Hunting (Teignmouth) beat D. Barron (Barnstaple); S. Willis (Teignmouth) beat M. Marriott (Capstone Hill); P. Pile (Teignmouth) beat A. Shaddick (Bideford); G. Westlake (Teignmouth) beat J. Dowling (Exmouth); P. Cochrane (Capstone Hill) beat G. Redfern (Teignmouth).

RESULTS

Team bouts: A. Cioffi (Devonport) beat T. Williams (Barnstaple); D. Morgan (Devonport) bt C. Summerwill (Ilfracombe); E. Cochrane (Ilfracombe) bt H. Roberts (Devonport); S. Whitting (Devonport) bt P. Coates (Ilfracombe); T. Shepherd (Devonport) bt R. Smith (Barnstaple), r.s.b. second round; R. Bigland (Devonport) bt M. Griffiths (Barnstaple); P. Dart (Devonport) bt T. Coates (Ilfracombe); N. Lane (Barnstaple) bt M. Chinn (Devonport); P. Hardwick (Ilfracombe) bt B. Jefferis (Devonport).

Special bouts: R. Warrey (Devonport) bt M. Jones (Plymouth Mayflower); A. Dart (Devonport) bt I. Clarke (Mayflower); C. Cusack (Devonport) bt P. Pile (Teignmouth); M. Cusack (Devonport) bt C. Attrill (Mayflower); P. Lance (Devonport) bt N. Westlake (Teignmouth); G. Payne (Teignmouth) bt P. Jefferis (Devonport); I. Nathan (Teignmouth) bt G. Johnson (Mayflower); C. Morgan (Pegasus, Plymouth) bt A. King (Devonport); C. Lewis (Barnstaple) bt M. Swift (Virginia House, Plymouth).

CAPSTONE HILL, ILFRACOMBE BOXING CLUB!

Brooking's devastating left hook too much for Exeter's Rowe

By JACK TRANTER

KEITH BROOKING, the young Torbay light-middleweight, was in devastating mood at the Town Hall, Kingsbridge, on Saturday, when he gained the only knock-out victory in a programme of exceptionally evenly matched bouts.

20·1·68

Southpaw Brooking's victim was the sturdy Alan Rowe, of Exeter, who in the first round looked as though he was going to give the somewhat lethargic Torbay man plenty of trouble.

The Torbay boxer, however, sprang to life in the next round and produced the kind of punch which should carry him a long way in the forthcoming A.B.A. championships — a crippling left hook with all his weight behind it.

Brooking paved the way for this punch with a hard right to the solar plexus and, as Rowe buckled up, he sent over the left which dropped the Exeter boxer for eight.

He had no sooner risen to his feet when Brooking sprang in with another left which hurtled Rowe halfway through the ropes, where he was counted out.

QUICKEST

Quickest win of the night was achieved by Harold Lightfoot, the Plymouth Mayflower heavyweight and reigning three counties A.B.A. champion. He stopped Mrs. George Stables (Virginia House) in the first minute of the opening round, the referee intervening to save Stables from further unnecessary punishment.

In a classic all-action junior contest, Timothy Williams of Barnstaple, failed to get revenge over Alex Cloffi (Devonport), who had outpointed him in their first meeting at Devonport recently.

This time it was an even closer contest, but the Devonport boy again scored well with his long-range boxing, and this must have swayed the judges in awarding him the points victory.

RESULTS

Feather— A. Nudge (Torbay) beat J. Gamble (Barber Mormon, Plymouth). Light— T. Tooley (Teignmouth) bt J. Issac (Barney Mormon). G. Clatworthy (Teignmouth) at L. Hawke (Virginia House, Plymouth). Light-welter — P. Denley (Teignmouth) bt W. J. Hawke (Barnstaple). Welter — J. Harmett (Barney Mormon) bt P. Mooney (Plymouth Mayflower). Light-middle — D. Cloffi (Exmouth) bt R. Knott (Exeter). K. Brooking (Torbay) knocked out A. Rowe (Exeter). Heavy — H. Lightfoot (Plymouth Mayflower) bt G. Stables (Virginia House).

CAPSTONE HILL BC
N. Devon

2–12–68

Seniors: D. Scott (Torbay) outpd P. Kersey (Bideford); A. Kirkham (Torbay) outpd B. Gregory (Ilfracombe); R. Ellis (Bideford) outpd R. Barlow (Virginia House, Plymouth); A. Jury (Bideford) outpd D. Doidge (Ilfracombe); D. Walker (Virginia House) outpd J. Pincombe (Ilfracombe).

Juniors: G. Lane (Barnstaple) outpd D. Brooking (Torbay); T. Williams (Barnstaple) outpd C. Summerwill (Ilfracombe); T. Coats (Ilfracombe) outpd A. Spry (Bideford); R. Kerswell (Barnstaple) outpd P. Coats (Ilfracombe); J. Cochran (Ilfracombe) stpd L. Jones (Camborne) 2; M. Shaddick (Bideford) outpd T. Dumbrick (Torbay); M. Bayliss (Barnstaple) outpd P. Hardwick (Ilfracombe); D. Manley (Barnstaple) outpd D. Barrett (Bideford); A. Quick (Virginia House) outpd J. McNiell (Ilfracombe); P. Jenkins (Barnstaple) outpd P. Marriott (Ilfracombe).

2-3-68

RESULTS

Senior bouts: Bantam—H. Clatworthy (Teignmouth) bt R. Issac (Barnstaple) r.s.f. third round cut eye. Feather—G. Tooley (Teignmouth) bt J. Issac (Barnstaple). Light—G. Clatworthy (Teignmouth) bt D. Prouse (Barnstaple). Welter—R. Denley (Teignmouth) bt S. Kalne (Kingsbridge) r.s.f. first round; D. Clargill (Exmouth) bt P. Edwards (Kingsbridge); R. Ellis (Bideford) bt P. Leyton (Teignmouth). Light-heavy—D. Short (Barnstaple) knocked out P. Tooley (Teignmouth) second round. Juniors: A. Cloffi (Devonport) bt S. Willis (Teignmouth); A. Shepherd (Devonport) bt P. Pile (Teignmouth); J. Nathan (Teignmouth) bt G. Doyle (Kingsbridge); D. Redfern (Teignmouth) bt D. Morgan (Devonport); S. Whitton (Devonport) bt O. Ebdon (Teignmouth); N. Westlake (Teignmouth) bt A. Duran (Bideford); P. Wakefield (Exmouth) bt T. Williams (Barnstaple); G. Payne (Teignmouth).

Championship bouts: Junior B 10st. semi-finals.—C. Simons (Exeter) beat S. Nuciforo (Camborne); A. Davis (Gillingham) beat W. Owen (Poole), r. s. b. first round. Final— Simons beat Davis, r. s. b. second round. Class B 9st. final.—L. Caines (Gillingham) beat R. Smith (Barnstaple). Class A. 10st. semi-final.—P. Goss (Barnstaple) beat G. Bashford (Gillingham), R. Bigland (Plymouth Mayflower) bye. Final.— Bigland beat Goss. Walkovers.— T. Pinder (Mayflower), V. S. Whitting (Mayflower), N. Shaddick (Bideford).

JUNIOR A.B.A.

Senior inter-club contests. Light —P. Smith (Truro) beat K. Ford (Teignmouth). Light-welter — R. Jennings (Mayflower) beat M. Bayliss (Barnstaple). Light-middle—M. Shaddick (Bideford) beat G. White (Exeter). Juniors: D. Pinder (Mayflower) beat P. Jenkins (Barnstaple), R. Knott (Exeter) beat D. Catterall (Mayflower), D. B. Williams (Barnstaple) beat P. Wakefield (Lympstone).

26/4/67

NEWCOMERS DOMINATE TOURNAMENT

One of the best-ever junior boxing tournaments to be seen in North Devon was staged at the Barnstaple Y.M.C.A. on Saturday.

Teams from Barnstaple, Bideford, and the newly-formed Capstone Hill Sports Club, Ilfracombe, competed for the Ken Winkle Cup.

And by virtue of winning four of the six competition bouts the trophy went to the Seasiders.

Other North Devon boxers fought juniors from the Exeter and Exmouth clubs.

During the evening, Michael Bavlis, of Barnstaple, was presented with the Alex Mason Cup for being North Devon's outstanding schoolboy boxer of the year.

Results: T. Williams (Barnstaple) lost on points to P. Marriott (Ilfracombe); P. Jenkins (Barnstaple) lost on points to D. Wakefield (Exmouth); Dan Manley (Barnstaple) bt K. Bates (Exmouth) on points; T. Coats (Ilfracombe) bt A. Spry (Bideford) on points; A. Maddison (Ilfracombe) lost on points to B. Houghton (Exeter); P. Coates (Ilfracombe) bt S. Bates (Exmouth) on points; David Manley (Barnstaple) bt G. Donovan (Exmouth) on points; A. Shaddick (Bideford) bt G. Edwards (Exmouth) on points; C. Blackmore (Ilfracombe) bt J. Lamont (Bideford) on points; M. Bavlis (Barnstaple) bt P. Hardwick (Ilfracombe) on points.

26/4/67

JUNIOR BOXING PULLS IN CROWDS

THE crowd-pulling potential of the junior tournaments run by Barnstaple Boxing Club was again demonstrated when the local Y.M.C.A. headquarters were filled to capacity for the latest show.

Boxers from five Devon clubs took part in the tournament, which produced some top-class displays.

Among the clubs involved was the newly-formed Capstone Hill Sports Club of Ilfracombe. In a local contest against the Barnstaple and Bideford boxers, Capstone Hill made a good start by winning the Ken Winkles Cup.

Results: P. Marriott (Ilfracombe) beat T. Williams (Barnstaple); P. Wakefield (Exmouth) beat P. Jenkins (Barnstaple); D. Manley (Barnstaple) beat K. Bates (Exmouth); T. Coates (Capstone Hill) beat A. Spry (Bideford); D. Houghton (Exeter) beat A. Maddison (Capstone Hill); P. Coates (Capstone Hill) beat S. Bates (Exmouth); D. Manley (Barnstaple) beat G. Donovan (Exmouth); P. Hopkins (Exeter) beat P. Bull (Exmouth); A. Shaddick (Bideford) beat G. Edwards (Exmouth); C. Blackmore (Capstone Hill) beat J. Lamont (Bideford); M. Bavliss (Barnstaple) beat P. Hardwick (Capstone Hill); C. Symons (Exeter) beat K. Wakefield (Exmouth).

There was also an exhibition bout given by R. Kenwood (Barnstaple) and T. Hoods the new Army and Inter-Services champion, who was formerly with the Barnstaple club.

QUICKEST

Quickest win of the night was achieved by Harold Lightfoot, the Plymouth Mayflower heavyweight and reigning three counties A.B.A. champion. He stopped Mne. George Stables (Virginia House) in the first minute of the opening round, the referee intervening to save Stables from further unnecessary punishment.

In a classic all-action junior contest, Timothy Williams, of Barnstaple, failed to get revenge over Alex Cioffi (Devonport), who had outpointed him in their first meeting at Devonport recently.

This time it was an even closer contest, but the Devonport boy again scored well with his long-range boxing, and this must have swayed the judges in awarding him the points victory.

RESULTS

Feather — R. Mudge (Torbay) beat J. Gamble (Hartley Mormon, Plymouth). Light — T. Tooley (Teignmouth) bt J. Little (Hartley Mormon); G. Clatworthy (Teignmouth) bt L. Hawke (Virginia House, Plymouth). Light-welter — R. Denley (Teignmouth) bt B. Hawkins (Barnstaple). Welter — J. Marshall (Hartley Mormon) bt P. Mooney (Plymouth Mayflower). Light-middle — D. Clarbull (Exmouth) bt R. Barlow (Virginia House); K. Brooking (Torbay) knocked out A. Rowe (Exeter) second round. Middle — A. Quirk (Virginia House) bt R. Salisbury (Plymouth Mayflower); D. Jarvis (Kingsbridge) bt K. Bates (Exmouth). Heavy — H. Lightfoot (Plymouth Mayflower) bt G. Stables (Virginia House) first round. Juniors — A. Cioffi (Devonport) bt T. Williams (Barnstaple); R. Warry (Devonport) bt S. Bavlis (Kingsbridge).

ACTION-PACKED BOUTS

ALTHOUGH Alan Rowe, of Exeter, started off well in the first round of his bout with southpaw Keith Brooking, the young Torbay light-middleweight, at the Town Hall, Kingsbridge, on Saturday, he was knocked out by a left hook in the second round.

After a competent first round, Rowe was caught with a right and a left which dropped him for a count of eight. Soon afterwards Rowe ran into another punch which hurled him half-way through the ropes and he failed to make the count.

AGGRESSION CARRIES THE DAY

By JACK TRANTER

THE junior tournament staged by the Devonport Boxing Club at the Johnston Memorial Hall on Saturday developed into a battle between the skilful boxing of the North Devon team and the continually aggressive and harder punching of the Plymouth boxers.

In the end it was that little extra power punching that enabled Plymouth to win by 6 bouts to 5.

Classy Ernie Cochrane triumphed over the tough and much fancied Harry Roberts, of Devonport, despite a grand rally by the Devonport boy in the last round. On this performance Cochrane could do well in the forthcoming schoolboy championships.

Timothy Williams (Barnstaple) boxed brilliantly against David Arnott (Plymouth Mayflower) and I thought the Plymouth lad was lucky in clinching the points verdict. It must have been Arnott's forceful infighting tactics that swayed the judges in his favour.

Sam Adair (Barnstaple), making his first ring appearance, brought off a grand points victory over Bob Adams (Mayflower) after three all-action rounds.

Team bouts: E. Cochrane (Ilfracombe) beat H. Roberts (Devonport); M. Cusack (Devonport) bt D. Barlow (Barnstaple); T.J.b second round; T. Coates (Ilfracombe) bt A. Dart (Devonport); D. Arnott (Plymouth Mayflower) bt T. Williams (Barnstaple); V. Stade (Hartley Mormon Club, Plymouth) bt B. Winnard (Ilfracombe); P. Reid (Barnstaple) bt G. Vincent (Mayflower); S. Whiting (Devonport) bt R. Kerswell (Barnstaple); S. Adair (Barnstaple) bt R. Adams (Mayflower); T. Shepherd (Devonport) bt R. Smith (Barnstaple); P. Mallit (Barnstaple) bt C. Tipton (Mayflower); S. Barrass (Mayflower) bt M. Griffiths (Barnstaple).

Special contests: G. Catterall (Devonport) bt G. Johnson (Mayflower); D. Morgan (Devonport) bt M. Slade (Hartley Mormon Club).

In an all-action junior contest, Timothy Williams, of Barnstaple, failed to get revenge over Alex Cioffi (Devonport), who had outpointed him in their first meeting recently, Cioffi again won on points.

In a welterweight contest, Exmouth A.B.C. boxer D. Clarbull earned a points decision over R. Barlow (Virginia House, Plymouth) after three hard-fought rounds, flooring his man twice in the final round.

Results included — Lightweight: T. Tooley (Teignmouth) beat J. Little (Hartley Mormon); G. Clatworthy (Teignmouth) bt L. Hawke (Virginia House, Plymouth); Light-welter: R. Denley (Teignmouth) bt B. Hawkins (Barnstaple); Light-middle: D. Clarbull (Exmouth) bt R. Barlow (Virginia House); K. Brooking k.o.d A. Rowe (Exeter); Middle: D. Jarvis (Kingsbridge) bt K. Bates (Sid...

A. Cioffi bt T. Williams.

20-1-68.

228

RONNIE ISAAC

RONNIE ISAAC

Ron Isaac   ## BARNSTAPLE ABC

My Boxing Career

My Amateur Boxing Career is rather
unusual. compared with most
that take up the sport.

I first Put on a Pair of
Boxing gloves when I was about
11 years of age.
My father came Home one day with
2 pairs of boxing gloves, witch a
friend of his had given him.
My father was a regular Soldier
before the 2nd World war broke out.
and was quit an all round sportsman
Boxing was one of the sports
he participated in.
He asked if I and my younger
Brother Jimmy if we wanted to
Have a go at sparring with Him
I remember him taken us into
our Bedroom pushing the bed
back against the wall, He then
Put on a Pair of gloves, Put a
Pair on me, went down on his
nees, and then incorouged
me to have a spar with him
after a little while, My Dad
asked if my younger brother
wanted a go, Jimmy was only

4 years old at the time.

My father proceeded to instruct and incorage us for a while, then he asked did we want to have a go against each other.

And that was the start of many years and hundreds of rounds of boxing that I and brother Jim competed against each other.

At the age of 11 I left junior school and started at the Barnstaple Bay Secondary school. this is where I was introduced to the game of rugby.

At this moment of time, there was not a ametuer Boxing club in Barnstaple and so my efforts of sport were consentrated in school, where I proceeded to over the next couple of years to represent the school both at rugby and cricket.

When Jim reached the age of 10 years old, A gentleman named Alex Mason, started a Boxing club for the local Cadet forces in Barnstaple, Jimmy joined the navy cadets so he could join the club.

Jim then went on over the next decade, to become one of the top Amateur Boxers in the Country, Winning 3 Junior national titles, and reaching the A.B.A. Semi finals and finals 4 times.

Although I never took up Boxing at the time, concentrating on playing Rugby. I often went to the boxing club to spar with Jim and the other boys at the club.

At the age of 23, A Married man with a family and still a playing member of Barnstaple R.F.C. I was still going to the Boxing club training and sparring with its members,

I was Very Proud of my brothers Achievements as an Amateur Boxer And probably, apart from my Father his no 1 fan.

One night whilst training at the boxing club. I said to the clubs Coach A man called Wilf Cooper, Wilf if you fix me up with a contest I'll have a go and see what I can do.

Wilf fixed up a contest against a lad down on a Tournament in Cornwall. We went to the tournament, and I proceeded to stop him in the 1st Round. That was the start of my Boxing Career in the public eye. My next fight was against a lad from Bideford at the Queens Hall in Barnstaple. I proceeded to stop him in the first Round.

After these Contest, and with people saying how impressed they were with me I wonderd how far I could go in the Amateur Boxing Circle.

I set myself a target of trying to achieve what my younger brother had achieved and become an international Amateur Boxer.

My Boxing Career lasted for 3 Seasons from 1965 to 1968 in that time I boxed many top ranking boxers all over the Country. In only my 5th fight I boxed and beat an england internatoinal, so my trainer felt Confident in me to compete against any apponent

I boxed in the A.B.A. Championships
3 times. First year in only my
3rd fight I fought in the Devon
Dorset & Cornwall championships.
I Boxed against a lad from
Torquay, who had already
boxed as an England International
and lost on a majority Decerison.
The Second year I reached the
A.B.A Quarter finals at Coventry
and fought the welsh Champion
a lad called Steve Curtis after
a tremendus bout he was given
the desicion, and went on that
year to win the A.B.A title.
I ranked steve as possibly
the best apponant I ever fought
Over the previouse two Seasons I
had established myself as one
of the top Ametuer flywights in
the Country
In January. 1968 I was informed
by the president of Devan A.B.A.
that I had been selected by the
English A.B.A. to represent England
against Iceland in Dublin the
following Month.
I fought for England against
Iceland in Dublin in front of
a crowd of over 2000, at the
national Stadium, my apparent
was a lad called Brendon Mcarthy
who the previouse year had Won

A Silver Medal, in the Iceland
championships, Although I
tried my best, he was a
tall rangey lad for a flyweight
he went on to win the Contest
Before the tournament began
both teams paraded into
the ring, where I had the
honour of carrying the union
Jack for my Country and stood
proud there while the national anthem
were played.
After this I had a few more
bouts, before entering the ABA
championships, for a third year
I went on to reach the
ABA Semi finals at Bell Vue.
Manchester on the 25th April 1968
Here I boxed M. Stevens the
London champion, and lost a
very close contest on a majority
Desision, even the report in the
Boxing news Paper thought
I was unlucky to lose the
contest.
That was the last Bout of
my Career, when I was in
the changing room after the
Bout, I said to my trainer
that was it, I have achieved
what I wanted to Do. I was
calling it a day.

I was a married man with
3 young children, and the
time spent training and travelling
the Country, Had to come to
an end.

I needed to spend more.
time with my family being
a Husband & Father to my
young family.

During the 3 years of my
career, I competed in around.
2. Dozen Contest, and I can.
only speculate losing to 4 of.
my opponents.

Colin Bovey. England International

Steve Curtis Welsh & A.B.A. Champion

Brendan McCarthy Irish Champion

Maurice Steeves A.B.A Finalist.

Ron Brace
2016

RON ISAAC WINS BY K.O. IN DEBUT

THE name of Isaac, which has become famous in Westcountry boxing circles with the exploits of Barnstaple's international, Jimmy Isaac, may become even more well-known in future.

For on Saturday, Jimmy was joined on the bill in a tournament at Camborne by his brother, Ron Isaac.

In the first contest he has had, Ron Isaac showed that boxing skills are not confined to one member of his family by securing a first-round knock-out over Harold Vinicombe (Truro), a fly-weight.

Jimmy Isaac won his feather-weight bout with Truro's Don Cunnick when the referee stopped the contest in round two.

Other Barnstaple boxers were Geoff Yeo, who outpointed A. Richards (Penzance) in a light-welterweight bout; and light-middleweight John Bracher, who lost on points to P. Hooley (St. Austell).

EXCITING BOUT

Arthur Tyrrell, Exeter's prospect, confirmed his superiority over Basil Withers, the hard-punching Truro middleweight, in an exciting bout which he won on points.

Other Exeter successes included W. Charles, who knocked out B. Jones (St. Austell) in the third round, and Allen Rowe, the novice welterweight, who improved upon a previous narrow points win over D. Hicks (Camborne) with a clear points win.

M. Choules (Exeter), novice light-welterweight, lost narrowly on points to B. Foster (Truro).

Rodney Seatherton, of the Royal Navy, and former Exeter junior star, scored his second win for his old club within a few days when, in a welterweight contest, he beat Peter Hayfield (Exmouth) on a narrow points decision.

RON STEALS SHOW FROM HIS FAMOUS BROTHER

BARNSTAPLE'S international boxer Jimmy Isaac was almost pushed into the background on Saturday at the Queen's Hall, Barnstaple, when he topped the bill, for it was Jimmy's elder brother Ron who produced the most convincing win of the evening.

This was Ron's second public appearance in a boxing ring, once again he knocked his man out in the first round.

His bantamweight victim this time was T. Staddon, of Bideford.

Staddon came out from his corner and made good use of left jabs to the side of Isaac's head, but Isaac returned with two well placed blows to the body.

In the second minute Staddon allowed his caution to waver for but an instant, but this was enough for Isaac, who came in hard with a vicious right to the head that dropped his opponent like a stone.

Jimmy Isaac had himself a comfortable points win over A.B.A. quarter-finalist M. Bryson, from Bath.

Bryson provided the packed hall, with a good display of steady boxing, but as the contest progressed Isaac found a way through his resolute opponent's defence with a series of hooks and short jabs to the body and head.

UNPOPULAR DECISION

An unpopular decision came early in the evening when Barnstaple's John Bracher was disqualified during the third round of his bout against G. Gaston, of Exeter.

Several Barnstaple boxers had good victories at this tournament—notably Ron Kenwood, who won his junior bout against D. Bryne, of Exeter. Success came to him after a fine display in the final round.

Barry Hawkins also won his lightweight contest against I. Mitchell, of Penzance, and it was Mitchell's faulty footwork that cost him this points defeat.

Other results: G. Yeo (Barnstaple) points victory over A. Richards (Penzance); H. Laird (Barnstaple) lost by technical knock-out to J. Sedgmore (Exmouth); P. Hayfield (Exmouth) points victory over K. Brooking (Torbay); P. Salter (Virginia House) lost on points to T. Cook (Bristol); M. Brady (Virginia House) points victory over R. Mudge (Torbay); D. Lewis (Watchet) points points victory over D. Barnes (Penzance); and R. Fisher (Bristol) points victory over J. Banks (Torbay).

Ronnie Isaac to box for England

AFTER only two full seasons in boxing, Ronnie Isaac, of Barnstaple, has been selected to fight for England.

Ronnie, who is 26, thereby creates a notable 'double.' His younger brother Jimmy already has eight international boxing caps.

"I think Jimmy was more excited than anyone at my selection," said flyweight Ronnie this week.

From an early age the Isaac brothers were encouraged by their father to box.

"Our father practically lived for boxing," said Ronnie, "and it

RON ISAAC

came as practically second nature to us."

It was Jimmy, however, who first captured all the headlines on the sports pages. After leaving school, Ronnie took up rugby.

For several seasons he played with the Barnstaple club, and at the time of his retirement two years ago he was captain of the third team.

"I found I didn't have time for both sports, so I decided to concentrate on boxing. From the look of things it appears that I made the right choice," he said.

In 25 bouts he has lost only to three opponents, and two of these, Colin Bovey and Steve Curtis, were internationals.

Ronnie lives at 69, Lethaby Road, Barnstaple, with his wife, Janet, and three children — Darren (4), Mandy (2), and Julie (11 months). He works as a checker with Messrs. Shapland and Petter.

RONNIE ISAAC

BARNSTAPLE ABC

RONNIE ISAAC, JIMMY ISAAC, Trainer WILF COOPER, DAVID VINE.

THREE CHAMPIONS : Three of these boxers—featherweigh[t]
Jimmy Isaac, his flyweight brother Ron, and lightweight Si[d]
Phillips, returned to Barnstaple from Gillingham wit[h]
South-West Counties titles. The fourth, heavyweight Joh[n]
Pincombe, of Ilfracombe, can only try again.

Barum boxers win SW. titles

TRIO RETURN IN TRIUMPH

BARNSTAPLE'S fighting brothers, Jimmy and Ron Isaa[c]
returned home on Saturday night after adding two mor[e]
triumphs to their ever mounting list. Sharing this hour o[f]
glory was another Barum boxer, Sid Phillips.

Earlier in the evening Jimmy had won the feather
weight title in the South West Counties championships, an[d]
Sid had taken the lightweight crown. But lucky Ron, wh[o]
like his brother, is an international, had enjoyed [a]
walk-over en route to the
flyweight title.

Two other North Devon boxers,
Robert Ellis, of Bideford, and John
Pincombe, of Ilfracombe, who also
took part in these championships
at Gillingham, were certainly not
entitled to regard it as a night to
be remembered.

Pincombe was outpointed by the
eventual heavyweight champion,
and Ellis suffered the frustration of
being three ounces over the welterweight limit. So he did not box.

Jimmy Isaac used all his experience and ring craft in the
semi-final when he defeated his
hit-and-run opponent, R. Mudge, of
Torquay, who proved an elusive
target.

Worthy champion

The Barnstaple boxer proved a
worthy champion in decisively
beating Gamble, of Plymouth, in
the final. He used his left hand in
stopping Gamble's rushes and then
punished him with his right.

After defeating Morgan, of
Plymouth, in the semi-final,

RONNIE ISAAC

North Devon Journal-Herald   October 19, 1967

ISAAC BROTHERS WIN FIGHTS FOR COUNTIES

THE Barnstaple boxing brothers, Ron and Jimmy Isaac,
won their fights when they appeared at Gillingham on
Saturday for Devon, Dorset and Cornwall A.B.A. in a match
against Jersey.

Bantamweight Ron outpointed Jersey's E. Hollevan, a
fast-moving boxer with a
good left hand.

In the second round Ron got his
range and hurt Hollevan with combination punches to the body. Isaac
was warned to keep his punches up.

Ron chased his man with devastating body punches in the third round
to get the verdict.

Featherweight Jimmy Isaac, recovered from a cut eye which caused
his retirement the previous week,
beat Channel Islander M. Micheletti.

TRUE FORM

Jimmy was slow in the opening
round against an awkward but fast
puncher.

His experience and footwork kept
Isaac out of real trouble, although
he was caught with swinging right
hands.

Halfway through the second round
Isaac showed his true form with
quick lefts and rights to the body.

In the third, Jimmy's combination
punches and speed got him the
points verdict.

North Devon Journal-Herald   April 4, 1968

JIMMY ISAAC

RON ISAAC

The battling Isaacs make history as they enter A.B.A. semis

TWO brothers have entered the A.B.A. semi-finals for the first time in the history of the championships. And the brothers are none other than the Barnstaple battlers, Jimmy and Ron Isaac.

Featherweight Jimmy and flyweight Ron are now just two bouts away from becoming national champions. The semi-final hurdle lies ahead at Manchester on April 25.

Both of them touched top form when they won their quarter-final fights at Wolverhampton.

Ron was well ahead on points against F. Laverty, of Coventry Irish, when the referee stopped the fight in the third round.

He stepped in when Ron dealt his opponent a hard right hand, and two cuts appeared above Laverty's right eye.

Ron had been the more aggressive boxer, although both fighters were slowed down by a collision of heads in the second round.

In the third round the Barnstaple boxer put on the pressure and caught Laverty with some crisp punches.

Unanimous decision

A unanimous decision gave Jimmy Isaac a points verdict against Danny Polak, of Park Farm.

After a promising first round, Jimmy was dazed in the second when Polak was severely warned by the referee for careless use of his head.

When Jimmy's head cleared in the latter part of the third round he punished Polak with good combination punches and hard rights to th head.

Displaying his best form Jimmy stopped old rival Mick Bryson (Bath) in the third round to win his fifth Western title.

Bryson never really recovered from a right hook to the chin that dropped him for "8" in the first round. After more punishment and another count the referee intervened.

Younger brother Ron had a much harder task retaining his flyweight crown. He had to battle hard for his points win over Harry Butt, a new recruit to Bristol from Ireland.

Neat-boxing Jimmy Banks, the young Torbay light-welter, had an exceptionally tough struggle with Bobby Gwynne (Bristol) before taking the verdict.

Only his durability enabled Mick Tuck (Bath) to go the distance with Arthur Tyrrell, the hard punching Exeter southpaw.

Welter hot-shot Dave Simmonds (Cinderford) took the decision in an exciting bout with Tony Sly (Poole).

With five champions each, Devon, Dorset and Cornwall shared the honours with Glous., Somerset and Wilts.

RESULTS: Fly, R. Isaac (Barnstaple) outpd H. Butt (Bristol); Bantam, S. Rendall (Poole) outpd N. Hynes (Bristol); Feather, J. Isaac (Barnstaple) stpd M. Bryson (Percy); Light, R. Fisher (Hartcliffe) outpd S. Phillips (Barnstaple); Light-welter, J. Banks (Torbay) outpd R. Gwynne (Swindon); Welter, D. Simmonds (Cinderford & Gloucester) outpd A. Sly (Poole); Light-middle, K. White (Wells) outpd F. Strawbridge (Gillingham); Middle, A. Tyrell (Exeter) outpd M. Tuck (Percy); Cruiser, D. Lewis (Watchet) ko'd P. Stacey (Gillingham) 2; Heavy, E. Stanley (Bristol) outpd D. Gatehouse (Gillingham).

JIMMY and Ron Isaac, the fighting brothers from Barnstaple, triumphed again in the WESTERN COUNTIES Championships at Salisbury.

BOXING NEWS   MARCH 22, 1968

HARRY BUTT crashes a right to the head of England international RON ISAAC in their Western Counties final. Isaac won on points.

It's The Isaacs' Again

Ron Isaac Halted With 6 Seconds To Go In Flyweight Thriller

MIDLAND COUNTIES send six men to Manchester next week for the ABA semi-finals following the MIDLAND AND WESTERN COUNTIES VERSUS WALES QUARTER-FINALS held at the Humber Works canteen, Coventry, last Friday. With the two Western Counties contenders —flyweight Ron Isaac and welterweight Dave Simmonds—crashing to inside-the-distance defeats, Wales provide four winners to complete a line-up which, on paper, stands a remarkably good chance of marching through to the finals at Wembley on May 5.

Highlight of the evening was Isaac's sparkling bout with 18-year-old Welsh champion Stephen Curtis. Brother of former England international Jimmy Isaac, and taking part in only his ninth contest, the 26-year-old bearded Devonian nearly caused a sensation when he rocked the classy moving Welshman with a number of sledgehammer blows in the opening seconds.

Curtis, of the Roath Youth ABC came back brilliantly to stop his man in the third round but Isaac was probably edging matters when the bout was stopped with only six seconds left on the clock.

A left and right to the chin caused Curtis to buckle at the knees during the first round and the Barnstaple boxer stormed in looking set for a quick win. The baby-faced Welshman was somewhat distressed as Isaac thumped over more numbing swings to the head and only his nimble footwork saved him from a sticky end.

Towards the end of the second round Curtis began to come into his own, catching Isaac with brilliant combinations of punches. And although Isaac still forced the pace Curtis gradually began to dictate the course with superb counter punching.

Delbridge Dazzled

In the third Curtis swung over a perfect left hook which sent Isaac crashing to the canvas for a count of "eight." Then the smoothmoving Welshman began to force the pace and sent Isaac spinning to the canvas yet again, when he connected with four dynamic punches to the jaw. Isaac was still reeling after the count and the contest was stopped in Curtis's favour.

TWO MORE WINS FOR ISAAC BROTHERS

Ron and Jimmy Isaac, the Barnstaple boxing brothers, fought well in Devon A.B.A.'s win by six bouts to five against the Oxon, Berks and South Bucks A.B.A., at Oxford, on Saturday night.

Devon threatened a runaway win when they took the first five bouts, but then the Home Counties lost only one of the remaining fights.

There was a close win for Ron Isaac in his three strenuous rounds with Ray Flowers (Battersea). He was the better puncher, but he had to weather some tricky moments early in the last round.

Jimmy Isaac was too formidable for Frank Read, whom he put down for a count of eight in the first round.

When he again floored Read with a right to the head, the referee stopped the bout to save the Reading fighter from further punishment.

A Bideford welterweight, R. Ellis, was beaten in a senior bout by G. Daniels (Reading), when the referee stopped the fight in the third round.

ISAAC v BUTT

RON ISAAC, the new England flyweight international from Barnstaple, and Irishman Harry Butt, a new recruit to Bristol, meet in what could be the highlight of the Western Counties Championships at the City Hall, Salisbury, tomorrow (Saturday).

Winners go forward to meet Midland Counties in the new-style ABA quarter-final at Wolverhampton on March 28.

Pairings—Fly: H. Butt (Bristol & D.) v R. Isaac (Barnstaple). Bantam: N. Hynes (Bristol & D) v S. Rendall (Poole). Feather: M. Bryson (Percy BC, Bath) v J. Isaac (Barnstaple). Light: R. Fisher (Hartcliffe) v S. Philips (Barnstaple). Light-welter: R. Gwynne (Swindon) v J. Banks (Torbay). Welter: D. Simmonds (Cinderford) v A. Sly (Poole). Light-middle: K. White (Wells) v F. Strawbridge (Gillingham, Dorset). Middle: M. Tuck (Percy BC, Bath) v A. Tyrell (Exeter). Light-heavy: D. Lewis (Watchet) v P. Stacey (Gillingham, Dorset). Heavy: E. Stanley (Bristol & D.) v D. Gatehouse (Gillingham, Dorset).

* * *

Isaac brothers reach last eight—but bad luck for Phillips

BARNSTAPLE'S international boxers, Jimmy Isaac and his brother Ron, have reached the quarter-finals of the A.B.A. championships at Wolverhampton on March 28.

They earned this right with victories at Salisbury in the Western Counties stage on Saturday and, in the opinion of the crowd, a third Barnstaple boxer, Sid Phillips, was cruelly unlucky not to go forward with them.

Many of the spectators claimed that the bell went a minute early in the third and last round, and at that time lightweight R. Fisher, of Bristol, was facing imminent defeat in his lightweight contest with Phillips.

He had already been given a public warning by the referee for "lying on," and he seemed certain to go down at any time. Booing greeted the decision.

Fisher had won the first round, when he did not allow Phillips to settle down, and the second round was even. But the last round it was all Phillips, who delivered solid punches to the head and left hooks to the body.

All-action bout

Ron Isaac's success in the flyweight class was against an Irish international, R. Butt, of Bristol.

It was a great, all-action contest from the first bell to the last, and Isaac won because of his greater variety of punches.

His brother, Jimmy, was an even more comfortable winner of his featherweight fight against M. Bryson, of Bath, who was receiving so much punishment that the referee stopped the bout in the second round.

After opening well, Bryson went down for a count of eight in the first round and was saved by the bell.

Bryson was in more trouble in the second round, when he again took a count of eight and was then floored by two left jabs and a hard right. The referee stepped in at this point.

RONNIE ISAAC

JIMMY ISAAC

RON ISAAC

SID PHILLIPS

JOHN PINCOMBE

THREE CHAMPIONS : Three of these boxers—featherweight Jimmy Isaac, his flyweight brother Ron, and lightweight Sid Phillips, returned to Barnstaple from Gillingham with South-West Counties titles. The fourth, heavyweight John Pincombe, of Ilfracombe, can only try again.

Barum boxers win SW. titles

ISAAC BROTHERS BID FOR PLACES IN A.B.A. FINALS
By JACK TRANTER

JIMMY and Ron Isaac, the two Barnstaple boxing brothers, will be tackling the last but one hurdle in the long and hard road to gaining national A.B.A. titles when they compete in the semi-finals at Belle Vue, Manchester, on Thursday.

Jimmy, now one of the most ringwise of Britain's amateur featherweight boxers, has reached this stage of the championships on four occasions, twice winning through to the finals at Wembley.

His biggest rivals in the featherweight division could be Johnny Cheshire (Repton), who has won all his six bouts for England this season, and Alan Richardson (Wakefield), who brilliantly outpointed ex-champion Bobby Mallon in the quarter-finals.

The other contender for the title is Jamaican Gilbert Gunn (R.A.F.).

Brother Ron, who caused a big surprise by reaching the quarter-finals last season after a short boxing career, is one of the hardest punching flyweights in the country and he will naturally be relying on this asset to carry him through.

The Barnstaple man's conqueror in last year's quarter-finals was Steve Curtiss (Cardiff), who went on to win the national title. This season, however, the Welshman was surprisingly eliminated in the quarter-finals by Johnny McGonigle (Army).

I think Isaac has the beating of McGonigle but he will need all his stamina and punching ability should he come against either Maurice Steeves (Wandsworth) or Alex McHugh (Kelvin).

Compared to brother JIMMY, RONNIE'S BOXING CAREER was of a very short duration, but he achieved so much.

BARNSTAPLE ABC

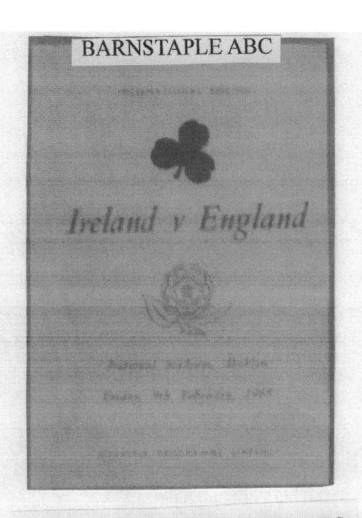

RONNIE ISAAC, NATIONAL HONOURS.

WHO'S WHO ON THE ENGLISH TEAM

Flyweight—R. ISAACS. 26 years. Western Districts Champion 1967. First International.

Bantamweight—F. TABERNER. 21 years. Represented England in Representative matches on a number of occasions.

Featherweight—J. CHESHIRE. 21 years. English representative on several matches.

Lightweight—G. MOUGHTON. 20 years. English Youth representative.

Light/Welterweight—C. BOOTH. Corporal in R.A.F. Represented Imperial Services on a number of occasions.

Welterweight—T. HENDERSON. 20 years. English Youth Rep.

Light/Middleweight—E. BLAKE. 21 years. Represented England in a number of International matches.

Middleweight—C. FINNEGAN, A.B.A. champion, 1966/'67. Has boxed for England on a number of occasions.

Light/Heavyweight—M. SMITH (Royal Marines). A.B.A. Champion 1967.

Heavyweight—R. DUNNE. 25 years. Northern Counties Champion.

244

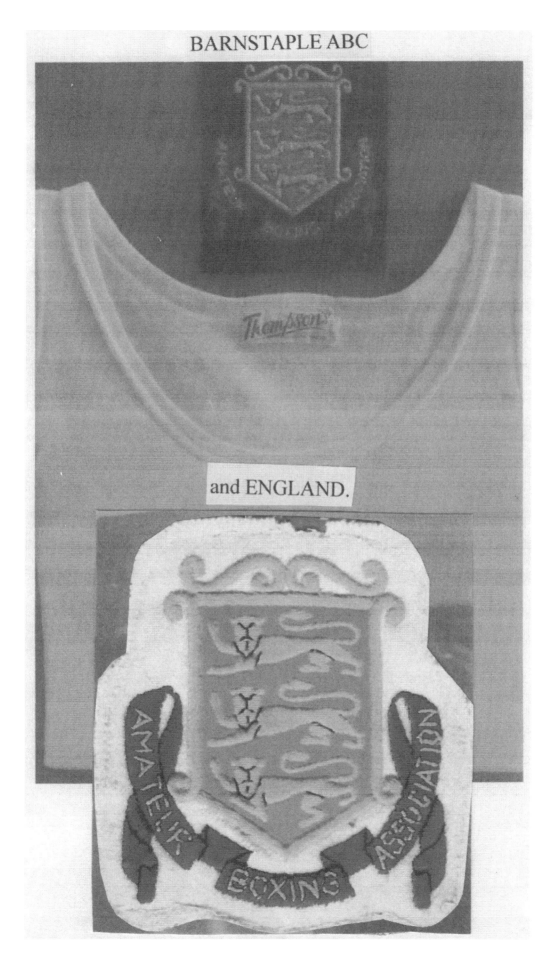

and ENGLAND.

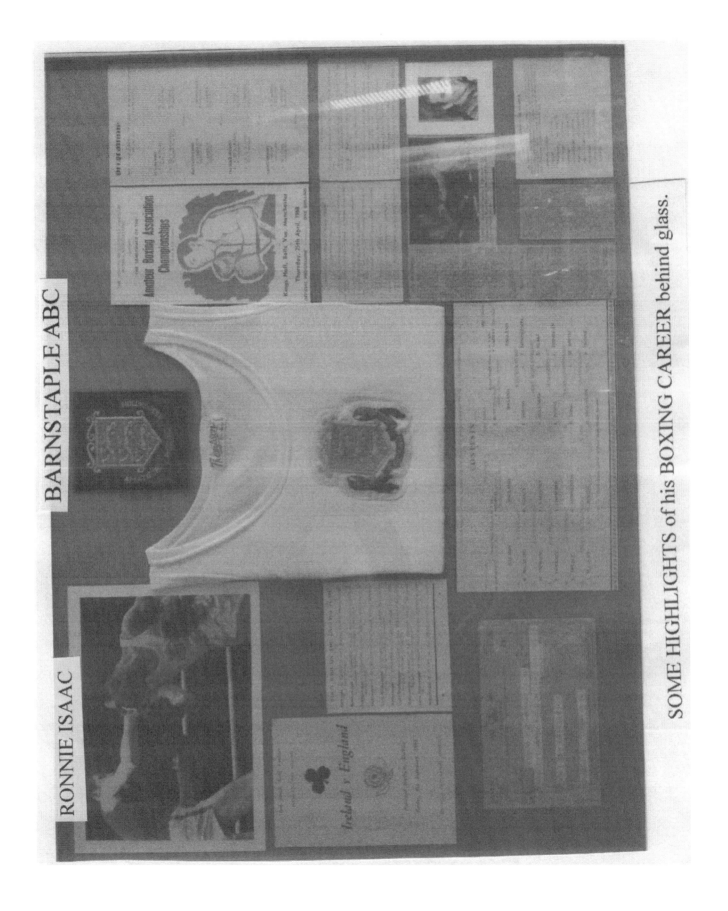

BARNSTAPLE ABC

RONNIE ISAAC

SOME HIGHLIGHTS of his BOXING CAREER behind glass.

IRELAND V ENGLAND
BRENDAN McCARTHY V RONNIE ISAAC,
9th FEBRUARY 1968.

BARNSTAPLE ABC

RONNIE ISAAC

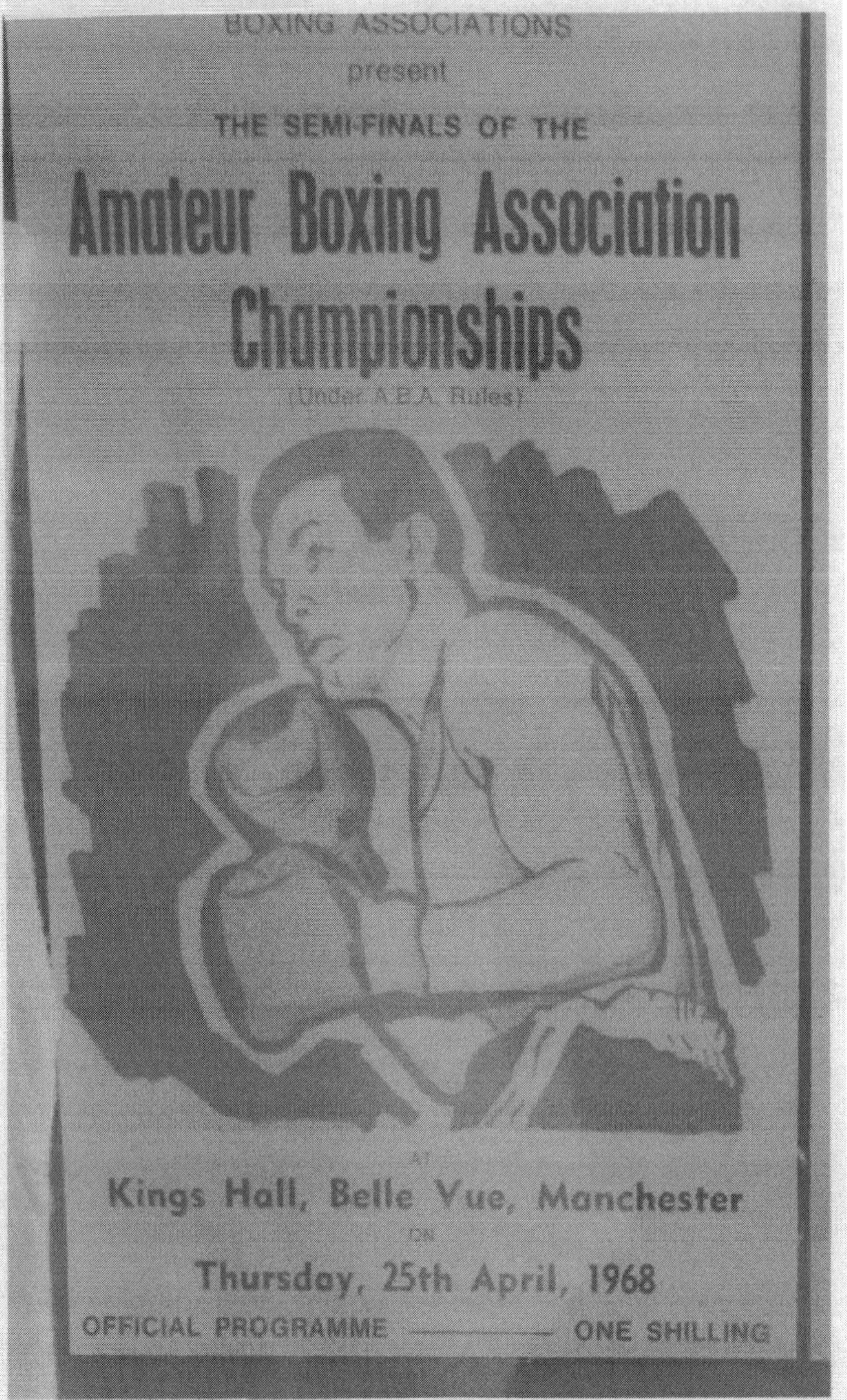
BOXING ASSOCIATIONS
present
THE SEMI-FINALS OF THE
Amateur Boxing Association
Championships
(Under A.B.A. Rules)
AT
Kings Hall, Belle Vue, Manchester
ON
Thursday, 25th April, 1968
OFFICIAL PROGRAMME —— ONE SHILLING

HIS LAST BOUT,
HE RETIRED, 1968.

GLENN ADAIR

The AMATEUR BOXING ASSOCIATION HEAVYWEIGHT TITLE came back to NORTH DEVON after eleven years. TONY BROGAN, also from BARNSTAPLE ABC won the coveted title in 1966. The 1977 NATIONAL TITLE was hotly contested by boxers from all clubs in GREAT BRITAIN and GLENN ADAIR'S victory must never be under rated. His brother SAM, always to be over-shadowed by GLENN'S success, had a distinguished amateur boxing career achieving representative honours and went on to be a successful BOXING PROMOTER. Their father, also SAM and a former boxer himself, had a great bearing on the brother's careers and was certainly an inspiration to both his sons.

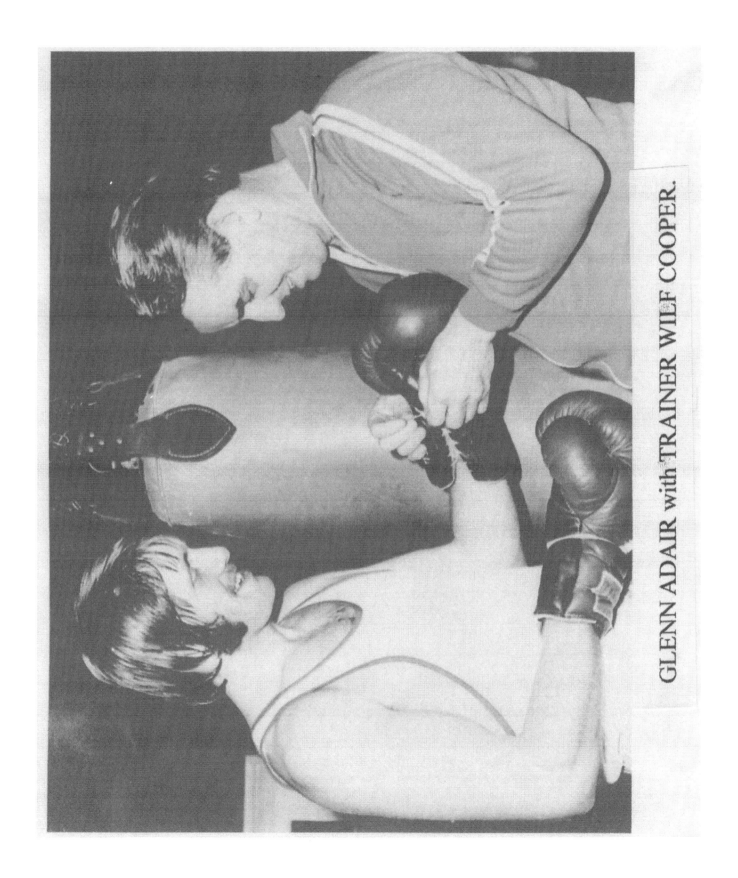

GLENN ADAIR with TRAINER WILF COOPER.

Amateur Boxing Association
Quarter Finals

Combined Services A. B. A.

versus

Western Counties A. B. A.

IN HMS NELSON, PORTSMOUTH

ON SATURDAY, 18th MARCH, 1978

AT 7.30 pm

Official Programme   Price 10p.

RED CORNER
(Western Counties)

BLUE CORNER
(Combined Services)

LIGHT FLYWEIGHT

S. Bailey *WON W.OW*
(Torbay A.B.C.)

L/CPL B. Oxley
(1 D.W.R.)

FLYWEIGHT

R. Jones *WON* — 60-56, 60-57, 59-58
(Hartcliffe A.B.C.)

SEA C. Storey
(HMS Antrim)

BANTEMWEIGHT

J.J. O'NEIL
~~L. Haydon-Foster~~
~~(Camborne A.B.C.)~~ GLESTER *WON*

CEM M. Chance — *WON* 60-57, 60-59, 58-59
(HMS Defiance)

FEATHERWEIGHT

S. Eden-Winn *WON* 58-57, 59-56, 56-60
(Marlborough A.B.C.)

L/CPL I. McKinnon
(2 L.I.)

LIGHT WEIGHT

M. Nicette
(Torbay A.B.C.)

Rct. T. Marsh — 60-57 *WON*, 60-57, 60-57
(C.T.C.R.M.)

LIGHT WELTERWEIGHT

S. Santigar — *WON*
(Empire A.B.C.)

AB W. Green
(HMS Ajax)

RED CORNER
(Western Counties)

BLUE CORNER
(Combined Services)

WELTERWEIGHT

K. Brooking
(Torbay A.B.C.)

RO M. Lescott — 60-58 *WON*, 60-57, 60-57
(HMS Dolphin)

LIGHT MIDDLEWEIGHT

S. Cobourn — *WON* 60-56, 60-55, 59-60
(Exeter A.B.C.)

AB N. Croombes
(HMS Kent)

MIDDLEWEIGHT

R. Squires
(Gloucester A.B.C.)

SAC D. Parkes — 60-58 *WON*, 58-59, 60-59
(RAF Halton)

LIGHT HEAVYWEIGHT

S. Adair
(Barnstable A.B.C.)

AB T. Taylor — 60-57 *WON*, 60-57, 60-56, 60-60
(HMS Hubberston)

HEAVYWEIGHT

G. Adair — *WON* 60-56, 60-57, 58-59
(Barnstable A.B.C.)

SA R. Greenacre
(HMS Vernon)

SAM ADAIR, TRAINER WILF COOPER, GLENN ADAIR.

Out for a run with brother SAM.

ANOTHER STEP NEARER

LOCAL boy Glen Adair took another step towards retaining the coveted A.B.A. heavyweight title with a victory in the English semi-finals at Gloucester.

Glen, who lives at Hiscott, just outside Barnstaple, beat L. McDonald of London's Alexandra A.B.C. on a disqualification and now goes into the British semi-finals at Belle Vue, Manchester on Wednesday.

His performance against McDonald —a giant of a man at 6 ft. 5½ in. and 17 stone—was one of the best of his career and he was well in front on points when the referee stopped the bout.

Glen, who is only 5 ft. 10 in. and just over 13 stone, started the David and Goliath contest at a tremendous pace. He caught McDonald well with his jab and then moved inside to punish him with left hooks.

The bigger man, made to miss with many of his punches, was given two public warnings for pulling Adair onto punches in the first round and, as he got more and more frustrated in the second, was warned again and then disqualified for the same offence.

On Thursday his young club-mate, lightweight Stephen Brown won the second fight of his career with a unanimous points decision over A. Potter of Camborne at Torquay.

Light middleweight Peter Mallett's third comeback fight also ended in victory—over J. Vowden of Mayflower —but light welterweight Chris Brown lasted only until the second round against Mayflower's P. Tuck before the referee stopped the bout.

Adair on top of his form

GLEN ADAIR is just nine minutes away from retaining his A.B.A. heavyweight title.

Barnstaple's champion outpointed the Welsh title holder R. Morgan at Manchester and now meets 24-year-old Joe Awome of Woking in the Wembley Pool final on May 5.

Glen, the first North Devon fighter to win an A.B.A. title since Tony Brogan in 1966 was at his very best against the tough Welshman.

He went straight into action from the first bell, pinning Morgan on the end of his left jab and catching him with some hard rights to the body.

GLEN ADAIR

Towards the end of the round he put his man down for a count of eight with a perfectly timed right to the chin, but the bell prevented him finishing the bout.

Morgan came more into the fight in the second round with several strong rallies but Glen's speed kept him on top and, in the final three minutes, his left jabs and hooks took him to a brilliant victory in one of the best bouts of the night.

The man who stands between Glen and a remarkable double title beat the Scottish champion, Rafferty, in his semi-final. Awome, who bears a striking facial resemblance to John Conteh has been boxing for only three years,

A FAMILY GROUP.

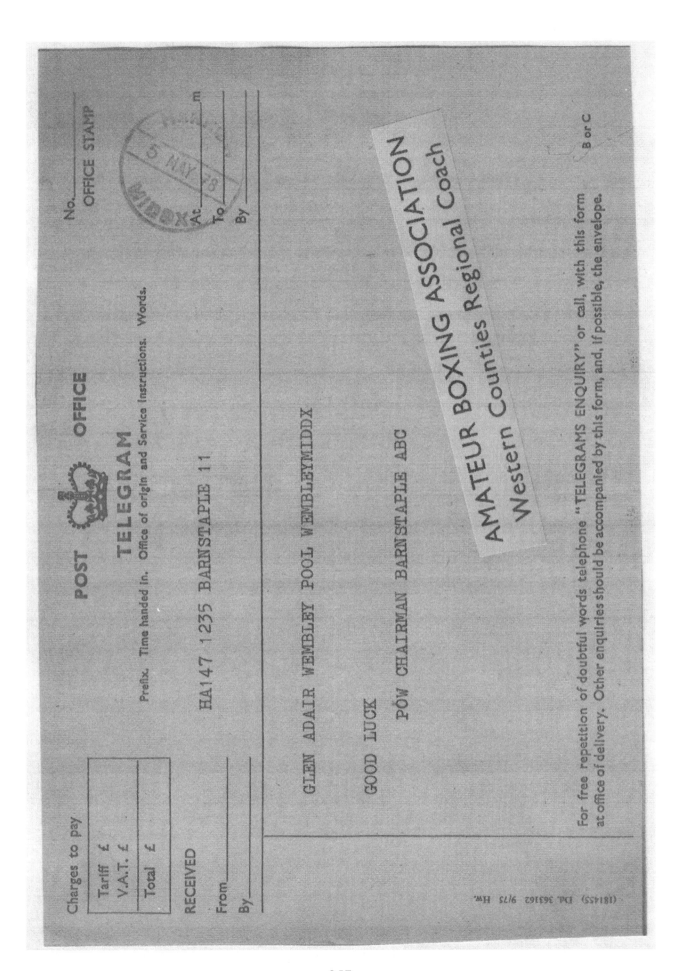

POST OFFICE

TELEGRAM

OFFICE STAMP

No.

At _____ m

To _____

By _____

5 MAY 78 MIDDX

Prefix. Time handed in. Office of origin and Service instructions. Words.

HA147 1235 BARNSTAPLE 11

GLEN ADAIR WEMBLEY POOL WEMBLEYMIDDX

GOOD LUCK

POW CHAIRMAN BARNSTAPLE ABC

AMATEUR BOXING ASSOCIATION
Western Counties Regional Coach

Charges to pay

Tariff £
V.A.T. £
Total £

RECEIVED

From _____

By _____

For free repetition of doubtful words telephone "TELEGRAMS ENQUIRY" or call, with this form at office of delivery. Other enquiries should be accompanied by this form, and, if possible, the envelope.

B or C

(181455) Dd. 363162 9/73 H.W.

THE MAYOR'S PARLOUR.
GUILDHALL,
BARNSTAPLE. EX31 1BL.
DEVON.

3rd May, 1977.

Dear Mr.Adair,

I note that you have reached the finals of
the A.B.A. Boxing Championships. I am sure
Barnstaple would wish me to congratulate you on
this achievement and wish you every success in the
Finals.

Yours sincerely,

Mrs.E.M.Fern.
Mayor.

Mr.Glen Adair,
South View Farm,
Hiscott,
N.Devon.

AMATEUR BOXING ASSOCIATION

A.B.A. CHAMPIONSHIPS

EMPIRE POOL
WEMBLEY

Friday, 6th May, 1977

OFFICIAL PROGRAMME 15p

HEAVYWEIGHT

GEORGE SCOTT, a 6ft. 4ins. Geordie who has boxed for Young England, will be glad to see action tonight. In the English semi-finals at Hull he received a walk-over and then drew a bye at the national semis in Manchester. George is 21 and unbeaten in 13 contests so far this season.

GLEN ADAIR is 25 and returned to boxing this season after a year's absence. He was a light-heavy before his short retirement and has now moved up a weight. This is his best season but his previous honours include the Cornwall, Devon and Dorset title as a light-heavy. His brother Sam boxes as a middleweight.

259

ADAIR TAKES TITLE ON POINTS

BARNSTAPLE'S Glenn Adair is the new ABA heavyweight champion. He outpointed George Scott (Perth Green) at Wembley last night to clinch the title.

Adair (20), trained by his father, Sam, was the favourite for the most important bout of his 36-fight career, having already beaten highly-rated Ricky James and Royston Hunt on his way to the final.

But Scott was a formidable opponent at 6ft. 4in. compared to Adair's 5ft. 11in. frame. Now he is established as the best amateur heavyweight in Britain, the North Devon hope will aim for next year's Commonwealth Games and after that he could be turning professional like his father before him.

Vernon Penprase, the 18-year-old Devonport bantamweight, failed albeit gloriously in his bid for the ABA title.

He was outpointed in three hard rounds by Hull boxer Jackie Turner, and the decision, a unanimous one in favour of the 17-year-old Northerner, nearly brought the Wembley roof down with boos and cheers of derision.

Although it was close, the margin was in no way as wide as the judges made it. A crestfallen Devonport camp retreated to the dressing room amazed at the unfairness, at times, of boxing judging.

Penprase was put down with a short right in the opening round, but did enough to perhaps share it.

In the second, however, it was all Penprase. He boxed brilliantly and scored heavily with heavy right hand and left hooks. By the end of the round Turner had a bloody mask for a face.

It looked only necessary for Penprase to continue in the same vein in the last round to win a convincing decision. Then came the bombshell, and the crowd erupted.

It was small consolation for Penprase and the bout was regarded as one of the finest seen at Wembley for years.

If ever the old slogan "we was robbed" could be fairly applied, then it was surely at Wembley last night with gallant brave Vernon Penprase the victim.

Charlie Magri, from Stepney, won his fourth successive ABA title at the tender age of 20 when he outpointed Mohammed Younis, of West Bromwich.

Magri produced the old familiar performance of skill and fire to win a unanimous verdict, and has now reigned for one year as the best light-flyweight in Britain and three years as the best fly-weight.

If he carries on chasing the titles he may have to decide to step up a weight next year because there were definite signs of flagging in the final rounds against Younis.

Feather-weight Pat Cowdell also claimed his fourth title when he outpointed Ian McLeod, from Edinburgh, but, like Magri, he did not quite produce a vintage performance.

McLeod was partly responsible for this, and his negative boxing gave Cowdell, Britain's only medal winner in the Montreal Olympics, few chances to show his paces.

The result was a dull contest and a clear win for Cowdell, who has been appearing in ABA finals since 1971.

In the light flyweight final, Paul Fletcher, from Merseyside, retained his title with a points win over Russell Jones, from Rhondda.

Glenn Adair . . . happy winner.

260

GLENN ADAIR versus GEORGE SCOTT.
AMATEUR BOXING ASSOCIATION of GREAT BRITAIN.
HEAVYWEIGHT TITLE, 1977.

GLENN ADAIR
WINNER
BARNSTAPLE ABC.

Home to Barnstaple comes boxing's new heavyweight champ

By GRAHAM ANDREWS

SAM ADAIR, boxing fanatic and Britain's proudest father, squeezed his son's biceps and said : " He's still got a bit of puppy fat left, but it won't be long before that's turned into muscle ".

Puppy fat or no, his Australian-born son Glen has returned to the Barnstaple village of Hiscott with amateur boxing's biggest prize—the heavyweight championship of Britain.

Glen, 20, last week became North Devon's first ABA winner since Tony Brogan ten years ago and only the second from the region in 89 years.

A more unlikely setting for a budding professional would be hard to find. Glen, his parents Sam and Elsie and boxing brother Sam junior, live on an eight-acre smallholding and spend their working hours breeding Yorkshire terriers.

But behind Glen, the soft-spoken and animal-loving country lad, is an agile fighter with a left hand that becomes more feared each time he enters the ring.

In the final at Wembley last week Glen outpointed George Scott from Jarrow in a David v Goliath clash. Scott, 6ft 4ins. against Adair, 5ft. 11ins.—and as in the Bible story it was precision that won.

Glen, who trains under Wilf Cooper of Barnstaple ABA, is coached, criticised, praised and willed on by his father. Sam senior, now 55, fought 200 fights as an amateur and around 20 as a pro and knows the game like the back of his glove.

In the fields

As well as a three-nights-a-week workout at the Leisure Centre, an hour-long sparring and skipping session at home, the rest of Glen's time is spent pacing the network of fields, woods and hills round the farmhouse.

After his boxing heyday, Sam migrated to Australia with his wife soon after the war. There, as a five-year-old, Glen had his first fight and taught a nine-year-old a thing or two about boxing.

All through his teens he matured and now looks to becoming British heavyweight champion as a pro. Sam goes one better.

" He'll be world champion one day," he said, admiring the trophies that decorate their living room. " Glen's got style, pace, strength and stamina.

" He's got plenty to learn. But winning is in his blood and that's why I know he'll go far."

Glen's next date in the ring—the European championships in East Germany next month.

BOXING NEWS, December 9 1977

Adair award makes history

ABA HEAVYWEIGHT champion Glenn Adair of Barnstaple created history when he was presented with the Sportsman of the Night's silver salver by Bristol Sporting Club president Douglas Mearns Milne at the Grand Hotel.

He became the first amateur boxer to receive the award and joins a roll of honour that includes Freddie Trueman, Jim Laker, Tommy Lawton, Bobby Charlton, Tommy Farr, John H. Stracey and Richard Dunn.

The club has revolutionised amateur boxing in the Western Counties by bringing top-class sides from Britain and the Continent to face the home selections.

But in its 10 years existence, no amateur boxer had been honoured. Adair was a fitting choice as the first West man to win the heavyweight crown since Tony Brogan, also of Barnstaple, in 1967.

Club chairman Cliff Hill also presented tankards to Wembley finalists Vernon Penprase of Devonport and Chris Sanigar of Empire, Bristol.

ABA secretary Bill Cox presented the ABA life vice-president jewel to Western Counties secretary Len Mills, the club's matchmaker, and chairman of the England selectors.

Dad comes before England

Bristol Sporting Club recognised the feat of Barnstaple's Glenn Adair in winning the Amateur Boxing Association heavyweight championship this year by making him sportsman of the night at their first show of the season at the Grand Hotel on his 21st birthday.

But Glenn admitted to me afterwards that a more important recognition will always elude him. He is sure he will never be selected to box for England.

The reason: Glenn thinks more of his father Sam, a former professional boxer, than he does of ABA officials.

He told me: "I travelled to Crystal Palace to attend an England squad session to prepare for the international against Ireland, in Dublin. My father, who trains me, came along. But when we got there I was told fathers weren't allowed. I wasn't prepared to accept that, so I packed my bag and went home.

"It turned out to be a 600-mile round trip for 10 minutes — and I know they will never pick me now."

Glenn, confident and outspoken, is very much an individualist. "Obviously it would be nice to box for England, but you can join the Army if you want to take orders," he said. "I don't. My father has been with me and trained me since I started. I'm certainly not going to drop him now.

"I reckon the attitude of some officials, who have probably never laced on a glove, is the reason why we seem to have so few good amateurs."

But Glenn's feud with the amateur administration is unlikely to last much longer. He told me frankly that if he retains his ABA title next year he will turn professional. In fact, he will probably turn anyway.

And the confidence came spilling over again when he added: "I think I could do all right. There isn't really much about in the heavyweight division."

Glenn, who at 12 stone 12lb and 5ft 10in is the smallest heavyweight ever to win the ABA title, started boxing at five. He has had 16 fights as a senior and won them all.

During the evening veteran administrator Len Mills, chairman of the England selectors and secretary of the Western Counties, was presented with a jewel as one of the ABA's six life vice-presidents.

The presentation was made by ABA secretary Bill Cox and it was the first time the ceremony had been performed in public.

Glenn Adair . . . overlooked by England.

BARNSTAPLE AMATEUR BOXING CLUB

A.B.A. FINALS

WEMBLEY   FRIDAY, MAY 6

Support

GLEN ADAIR

BARNSTAPLE'S HEAVYWEIGHT FINALIST

Tickets etc apply L. H. Codd (Distributors) Silver Street, Barnstaple
Telephone 2064

Unsung Glenn can score a double ABA win

GLENN ADAIR, heavy-weight boxer from a region far removed from the big-time centres of amateur boxing, has done it again.

In a few weeks time he will step into the ring at the Empire Pool, Wembley before thousands of fight fans (and millions of television viewers) to contest the most prestigious, if not the richest prize in the amateur game — the ABA heavyweight title.

Barnstaple, tucked away in the upper reaches of North Devon, is not a fashionable boxing club. But it is Adair's club — and he has put it on a map which for all too long has been the province of the Reptons, the

Belsizes, the Bristols and Glosters of the ABA game.

Last year Adair went all the way to Wembley. He won through the "Three Counties" stage (the first); then the "Six Counties" — the Combined Services stage — the English semi-finals — then the British. And on a never-to-be forgotten night at the Empire Pool, in May '77 he became Britain's top amateur heavyweight, winning a points decision.

Adair confounded all the critics in doing so.

This unsung boxer, from a relative boxing backwater, beat them all.

Now he is back again — and bidding to pull off an incredible "double." Next month he will be at Wembley once again to defend his title.

Winning through all the preliminary rounds for the second successive year as he has done, represents a major achievement by any standards — be they London or North Devon — and if Adair should retain his title, then the Westcountry in general, and North Devon in particular, have every reason to be more than inordinately proud.

Adair — he has a fighting brother, Sam, who went three-quarters of the way to this year's Wembley finals himself at cruiser before bowing out — was formerly a middle, then a cruiser.

In his years at this weight he developed a combination of punch and speed. He retains the left-hand skill of a lighter man — and the weight of punch so necessary at this "dreadnought" level. He is also durable.

At Belle Vue recently Adair took the final step to the Wembley showpiece when he outpointed Welshman K. Morgan. His progress to the final stage has, as last year, passed by some sections of the media almost unnoticed.

North Devon is off the beaten track, both geographically and pugilistically. If Glenn should win again then he will have rectified things in the most positive way possible.

As was the case at last year's finals, a strong contingent of North Devon supporters will be travelling for the contest.

Of especial interest to Westcountry fans apart from the amazing success of Adair, is that last year's bantam champion, Jackie Turner (Hull) is at Wembley again.

In a memorable final in '77 he beat Devonport's Vernon Penprase on points in the final, a bout regarded by the experts as one of the best at Wembley in years.

Since then Penprase has turned pro with Eddie Thomas. Turner got to Wembley by ko'ing Bambrick in two rounds at Belle Vue.

A NEAR MISS in 1978, but still a GREAT ACHIEVEMENT in the days when all GREAT BRITAIN contested ABA BOXING TITLES.

Devon ABA hero aims for

Canada and 'pro' ranks

GLENN BIDS FOR DOUBLE AND MORE

By GEOFF SWEET

ABA HEAVYWEIGHT champion Glenn Adair boxes for a unique double on Friday night that could turn into a monumental treble. For if he successfully defends the title against Woking's Joe Awome at Wembley, victory could be a ticket to the Commonwealth Games followed by a passage into the professional bracket.

The 21-year-old Barnstaple club boxer is lighter, fitter and more confident than when he outpointed Ricky James to take the prize amateur championship in 1977.

He will climb into the ring at about 12st. 11lb., compared with the 13st. 2lb. fighting frame he sported against James. Two hours hard running over the Saunton sand dunes, plus an hour's workout in the club with trainer Wilf Cooper each day have produced a more mobile Adair.

Speed could be the essence for the 5ft. 10th. North Devon champion, who in Awome faces a taller, very forceful fighter.

"I'm not worried about that. I've seen him twice and know I'm faster, can box better and slug it out if I have to," said optimistic Adair.

Remote

The routes to both Wembley appearances have seen Adair account for 13 different opponents. The ABA's are his only serious competition — his only other fight outside the championships during the last year lasted just one minute.

"North Devon is a bit remote and it's hard to get good opposition," he explained. "Everyone knows that they may have to face me in the ABA's so they seem to wait until then.

"It may be different if I was in London, but North Devon is the best training area around and I'm still young for a heavyweight, so there's plenty of time."

Friday's double title bid could well be Adair's last fight as an amateur—unless he's picked for the Commonwealth Games in Canada. It's likely he'll turn pro in August, but would love to fight for his country in Edmonton before signing any dotted lines.

"I think I'll be lucky to make the Commonwealth team," he said. "If your face fits you're usually okay—mine doesn't seem to.

"I want to go to Canada. There's a fair gap between now and August—and nothing to say I'll sign pro then, anyway—and in between I want something to train for. Everybody needs something to keep them going."

Adair's road to Wembley this time round started with a walkover, was followed by a bout of 'flu before the Western Counties' stage when he beat Alan Hall.

"I was under the doctor for ten days and that put me back," he said. "I'd knocked out Hall twice before, but he put me down that last time. I got up all right and went on to knock him out again."

Roy Greenacre was the next to feel the force of the Adair punch in the Combined Services' stage before 6ft. 5in. muscle man Larry McDonald was beaten in the English semi-finals.

Maligned

To reach Wembley, Adair overcame Ken Morgan at the British semi-finals.

"I like to have a little fight when I'm in the ring and it may come to that on Friday," added the champion, whose battle with James last year was maligned as a slugging match.

"At Wembley you just want to win—it doesn't matter so much how you do it, I like to think I'm a good boxer, but remember I'm usually up against much bigger opponents and you have to show them you're as strong and can get involved."

Adair leaves this morning for his title defence with the Western country rooting for him. His weight of punch, durability and speed should see him through.

Glen's reign ends:
he may turn pro

(MAY 11 78)

THE FIGHTING Adair brothers of North Devon could both be earning money as professionals by the end of the year.

For this week's word from Mr. Sam Adair, father of former ABA heavyweight champion Glen and his 26-year-old brother Sam, was that both wanted to try their luck in the paid ranks.

But he added: "As far as Glen is concerned, he has the summer to make up his mind."

Glen was back on his father's farm near Newton Tracey this week after narrowly losing his ABA crown at Wembley on Friday to Joe Awome of Woking.

Mr. Adair senior said he thought his son had just shaded the verdict.

"He took the first, lost the second, and I thought he was a clear winner in the third. Glen doesn't get bothered about such things, but I know he thought he had done enough to win it.

"He was pleased that he put up a good showing in front of millions of televiewers. They showed all three rounds — the only bout to get such covarage — and it was a good scrap which pleased him."

Elder brother Sam has only had three contests in three years as a light-heavy.

But top London managers Terry Lawless and George Francis are both reported to be showing an interest in Glen's future and an offer could soon be coming his way.

TITLE ACTION. Glen gives Awone a taste of his left hand (above) but then has to cover up as the new champion demonstrates the power of his punching to the Wembley crowd (below).

JOE AWOME on the attack, ABA HEAVYWEIGHT FINAL 1978.

J. Awome (Woking), the new A.B.A. Heavyweight Champion, raises his arms as the saddened G. Adair (Barnstaple) leaves the ring after his defeat.

Adair brothers to join the paid ranks

By CLIVE ANGEL

NORTH DEVON heavyweight, Glenn Adair, scorned by the England selectors after winning the Amateur Boxing Association title two years ago, is turning professional.

In fact 22-year-old Glenn has timed his decision to join the paid ranks to coincide with that of his brother, Sam. Four years his senior, Sam is also a former ABA heavyweight contender.

And the date they have chosen to become pros is tomorrow week (Feb. 7) the day when Glenn marries Miss Deborah Sharp at St. Peter's Church, Tawstock.

Indeed February 7 is quite a day in Adair family life, because it is also the birthday of their father, Sam Snr., a former boxing professional.

Both Glenn and Sam Jnr. have been coached by Sam Snr. "It's always been our ambition to follow in his footsteps," says Glenn, who used to box under the banner of the Barnstaple ABC.

Both the Adair boys will be joining the Highgate, London stable of manager George Francis, who has guided the careers of many well-known British boxers, including ex-world champion John Conteh.

They expect to get their first paid fight in March or April. "We plan to do some hard training in the next month or two, because it's a little different over eight or ten rounds, compared with the three in amateur boxing," says Glenn.

Naturally, Glenn and Sam would like to appear on the same programme, but that will be up to the promoters and matchmakers.

The Adairs, who live with their parents in the North Devon village of Hiscott, near Barnstaple, fought under amateur rules for several years.

Highlight

The highlight for Glenn—who had 42 amateur fights—came in 1977 when he lifted the ABA heavyweight crown. He was back defending it again last spring, losing in the final to Joe Awome, who went on to win the Commonwealth gold medal in Edmonton, Canada.

Sam's greatest achievement in 60 amateur contacts was his ABA quarter-final appearance, losing to Tom "Buck" Taylor.

How do the Adairs rate their chances of progressing as professional fighters?

"At present the title chances are wide open," says Glenn, adding: "Ricky James, who lost in the ABA semi-finals two years ago and turned pro last May, is now ranked at No. 8. Not bad progress after nine months and just three fights as a professional."

And Glenn rates himself a better prospect than James.

Glenn Adair. . . going professional on the same day as brother Sam.

Glenn in the big time—if he wins

BY CLIVE ANGEL

NORTH Devon heavyweight Glenn Adair faces the biggest challenge of his boxing career next Tuesday, when he is matched against British title contender Joe Awome at London's Royal Albert Hall.

Adair, now 22, and Awome are old adversaries from their preprofessional fight days, last meeting in the ABA heavyweight final at Wembley in 1978.

"Joe got the verdict then, so I've got a score to settle," the Newton Tracey boxer, who helps run his family smallholding and dog kennels, told me last night.

But since he turned professional in February, Glenn has had only one contest, against Kettering's Colin Flute in April, which he won on points, Awome, who turned pro about the same time, has been more fortunate, fighting eight times and winning seven bouts — a success rate that has put him among the top dozen heavyweights in the land. His latest success was against the promising Austin Akoye.

But whatever happens — and Glenn says it won't be a miracle if he succeeds — the North Devon fighter won't be unprepared.

"I've been training hard in my gym morning and evening, interspersed with plenty of road work and sparring with my brother Sam," he says.

A winning night for Adair in London next Tuesday would alter the British ratings quite a bit. Then Glenn would be making a choice of staying in Devon or moving to the big city.

270

GLENN with BIDEFORD ABC PRESIDENT, RAY PENFOLD.

....and with BIDEFORD ABC BOXER, RAY PENFOLD JNR.

DURRANT HOUSE HOTEL BOXING SHOW.
DERRY BROWNSON, GLENN ADAIR, JOHNNY KINGDOM,
DB, JIMMY ISAAC, PHIL COX.

Deep in conversation with brother SAM.

With DB and JIMMY ISAAC.

JIMMY ISAAC, GLENN ADAIR, DB, RONNIE ISAAC at a
BIDEFORD PANNIER MARKET BOXING SHOW.

273

PRESENTING TROPHIES.

Boxing returned to Appledore for the first time in more than half a century with Bideford Boxing Club's charity show in aid of North Devon Children's Foundation.

Boxers from Bideford, Barnstaple, Torrington and Tiverton clubs took part in a total of 16 skills exhibitions and former British amateur heavyweight champion Glenn Adair gave his support, presenting commemorative medals to the boxers.

GLENN ADAIR receives his LICENCE from DICK BROWNSON, a former MEMBER of the B.B.B. of C. and STEWARD for the WESTERN AREA.

Pro licence for ex-champion

A FORMER British amateur boxing champion has become the only licensed professional trainer in North Devon.

Glenn Adair, the 1977 British amateur heavyweight boxing champion, was awarded his professional trainers' licence by the British Boxing Board of Control last week after extensive training and interviews and becomes the first person in the area to hold a pro licence since Dick Brownson over 30 years ago.

Glenn's achievement will give the area's talented amateur boxers who are keen to enter the professional ranks a chance to train locally.

"It's a breakthrough which will enable young boxers who turn pro to train locally and not have to move away, which has happened so often over the years and led to career failures," said Dick.

Glenn is now on the lookout for suitable premises to equip a gym in the local area.

Trainer aims to build a champion in his garage

By MARK JENKIN
mjenkin@northdevonjournal.co.uk

GLENN ADAIR

"A CHAMPION isn't made from a brand new gym," says Glenn Adair. "A champion is made from within. What makes a champion? It's that spark when you're tired."

Looking at his Polish protégé Kamil Sokolowski after a punishing training session on the hottest day of the year, Glenn points out: "He's got that spark that will drag him over that tiredness."

Unsurprisingly, Kamil is "very tired" after some brutal hitting on the pads in the soaring temperatures. And this is a long way from the relative comfort of a brand new gym.

Between the mopeds, bikes, paint tins and wellington boots, Glenn is training a hungry heavyweight in a garage at his Northam home.

"You're not going to believe it but that was a reasonably easy session," says Glenn as he rings a bucketful of sweat from Kamil's discarded shirt onto the driveway.

Watched by his wife Ilona and young son Marcell, the 28-year-old former Polish kickboxing champion has pushed himself to exhaustion on the skill ball, skipping rope and road run.

Originally from Czestochowa and now living in Chivenor, Kamil looks determined to make a name for himself in North Devon.

"I have been with Glenn since March and I feel better every day," says Kamil in his broken English.

Does he have what it takes to be successful in the UK? His coach should know.

Taught the skills of boxing by his father, Glenn had his first amateur bout at the age of five.

After moving to North Devon from Australia, he trained at Barnstaple ABC with Wilf Cooper and became England ABA heavyweight champion in 1977, aged 20.

He reached the final again the next year and was beaten by Joe Awome who went on to win the gold medal for England at the Commonwealth Games.

When he turned pro soon after, Glenn was rated 12th in the country before returning to live in Australia.

Sporting talent was part of the family. Glenn's brother Sam was the No 1 light heavyweight in the country and sister Babs Spear became the UK's first female licensed pro trainer for 60 years. They guided Richie Wenton to victory in a British title fight.

Having moved back to North Devon in 2011, now Glenn is enjoying passing his knowledge on to other emerging boxers.

This year he gained his professional trainer's licence, becoming the only person in the region to hold the certificate.

A small but enthusiastic group, mainly amateurs training alongside Kamil, have been going through their paces at the garage every week.

"I don't just want to train Kamil," says Glenn. "It would be nice to get something up and running for the youngsters. Girls, boys, men, women, anyone who wants to train. I do it for nothing."

Dermot McGeough, 32, is a former strongman competitor who has lost two-and-a-half stone since joining the group to keep fit; Matt Jeffery, a former amateur competitor, is now training purely to stay in shape; James Turner, a Barnstaple ABC member, does extra training at the garage.

They are all helping Kamil get ready for his big date in Blackburn. Machaj is ranked 17th in the country, having stopped three of his first four opponents, but Glenn believes his boxer can make an impact.

"It's hard to get big men who are good on their feet," says Glenn. "He's a very good mover.

"As long as it's a good fight, sometimes you can learn more from a loss than a win (but) he has got the skill to win."

Glenn Adair would like to hear from potential sponsors and anyone with a suitable space to set up a gym. Call 07427 565553.

On September 6 at St George's Hall in Blackburn, he will make his UK professional debut against unbeaten Adam Machaj.

The Journal Thursday August 7, 2014

■ WORKOUT: Glenn Adair puts Polish professional boxer Kamil Sokolowski through his paces in the trainer's garage in Northam.

277

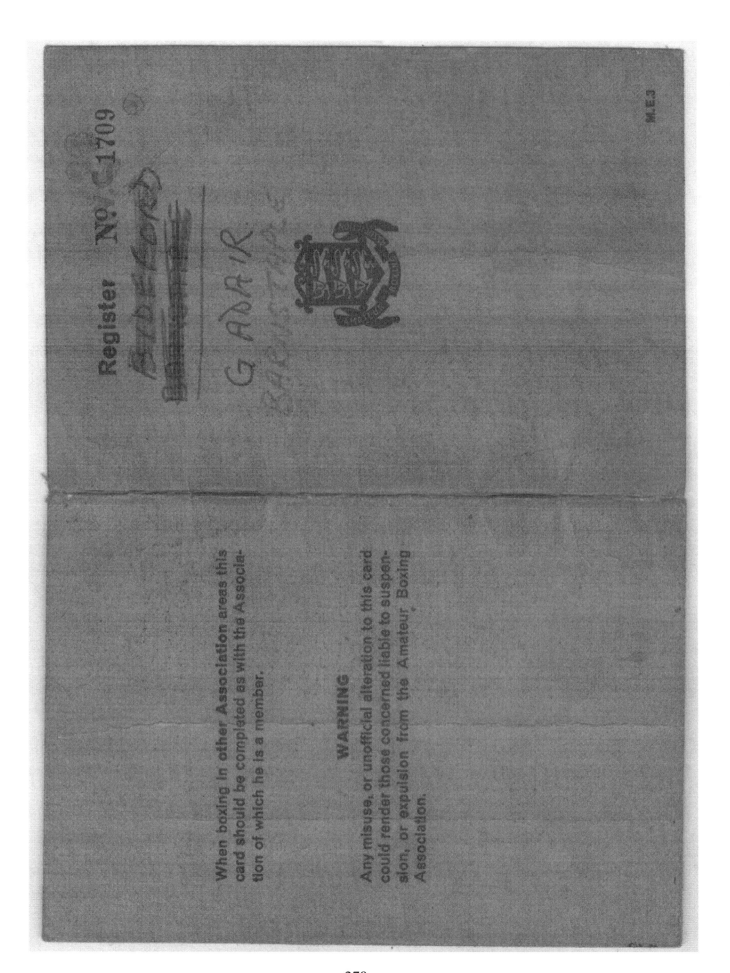

Register Nº C1709

BIDEFORD

G ADAIR
RACKISTAPE

When boxing in other Association areas this
card should be completed as with the Association of which he is a member.

WARNING

Any misuse, or unofficial alteration to this card
could render those concerned liable to suspension, or expulsion from the Amateur Boxing
Association.

M.E.3

278

AMATEUR BOXING ASSOCIATION

Association:

WESTERN COUNTIES

AMATEUR BOXING ASSOCIATION

MEDICAL AND RECORD CARD OF

Holder's Signature _Glenn Adair_

Christian Names _GLENN LEWIS_

Surname _ADAIR_

Address _SOUTHFIELD FARM HISCOTT_

Club _BARNSTAPLE_

Date of Birth _18-10-56_

Parent's Signature (where junior) _B. Adair_

MEDICAL CERTIFICATE

This is to certify that the above named boxer has been examined, found medically fit, and duly registered with the affiliated association as above.

Date of Examination _4-3-69_

Association Stamp _WESTERN COUNTIES_

CLASSIFICATION

NOVICE | INTER

BOXING DATA
For Contest purpose only

Experience prior to issue: _1_ Contests — W. _1_ L.

MEDICAL DATA
for boxers concussed or sustaining injury

Date	Opponent's Name	Reg. No.	Club	Result	M.O.	Date	Nature of Injury	Rest Period Specified	Doctor's Signature
11-12-71	M. PORTER	WC 1704	TORBAY	WON PTS					
22-1-72	A. GROSS	VC 1777	Budleigh Salterton	Lost 16					
25-3-72	R. WALKER	3343	BARNSTAPLE	WON PTS					
1-4-72	E. TRIGGS	296	PENZANCE	WON PTS	R.SD				
8/4/72	A. CROSS	1777	MAYFLOWER	D.S. LOST PTS					
15-4-72	K. W COMBER	WC 126	N.S. GT.	LOST PTS					
12-4-73	K. OUGH	KO 6977	DEVONPORT	WON Premila					
1/10/73	K. OUGH	WC 6977	Davenport	WON PTS					
22-10-73	M. BECKWICK	2513	MORTHOE	WON PTS	JB	22.10.73	R. supra-orbital (bullet by sutures)	3 weeks	S. Khull
17/11/73	G. HALL	358	MAYFLOWER	WON PTS					
30/4/73	N. AUSTIN	WC 12	PLRIGBY	WON R.S.Lo					
1-12-73	L. GARRET	344	MAYFLOWER	WON PTS					
9.2.74	J. VOWDEN	1862	CALSTOCK	LOST PTS					
11/2/74	G. FRANKISH	1448	CHERLESHOLT	LOST PTS					
8/3/74	DUNCELLY	152	EMPIRE	LOST PTS					
20/3/74	H. ROYLES	RM	GRAVESSTON	WON DISQ 2					
30 3 74	T. M GUNNING	36-350	EXETER	LOST PTS					
22-10-73	D. CRAWFORD	WS 7960	TORISAY	WON PTS					
4/11/73	1) CRANFORD		TORBAY	WON RSB3					

BOXING DATA
For Contest purpose only

MEDICAL DATA
for boxers concussed or sustaining injury

Experience prior to issue: Contests   W.   L.

Date	Opponent's Name	Reg. No.	Club	Result	M.O.	Date	Nature of Injury	Rest Period Specified	Doctor's Signature
19/11/75	S. FERRIS	5266	Austin.	WON					
26/11/75	L. DUNN	27510	R.N.	WON PTS					
24/12/75	FITZPATRICK	1647	LEWIS	L/PTS					
	T. PALMER	9996	ClaktonHeath	WON					
10·1·76	A. HALL	WC 1820	Gillingham	WON ABA 2nd					
4/1/76	W. OSBY3		MASTERS	Not PTS					
28/1/77	1) SMITH	WC 1841	Met. Police	WON PTS	P				
6·3·76	A. HALL	WC 1820	Gillingham ETSK 2nd	WON					
42.77	WALSN	18443	EXETER	WON			DEVON		
14.2.77	T. SINCOE	18442	BINCOTH APPRENTICES	WON			DORSET ¥ GANTS CHAMPION		
3/3/77	R. FULLER	34	EASSTOCK	WON			WESTERN COUNTIES CHAMPION		
18·3·77	K.P. HUNTE		R.B.F.	WON FINALS					
6.4.77	K. JAMES	5027	Golly Jah	WON A	M.O.		ABA SVATGER FINALS ABA ENGUSH SEMI-FINALS		
2·4·77	O. THOMAS	3500	British Semi Finals	WON PTS			A.b.A. Gt. BRITAIN Semi-Finals		
15.7.77	SCOTT	2160	JARROW	WON			A.B.A. HONYBRATI CHAMPION		
28/1/78	J. MOXTON	366	EXETER	WON RSR 1					
4·3·78	A. HALL	WC 1820	Beckenham	WON RSR 2nd			Vc SENIOR CHAMPS		
18·3·78	R. Kanner		ESSEX	WON			A.B.A QVATER FINALS		
5·4·78	L. McDonald	5518	ALEXANDRA	DISQ 3rd			A.B.A ENGUSH Semi. Finals.		

BOXING DATA
For Contest purpose only

MEDICAL DATA
for boxers concussed or sustaining injury

Experience prior to issue:		Contests	W.	L.				
Date	Opponent's Name	Reg. No.	Club	Result	M.O.	Date	Nature of Injury	Rest Period Specified	Doctor's Signature
19.4.78	K MORGAN	52,341	MORGAN	Won	P's	A.B.A	Semi Final		
5.5.78	J. AVOME	15063	CHERTSEY	L P/S		A.B.A.	Heavyweight Finalist		

SAM ADAIR...BOXING PROMOTER.

1995...
I WAS a DIRECTOR of THE BRITISH BOXING BOARD OF CONTROL
LTD., and STEWARD for the WESTERN AREA of GREAT BRITAIN.
NORTH DEVON had not seen a PROFESSIONAL BOXING SHOW SINCE
1952.
I approached SAM ADAIR who had always shown a flair for the showmanship
side of boxing and suggested he promote in this area. He agreed.
He first promoted a show in Plymouth and then followed his THREE in
NORTH DEVON. They were a great success. His LAST PROMOTION on 18th
OCTOBER 1996 featured a bout for the WESTERN AREA SUPER-
BANTAMWEIGHT TITLE.
Sadly his extensive business commitments then took up all his time.
There has been no further PROFESSIONAL BOXING PROMOTIONS in
NORTH DEVON since 1996.

A. B.

A GENTLEMEN'S EVENING OF PROFESSIONAL BOXING, DINNER & CABARET

(Licenced by the B.B.B. of C. Ltd.)

THE NEW CONTINENTAL HOTEL, PLYMOUTH

TUESDAY, 19TH SEPTEMBER 1995
DINNER: 7.30 p.m.

Programme
No.

PROGRAMME
£2.00

Programme sponsored by

GOOD Evening My Lords and Gentlemen. Tonight marks another step towards the target of restoring the City of Plymouth as a major professional boxing centre. With feet firmly on the ground, that ambition of mine would be impossible without the continued support of you, the boxing public, and the essential support of the sponsors and advertisers. Given that, the staging of at least two Area Title Contests in the not too distant future can be achieved.

This evening, I am delighted to welcome, as my Guest of Honour, the popular and talented Ross Hale from the Chris Sanigar Stable; Ross should be fighting for a World Title this year, and I trust he will have a pleasant evening with us. The visiting boxers have travelled long distances to match their skills against your local favourites and, whatever the outcome, I know that they can be assured of a real westcountry sporting welcome. The programme has all the potential for an exciting evening of boxing so, whoever you support, I wish you once again a great evening of boxing.

SAM ADAIR

BOXING PROGRAMME

6 Rounds (2 minutes)
SUPER-MIDDLEWEIGHT CONTEST

	1	2	3	4	5	6	TOTAL
VOSPER			W3				
ALTON							

PETER VOSPER v **SPENCER ALTON**

6 Rounds (2 minutes)
LIGHT-MIDDLEWEIGHT CONTEST

	1	2	3	4	5	6	TOTAL
SIMMONS							PTS
CASEY							

JUSTIN SIMMONS v **SEAMUS CASEY**

6 Rounds (2 minutes)
LIGHTWEIGHT CONTEST

	1	2	3	4	5	6	TOTAL
EVANS							
HINDS							

MARTIN EVANS v **DAVE HINDS**

6 Rounds (2 minutes)
MIDDLEWEIGHT CONTEST

	1	2	3	4	5	6	TOTAL
ANDREWS							
HARPER			WRC				

SIMON ANDREWS v **ROBERT HARPER**

P. MATHEWS

Officials as appointed by the Western Area Council

Sam Adair Promotions
PROUDLY PRESENTS

Walter 'Tiny' Green V Terry Allen (World Fly-Weight Champion)
The Pannier Market   Barnstaple   September 8th 1952

PROFESSIONAL BOXING
DINNER & CABARET

ON

13th November 1995

AT THE

BARNSTAPLE HOTEL
BRAUNTON ROAD
BARNSTAPLE

Tickets and Programmes
Sponsored By
The Pelican Restaurant

Picture by courtesy of M.S. Green and family

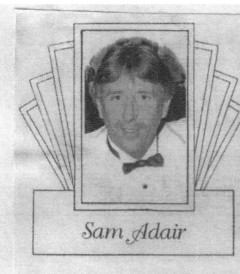

Sam Adair Promotions

PROUDLY PRESENTS

Sam Adair

A LADIES AND GENTLEMENS EVENING OF
PROFESSIONAL BOXING
DINNER & CABARET

(LICENSED BY THE B.B.B. OF C. LTD)

AT THE BARNSTAPLE HOTEL
BRAUNTON ROAD   BARNSTAPLE
13th November 1995
7 for 7.30p.m. Dress Formal

 Featuring Professional Boxing for the FIRST TIME in North Devon for 43 years

MARK HICKEY Barnstaple Making His Pro Debut	V	Selected Opponent
PAUL SALMOND Plymouth	V	Selected Opponent
JUSTIN SIMMONS Plymouth	V	Selected Opponent
SIMON ANDREWS Plymouth	V	Selected Opponent

288

SAM ADAIR and DB.

PRO BOXING BACK IN BARUM

■ **FLASHBACK:** World flyweight champion Terry Allen in exhibition action against local man Walter "Tiny" Green in September, 1952 - the last time professional boxing was staged in Barnstaple. Now, 43 years later, it's back. Promoter Sam Adair stages a 4-bout dinner show at the Barnstaple Hotel on Monday which includes the professional debut of local light heavyweight Mark Hickey, a former amateur with both the Barnstaple and Bideford clubs.

Good Evening Ladies and Gentlemen

When Tiny Green climbed in to the ring to box the World Flyweight Champion Terry Allen in the Barnstaple Pannier Market over forty years it was goodbye to professional boxing in North Devon until tonight. Now the British Boxing Board of Control Ltd., have in Sam Adair a promoter who plans this show to be the first of many in this area and featuring West Country Boxers.

North Devon has produced a number of professional boxers in recent years. Sam and Glen Adair, Steve Huxtable and Tony Cloak who all travelled far and wide for contests. Between the two world wars local boxers fought and beat the best in the country and climbed in the ring with some of America's greats. Professional shows were regularly held in Barnstaple and at the Forresters' Hall and in the Pannier Market at both Barnstaple and Bideford. Bert Griffiths and Pat Sullivan were both licensed promoters who were active in this area before the second world war.

Tonight Sam Adair brings professional boxing back to North Devon and would like to thank all of you for your support. A special mention to Micky and Annette Forrest for the hours spent preparing this event, Ian Holtby for his support, all the sponsors and a big thank you to my wife Anne for her patience.

Officials Appointed
By British Boxing Board Of Control

Steward In Charge
Mr Dick Brownson

Timekeeper
Mr Roger Bowden

Referees
Mr Denzil Lewis
Mr Grand Wallis

Inspectors
Mr David Brown
Mr David Renwieke

Doctors
Dr Robin Buckland
Dr Ian Longhorn

SAM ADAIR PROMOTIONS

Proudly present

A LADIES & GENTLEMENS EVENING

of

PROFESSIONAL BOXING, DINNER & CABARET

AT THE BARNSTAPLE HOTEL
BRAUNTON RD,
BARNSTAPLE

SATURDAY 16th MARCH 1996

Tickets and Programmes
Sponsored By

PRB
Brend Hotels

Good Evening Ladies and Gentlemen

Tonight I am proud to present our second professional tournament, our last show was so well received that tonights bill is almost by public demand !!

So, here we are again and once more the support has been vastly encouraging, with all the many sponsors proving that, in North Devon , we do have a solid interest in professional boxing.

It is because of your continued support that I have decided to accept a recent invitation, from The British Boxing Board of Control, to bring National Championship eliminators to our locality, by way of thanks to each and every one of you for supporting tonights bill.

Forgive me for seeking out those, among so many, who deserve special mention tonight because I have to record that The Brend Hotel Group have provided enormous help in making tonights show possible, they are undoubtedly one of North Devons great family success stories but still willing to provide help where needed and for which I thank them tonight. Also Phil Vanstone, Peter Mallett & gang member Bill James three tremendous friends who have always supported me. Not forgetting Ian Holtby who has been around longer than Tesco's and my special thanks to Mel Green for the many hours spent preparing for this show.

Finally !!!!

Finally to my ever patient wife Anne - who deserves an entire page but, I hope, will settle for a sincere 'thank you' from me.

Lets get Ready to Rumble

===== MAIN SPONSORS =====

BREND HOTELS
WILLIAM C. HOCKIN TRANSPORT LTD
J.V. JONES
NORTH DEVON DEVELOPMENT LTD
PETER MALLETT
PHIL VANSTONE
P.V. PLANT

For Sponsoring The Boxers

PHIL VANSTONE   PETER MALLETT
W. C. HOCKIN & J. V. JONES   PAUL CASSINELLY
CAR CARE CENTRES   FLEETWHEEL PLC
SIMON LITTLE   K & J PLANT

Officials Appointed
By British Boxing Board Of Control Ltd

Area Secretary
David Corp

Steward In Charge
Dick Brownson

Referees
Denzil Lewis
Grant Wallis

Inspectors
David Brown
David Renwick

Timekeeper
Roger Bowden

House Second
Les Booth

Medical Team
Dr Robin Buckland
Dr Brian Malcolm
Dr Alison Diamond

SIMON ANDREWS Plymouth	V	CARL WINSTONE Newport
JUSTIN SIMMONS Plymouth	V	JOHN JANES Newport
PETER VOSPER Plymouth	V	MARTIN JOLLEY Chesterfield
BARRIE BESSANT Plymouth	V	PETER MITCHELL Southampton

SAM ADAIR PROMOTIONS

Proudly Present
A Ladies and Gentlemens Evening of

CHAMPIONSHIP PROFESSIONAL BOXING

Licensed by The British Boxing Board of Control Ltd.

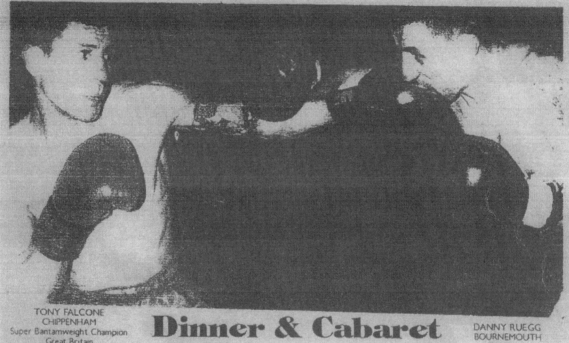

TONY FALCONE
CHIPPENHAM
Super Bantamweight Champion
Great Britain
(Western Area)

DANNY RUEGG
BOURNEMOUTH
Challenger

Dinner & Cabaret

Friday 18th October 1996

AT THE BARNSTAPLE HOTEL
BRAUNTON ROAD
BARNSTAPLE

Tickets & Programmes Sponsored By

Phil Vanstone
P V PLANT

Sou
Prog

294

18th October 1996 • Barnstaple Hotel

SAM ADAIR PROMOTIONS

presents

THE RETURN OF THE WARRIORS

10 (3 minute rounds) of BOXING)

SUPER-BANTAMWEIGHT CHAMPIONSHIP OF GREAT BRITAIN

WESTERN AREA

TONY FALCONE
CHIPPENHAM

v

DANNY RUEGG
BOURNEMOUTH

SPONSORED BY
PHIL VANSTONE

SPONSORED BY
PETER MALLETT

Steward in Charge
Dick Brownson

Referees
Denzil Lewis • Grant Wallis

Timekeepers
Roger Bowden

Inspectors
David Brown • David Renwick

House Second
Les Booth

Medical Team
Dr Robin Buckland • Dr Brian Malcolm
Dr Alison Diamond

Good Evening Ladies and Gentlemen

It gives me great pleasure to be able to promote tonights show. The first ever Championship Boxing held in North Devon and also to be able to promote it on my brother Glenn's 40th birthday who just happens to be the last champion to come out of North Devon - he won the A.B.A. Heavyweight title in 1977. I would like to wish both Tony Falcone and Danny Ruegg the best of luck for tonights championship.

Many thanks to all the sponsors and for your support. I would personally like to thank Tony Rutherford for his tremendous support (a man who will have a go at anything, win lose or draw.) Phil Vanstone for the many hours spent on the phone and his support throughout my career which has always been total, also Wendy and Peter Mallett for their support.

Tonight's winner of the championship will be presented with the Santolo Alaia trophy in recognition of my father, for his achievements in Boxing during the early 1940's - 1950's. 300 fights and one defeat **A real champion.**

Finally

A recipe to success is a short wife with a short memory
Sincere thanks to Anne, Victoria and James.

Lets get Ready to Rumble

MAIN SPONSORS

PHIL VANSTONE • P.V. PLANT

TAW TORRIDGE FISHERIES
PETER MALLET
MICKY FORRESTT
KEITH CURTIS • K & J PLANT

P V PLANT	WEST OF ENGLAND
PETER MALLETT	FIRE PROTECTION
K & J PLANT	LETS GO SUPERBOWL
ERASADOR	COLINS REMOVALS
	ALTER START

For Sponsoring The Boxers

SAM ADAIR PROMOTIONS

In Association With

PHIL VANSTONE

MATCHMAKER
JOHN GAYNOR

Proudly Present

Professional Boxing

The British Super Bantam Weight

Championship of Great Britain

(Western Area)

TONY FALCONE

Champion (Chippenham)

V

DANNY RUEGG

Challenger (Bournemouth)

10 x 3 Minute Rounds
Plus Supporting Bouts

Cabaret & Dinner

At THE BARNSTAPLE HOTEL

FRIDAY • OCTOBER 18th

7pm for 7.30pm

LEE BISHOP

THREE GENERATIONS of the BISHOP FAMILY.

STANLEY BISHOP with Grandson KYLE and SON LEE.

STAN boxed on the BARNSTAPLE ABC SHOWS in 1951 in the
PANNIER MARKET. He previously boxed many times for
BICKINGTON BOXING CLUB.

BARNSTAPLE ABC

LEE BISHOP in ACTION!

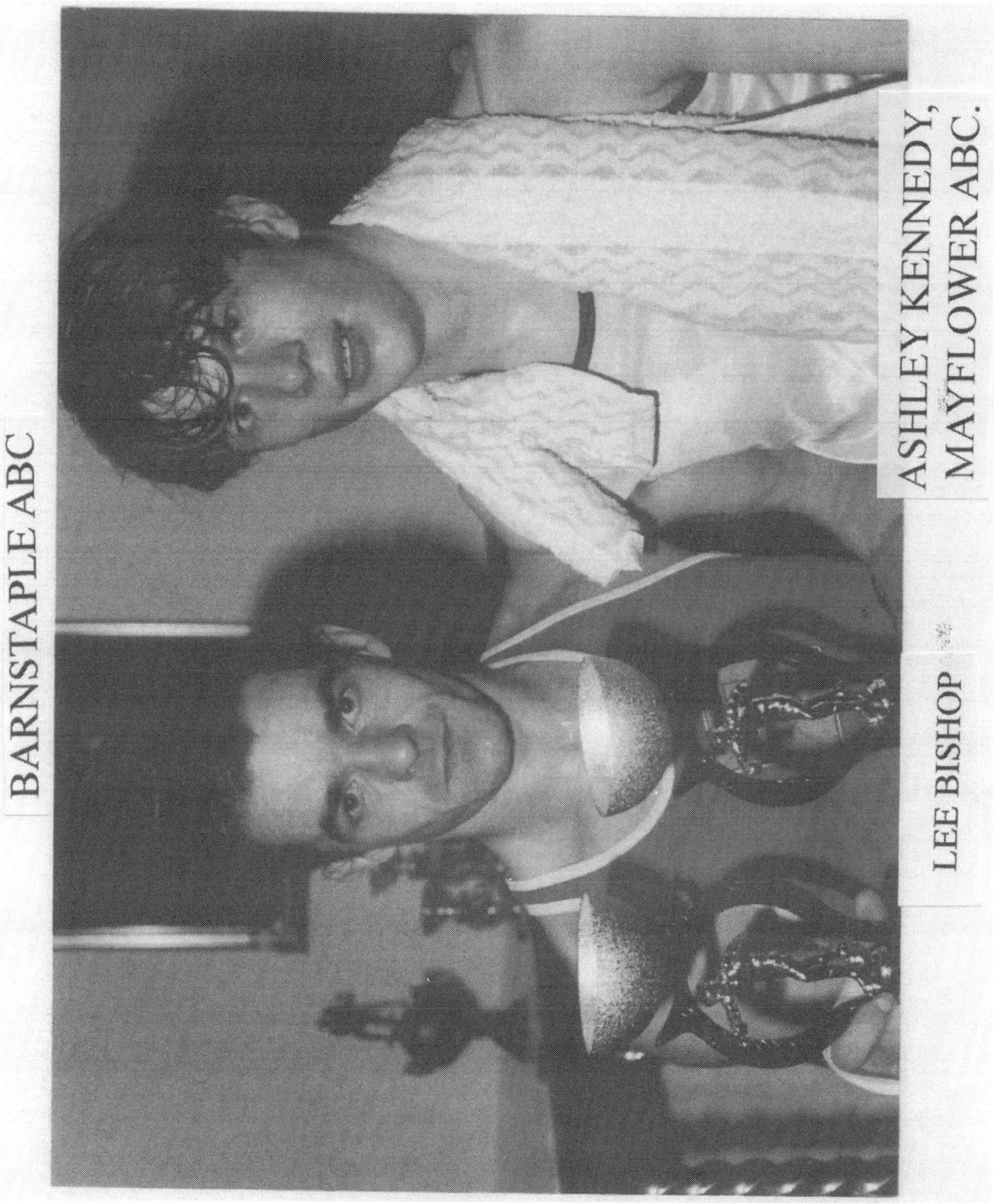

BARNSTAPLE ABC

ASHLEY KENNEDY, MAYFLOWER ABC.

LEE BISHOP

BARNSTAPLE ABC

LEE and KEVIN DUNN

Name of the game

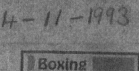

4 - 11 - 1993

Boxing

All over the place

BARNSTAPLE's boxers were in action at three different venues in a week.

And the two who went to Torbay came home with the spoils.

Junior Kevin Dunn gave another compelling display of his boxing skills, showering his opponent S. Watson of Apollo with punches on his way to a clear points victory.

And Lee Bishop also got the nod from all three judges after a composed and powerful performance against T. O'Leary of Torbay.

No luck, though, for Nicky Luxton at Axe Valley. He gave L. Warrey of Devonport a tough fight but got caught by too many punches to lose on a majority verdict.

At Taunton, Jethro Allen spoiled a good performance by losing his composure — and the fight — in the final round against K. Chaffer of the host club and Michael Sanders was stopped by the more powerful L. Leavy of Taunton.

ROCKY HUXTABLE (left) certainly has the name to be a boxer and, judging by his ring debut at Exeter, the talent too.

The 13-year-old Barnstaple boy conclusively outpointed W. Western of Exeter with a great display of quick, straight and varied punches, forcing his opponent to take a standing count in the first round.

Senior Lee Bishop also scored a unanimous victory over S. Gidley of Kingsteignton, mixing classical points scoring with equally effective defence.

IN-FORM Barnstaple boxers Kevin Dunn, above, and Lee Bishop, below, went home with bonuses from the Otter Vale show at Honiton.

Both were awarded best boxer of the night awards, Kevin taking the junior trophy.

He did a great job in beating L. Warrey of Devonport, punishing his opponent with waspish jabs and flurries of hooks to head and body as he outclassed Warrey in all three rounds.

And Lee survived an anxious opening to stop the host club's W. Keen.

Keen came out with all guns blazing but the Barnstaple man showed great composure to box his way out of trouble and pummelled his opponent to defeat with some telling two-fisted attacks.

Barum's Nicky Luxton, meanwhile, earned a unanimous verdict over P. Evans of Cwmbran on the Welsh club's show but there was no joy for brother Andrew, who lost a cracker to L. Brook of Cwmbran.

4 - 11 - 1993

Boxing

All over the place

BARNSTAPLE's boxers were in action at three different venues in a week.

And the two who went to Torbay came home with the spoils.

Junior Kevin Dunn gave another compelling display of his boxing skills, showering his opponent S. Watson of Apollo with punches on his way to a clear points victory.

And Lee Bishop also got the nod from all three judges after a composed and powerful performance against T. O'Leary of Torbay.

No luck, though, for Nicky Luxton at Axe Valley. He gave L. Warrey of Devonport a tough fight but got caught by too many punches to lose on a majority verdict.

At Taunton, Jethro Allen spoiled a good performance by losing his composure — and the fight — in the final round against K. Chaffer of the host club and Michael Sanders was stopped by the more powerful L. Leavy of Taunton.

❖ ❖ ❖ ❖

BARNSTAPLE junior Kevin Dunn was a convincing winner on the bill at Torbay.

His waspish jabs and flurries of hooks to head and body kept him in control from first bell to last against K. Western of Exeter.

But Lee Bishop lost his unbeaten record to P. Kamara of Bridport.

He was still recovering after a bout of 'flu and, although he kept going gamely to the end, couldn't find his sparkling recent form and went down on points.

19 - 11 - 1993

Confidence growing

LEE BISHOP, growing in confidence with each bout, notched another win at the weekend.

The Barnstaple boxer, took control of his scrap with host club Sydenham's A. Lloyd with a battery of thunderous punches in the second round and ran out a convincing points winner.

Barnstaple host their dinner show at the Barnstaple Hotel on December 16.

5th FEB. 94

Boxing

Profitable

A JOURNEY to Devonport proved highly profitable for three of the four Barnstaple boxers on the bill.

Andrew Luxton took control from the first bell of his junior bout with D. Taylor of Devonport and his mobility and range of punches earned him a unanimous decision.

The judges had no doubts, either, about bright young prospect Kevin Dunn's stylish display against L. Warrey of Devonport.

And Lee Bishop didn't need them. His composure saw off an opening burst from Appollo's C. Watson and he had his man down three times before the bout was stopped.

No joy, though, for Jethro Allen, who lost a split decision against K. Ardis of Devonport.

● Barum host the Western Counties ABA Championships at the Barnstaple Hotel this Saturday.

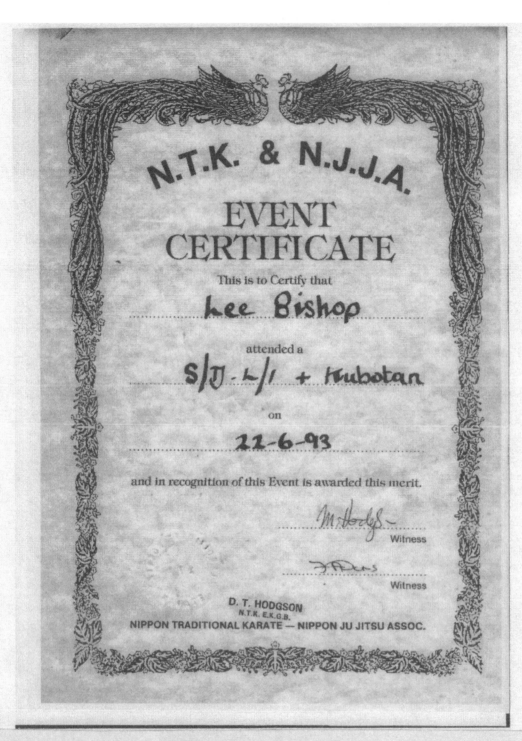

N.T.K. & N.J.J.A.

EVENT CERTIFICATE

This is to Certify that

Lee Bishop

attended a

S/JJ - L/1 + Kubotan

on

22-6-93

and in recognition of this Event is awarded this merit.

Witness

Witness

D. T. HODGSON
N.T.K. E.K.G.B.
NIPPON TRADITIONAL KARATE — NIPPON JU JITSU ASSOC.

LEE followed a successful BOXING CAREER with BARNSTAPLE ABC by adding HONOURS to his NAME in the Ju-Jitsu ARENA.

■ **STYLE:** Lee Bishop (back) and John Pullen of Barnstaple Ju-Jitsu Club give an exhibition of the style that won them medals at the Southern Area championships. Lee took gold in the U65k class and John silver in the U78k - and both of them were awarded trophies for showing the best technique in their categories. CH0046

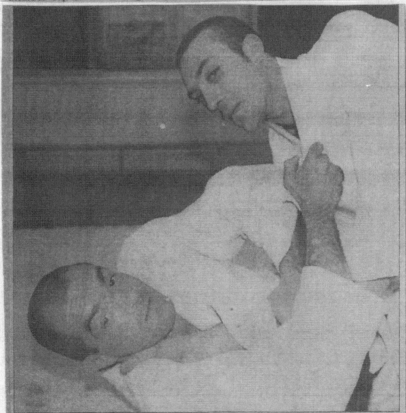

■ **MEDAL MEN:** Two martial arts men from Barnstaple took the Ju-Jitsu world by surprise by winning titles in the Southern Championships.

■ Neither Lee Bishop (left) nor Paul Passmore have belts in the sport - a combination of karate and judo - because they have only been involved in it since January when the Yeo Valley Karate Club became the Yeo Valley Ju-Jitsu Club.

■ Lee, who is a black belt in both karate and judo, won gold in the U65k class and Paul - a karate brown belt and judo blue belt - triumphed in the U78k class. The competition was a first time out for both of them.

■ The Yeo Valley club where they train meets on Monday and Thursday evenings at Yeo Valley School in Barnstaple. i621/5

LEE BISHOP

LEE shows LEIA his LATEST AWARDS.

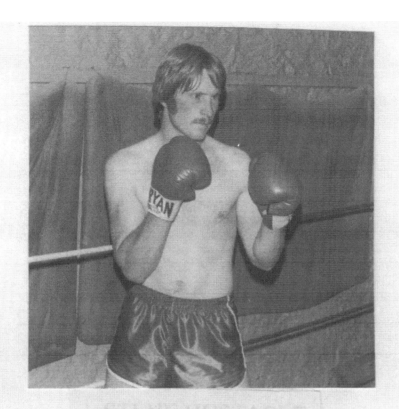

STEVE HUXTABLE

DB, STEVE signing PROFESSIONAL FORMS,
TRAINER WILF COOPER.

TONY CLOAK, TRAINER WILF COOPER, STEVE HUXTABLE.
At the SILVER STREET GYM, BIDEFORD.
Both TONY and STEVE had long AMATEUR boxing careers.
They fought each other at least six times on local shows!

Boxing: Tim Metcalfe reports on new stable

Second fighter signs

A SECOND boxer has joined North Devon's newly-formed stable of professional fighters.

Stable manager Dick Brownson has signed Barnstaple builder Stephen Huxtable, a 22-year-old light-middleweight.

He has boxed for the past seven years with Barnstaple Amateur Boxing Club under the guidance of trainer Ken Manley.

The new recruit is likely to fight his first pro bout before the end of this month, either in Brighton or London.

He partners former rival, Tony Cloak, of Bideford, in the professional stable which was formed only last month.

Tony, a 24-year-old butcher, also fights in the light middleweight division and has one victory under his belt already.

The two have fought each other six times in the amateur ranks.

Manager Mr. Brownson said: "They won three fights each so they're all square."

He added: "I'm pleased that the new stable has a fighter from both Barnstaple and Bideford."

Both will be guided in their professional careers by stable trainer Wilf Cooper.

They could both be fighting in North Devon within six months when Mr. Brownson hopes to stage the area's first professional promotion for 30 years.

The Gazette, November 6th, 1987

Defeat on his debut

BARNSTAPLE light-middleweight boxer Steve Huxtable tasted defeat in his first professional fight in Brighton this week.

He was beaten on points in a six-round contest by local man Lou Ayres.

It was a hard-fought contest which had the crowd on its feet and Steve was given a big cheer at the end.

Steve's next fight is in Weston-super-Mare on November 19.

6 × 2 minute rounds Light Middle weight contest at 11st 2lb

LOU AYRES v. STEVE HUXTABLE
MITCHAM   BARNSTAPLE

PADDY BYRNE PRESENTS

PROFESSIONAL BOXING

LICENSED BY B.B.B. of C

CORN EXCHANGE BRIGHTON

TUESDAY OCTOBER 27th 1987

The Western Morning News

Tuesday, January 5, 1988

Boxing: Westcountry pros take to London

Capital ideal for Devon rookies

by TIM METCALFE

NORTH Devon's rookie boxing professionals Tony Cloak and Steve Huxtable are heading for the tough rings of London to learn the rough ropes before starring in the area's first fight promotion for 36 years early in the New Year.

Since turning pro three months ago, 23-year-old Bideford butcher Tony and his stablemate Steve, a 22-year-old Barnstaple builder, both have three provincial fights under their belts.

Now manager Dick Brownson wants them to experience contests in the capital.

"I'll be taking them up to London in early January," he said.

Middleweight Tony, who has won twice already, is likely to be matched against tough Steve Aquilano of Wolverhampton, who is also a newcomer to the professional ranks.

Steve, a light-middle-weight, who has also won two bouts, will probably be fighting fellow rookie Nigel Dobson of Newbury.

A venue for their North Devon debut in February has not yet been confirmed, although it is likely to be either at the Kingsley Leisure Centre or the Elizabethan Rooms in Westward Ho!

"I would have liked to promote between four and six fights in Barnstaple, but there's nowhere suitable," said Brownson.

North Devon's last professional promotion was in 1952 to raise funds for victims of the Lynmouth Flood Disaster. It was staged in Barnstaple's Pannier Market.

Brownson added: "It's taken me two years to start the boxing stable and I'm very pleased with progress so far. I couldn't have started with two better fighters — I only wish there were more, especially as sparring partners."

Building to success: Steve Huxtable.

Building new career

THE GAZETTE 23-10-1987

NORTH Devon's professional boxing strength is growing — Instow manager Dick Brownson adding Barnstaple light middleweight Steve Huxtable to his stable.

Steve, a 22-year-old builder and former amateur with Barnstaple Boxing Club, joins his former Bideford rival Tony Cloak, who recently won his first professional fight.

The Barnstaple boxer is expecting his first paid fight at the end of this month, either in Brighton or London.

Both local boxers are hoping to be on the bill in promotions in Weston-super-Mare on November 19 and in Gloucester on December 5.

By the spring, Dick is hoping North Devon will have made enough of an impact on the national scene for him to stage the region's first professional promotion for 30 years. He is currently looking for a suitable venue.

BARNSTAPLE ABC

JIMMY RANDALL

The boy with the Golden Gloves

BARNSTAPLE fighter Jimmy Randall has won the Western Counties Golden Gloves title.

Randall was simply untouchable – in fact, opponent Joseph Rees wasn't even able to land a single punch in their scrap for the regional championship at Walcot ABC on Saturday.

And at the end of the opening round, Rees' cornermen opted against sending their charge out for another round with the Barum big-hitter.

As a result, Randall will now miss the next Barnstaple ABC show on February 25 – instead he will be in Gloucestershire to fight the Southern Counties champion for a semi-final spot in the national competition.

Club mate Tommy Hammett, meanwhile, once again proved to be too strong for Pilgrims rival Jamie Quinn.

Hammett has beaten Quinn in both Barnstaple and Bideford, and has now bettered the Plymothian on his own patch as well.

He was in charge for all three rounds against Quinn at the city's New Continental Hotel, and deservedly took the unanimous decision.

■ Tickets are now on sale for Barnstaple ABC's show at the Ex-Servicemen's Club on Saturday week.

Get them from the Corner House pub in Barnstaple, or from coach Mark Simpson on 01271-326148.

Contact the Sports Desk: call Dave Pedler on 01271-347421 or Chris Rogers on 01271-347458; fax on 01271-322115 or e-mail to: sportsdesk@northdevonjournal.co.uk

■ Jimmy Randall (A)

Golden Gloves national competition

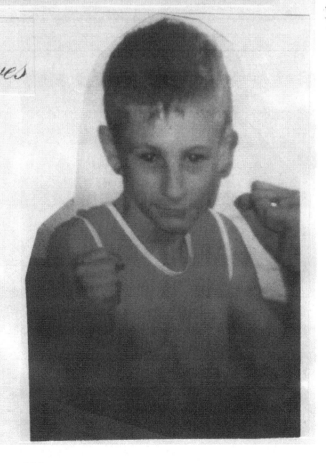

Home advantage did not help **Joe Rees** in the only Class 3 encounter when he faced more experienced Barnstaple southpaw **James Randell** at 50 kgs.

The Devon teenager launched a succession of lefts off the right lead and his dominance prompted the Walcot corner to withdraw their boxer after the bell to end the opener.

BOXING

The boy with the Golden Gloves

BARNSTAPLE fighter Jimmy Randall has won the Western Counties Golden Gloves title.

Randall was simply untouchable – in fact, opponent Joseph Rees wasn't even able to land a single punch in their scrap for the regional championship at Walcot ABC on Saturday.

And at the end of the opening round, Rees' cornermen opted against sending their charge out for another round with the Barum big-hitter.

As a result, Randall will now miss the next Barnstaple ABC show on February 25 – instead he will be in Gloucestershire to fight the Southern Counties champion for a semi-final spot in the national competition.

Club mate Tommy Hammett, mean~~~~~~ again proved to be too strong for Pilgrims ~~~~

Hammett has beaten ~~~~~~~~~~~ d Bideford, and has now ~~~~~~~~~~~~~~~~~ patch as well.

~~~~~~~~~~~~~~~~~~~~~~~~~~~~~ n at the cit~~~~~~~~~~~~~~~~~~~~~~~~~~ unanimous~~~~~~~~~~

■ T~~~~~~~~~~~~~~~~ nstaple ABC's show at the Ex-Se~~~~~~~~~~~~~ Saturday week.

Get ~~~~~~ e Corner House pub in Barnstaple, or from coach ~~~~~ Simpson on 01271-326148.

NORTH DEVON JOURNAL
SPORTS EDITOR,
DAVE PEDLER
spots the
EARLY TALENT of JIMMY RANDALL.

Contact the Sports Desk: call Dave Pedler on 01271-347421 or Chris Rogers on 01271-347458; fax on 01271-322115 or e-mail to: sportsdesk@northdevonjournal.co.uk

Bumper bill as Barnstaple Pannier Market stages show

BARNSTAPLE ABC are gearing up for their biggest show of the year.

On Sunday, at Barnstaple Pannier Market, a bumper bill will feature more than 20 bouts.

After the success last year when boxing returned to the historic venue for the first time since the 1960s, it looks set to be another exciting afternoon.

Barnstaple, Bideford and Combe Martin all have boxers in action and there are prospects from across the South West as well as London and Wales.

Doors open at 1pm and the boxing starts at 2pm. Tickets are available on the door or can be purchased from Barnstaple ABC or the Corner House.

For more information call Mark Simpson on 07749 231121.

Bouts (Barnstaple ABC unless stated): Bailey Murphy v James Stowell (Blandford), Mitch Turner v Wallace Atwell (Weston-super-Mare), Zac Jones (Tiverton) v Joe Henson (Weymouth), Brad Ingram (City of Gloucester) v Jack Barlow (Weymouth), Patrick Morton v Jake Barnard (Pilgrims), Aiden Vitali (Bideford) v Ryan Coogan (Hornchurch and Elm Park), Joe Freeman v Morgan Hart (Downend), Connor Adaway (Pilgrims) v Paul Claydon (Romford), Nico Faassen v Rob Collins (Tavern), Robbie Squires v Morgan Burgess (Llanharan), Alex Jones (Tiverton) v Georgio Guidotti (Hornchurch and Elm Park), Ricky Dymond (Bideford) v Tom Williams (Downend), Liam Laird v Jake Demery (Downend), Becky McMillan (Plympton) v Zoe Young (Navy), Lewis Hughes (Romford) v Callum Anderson (Barry East End), Jordan Jones v William Jefferies (St Ives Bay), Aaron Edwardes (Tiverton) v Dan Ruddell (Blandford), Kai Avery v Fabien Peterkin (Weymouth), Wayne Ingram (City of Gloucester) v Callum Harper (Tavern), Harry Sugars v Rhys Geisheimer (Barry East End), Billy Stanbury (Combe Martin) v Toby Osmond (Weymouth), Kyle Bishop v Darren Townley (Pilgrims), Tom Allum v Joe Smith (Tavern).

■ KID GLOVES: Barnstaple ABC boxers took a break from training for this weekend's Pannier Market show to meet the club's star boxer Jimmy Randall's baby son Ronnie.

Randell digs deep

By CHRIS ROGERS
crogers@northdevonjournal.co.uk

JIMMY RANDELL dug deep to engineer a stunning fightback at the Barnstaple ABC curtain-raiser on Friday.

Randell looked down and out after two rounds of his battle with Devonport's Howard Hart at the Ex-Servicemen's Club.

But the Barum boy whipped his home crowd into a frenzy with a truly gritty display in the third.

After struggling in the first, and seeing his steady progress in the second halted by a fierce Hart right hook, Randell was desperate for a big finale.

And how he delivered. . . he exploded into action and, in the opening moments of the round, sent Hart crashing to the canvas.

He dominated the rest of the round with some rapid combinations, and ended up taking a majority decision.

Randell wasn't the only one to leave his most devastating offence for the finale. Barum club mate Tommy Hammett also grew in stature as his bout with Torbay's Mario Montenara developed.

It took until midway through the second round for Hammett to start using his left jab effectively, and it was a weapon to which his opponent had no protection.

The home fighter then took total control and, in the final round, delivered flurries of blows so hard they knocked Montenara's headguard into the crowd. . . twice.

It was no surprise to see Hammett get the unanimous decision – the only home whitewash of the night.

In fact, there was only one other North Devon winner, and that was Barum's Jimmy Briggs in the show's finale.

He constantly had Golden Ring opponent Jamie Ferguson up against the ropes

■ BREACHED DEFENCE: Tommy Hull comes under attack from Lympstone's Tristan Kelso-Spur at Barnstaple ABC's show. Order this picture at www.ndjphotos.com

in the first round, although the visiting Southampton boxer did enough in the next round to trouble Briggs.

Seconds before the bell, Briggs followed up a rasping right with a good combination and Ferguson took a standing count.

Another one soon followed in the opening half of the third and, for Ferguson, there was no way back. . . he lost on a majority verdict.

In other action, Tommy Hull was unlucky to be beaten unanimously by Lympstone's Tristan Kelso-Spur.

Hull landed some good right hands in the opening round, but was rocked by a stinging left jab in round two.

The Barum boxer then suffered further punishment, resulting in a standing count in the third.

Bideford's Gary Roberts, meanwhile, lost out on a majority verdict to Pilgrims' Dean Coots.

He too was forced to take a standing count, this time early in the second round after tasting a powerful punch during a thrilling exchange.

Roberts' club mate Ben Morris fared no better against Pilgrims' Jason Dann, who used a cracking left jab to claim a unanimous decision.

And the referee ended Chivenor boxer Chris Alexander's suffering midway through the third round.

The 59 Commando Regiment man had just taken his third standing count when the man in the middle raised the hand of Bodmin's Sean Crosby.

The ref also stopped Barum's Sam Baird after he took a great deal of punishment in the first round of his fight with Devonport's Michael Chapman.

TRAINER GRAHAM DAVIES
watches JIMMY closely.

ALL OVER...ANOTHER WIN!

N.A.J. 26-10-2006

■ WINNING START: Stefan Davis-Ross got his Barnstaple ABC career off to a successful start after pounding Dorchester's Peter Pring unanimously.

■ RING WARS: Jimmy Randall goes to work against Welsh boxer David Innes en route to claiming the prize for best Barnstaple boxer of the night (above). Meanwhile, Bryn Haywood (right) was on the wrong end of the judges' decision against Jamie McIntosh but Craig Lavercombe (below) claimed a debut win. See page 67 for the full report.   Pictures by Tom Teegan 071014223 / 09 / 15

The host club introduced the crowd to an exciting crop of new boxers.

He was followed by another Barum debutant, Stefan Davis-Ross, who can throw one big right hand.

His wild swings soon got the better of Dorchester's Peter Pring as he unloaded his heavy artillery immediately.

Pring hung in there for the best part of the opening two rounds, but the damage began to take its toll in the third.

Davis-Ross landed a hard left square on his opponents nose in the early going, and was soon named the bout's unanimous winner.

Welsh win for Jim

BARNSTAPLE'S most experienced boxer Jimmy Randall was in action on Friday night in Cardiff, winning an all-action three round contest against Welshman Ryan McCarthy.

McCarthy tried his hardest to unsettle the Barum southpaw, but Randall stuck to his game plan, moving constantly and landing some blistering combinations to earn a well deserved victory on all the judges' cards.

The prize for Barnstaple's best boxer of the night went to Jimmy Randall who showed his poise and precision in a real tactical tussle against Welsh number one David Innes.

Silky combinations and speedy footwork made for a high-quality bout and both lads were congratulated by the referee for an excellent contest.

After two tighter-than-tight rounds, Randall went into the third with added aggression and he shaded the judges' verdict by the narrowest of margins.

The Amateur Boxing Association
of England Limited

This is to certify that at the

Western Counties ABA
Vs
Home Counties ABA

Seniors
2011

Jimmy Randall
of
Barnstaple Amateur Boxing Club
Was

Winner
60kgs-63.5kgs

Date 20th March 2011

Plymouth Albion

320

BOXING

Sportsdesk: 01271 347448

Randall can join the top brass

By MARK JENKIN
mjenkin@c-dm.co.uk

NOT many amateur boxers can say they have fought in 75 bouts before their 20th birthday.

Jimmy Randall reaches that milestone this weekend and the occasion could not be much bigger.

On Saturday night in Dagenham, Essex, he has a chance to reach the England ABA Senior Championship final.

Randall, 19, is the first senior boxer from Barnstaple ABC to get this far in the national competition for more than 30 years.

Louis Adolphe, of Barnsfield, is blocking his path in the 60.5kg division.

Randall may be in the form of his life but, a member of the Army's boxing squad, he is keeping things in perspective.

"I'd be in Afghanistan now if I wasn't boxing," he said, aware many of his colleagues in the Airborne Gunners risk more than bruises in a boxing ring.

The Army gym in Aldershot is one of the top facilities in the country and full-time training there has been central to Randall's huge improvement.

But there is no place like home and he returns regularly to the less glamorous Mill Road.

Randall first walked through the doors of the Barum gym at the age of 12 and became hooked on "the atmosphere, the buzz".

"It means a lot to me," he said. "I wouldn't go to anywhere else, that's for sure. Stick to your roots as they say.

"With the Army, it's all well and good but they don't know you like your original coach. Graham has been there from the start."

For the last seven years, Graham Davies has been in Randall's corner at shows all over the country.

Helping nurture young talent and teach discipline is the aim at Barnstaple.

Davies said: "If you're honest with them, that's the most important thing.

"If they were rubbish you tell them they were rubbish rather than try to big them up all the time."

Not that Randall, aside from the occasional sluggish start, has needed too many harsh words.

"He's always trained hard, that was never a problem," said

■ GOOD SIGN: Mill Road may soon be the home of a present champion. Ref: BRMSD110050F-001_C

■ SOLDIERING ON: Jimmy Randall, who is in the Army boxing squad, has come through four fights to reach the England ABA Senior semi-finals. Picture: Anna Staunton. To order this picture, call 01944 4000 3303 and quote Ref: BRMSD110500F-0002_C

Davies. "He used to start slowly and he'd be chasing the points.

"(But) he always had the capability and he's starting quicker now."

The new, fast-starting Randall has yet to fall behind in four rounds of ABA competition.

After stopping Ben Zacharkew, he outpointed Craig Ryder to be crowned Western Counties champion.

England internationals Liam Shinkwin and Adam Dingsdale were victims in the next two rounds.

Now Randall stands on the verge of an England call-up that he admits would mean "everything".

"This weight category this year is widely regarded as the best competition and to get through to the last four is an achievement in itself," he said.

'I would be in Afghanistan now if I wasn't boxing'

Jimmy Randall

"If I could win this next one it would be massive.

"If you can reach the ABA finals, basically it's set in stone that you should be representing England."

The head injury that has hindered him since the win against Zacharkew has been given time to heal.

And Adolphe might want to take note when the Barum boxer says: "I have probably only given 75 per cent of what I have to get this far."

Randall may need that extra 25 per cent to get past a man who caused a shock in the previous round.

Adolphe beat Martin Stead, the three-time ABA champion and Randall's Army stablemate.

Do not underestimate the value of experience for a seasoned 74-bout 'veteran' though.

It was only a few years ago that Randall walked out to win his first fight against Tristan Kelso-Sur at Exmouth Pavilions, to the sounds of We Will Rock You by Queen.

We Are The Champions may be a more suitable tune if he can continue his current form.

Randall thrilled by England call

By MARK JENKIN
mjenkin@c-dm.co.uk

BARNSTAPLE boxer Jimmy Randall is set to fulfil his dream of representing England.

The Army squad member has been selected for an England v Great Britain show in Basingstoke tomorrow night.

Randall, who started out with Barnstaple ABC at the age of 12, received the call on Monday after spending time at a training camp in Scotland.

He said: "I was absolutely over the moon.

"It's been an ambition since I first started boxing. It's the biggest honour you can have.

"It will be my 30th fight on Friday and it's fitting that it's on the biggest stage.

"Coming off the back of last year and having one of the best seasons I've had, I'm obviously reaping the rewards now."

Randall's opponent will be Louis Adolphe, the boxer he lost to in the semifinals of the England ABA Championships in Dagenham last year.

Adolphe, who recently won gold in the Great Britain Championships, provide a stern test in the interweight clash.

"He's a hell of a strong lad and fit as well," said Randall.

"I learnt a lot the last time I boxed I can't play into his hands. I've got to be a bit more this time. It should be an interesting bout."

Randall, 20, was disappointed when his bout in the Barum Show was cancelled because he was unable to travel.

Since then he has been in sparring with members of the England team.

"I've had four bouts this season and got in with some of the top lads and good experience," he said.

"Everything is ready and hopefully I can perform to the best of my ability."

● Bideford ABC are to have a show at the Pollyfield Centre in East-the-Water on Saturday.

Doors open at 7pm and the boxing at 7.30pm. To order tickets call Dave Hersey on 07841 846552.

■ INTERNATIONAL DEBUT: Jimmy Randall.

■ THIRD WIN: Jimmy Randall.

Randall wins in 30 seconds

A LONG journey to Durham proved worth it for Barnstaple ABC's Jimmy Randall with his best performance yet.

Randall took his tally to three wins this season by stunning local favourite Jamie Archer by first-round stoppage.

The experienced North East boxer was left with a broken nose as Randall landed a huge overhand left in the early exchanges.

And the Army man followed up with a flurry of punches to floor Archer inside 30 seconds, winning by stoppage for the second time in three bouts.

National titles get closer

JIMMY RANDALL and Jack Langford are both one fight away from a Golden Gloves national title shot.

And for both fighters, the big bout takes place this Saturday night at amateur boxing's hallowed hall at Bethnal Green.

The North Devon duo raised Southern Counties titles at the quarter-finals in Bridport.

Bideford ABC's Langford got the better of Herne Bay boxer Jay Lipton to book his place in the semis.

He kept Lipton at bay with a series of straight shots, and got stronger in each round to take a unanimous judges' decision in the 42kg Class 2.

And Barnstaple ABC's Randall will join Langford on the trip to London after battering Dorking's Allen Pullen.

The Barum boy was expecting it to be tough – Pullen is a strong come-forward fighter.

But south paw Randall threw some good left hands to dictate the first round, before catching Pullen in the second when the Dorking fighter tried to get a bit more physical.

By the third, Randall scored well with good lefts and rights, and took a unanimous verdict to set up a tough semi-final showdown with former Four Nations winner and England boxer George Langley.

Randall ends Barum title wait

JIMMY RANDALL has become Barnstaple ABC's first Western Counties senior ABA champion since the 1980s.

The trip to Camborne on Saturday night was worth it for Randall who faced Frome's Craig Ryder over three three-minute rounds.

Although nursing an injured left hand from the previous week's stoppage win, the Barum southpaw produced a classy display of boxing.

The first round of the light welterweight clash started at a decent pace with Randall finishing 4-2 up on the computer scoring system.

He stepped up a gear in the second, going 10-3 up after landing some powerful combinations and using his footwork to make his opponent miss.

In the third round, Randall continued to move well and score points while holding back the power in his injured hand.

After earning a 17-4 win with a confident display, he now takes on home counties boxer Liam Shinkwin, of Bushey ABC, in Plymouth.

Randall's influence seems to be inspiring the younger members at Barnstaple.

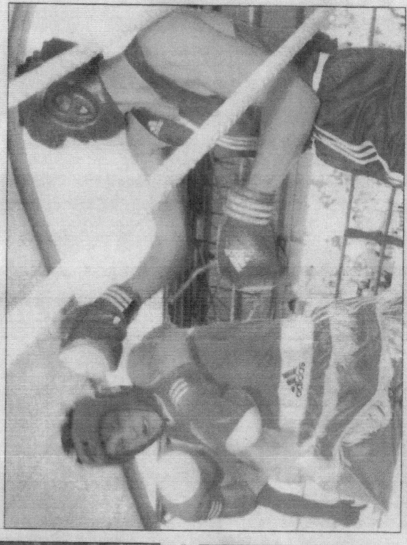

■ FOND FAREWELL: Jimmy Randall beat Launceston fighter Jameel Sandham unanimously in his final fight for Barnstaple. 0805.90.28

■ SWINGING: Brook Hawkins goes on the attack on his way to a majority decision over Portland's Tom Gardiner at Barnstaple RFC. 0805.96.02

Barnstaple ABC results ...

Juniors: Sam Burden (Ilfracombe) beat Jake Chiswick (Dorchester) - majority; Willy Price (Sturminster Newton) beat Liam McCormack (Leonis) - majority; Dan Watters (Ilfracombe) beat Tom Farnthorpe (Tivvy South Molton) - unanimous; Joe Singh (Finchley) beat Billy Hammett (Barnstaple) - majority; Scott Wilson (Pilgrims) beat Tommy Hull (Barnstaple) - unanimous; Jake Langdon (Barnstaple) beat Jake Foley (Finchley) - majority.

Seniors: Marcus Hodgson (Launceston) beat Ricky Prior (Leonis) - unanimous; Tom Herd (Barnstaple) beat Boston James (Downend) - 3rd round KO; Brook Hawkins (Barnstaple) beat Tom Gardiner (Portland) - majority 8-10, 25-14, 17-16; Josh Williams (Launceston) beat Warren Lilly (Sydenham) - unanimous; Desio Ferreira (Leonis) beat Byryn Haywood (Barnstaple) - unanimous 35-14, 20-11, 26-10; Thomas Gormal (Bodmin) beat Alex Burnett (Leonis) - unanimous 17-14, 18-6, 19-9; Shane Goggins (Leonis) beat Lee Slade (Barnstaple) - unanimous 33-10, 22-14, 38-11; Jimmy Randall (Barnstaple) beat Jameel Sandham (Launceston) - unanimous 24-10, 16-8, 21-9; Valantin Bumbul (Barnstaple) beat Dan Foster (Dorchester) - 3rd round KO.

From: Major General PW Jaques

President Army Boxing Association

Army Headquarters
IDL 12, Blenheim Building
Marlborough Lines
Monxton Road
Andover SP11 8HJ

Email: lf-dg-lee@mod.uk

Telephone: 01264 886551   Fax: 01264 886547
Military: 94393 6551   Military: 94393 6547

Feb 2013

Gunner Jimmy Randall
Army Sport Control Board
McKenzie Bldg
Fox Lines
Queens Avenue
Aldershot
GU11 2LB

27ᵗʰ February 201:

Dear Gunner Randall,

Seriously well done on being selected for your country to box Sweden. It is a real achievement to have your second national call-up and I hear that after an excellent and close bout you were the wrong side of a very tight points decision. Gutting for you I've no doubt, but take heart from your success in getting to this level.

Good luck for your next fight!

Yours Sincerely

Paul

325

Name: Gnr Jimmy Randall
Weight: Welter
Unit: 7 Para RHA
Age: 22
Honours Won: England Representative

A GREAT COMBINATION...
HATTON and RANDALL !

ARMY BOXING TEAM RECEIVING
THE COMBINED SERVICES SPORTS TEAM OF THE YEAR 2013
FROM HRH THE COUNTESS OF WESSEX

Randall looks forward to support from home fans

By MARK JEMKIN

mjemkin@northdevonjournal.co.uk

THREE years after he last boxed in North Devon, Jimmy Randall cannot wait to return for the Barnstaple Pannier Market show.

The Army boxer will be back in his home town to take on Lloyd Johnson, of Southampton's Golden Ring ABC, on June 2.

Not since his stoppage victory against Ben Morrish at Petroc in April 2010, has Randall heard the roar of the home fans.

"It will be good to box in Barnstaple again," he said. "I miss it, big time.

"Boxing in front of my friends and family. I get really good support. Boxing for Barnstaple will always have a fond place in my heart. It's my roots. It's where I learnt the tricks of the trade."

With the possibility of turning professional next year, the 21-year-old is keener than ever to impress the fans.

"I've lost track of how many times I have boxed for Barnstaple over the years at all the different shows," he said.

"The British Legion, certainly for the atmosphere, was probably one of the best venues we had.

"Now we have got the Pannier Market and if we fill it, you couldn't have a better venue for boxing."

In the 66kg contest, Johnson, a former NACYP national champion, should provide a stern test.

"We are both southpaws so it should prove to be a good fight," said Randall.

"I normally box at 63.5 kilos but I make 66 kilos a lot more comfortably so I should be nice and strong for it."

Randall's reputation has grown over the last two years with two appearances for England.

He trains daily with the Army at his base in Aldershot but that could change next year with the possibility of a redundancy package.

"If the opportunity is there, I want to try to turn over (to professional boxing) as soon as possible," he said.

"It's always been something I have had in the back of my mind.

"Amateur boxing is all about point scoring. Professionally you have got to look for the bigger, harder shots and you need to be fitter to last for more rounds."

Last time he was due to box in Barnstaple, in February 2012, the evening ended in disappointment without a punch being thrown. His scheduled opponent Tamuka Muchapondwa was held up in snow and did not travel to North Devon.

Randall will be more determined than ever to put on a show this time and will be joined by a selection of the best young boxers in North Devon.

Tickets, at £10, are available from Barnstaple ABC, the Corner House or by calling Mark Simpson on 07749 231121.

■ RETURN: Army boxer Jimmy Randall is looking forward to fighting in his home town of Barnstaple.   Picture: Mike Southon   To order this photograph call 0845 4090 285 and quote Ref: DEVAS3011Q407F-007_C

Faassen gets the decision he deserves

NICO FAASSEN was in fine form to beat Jordan Platt, of Launceston ABC, at the Mayflower Show in Plymouth.

The Barnstaple boxer has been on the wrong end of some tough decisions this season and responded with a classy performance.

Platt was strong and aggressive but Faassen soaked up pressure and picked ins, at times drawing his opponent into a clinch and scoring on the break.

At the end of three entertaining rounds, he took the victory.

Rob Squires took on Callum Belcher, of the Empire Gym, in a fast-paced encounter. The tempo suited the Bristolian and Squires, a southpaw, found himself being caught on the way in.

While the Barnstaple boxer battled well, Belcher showed his greater experience for a unanimous win.

329

BARNSTAPLE ABC

TRAINING SESSION. Four North Devon boxers with but a single thought—the A.B.A. championships—do some training at Barnstaple, watched by their coaches. Left to right: Ron Isaac, Sid Phillips, Jimmy Isaac, and Tony Brogan.

TONY BROGAN, ABA HEAVYWEIGHT CHAMPION, 1966. VERY FEW PHOTOS. EXIST of him TRAINING.

'FLASH-BACK STORY...
it would be great to name them all!

Sixties Spot

BARNSTAPLE and BIDEFORD BOXING CLUBS.

THESE young North Devon boxers made a name for themselves in April 1960 when they won the team championship against South Devon in Exeter for the Alex Mason trophy.

One of the smiles belongs to Jimmy Isaac, then in his mid-teens, who went on to become the region's most celebrated boxer at bantamweight and featherweight.

In 1960 he was already a 12-counties schoolboy champion; later he went on to lose three times in the ABA finals, once on points to none other than Ken Buchanan who later became world featherweight champ.

Now 44, Jimmy is a Barnstaple fireman and still keeps fit, not in the ring but on the roads.

Others in Barnstaple and Bideford who triumphed 29 years ago were G. Yeo, J. Neale, D. Williams, P. Davey, M. Henry, R. Burridge, J. Webber, M. Smith, R. Fishleigh and M. Christie, with R. Slade, M. Orchard, J. Smith, P. Ray, A. Sherborne, J. Spiller and K. Graham the gallant losers.

BARNSTAPLE ABC

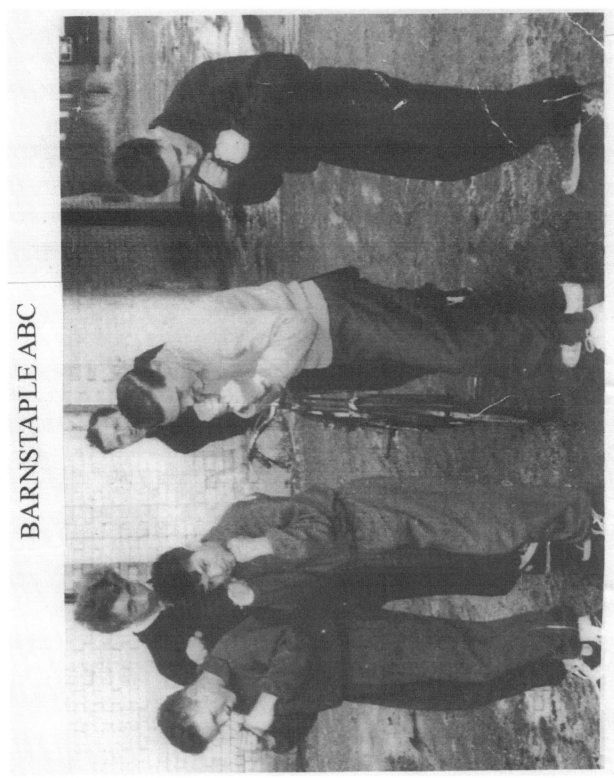

ROGER BURRIDGE, ALBERT TITHECOTT, JIMMY ISAAC,
JIM BARTLETT, BRIAN TUCKER, GRAHAM HALLET.

Not a clear photo, but worth including for the number of boxers present.

BARNSTAPLE ABC

DEVON *versus* NOTTINGHAM at WESTWARD HO!

RONNIE ISAAC, GRAHAM TOOLEY, JIMMY ISAAC, DAVE STACY,
FRED TOOLEY, KEITH BROOKING, JIMMY BANKS,
DAVE SHORT, PETER HAYFIELD, DAVE CRAWFORD.

...off to a BOXING SHOW.

DANNY KEENOR

BARNSTAPLE ABC

On the left, DEAN SAVAGE.

On the right...ROY SMITH.

BARNSTAPLE ABC

PAUL HALLET with DAVE SHORT.

BARNSTAPLE ABC

MARK SANDERS

Boxing

FISTFULS OF SILVER: Barnstaple Boxing Club's top performers flanked by coach Bobby Shaddick (left) and his assistant Mark Sanders after the club's prize-giving.

The major trophy, the Arthur Cole Cup for the club's outstanding boxer of the year, was one of three collected by Lee Bishop — a tally matched by Tommy Simpson and Nick Crossley.

Winners: Fred Fewings Memorial Shield for dedication, courage and style — Rocky Huxtable. D. Short/R. Handford Trophy for best all-rounder — Tommy Simpson. Club Captain Cup — Lee Bishop. Bale Cup for most promising boy — Nick Crossley. Tom Pow Cup for courage — Gary Stamp. Boulding Cup — Craig Lavercombe. Lewis Cup for most stylish boxer — Tommy Simpson. Wilf Cooper Memorial Cup — Tommy Simpson.

Senior awards: Three Tuns Trophy for achievement — Danny Keenor. Senior Trophy — Lee Bishop. Senior club member — Gary Stamp.

Junior awards: Fred Fewings Junior Trophy — Mark Lavercombe. David Short Cup for dedication — Bill Simpson. J. C. Barfoot Cup for best prospect — Rocky Huxtable. Most improved boxer — Nick Crossley. Alex Mason novice trophy — Bill Simpson. 14-18 year-old trophy — Nick Crossley.   *17829*

MARK SANDERS in the corner.

Show revives the old market forces

■ TRADITIONAL VENUE: Barnstaple Pannier Market, where Tiny Green fought Terry Allen in 1952 (inset).

By MARK JENKIN
mjenkin@c-dm.co.uk

THE RETURN of boxing to a traditional venue in North Devon has revived memories for fight fans.

On June 19, the Pannier Market in Barnstaple will host its first boxing show since the 1960s.

Some respected names from both the amateur and professional ranks have boxed under the arches in years gone by.

In August 1940 – three years after going the distance with Joe Louis in New York – Tommy Farr appeared in Barnstaple. One of the most famous British boxers of his generation, Farr stayed at the Bell Hotel on the Strand.

Taking place during the Second World War, the event was billed as Fund for the Fighting Forces. It was organised by Cyril Blackmore, a one-time Mayor of Barnstaple, and promoted by Dai Morgan, a Welsh ex-professional boxer who was also a pub landlord in Barnstaple.

Dick Brownson, a former president of both Bideford and Barnstaple ABC, is a keen boxing historian and has a programme from the show.

He said: "Tommy Farr topped the bill against Zacky Nicholas who was billed as West of England heavyweight champion. Tommy won in the fourth round.

"He'd not long come back from America where he fought Joe Louis. He fought five times in America and he lost every one but he stayed on his feet."

There was plenty of local interest in the show with Barnstaple's Albert Turner, who died recently, fighting Eric Moyse, of Bideford.

"Because it was such a good fight, Tommy Farr gave Albert a £5 note after," said Brownson.

Another all-North Devon clash took place between Ernie Skinner, of Bideford, and Ken Baglow, of Barnstaple.

And Tiny Green, of Barnstaple, took on the Welshman Kid McCoy. Green, from a renowned boxing family, was also in action at the Pannier Market 12 years later.

"The last recorded pro show was a fundraising event for the Lynmouth flood disaster in 1952," said Brownson. "Top of the bill, Terry Allen, the flyweight champion of the world, did an exhibition with Tiny Green."

One of North Devon's finest amateur boxers, Jimmy Isaac, has fond memories of the venue as a spectator and fighter.

He said: "I can remember sitting on my father's shoulders and watching a boxing tournament down there. I could only have been five or six years old.

"It was packed. There were a few seats around ringside and everybody else was standing.

"I boxed there myself in the 1960s. I fought Bobby Arnott from Mayflower in Plymouth. He was a good lad, a good boxer and I beat him but it was a very close bout."

It was the only time Isaac, who went on to represent England seven times, boxed at the market. Later his big shows in Barnstaple were hosted at the Queen's Theatre where on one occasion more than 200 people were turned away, unable to get a ticket.

Isaac and Arnott had the opportunity to reminisce last year after a chance meeting at a boxing reunion in Wales.

The new generation of North Devon boxers will develop their own rivalries and friendships at next week's show.

Some of the area's best young boxers are expected to be in action with up to 20 bouts scheduled for the Sunday afternoon meeting.

Tickets cost £10 and can be ordered from the club on Mill Road or from Sarah Simpson on 01271 345638.

North Devon Journal-Herald   June 26, 1986

BOXING

CLUB'S NEW PRESIDENT

A GREAT HONOUR for me to become PRESIDENT of BARNSTAPLE ABC. KEITH ABRAHAM had done a tremendous job.

DICK BROWNSON, until recently the landlord of the Royal Exchange, is the new president of Barnstaple Boxing Club.

Mr Brownson, who takes over from Keith Abraham, has been involved in boxing for over 30 years and during his seven years in the Joy Street pub it became a meeting place for everyone interested in the sport.

The top trophies at the Boxing Club's presentation evening went to Dave Short as the outstanding junior and Steve Huxtable, the outstanding senior.

Other trophy winners were: Junior - Barnstaple Amateur Sporting Cup — Robert Shaddick; Ken Williams Memorial Cup — Wayne Sheppard; Best Junior Member Cup — Steve Bailey; Alex Mason Trophy for courage — Danny Keenor; Bales Cup (most promising junior) — John Roberts; J. C. Barfoot Cup (best prospect) — Kelly Roberts; Dave Short Cup (dedication) — Billy Hayward.

Senior: Arthur Coles Cup (most improved boxer) — Mark Saunders; BABC Cup (best senior member) — Mark Hutchings; Tom Lewis Cup (best stylist) — Darren Todd; Tom Powe Cup (courage) — Paul Hallett; Tom Barrow Trophy (best first year novice) — Shaun Hopkins.

Tom Powe, who retired as club chairman, was made a life vice-president and presented with some cut glass to mark his 20 years service with the club, and the club's long time MC, Ron Herniman, was also made a vice-president.

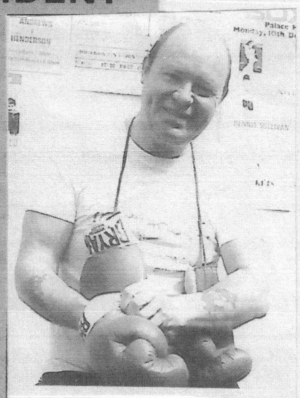

Honorary Burgess Keith Abraham with town mayor Lesley Brown

BARNSTAPLE AMATEUR BOXING CLUB
(Affiliated to the A.B.A. and N.A.B.C.)
President : RICHARD BROWNSON Esq.

CHAIRMAN
Mr. M. Davis
11 Wrafton Road,
Braunton.

VICE CHAIRMAN
Mr. J. Todd
37 John Smale Road,
Barnstaple.
Telephone 76349

HON. SECRETARY
Mr. J. Xavier
5 South Molton Street,
Chulmleigh
Telephone 80558

HON. TREASURER
Mrs. L. Davis
11 Wrafton Road,
Braunton.
Telephone 813578

COMPETITION SECRETARY (Club Coach)
Mr. K. Manley, 42 Weirside Way, Silver Leat Estate, Barnstaple.
Telephone 71012

16th February, 1988

BOXING TOURNAMENT - DINNER - CABARET

The event will take place at the Barnstaple Motel, Braunton Road on
Wednesday the 9th of March, 1988.

Tickets are now available from Mr. J. Facey, Edward Thomas, 30 Joy Street,
Barnstaple.

CABARET: EXOTIC DANCER: Nina
                  COMEDIAN: Mike Swan

Your sponsorship would be appreciated.

Dinner Jackets or suits to be worn.

We regret that no refunds can be made.

J. Xavier
Secretary

R.A.O.R.

MEN ONLY

BARNSTAPLE Boxing Club is 30 years old this year and our picture shows some of the young men who hope to follow in the footsteps of past champions.

Canadian Alex Mason founded the club and, in the early days, he, Jim Bartlett, Fred Knill and Wilf Cooper coached the town's boxers in the secondary school gym in Vicarage Street.

The Isaac brothers were among the early successes. Jimmy was a youth champion in 1961, going on to box seven times for England, and Ron won an England vest in 1968.

In between them, Barnstaple produced Devon's first ABA heavyweight champion, Tony Brogan, in 1966 and his achievement was matched, 10 years later by Glen Adair.

Mike Bayliss was an ABA semi-finalist in 1970, Dave Barrow a quarter-finalist in 1978 and among the club's Western Counties champions have been Sid Phillips, Dave Short, Peter Mallett and Sam Adair.

The club's current crop of hopefuls train three nights a week under Ken Manley and Dave Short at the North Devon Leisure Centre and in the picture are (L to R): standing — K. Manley, D. Short jnr, A. Hickey (committee), D. Keenor, N. Squire, F. Huxtable (committee), S. Huxtable, M. Hickey, G. Xavier, D. Short snr; kneeling — B. Hayward, K. Saunders.

In the preliminary round of the Devon Schoolboy Championships three Barum boys, D. Keenor, S. Bailey and D. Short had byes through to the finals but B. Hayward was beaten on points by J. Glasser of Paignton.

The next Barnstaple club tournament is at the Barnstaple Motel on Saturday.

Barnstaple's Robert Shaddick (left) forces Eric Kelly of Bideford into a corner before the referee stopped their bout in his favour.

Six memorable minutes

SIX memorable minutes of skill, strength and bravery climaxed Barnstaple Boxing Club's dinner show at the Barnstaple Motel, writes DAVE PEDLER.

The final bout of the night matched local favourite Paul Hallett with Exmouth middleweight Steve Cockayne, and what a contest they produced!

Cockayne's lightning jab and super skills left Hallett red-faced — literally — and bemused after two rounds of torment.

But the Barnstaple boxer somehow summoned up reserves of strength and character to match his elusive opponent blow for blow in a marvellous last two minutes of non-stop action.

He couldn't prevent Cockayne winning a unanimous points decision but no two fighters have been more deserving of the standing ovations they received.

Barum had only two other boxers on the bill . . . and both won against opponents from Bideford.

Robert Shaddick's two-fisted attack quickly persuaded the referee to stop his bout with Eric Kelly in the opening round and, in a lively schoolboy bout, Mike Tipper won a unanimous decision against John Stevenson.

The rest of the bill — high on endeavour but with little for the purist to savour — was a tale of woe for an eight-strong team from the RAF.

Seven of their men met defeat in one form or another and it was left to Geordie Taylor to salvage their honour with a thundering right hand which lifted Exeter welterweight Kevin Mitchell off his feet and laid him out in the first round.

Boxing

A TRIO OF TITLES

THREE Barum schoolboys won Western Counties titles at Paignton on Saturday — two with first round stoppages and the third by a majority verdict at the end of a gruelling battle.

It was Danny Keenor who earned his triumph the hard way, showing tremendous courage and strength after recovering from a bout of 'flu in the week leading up to his fight in the senior 60kg class.

He was peppered by a series of stabbing left jabs from S. Press of Weston-super-Mare early in the first round but walked through the punches to land his own solid right hands and left hooks.

The action stayed fast and furious through the second round, in which Keenor had his opponent back-pedalling under a non-stop onslaught.

And, in the third, he threw caution to the winds, calling on all his strength to survive a standing count and take the verdict with a gutsy display of in-fighting.

Two previous byes in the junior A 54kg class meant that Jason Orton was having his first bout in the schoolboy championships — and he made short work of it, too.

After weathering an early attack from A. Holyday of Swindon he had his opponent wilting under a barrage of right hands and the towel came in from the Swindon corner after only 30 seconds.

Billy Hayward's junior B 51kg progress was almost as swift. He put A. Derrick of Taunton down for an eight count early in the opening round and another furious attack quickly persuaded thereferee to step in and stop the fight.

All three boys will be on Barnstaple Boxing Club's 18-bout bill at the Barnstaple Motel on Saturday and the next stage of the schoolboy championships is the quarter-finals at Bovington in Dorset on February 27.

DANNY KEENOR

JASON ORTON

BILLY HAYWARD

346

GARTH GOSS, CHAIRMAN of BARNSTAPLE ABC presents DB with an ENGRAVED TANKARD for his CONTRIBUTION to the CLUB during his time as PRESIDENT.

❏ THE Grand Boxing Tournament at the North Devon Leisure Centre will be featuring these three star boxers from the Barnstaple Boxing Club.

Stuart James, Daniel Keenor and Mike Tipper are all tipped as favourites for the tourament which will be attracting boxers from all over the Western Counties and Wales. From left: Stuart James, Daniel Keenor and Mike Tipper.

Boxing 17-OCT-92
AXMINSTER,

On his way to the top

STUART JAMES is a boxer on his way to the top.

The Barnstaple bantamweight made his senior debut at Bridport and soon showed the style which makes him one of the most exciting prospects in the West of England.

James's confidence and punching power swept him to a unanimous points victory over the more experienced N. Ware of Weston-super-Mare.

His club-mate Nicky Luxton, meanwhile, got the same verdict over P. Austin of Saxon on the Axe Valley bill.

His long reach and superior technique was too much for his opponent.

Boys' bill

BARNSTAPLE Boxing Club host the Western Counties Schoolboy championships next month.

And their own Mike Tipper will be on the bill at the Barnstaple Motel on February 15.

Danny Keenor, who begins his bid for an ABA title seven days earlier, stepped into a ring for the first time this season at Devonport.

And he climbed out again only a few minutes later after stopping R. Carless of Colyton in the second round.

Club-mate Dave Short, though, lost to J. Glasser of Paignton.

Andrew Davies scored a fine win over D. Graham of the Army at Newquay, where Darren Horsman was out-pointed in an action-packed bout with A. Hurt of Truro.

Davies, though, was pipped on points by M. Mills of Saltash on Saturday's Plymouth bill.

And the Barum flag was flown by Nicky Luxton, whose two-fisted attack ended the challenge of B. Lane of Taunton in the opening round.

Boxing

Double at Devonport

BARNSTAPLE Boxing Club have ended their season with a successful double-hander at Devonport.

First on was N. Luxton who, showing great technique and skill, won all three rounds against local opponent J. Carmichael.

Then J. Allen got back to winning ways. Showing courage in a hard-fought contest, he gained a split decision over M. McGarry, also from Devonport.

● The club's AGM will be held at Barnstaple Hotel on June 17 (7.30).

Boxing

IN-FORM Barnstaple boxers Kevin Dunn, above, and Lee Bishop, below, went home with bonuses from the Otter Vale show at Honiton.

Both were awarded best boxer of the night awards, Kevin taking the junior trophy.

He did a great job in beating L. Warrey of Devonport, punishing his opponent with waspish jabs and flurries of hooks to head and body as he outclassed Warrey in all three rounds.

And Lee survived an anxious opening to stop the host club's W. Keen.

Keen came out with all guns blazing but the Barnstaple man showed great composure to box his way out of trouble and pummelled his opponent to defeat with some telling two-fisted attacks.

Barum's Nicky Luxton, meanwhile, earned a unanimous verdict over P. Evans of Cwmbran on the Welsh club's show but there was no joy for brother Andrew, who lost a cracker to L. Brook of Cwmbran.

Boxing

Barum boy wins West title

TWO Barnstaple boxers were in action at the Western Counties schoolboy finals at Gloucester and one of them came home with a title.

N. Luxton's ability dominated every round as he outpointed Walcot's J. Evans.

But club-mate J. Allen, although full of aggression and skill, lost a majority decision to N. Wyatt of Bronx ABC after being warned for careless use of his head.

Boxing

Danny in the England squad

DANNY KEENOR has fought his way into the Young England squad.

The Barnstaple light-heavyweight's hard work over the season paid dividends when he was called up to box for his country in Bedfordshire on May 11.

And he celebrated with another great display on Friday to notch another victory over Welsh international C. Beck.

Danny was one of five Barum boxers in action at Aberavon and showed all his well known aggression in the re-match against a man he recently beat on home ground.

His power and skill wore down the Welshman, forc-

Nicky on points

NICKY LUXTON fought his way into the second round of the Schoolboys championships by notching a second win over Saxon's D. Edwards.

The Barnstaple youngster, under the watchful eye of new club coach Andrew Davies, lost the first round of the intermediate 48k bout at Plymouth.

But a powerful jab and plenty of determination saw him through.

Clubmates J. Allen (Class B, 51k) and M. Jefferies (Senior 66k) were also at the championship event, but neither saw action.

Allen went through on a bye and Jefferies was withdraw because his prospective opponent was too experienced for him.

DANNY KEENOR

ing him to take a standing count in round two, before destroying him in the final round, when the referee stepped in to save Beck from further punishment.

Barum's other winner on the night was Jethro Allen, who retained his unbeaten record by skilfully out-boxing J. Whitbread of Pembroke in all three rounds.

Nicky Luxton lost a close contest to G. Westacott of the Gwent Swansea club; Matthew Jeffery was beaten by Westacott's club-mate P. Ireland and Stuart James put up a great display before being pipped by Welsh international H. Jones.

Skilful and stylish

A SKILFUL and stylish display by Nicky Luxton earned the Barnstaple youngster victory at Devonport.

He dominated and outboxed L. Warrey of the host club from the first bell to warrant a conclusive points verdict.

Nicky's brother Neil and Dale Webber were also on the bill, but both missed out in close decisions.

Neil worked hard against J. Dart of Devonport and Dale surrendered his unbeaten record this season despite showing good footwork and aggression against C. Williams of Coed Eva.

BARNSTAPLE ABC

Little Stephen Bailey of Barnstaple (right) makes Bideford's Andy Butler flinch on his way to a second round victory on Barnstaple Boxing Club's bill on Saturday.

Barum boxers emerged with six wins in the nine contests, the quickest being light middleweight Stephen Huxtable's first round knock-out of C. Cox of Exeter.

Other results: Steve Davis (Barnstaple) beat H. Pettifer (Bideford) on points; Eddie Laing (Barnstaple) lost to R. Tully (Watchet) on points; Robert Shaddick (Barnstaple) lost to Gavin Dawkins (Lynton) on points; Michael Roode (Barnstaple) beat G. McGahey (Exeter) on points; Mark Taylor (Barnstaple) lost to G. Wright (Exmouth) on points; Mark Hutchins (Barnstaple) beat M. Hanley (Exeter) on points; Paul Hallett (Barnstaple) beat M. Wilson (Combe Martin) on points.

Another picture from the evening's boxing appears on page 35.

Five county champs

Five North Devon boys have won Devon schoolboy boxing titles.

Paul Coleman of Lynton and the Combe Martin pair, Shaun Doyle and Matt Theobold, had byes in the finals of the championships at Plymouth on Friday.

But the other two, Andrew Macdonald-Brown of Lynton and Dave Short of Barnstaple, both scored convincing victories.

Macdonald-Brown stopped his opponent, J. Collier of Plymouth in the first round and Short's power persuaded the referee to stop his bout with A. Davis of Devonport in the second round.

All five boys fight for the Devon and Cornwall titles in Cornwall tomorrow night.

CYMER AVON AMATEUR
BOXING CLUB

presents

Grand
Amateur Boxing
Dinner

(under WABA rules)

at the

Aberafan Hotel

on

Friday 24th April 1992

Dinner served 7 p.m. for 7.30 p.m.
Black bow tie

*In memory of the late Mr. Eddy Roberts, former coach of
Cymer Avon Boxing Club*

GRIPPING STUFF

Pirelli is pleased to support
Cymer Avon Amateur Boxing Club

	Red Corner		Blue Corner
1.	D. Entwhistle (Taunton)	v	N. Luxton (Barnstaple)
		(Schoolboys)	
	Sponsored by B Dann & Son (Builders)		
2.	K. Ardis (Devonport)	v	J. Allen (Barnstaple)
		(Schoolboys)	
	Sponsored by Hearn Matchroom Snooker		
3.	K. Rogers (Truro)	v	N. Ayres (Bideford)
		(Schoolboys)	
	Sponsored by Southway Service Station		
4.	J. Simms (Mayflower)	v 3x2	L. Dorman (Taunton)
		(Seniors)	
	Sponsored by Kenelly & Steadman		
5.	V. Bath (Mayflower)	v 3x2	C. Whitmore (Bideford)
		(Seniors)	
	Sponsored by Derek & Jean Bradbury		
6.	C. Phillips (Mayflower)	v 3x2	J. Short (Bideford)
		(Seniors)	
	Sponsored by Breakwater Breakers		
7.	M. Wakefield (Mayflower)	v 3x2	J. Hudson (Axe Vale)
		(Seniors)	
	Sponsored by M & S Amusements		

	Red Corner		Blue Corner
8.	A. Peters (Mayflower)	v 3x2	N. Gould (Bideford)
		(Seniors)	
	Sponsored by Allied Builders		
9.	P. Mann (Torbay)	v 3x2	N. Murphy (Truro)
		(Seniors)	
	Sponsored by P.R.Quick (Steel Reinforcing)		
10.	A. Derrick (Taunton)	v 3x2	P. Bailey (Torbay)
		(Seniors)	
	Sponsored by The Three Crowns (R. Shotman)		
11.	A. Morris (Mayflower)	v 3x2	K. Jeffery (Bideford)
		(Seniors)	
	Sponsored by B.D. Builders (0752) 780478		
12.	V. Powell (Mayflower)	v 3x2	H. Rogers (Truro)
		(Seniors)	
	Sponsored by Nurdin & Peacock		
13.	D. Keenor (Barnstaple)	v 4x2	S. Cockayne (Exmouth)
		(Seniors)	
	Sponsored by Valletort Public House (M Taylor)		

BARNSTAPLE ABC

DAVE SHORT Junior in action.

DAVE SHORT Senior,
an active
MEMBER of
BARNSTAPLE
ABC for many
years and GAINED
REPRESENTATIVE
HONOURS.

DAVE SHORT Junior in action.

DAVE SHORT Junior, a WINNER!

MAY 28th 1999

BOXING

BIG H TOPS THE BILL ON CHARITY NIGHT

NORTH DEVON fight fans turned out in their numbers on Friday night to help raise more than £2,000 for a Barnstaple youngster battling against Cerebral Palsy.

Boxers from Barnstaple's Amateur Boxing Club, including crowd favourite **Martin Elkins** - Big H to his fans - took on opponents from across the South West in the show at the Kingsleigh Entertainments Centre in Westward Ho!

All proceeds from the event, which included the auction of a pair of gloves worn by Prince Naseem which fetched £170, went towards the appeal set up in aid of five-year-old Tyler Bishop who was recently diagnosed with Cerebral Palsy.

Dad

Tyler's dad Lee has been with the BABC fro six years and is a valuable member of their training team.

Eight bouts were laid on during the evening including several junior bouts which produced some impressive performances.

But it was Big H the fans had come to see and he didn't disappoint.

Matched against 22-stone Bristol bruiser Mark Butler, Big H made the most of his significant height and reach advantage to keep his opponent at bay and ease to a comfortable unanimous points victory.

Butler was never a match for

By STUART AUSTEN

the more mobile Elkins - who weighed in four-and-a-half-stones lighter at 171/2 stoneand once the Barnstaple boxer had come to terms with the bulldozer approach of his opponent another Big H victory was never in serious doubt.

Unfortunately, younger brother **Carl Elkins** couldn't match the feats of his super-heavyweight sibling and slid to a unanimous points defeat in his junior bout against Joe Smith from Launceston.

Mixed fortunes

Other Barnstaple boxers in action included junior Bobby Davidson and senior Phillip Brogden who enjoyed mixed fortunes.

Davidson was impressive behind a solid jab and earned a deserved points verdict over Lee Sanders from Sydenham, while Brogden found the going tougher against Launceston's Underwood. Despite a good second round he tired in the third and slipped to a points defeat.

Elsewhere on the card there was a cracking contest in the bout of the night between Barnstaple boxers **Lee Slade** and **Justin Francis**.

These two seniors gave it everything in an action-packed three rounds and although Slade deserved victory it was a little surprising the judges gave him the verdict unanimously.

Riveting contest

With only one fight between them - Slade was the one with a previous outing under his belt - they belied any inexperience to produce a riveting contest.

Slade was given a standing eight count in the first after he was rocked by a Francis combination, but he bounced back to take command bloodying his opponents nose in the second with a flurry of punches and maintaining control in the third.

The final bout of the evening produced the most impressive performance as Sean Mulvihill from the Empire club in Bristol outclassed Barnstaple's **Mark Blanche**.

Support

Despite fervent support from the crowd Blanche was literally up against it from the start against his considerably taller opponent who enjoyed early success punching down to repel Blanche's attacks.

A standing-eight count at the start of the second round was followed by another as pressure told and Blanche was eventually floored by a short left hand cross before the round was out.

Blanche was quickly off his stool for the final round but Mulvihill never allowed him to settle and continued to pick him off with his neat left jab, forcing another standing-eight count.

With the fight nearing it's end Blanche was subjected to another barrage of blows and with their fighter trapped on the ropes, the Barnstaple corner men threw in the towel just as the referee stepped in to end the fight.

Juniors: Bobby Davidson (Barnstaple) optd Lee Sanders (Sydenham);

Joe Smith (Launceston) optd Carl Elkins (Barnstaple);

Lee Haskins (Bristol) optd Jed Saygi (Paignton);

Danny Kent (Bournemouth) optd Ross Saunders (Sydenham)

Seniors: Lee Slade (Barnstaple) optd

Justin Francis (Barnstaple); R Underwood (Launceston) optd Phillip Brogden (Barnstaple);

Sean Mulvihill (Bristol) beat Mark Blanche (Barnstaple) ref stopped fight r3

Super Heavyweight: Martin Elkins (Barnstaple) optd Mark Butler (Bristol)

Dick Brownson

A well known face in North Devon boxing circles has announced his retirement.

Due to failing health, Dick Brownson, from Instow, has just finished his duties with the British Boxing Board of Control.

In recognition of his sterling work in the region Dick was presented with an engraved tankard by Chairman of the Barnstaple Amateur Boxing Club Garth Goss before the start Friday's charity show.

355

BOXING

Big H 'loses' on his way to victory

MARTIN ELKINS has powered his way through the preliminary round of the ABA Boxing Championships in Plymouth – despite first seeing his opponent's arm raised.

Barnstaple's Big 'H' was initially declared the loser of his super-heavyweight showdown with Jersey powerhouse Dave Lund but, after a mix-up between ring announcer and judges was resolved, the Barum boxer was awarded the decision and the Southern Divisional Championship.

He must now prepare for a revenge clash with Frome's Henry Smith at Ashton Gate on February 28, while nursing a nasty eye injury inflicted by Lund in the opening round of their Devonport showdown.

It was one of the few times the Channel Islander could get past Elkins' left jab – the Barum man dealt with his ferocious starts in rounds two and four, and rocked him with some powerful right uppercuts on his way to the majority decision.

Fellow super heavyweight Paul Gumbley, stepping into the squared circle for only the second time, also picked up a win against Devonport's Mark Spooner.

Gumbley dished out a royal hammering, connecting with some jaw-jarring left hands which resulted in several standing counts, before being handed a unanimous decision.

Jimmy Briggs, meanwhile, missed out on making it a clean sweep for Barnstaple when he went down to Devonport's Jamie Eddy.

The Barum camp had no complaints about Briggs' fine effort, though, and the two boxers threw everything at each other in a sensational bout.

But despite being handed a standing count in the final round, it was Eddy who sneaked a majority ruling due to his disciplined work rate in the earlier stages.

BARNSTAPLE ABC

BARNSTAPLE AMATEUR BOXING CLUB

presents

GRAND DINNER SHOW
(MEN ONLY)

at

THE BARNSTAPLE HOTEL
Braunton Road

FRIDAY, 22nd JANUARY, 1999

featuring

TOMMY SIMPSON	MARK (BIG H) ELKINS
JOHN VANEMMENIS	JASON RIXON
WILL JAMES	CHRIS BWYE
TERRY DAVIDSON	BEN DOOLEY
BOBBY DAVIDSON	CLEEVE PUGSLEY
BRAD MUNDEN	IAN HAMMOND

Doors open 6.30 – Meal Commences 7.30 – Boxing Commences 8.45

Dress strictly formal (dinner jackets or lounge suits)

COMEDY ENTERTAINMENT
JOHNNY TAIT

GUEST CELEBRITY
GLEN CATLEY (IBF International Super Middleweight Champion)

This will be ticket only – Early booking advisable

TICKETS £25 ALL INCLUSIVE

**Tickets available from Ebberly Arms, Bear Street
or by telephone 01271 882063 (Tony) – 01237 472381 (Garth)**

Palmer succumbs to flamboyant fighter

THE FLAMBOYANT fists of four-times Welsh schoolboy boxing champion Mohamed Nasir proved too strong for home town hero Robert Palmer at Barnstaple ABC's 2003/04 curtain raiser, *writes Chris Rogers.*

Palmer, an ABA semi-finalist last season, diligently tried to contain the St Joseph fighter's snappy combinations and nimble footwork, but ended up on the wrong end of a unanimous judges' decision at the Ex-Serviceman's Club show.

Nasir's main danger was his unpredictability, and Palmer's composed and assured defence was forced to deal with a bombardment of blows from all angles.

On the attack, though, the Barum boxer looked every bit as dangerous – a blistering onslaught in the opening seconds of round three pushed Nasir against the ropes, and a combination of body blows found their mark in the fourth.

But Palmer's attacks were too few and far between to alter the judges' decision, and the speedy Nasir had his arm raised.

Downend fighter Matt White was also notable for his quickness, but he went down to impressive Barum man Karl Windsor – boxing his first competitive bout.

The debutant seemed keen to keep on the offensive, and the determination paid off midway through the second round when White was blasted back into his own corner with a fantastic combination followed by a rasping right hook.

Windsor's confidence had grown further by round three and, despite his slow start, he took the bout on a majority decision.

It wasn't such a memorable night for fellow Barum debutant Jamie Creek, who fell to a unanimous loss against Titans' Levi Dean.

Creek was quickly unsettled by Dean's left jab and, after several stinging blows found their mark, a bleeding nose began to stifle his breathing patterns.

Dean, deducted a point in the third, also rocked Creek with some measured right hooks to seal the win.

Creek wasn't the only Barum boxer to don the crimson mask – Jimmy Briggs' nose also gushed the red stuff after a bruising and bad-tempered encounter with Broadplain's Dan Butler.

The damage was done after just 20 seconds of the opening round when Briggs was worse off in a ferocious opening exchange.

The lightning-quick action continued for a further two rounds, but Briggs spent most of the contest on the back foot, and a unanimous judges' ruling went Butler's way.

And to make it an even more miserable night for the home club, both Brian Birchmore and Darren Hull suffered defeats.

Birchmore was simply outpowered by larger Paignton opponent Gez Langford and, despite valiantly trying to keep moving, he was rattled by two crushing right hooks and a left jab during the opening round.

And in round two, a smashing Langford square right deposited Birchmore unceremoniously onto the mat – wisely deemed to be 'game over' by the referee, who immediately stopped the contest.

Hull, meanwhile, saw his three rounds through, but ended up on the wrong end of a unanimous decision against Pilgrims' Damon Ware.

Confident Ware was occasionally rocked by the Barum boy – a rapid left-right combination shook him at the end of the third – but he remained in control throughout and deserved the win.

Jack Langford was Bideford ABC's only representative on the card, and many in the crowd felt he was robbed of a win after losing a unanimous decision to Broadplain's Joe Ashmead.

Ashmead took a standing count in the second and third rounds after absorbing some scintillating Langford blows but his superior work rate was rewarded with a win.

Elsewhere on the card, St Joseph's Adrian Morgan beat Paignton's Angelo Crowe, while the Paignton duo of Josh Gooding and Ben Murphy beat Aaron Screen and Pete Loworthy respectively.

■ Amateur boxing action returns to Bideford Pannier Market for an open tournament on Saturday night.

Thursday, October 23, 2003

■ DUEL: Young Bideford fighter Jack Langford trades blows with Broadplain's Joe Ashmead. Langford lost the fight by a unanimous judges' decision.

■ GRIMACE: Barnstaple's Jimmy Briggs feels the full force of Dan Butler's brutal offence during his unanimous loss to the Broadplain fighter.

Briggs salvages pride

JUNIOR fighter Jimmy Briggs made sure Barnstaple ABC did not suffer a treble knock-out at the hands of Mayflower ABC during Plymouth's Duke of Cornwall Hotel show.

Briggs was one of three Barum boxers who locked horns with Mayflower opposition, and was the only one to have his arm raised after Dan Davies and Lee Slade were both soundly beaten.

He won the closely-contested bout on a majority decision, but opponent Ben Parsonage put up a strong resistance.

Briggs, though, used some fast footwork and was able to skilfully box his way to victory.

Slade, meanwhile, had a much tougher time against the strong Lee Coleman.

Falling short on both height and reach, the chances of an upset looked quite possible after round one when Slade put up an almighty challenge.

He used the left jab to good effect, and was giving Coleman a rough time until the Mayflower man replied with two cracking rights.

But the opening 20 seconds of round two put an end to any hopes the Barum fighter had of victory – Coleman unleashed a vicious left and right-fisted assault to put Slade on the canvas.

Slade fought on valiantly to the final bell but he could not alter the judges' unanimous decision.

And it was another pair of lightening-quick fists that ended Davies' night.

Enrico Cutone's ferocious combinations rattled the Barum man, and a cracking right put him against the ropes.

Davis began to find some success with the jab as round two developed, but Cutone's ultra-fast style proved too tough to counter.

●Barnstaple ABC is holding a show at the Ex-Servicemans Club tomorrow evening. Doors open at 7pm, and there are still some tickets left.

BOXING

Revenge bid

MARTIN ELKINS fights for a title and revenge at Devonport on Saturday.

Barnstaple's "Big H" takes on Dave Lund from Jersey in the ABA Southern Division championships determined to erase the memories of two controversial defeats at the hands of his super heavyweight rival last season.

Barum's Jimmy Briggs, meanwhile, enhanced his reputation with an excellent performance to outpoint Nick Curtis of Camborne on the Plymouth bill.

■ LOCAL RIVALS: Ben Chapple of Barnstaple (right) and Bideford's Ben Owen do battle at Barnstaple Boxing Club's dinner show.

BOXING

Jimmy furious at stoppage

By CHRIS ROGERS
crogers@nrthdevonjournal.co.uk

FURIOUS Jimmy Briggs was stopped for the first time in his career by Apollo fighter Ben Wakeham at Barnstaple ABC's dinner boxing tournament.

The referee ended the bout with just five seconds of the final round remaining – a decision fiercely contested by the Barnstaple boxer.

Seconds before the controversial ending, Briggs had been handed a standing count after tasting a ferocious flurry of blows from Wakeham – his second of the fight.

The first came in the opening minute of round one when Wakeham landed a sweet right

glove, but Briggs was quick to recover and even launched his own dramatic attack midway through the second.

Only the ropes kept the Apollo fighter on his feet after he absorbed the full brunt of an awesome Briggs right hook, but somehow he recovered to deliver the quick-fire combination which caused the home-town fighter's downfall.

Bideford's Tommy Langford gained a measure of revenge for North Devon, though, when he beat old Apollo rival Jamie Spate on a majority decision.

Spate struggled to keep up with the quick-footed Langford who grew with stature and confidence as the fight went on.

Langford's club mate Ben Owen came unstuck against Barnstaple's Ben Chapple in an all-North Devon clash.

Chapple earned a majority decision largely due to his work in the opening two rounds.

A majority decision also ended Barum's Karl Windsor's hopes of a win over Torbay fighter Mike George, who landed some heavy right

hands throughout the bout.

And, in his debut bout, super heavyweight Paul Gumbley from Barnstaple lost a majority decision to Pilgrims debutante Mark Street in a thrilling finale.

Both 'men traded some jaw-jarring shots in round two - Gumbley was rocked by a stinging left hook, but he charged back and handed Street a standing count courtesy of a rasping right hand.

■ ON THE MIKE: Ron Hemiman – the voice of amateur boxing in North Devon for more than five decades – has been honoured for his 51 years of dedicated service to Barnstaple Boxing Club.

■ Ring announcer Ron (left) was presented with an engraved tankard by chairman Garth Goss before the club's dinner tournament at Barnstaple Hotel.

■ Garth told the crowd: "Ron must really love this sport to have continued doing it for all these years, and he really is the salt of the earth in North Devon."

Order this picture at www.ndjphotos.com ref.03126603

In the third, both were handed further standing counts after a vicious exchange of blows, but it was the Plymouth man who got the judges' nod.

■ Barnstaple soldier Richard Watson was stopped in the second round of his Devon and Dorset Regiment Inter-Company boxing final in Northern Ireland.

A Service to Celebrate the Life of

Ron Hernaman

who passed away on Easter Saturday
10th April 2004

aged 80 years

The Parish Church of St Peter, Barnstaple.
Friday 16th April, 3.00pm
followed by committal at The North Devon Crematorium.

Three out of six

SIX Barnstaple boxers were on the bill at Devonport and three of them got the right verdicts.

New senior Lee Bishop's outstanding skills dominated his bout against the host club's A. Kennedy for a comfortable points victory.

And both Stuart James and Jethro Allen won on disqualifications.

James was always in charge against former ABA champion D. Lawson and Allen had a real battle with his old adversary K. Ardis of Devonport, both receiving public warnings before his opponent was ruled out in the third round.

Andrew Luxton and southpaw Michael Sanders — both making their debuts in the ring — lost points decisions and Kevin Dunn suffered the same fate. He threw plenty of punches but couldn't penetrate a solid defence.

Barnstaple's show scheduled for October 23 has been cancelled but there is action in Bideford on October 30 when a full card at the Pollyfield Centre includes the Southern Division novice championships.

Great skill

BARNSTAPLE Boxing Club junior Nicky Luxton showed great skill and confidence to notch an outstanding victory over the more experienced D. Endtwhistle of Taunton on a Plymouth bill.

But there was no joy for club-mate Jethro Allen who lost his unbeaten record to K. Ardis of Devonport.

South best

NICKY LUXTON of Barnstaple Boxing Club is the new Junior ABA Southern Division champion at 51-54 kilos.

His boxing skills and punching ability forced S. Watson of Appollo to take two standing counts before the referee stopped the contest.

Club-mates Kevin Dunn and Andrew Luxton, meanwhile, were in action in warm-up bouts for the Royal Marines championships.

Kevin dominated his bout with L. Warey of Devonport, mixing up his punches well to earn a unanimous decision.

But Andrew, lost a close decision to Devonport's D. Taylor after a tough battle in which he matched his rival punch for punch most of the way.

Sparkling debuts

TWO Bideford Boxing Club youngsters made sparkling debuts in the ring at Devonport.

Billy Oliver rarely wasted a punch in a stylish display which outpointed the host club's M. Smith 60-56, 60-57, 60-56.

And Michael Morgan was even more impressive against D. Smith of Devonport.

He dictated from the first bell behind his left jab and a barrage of head and body punches persuaded the referee to step in in the second round.

Barnstaple's Nicky Luxton, meanwhile, lost a unanimous decision to J. Delaney of Dale Youth in the Schoolboys Championship despite a performance which illustrated all his improvement and promise.

Bideford stage a dinner show, in conjunction with the Rotary Club, at the Elizabethan Club, Westward Ho! on March 10 and, a week later, Barnstaple stage their dinner jacket show at the Barnstaple Motel.

As close as it gets

KEVIN JEFFERY lost his bout at Devonport, but it couldn't have been any closer.

The Bideford light middleweight was edged out 60-59, 60-59, 59-60 by Welshman N. Trinder after three action-packed rounds.

The first two were a classic boxer-fighter confrontation with Jeffery making excellent use of a solid left jab and plenty of good body punches.

The third was toe to toe, blow for blow, prompting a standing ovation and a comment from Bideford coach Ken Manley: "I have rarely seen a fight like it. I don't know how the judges separated them."

Bideford's other boxer on the bill, heavyweight Nicholas Gould, was rusty after a 15-month absence from the ring and lost 60-57 on all three cards, to Camborne's C. Thomas.

Boxing

BARUM ACTION: Nick Luxton (above right) and Stuart James (below) in the thick of the action at Barnstaple Boxing Club's dinner show.
Pictures by Andrew Entwistle.

BARNSTAPLE ABC

BARNSTAPLE's boxers scooped all but two of the winners' trophies at their club's dinner show.

The Barnstaple Hotel was the setting for six convincing wins by own-grown talent.

Schoolboy Andrew Luxton opened the evening with his bout against Devonport's Michael Lidstone.

Luxton was economical with his punches but found his target 80 per cent of the time to overwhelm Lidstone for a unanimous verdict.

Emphatic

Kevin Dunn produced the most emphatic victory after knocking down opponent Steve Watson from Torquay's Apollo Club only seconds into the first round.

When Watson rose from the count Dunn finished the job with a lightening jab before the bell.

Stuart James, one of Barnstaple's most promising talents, narrowly lost on points to Max Stuckey, another Apollo boxer.

■ ALL WIN: Barnstaple's Jamie Creek (centre) maintained his sparkling form this season with a 4th win in four bouts. Creek, who lost all his seven bouts last season, avenged two of those defeats with a convincing points win over Newton Abbot's Wayne Bellamy at the Race Course.

■ Danny Squire (left) marked his debut in the ring by stopping Sam Harvey of Torbay in the 2nd round of their contest and the third Barum fighter on the bill, Nico Faassen, notched his first win in his 2nd bout with a points verdict over Apollo's Dean Hunter.

■ All three of the boys are expected to be in action on the Barnstaple show at the Ex-Servicemen's Club on March 18.

■ Richard Grigg of Bideford, meanwhile, had an impressive win over Apollo's Tom Tracey.

■ He won the first round comfortably and then stepped up the pace to an even higher level to pummel his opponent until the referee stopped the contest in Round 2. (S)

In support bouts, Jimmy Randell gained a comfortable win by majority over Billy Davies, while Dan Squire and Tom Hammett weren't so lucky.

Squire looked good against Terry Richards until the referee stopped him in round two due to a bleeding nose.

And Hammett went down on points to Bristol boxer Daniel Belcher.

BARNSTAPLE ABC

N.D.J. May 2004

■ RETREAT: Barnstaple's Jamie Creek backs off during his unanimous defeat to Tamin Nassiri.

■ Junior ABA semi-finalist Rob Palmer prepares for action.

Boxer backing for our boys

June 2003

I WAS very pleased to see (*Journal* June 12) that the Royal Marine commandos are to be honoured at St Peter's Church, Barnstaple, but would like to point out that Barnstaple Amateur Boxing Club has already done so at our show of May 23.

Although the *Journal* carried an excellent report on the boxing for some reason our guest of honour was ignored. RSM Nick Garcia was introduced to the crowd and received a wonderful round of applause. Our club has always had a close relationship with 59 Commando, having helped with their training.

After the anti-war protesters got front page coverage and BABC none at all I was beginning to wonder if the *Journal* was also anti-war?

GARTH GOSS,
Chairman BABC,
Aysha Gardens, Westward
Ho!

BOXING Dec 03

Unanimous

DAN DAVIES and Billy Peach both took unanimous points wins at Mayflower ABC's Duke of Cornwall amateur boxing show.

Barnstaple fighter Davies completely dominated home town hero Enrico Cutone, while Bideford's Peach was equally impressive in his success over Truro's Charlie Scott.

Late blow for Lee

By CHRIS ROGERS
crogers@northdevonjournal.co.uk

IT STARTED cautiously, but Lee Slade's eagerly anticipated re-match with Tim Coupe at Barnstaple ABC's show on Friday evening climaxed with a crescendo of crunching exchanges.

Unfortunately for the home fighter, though, his fate was sealed in the latter half of the final round when a wicked right hook from Coupe forced him to take a standing count.

The Newton Abbot boxer was then given the unanimous decision at the Ex-Servicemen's Club show, gaining revenge for the beating Slade had given him in Plymouth eight days earlier.

It was a thrilling end to a bout which had started so cautiously – both fighters spent the opening 30 seconds sizing each other up, and a quick flurry from Coupe was the only action of round one.

But Slade soon grew in stature after an explosive start to round two – a cracking exchange of combinations worried Coupe, who was later pounded into the corner.

He was rescued with a standing count in the final seconds, though, and regained control in the third.

Slade was shaken by a smashing left hook and a big right, paving the way for his late standing count.

While he and Coupe were rewarded for their efforts with a 'fight of the night' award, Karl Windsor was named Barum's top boxer with a fantastic win over Exeter's Ryan Maine.

He was forced to taste Maine's gloves on a number of occasions in the early going, but soon found his feet with some powerful rights.

And after weathering the Exeter fighter's left jab, Windsor stayed in full control to get the judges' nod.

Quick lefts

Another fighter with a quick left hand – Torbay's Tamin Nassiri – proved too much for Barnstaple's Jamie Creek.

Nassiri landed some good left uppercuts and jabs which Creek struggled to contend with, and he went down on a unanimous decision.

His club mate Dan Davies was also on the wrong end of a unanimous result in his duel with Reading's Sonny Jury.

Davies looked promising early on, but the power in Jury's arsenal rose to the fore in round two when he dished out a standing count to his Barum opponent with a left jab and big right.

An inevitable second stand-

ing count came in the final moments of act three, and Jury's impressive right hand was raised.

The host club then experienced another loss when Paul Gumbley went down against Weston-Super-Mare fighter Sheridan Davy.

Gumbley gave away a colossal eight inches to the Somerset giant, yet still seemed intent on going for head shots rather than concentrating on the body.

Costly

And that decision proved costly – Davy bossed the bout, shaking off Gumbley's attacks to claim another unanimous success.

In fact, Barum's only other win on the night came from young Ben Chappell, who opened proceedings with a fine display against Titans' Curtis Manlow.

Chappell made all the forward moves during the contest, and backed up some solid left jabs with good combinations.

He began to struggle with an apparent rib injury midway through the second round, but the pain seemed to spur him on and, from there, he enjoyed his best spell of the bout.

And at the start of the third, he emphasised his dominance by giving Manlow a standing count.

■ TRADING BLOWS: Barnstaple's Dan Davies (right) wages war with Reading opponent Sonny Jury – Davies was beaten on a unanimous decision.

BOXING

No title for "Big H"

MARTIN ELKINS' hopes of a Western Counties were dashed at Bristol on Saturday.

Barnstaple super heavyweight "Big H" was below his best in the four-round final against Henry Smith of Frome and lost a tight contest on points.

His club-mate Rob Palmer also tasted defeat on a bill at Bournemouth.

He was matched with Peter Barney of Lymington in a repeat of last year's junior ABA quarter-final and the two teenagers produced a cracker of a contest.

But Palmer just lost out on points after four rounds of hard work and quality punching which earned them the fight of the night award.

■ There are still tickets available for Barnstaple's show at the Ex-Servicemen's Club on March 12. They can be bought at the Ebberley Arms or the Corner House.

BARNSTAPLE ABC

Thursday, June 23, 2005

N. D. J.

BOXING

■ **BOXING AWARDS:** Barnstaple's boxers gather before their presentation night at the Ex-Servicemen's Club when club captain Lee Slade and youngster Ben Chappell were named as best senior and junior. Chappell also won the most stylish boxer, while Jamie Creek also won two awards – best all-round achiever and best club boy.

■ **Awards:** Most promising junior - Tom Hull. 14-18yrs junior annual trophy - Joey Kerner. Best junior prospect - Tommy Hammett. Most improved senior (Wilf Cooper Trophy) - Mark Paddock. Most improved junior - Dan Davies. Most dedicated junior (David Short Cup) - Nico Faassen. Outstanding junior - Ben Chappell. Most stylish boxer (Lewis Cup and Adair Bros Cup) - Ben Chappell. Best senior (Davies Cup) - Lee Slade. Best all-round achiever - Jamie Creek. Best club boy (Chappell Shield) - Jamie Creek. All-round dedication and style (Fred Fewings Memorial Shield) - Jimmy Randall. Simpson Captain's Cup - Jimmy Randall. Medal winners: Tom Herd, Dan Squires, David Sewell, Mark Hunt, Karl Windsor, Jimmy Briggs, Rob Palmer, Joe Branch. Order this picture at www.ndjphotos.com ref. 05065701

Gutsy Palmer goes toe to toe . . . and loses

■ BLOODIED: Barnstaple's Rob Palmer is the man covered in blood during his battle with Rob Bowman of Camborne at the Ex-Serviceman's Club.

By CHRIS ROGERS

ROB PALMER got embroiled in an all-out war with Camborne power-house Rob Bowman at Barnstaple ABC's Ex Servicemen's Club show.

Though gutsy, the decision by crowd favourite Palmer to go toe-to-toe with the intimidating Cornishman was probably the wrong one – he came off second best and was beaten unanimously.

But nobody in the vociferous crowd would deny that the home boxer gave one mighty effort. . . especially when the fight exploded in round three.

Southpaw Palmer had been stung by a couple of hard right hands in the opening two acts, but he stormed out of his corner to pummel a shocked Bowman.

Never one to shirk a scrap, Bowman fired back with a barrage of blows in a furious exchange which lasted the whole round.

Palmer was clearly worse for wear but, with blood streaming from his nose, he stepped right back up for another head-on collision.

However, Bowman's retaliations were just too powerful and he was given the judges' decision.

There was still plenty for the Barum club to shout about, though – especially the performance of Ben Chappell.

He quickly set about dismantling Sturminster fighter Andrew Loveridge with his most professional display yet in the squared circle.

Loveridge was given a standing count in round two after being ambushed in a neutral corner, and was stopped again in the third after absorbing a cracking Chappell left hook.

Chappell earned a unanimous win for his efforts, as did club mate Jamie Creek for a methodical defeat of Taunton man Mark Cooper.

Scorcher

Newcomer Tom Herd wasn't so lucky in another scorcher with Mayflower's Sam Coney.

The Plymouth fighter took a majority decision after edging the final round with some solid combinations.

Earlier, Herd had enjoyed a blistering second round and clobbered Coney in a neutral corner, but the visitor had just enough left in the tank to get the job done.

Elsewhere, Billy Peach and Jimmy Briggs had remarkably differing fortunes with referee stoppages.

Peach was handed a standing count in the third round of his battle with Camborne's Rob Gammon and, after tasting yet more rasping blows, the man in white intervened.

Briggs, though, had his arm raised when outclassed opponent Danny Smith was disqualified after being given three warnings for holding.

Mayflower's Louis Spencer, meanwhile, was equally overwhelmed against a stronger Lee Slade, and lost unanimously after offering no reply to the Barum man's attacks.

BARNSTAPLE ABC

Revenge bid fails

Thursday, December 22, 2005

By CHRIS ROGERS

crogers@northdevonjournal.co.uk

JOEY KERNER was hoping a vociferous and partisan home crowd could spur him on to extract revenge on Mayflower's Daniel Clancy.

Seven days earlier, the Barnstaple fighter was beaten by Clancy down in Plymouth, but the tables were turned on Saturday night at Barum ABC's big Christmas show.

This time Kerner had home advantage but, despite that, it was the same outcome – the Mayflower man had his arm raised.

The fight followed a similar pattern to its predecessor the week before.

Clancy is a difficult opponent to get to – he is constantly on the move, in and out, and rarely gave Kerner chance to unload his heavy-duty artillery.

The Barum fighter improved as the bout went on, resulting in a furious start to the third in which he landed two cracking lefts on Clancy's nose.

But it was to no avail, and the visitor took the unanimous decision.

The battle was one of 16 put on by the club at the Ex-Servicemen's Club. . . and 13 featured local fighters.

The picks of the bunch were Barum duo Tommy Hull and Jimmy Randell.

Hull's contest with the much taller Tristan Kelso-Spur from Lympstone was a scorcher.

And despite giving away a few inches, the home fighter did exactly what was needed to get a unanimous verdict.

He crept in with some stiff shots in the opening round, although Kelso-Spur was able to take a much-needed breather when he needed his headguard readjusted.

It proved only to be a stay of execution, though, as Hull got right back to work in rounds two and three to dominate.

Randell, meanwhile, was named best boxer on the show at the end of the evening, and it was not a hard decision.

He was smashed to the canvas midway through the first,

but dusted himself off and also took a unanimous decision.

In reality, Warrington boxer Sam Birtwhistle's punch that put Randell down was a speculative one.

He had done little else before it, and ended up retaliating to a fierce combination of lefts and rights by swinging wildly.

Randell quickly got back in the zone, and scored points at will – countless punches went unanswered and, on two occasions, he trapped Birtwhistle in the corner and knocked seven bells out of him.

Bideford ABC also had boxers on the card, although two came out on the wrong end of majority decisions.

So close

Kyle de Banks' tussle with Devonport's Mike Chapman was extremely close.

It looked to be going the Bideford hitter's way at the end of the second round – Chapman appeared to be holding on in desperation after being worn down by de Banks' long and powerful left jab.

The fight was turned on its head in the third, though, when Chapman came out with all guns blazing.

In the first 20 seconds he hit de Banks with a flurry of wincing blows and forced the Bideford boxer to take a count.

De Banks struggled to find his rhythm after that, and the fight probably hinged on it – Chapman won 33-31, 23-29, 31-17.

Clubmate Ben Owen fared little better – he too was beaten on a majority by Blandford's Glenn de Lange.

And again the damage was done in the third – there was little to separate the two lads up to that point, but de Lange did just enough in the finale.

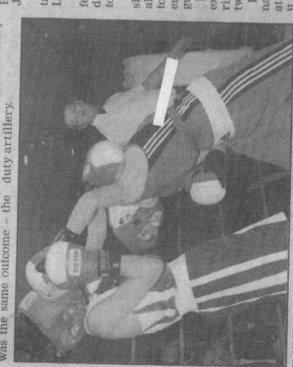

■ 'AVE IT: Jimmy Randell lands one during his unanimous win over Sam Birtwhistle. 051213928

Valantin's debut

The Journal   Thursday October 26, 2006

massacre

■ WINNING START: Stefan Davis-Ross got his Barnstaple ABC career off to a successful start after pounding Dorchester's Peter Pring unanimously.   0610-115-07

Billy Hammett also had to take a 10-second breather in his bout with Watchet's Callum Harper, and lost by majority as a result.

Hammett landed a great left in the second round, but was temporarily stopped in the third.

Jake Langdon got the home club back on winning form as he took a majority verdict over Mayflower's Jimmy Taylor.

He connected with some hard rights in the second and, shortly after, the referee stepped in for a count.

After that, Langdon was diving in with some quick combinations, leaving Taylor to fight his way out.

Tommy Hull took a standing count in the early going of his bout with Laurie Thomas from Dorchester.

Hull did well to get back into the fight, but his efforts weren't quite enough – he lost on a majority.

Jimmy Randall claimed his second big win in the space of four days at the Ex-Servicemen's show.

Having beaten Howard Hart in Plymouth last Tuesday, he faced the daunting prospect of Golden Ring's hot prospect Connor Malloy.

But Randall dominated the highly-rated Southampton fighter and won unanimously.

By now the Barum boys were on a winning role, and Bryrn Haywood's name was next on the list as he stopped Torbay's Martin Eales in an awesome first round display of dominance.

Jamie Creek then beat Pilgrims' Jamie Quinn by disqualification – the Plymouth fighter had twice had points deducted due to his approach and, on the third strike, he was out.

Joe Davis kept the home run going with a unanimous win over Titans' Carl Hartnip, who took a count in the third.

And the evening was rounded off superbly by Bumbul and Davies' action-packed antics.

■ Jake Langdon.   0610-115-19

BOXING

By CHRIS ROGERS

crogers@c-dm.co.uk

IT'S not February, but it was a real Valantin's Day Massacre in Barnstaple on Saturday.

And it had nothing to do with the sharp shooting of Bugs Moran and Al Capone . . . this was all about the furious fists of Barnstaple ABC's latest discovery.

Lithuanian powerhouse Valantin Bumbul tore the house down at the Ex-Servicemen's Club on Saturday night in one of the most explosive heavyweight debuts ever seen at the venue.

He traded brutal blows for three punishing rounds with gutsy Dorchester battler Dan Foster before having his hand raised via majority decision.

And what an impact he made – Foster was left chewing canvas after Bumbul's first blow of the fight, a blistering left jab as soon as the bell had rung.

For the next minute, the besieged Dorset man was pounded more times than an Iron Maiden snare drum and had to take two standing counts.

Even more astonishingly, Foster was able to shake off the cobwebs to blast his way back into contention in round two.

A cracking left hook in the third gave Bumbul a tempor-

ary visit from 'old Spaghetti legs' which resulted in his one and only standing count.

But it was to be his night and, before it was all done and dusted, Foster had been given another 10-second reprieve an eye-watering combination in a neutral corner.

Bumbul may have brought the house down, but Barum's Dan Davies literally did bring the ring down.

He was next up after Bumbul's war and, in the process of pounding Mike Jewell into oblivion, the blue corner turnbuckle gave way.

The damage was irreparable, so Davies was handed a unanimous win after just a minute.

It brought the evening to a slightly premature end, but there were still 10 other cracking bouts for the vociferous crowd to roar their support.

The host club introduced the crowd to an exciting crop of new boxers.

Young Liam Clarke got the evening off to an action-packed start with a fired-up display against Titans' Lewis Stacey in a Kid Gloves contest.

He was followed by another Barum debutant, Stefan Davis-Ross, who can throw one big right hand.

His wild swings soon got the better of Dorchester's Peter Pring as he unloaded his heavy artillery immediately.

Pring hung in there for the best part of the opening two rounds, but the damage began to take its toll in the third.

Davis-Ross landed a hard left square on his opponents nose in the early going, and was soon named the bout's unanimous winner.

Fellow debutant George Beveridge was unable to get past Minehead boxer Danny Wilson's left jab to continue Barum's winning start.

He squeezed a couple of blows through, but was handed a standing count in the second round after a pair of shots put him back against the ropes.

■ CHEERS FOR THE BEVERIDGE: Barum debutant George Beveridge lands one on Danny Wilson's cheek, but he was later beaten unanimously. Pictures by Mike Southon 0610-115-09

375

Barum's Benny Boy wins Golden Belt

By CHRIS ROGERS
crogers@c-dm.co.uk

BEN CHAPPELL has given North Devon boxing a massive boost by winning a national title in Liverpool on Saturday night.

The Barnstaple ABC fighter – known in amateur boxing circles as Benny Boy – was in superb form to lift the Golden Belt championship after beating Shrewsbury ABC youngster Tony Jones.

The convincing 8-3 points win came just days after Tommy Langford's controversial NACYP points defeat and has restored some real festive cheer among the region's boxing ranks.

Chappell is the first junior in Barnstaple ABC's history to win a national title, and he said: "I have waited a year to win an English title, having come so close last year."

In 2005, Benny Boy couldn't have come any closer to making the final if he had tried.

Computerised scoring could not separate him and semi-final opponent Joe Mc-Cauley, so countback was called. The Barum boxer then lost 13-12 – the equivalent of one punch.

This year, though, Chappell didn't have the worry of a semi-final as he received a bye into the final.

Jones, who had already beaten a fighter from Droylsden, was the only thing that stood between Chappell and the Open Class 3 38kg title.

And he was no match for Chappell, who is sponsored by Ian Geddes and Nick Jenkins and Paul Raynor from Combe Martin, where the youngster lives.

The triumphant boxer added: "I want to dedicated this fight to my granddad Mickie Davy."

■ THE MAN: Ben Chappell is the new English Golden Belt champ.

Bumbul brute force shakes Barum super show

BOXING

By MARK JENKIN

mjenkin@c-dm.co.uk

THE LAST punch landed at Barnstaple ABC's Saturday night show was the one that will live longest in the memory.

Home town hero Valantin Bumbul gave another demonstration of his ferocious power with a stunning third round knockout against Dorchester's Dan Foster.

With one swing of that brutal right hand, the imposing Lithuanian showed why he is such a popular choice to top the bill on Barum's big nights.

It was an explosive end to a cracking evening's entertainment at Barnstaple Rugby Club and it certainly sent the home crowd home happy.

Time seems to have flown by since Bumbul was first introduced to North Devon fight fans with his all-action debut against the same Dorset visitor back in October 2006.

On that occasion, both men traded blows furiously in a classic encounter before Bumbul took a majority decision at the Ex-Servicemen's Club.

But Foster had shown enough strength and spirit first time around to suggest the rematch could be another thriller.

As things panned out, it was the visitor who settled in for the scrap with a far more impressive opening.

Outworking the home favourite and scoring points with his tidy left jab, he looked to be winning the bout as the two warriors stepped off their stools for the final two minutes.

But beware! Bumbul can bang.

A shuddering right rocked Foster onto one knee and changed the whole complexion of the bout in a flash.

Although the Dorchester heavyweight steadied himself during a standing count, the respite didn't last long.

Bumbul was straight back in to finish the job with ruthless efficiency as the crowd roared to the rafters of the Pottington stand.

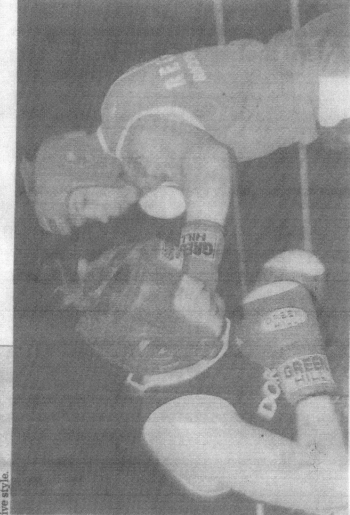

■ A BAD PLACE TO BE: Dorchester's Dan Foster is floored by a devastating Valantin Bumbul onslaught at Pottington. The Dorset cruiserweight was okay to leave the ring after being checked out by ringside doctors.
0605-96_35

Two more thunderous rights sent his opponent crashing to the canvas and suddenly the fight was over in comprehensive style.

● BARNSTAPLE ABC boxer Harry Sugars put his Western Counties middleweight belt on the line with a voluntary defence against Lewis Scutt.

The top-of-the-bill clash in Bridgwater had it all before Scutt, of Sydenham ABC, won on a split decision.

Coach Mark Simpson said: "There are no regrets in the Barnstaple camp. It is a contest he could have avoided but that is not in the nature of Harry. This title will return to North Devon soon, we have no doubt."

Liam Laird will represent the Western Counties at welterweight against Bristol Sporting Club's Ryan Fillingham on December 7.

Briggs targets revenge in pro debut

■ NICE ONE: Jimmy Briggs – just a week away from his pro debut – congratulates national amateur semi-finalist Tommy Herd.

By MARK JENKIN
mjenkin@c-dm.co.uk

NO DOUBT Jimmy Briggs was itching to get in on the action as he stood ringside at Saturday's big boxing show.

The popular welterweight was handing out the silverware to some of his old Barnstaple ABC club mates at the Ex-Servicemen's Club.

But the big-fight build-up is almost over for Briggs who is just a week away from his full professional debut.

On November 9, the 19-year-old will step into the ring at Plymouth Guildhall to face up to former amateur foe Ben Wakeham.

Briggs, who bases his come-forward style on his boxing idol Ricky Hatton, can't wait for the challenge.

"There's quite a big rivalry between us," admitted Briggs. "During our amateur days, we always had a few things to say to each other. Technically, he's a brilliant boxer, but I haven't trained this hard to lose.

"I know I'm the underdog and I'm up against it, but I'm hoping to prove a point."

While Briggs has twice missed out against Wakeham on points decisions in the past, he hopes the longer bouts of the pro game will suit his aggressive approach.

"I'm a puncher and he's quite a big puncher but I've got six rounds to wear him down now instead of the three we had in our amateur days."

A workaholic lifestyle now sees Briggs combining up to six hours a day training with his job as plumber. He said: "It's quite tough but I'm really enjoying it – it's a positive thing I'm doing with my life.

"At amateur level you just maintain a steady level of fitness because you might have to take a fight at just a week's notice. Now you just get one date and you spend so much time building up to it.

"I'm 100% fitter now. As an amateur, that was my problem, I was never fully fit, but now I'm in the best shape I have ever been in; I'm pushing myself to new limits all the time."

Briggs has just returned from six months working in Guernsey where he combined 12-hour working days with long hours in the gym.

Since coming back, he has been travelling to Plymouth to train three times a week under the guidance of coach Glyn Mitchell and manager Nigel Christian.

When he's in North Devon, Briggs still trains with Barnstaple ABC coach Mark Simpson, who he worked with for seven years as an amateur.

"Mark has been absolutely brilliant for me and he's the reason why I turned pro," said the ring prospect.

"I was going through a bad patch, like a lot of young people do with drinking, but he pulled me out and got me into the gym.

"I used to have the occasional drink, but now I realise there's no point. It just dehydrates you and doesn't do you any favours at all.

"I'm tee-total now. If you're an athlete and you drink lots, then you're probably not much of an athlete."

As he sets off on his pro career, Briggs is aiming for the top and he is encouraging North Devon's boxing supporters to get down to Plymouth to witness his debut.

"It should be an explosive night and I'm sure the people who come down will have a good night out in Plymouth afterwards. I'm hoping to put on a good show.

"I want to go places, I want to be at least British champ. You can never tell what's going to happen, but I'm aiming to be the best otherwise there's no point doing it."

If you want a ticket for the big fight, contact Briggs on 07982 468127 or promoters Bristol Boxing on 0117 949 6699.

Palmer pro bid given go ahead

BOXING

By CHRIS ROGERS
crogers@c-dm.co.uk

BARNSTAPLE fighter Robert Palmer is ready to become North Devon's third professional boxer after making a successful ring comeback.

Palmer has this week received his boxing licence after spending the past four months in intensive training, and is aiming to make his competitive pro debut by the end of July.

His former Barnstaple ABC club mate Jimmy Briggs and Bideford ABC star John Van Emmenis have both launched pro careers in the past year.

And now Palmer is determined to follow in their footsteps after seeking advice from Plymouth-based trainers Glyn Mitchell and Nigel Christian.

The pair are currently trying to put Plymouth boxing back on the regional map following the injury-enforced retirement of city hero Scott Dann.

And the 22-year-old Barum flyweight can't wait to get stuck into it.

"Devon boxing needs a superstar again," he said. "There's a spot to be filled and I think I can fill it.

"There's not too many other lads at flyweight at the moment, and they've got high hopes for me down there."

Palmer has only made one in-ring appearance in the past three years – and that was an impressive unanimous defeat of Exeter's England international Aaron Seldon at Barnstaple ABC's dinner show in February.

Before that, a disillusioned Palmer had taken some time out from the amateur game to deal with the heartbreak of his 2004 NACYP final defeat.

But now he is raring to go, and says he's in the best shape of his career.

"In February, I only trained for six weeks and won it," he added. "I've been training solidly for four months now, and I think I would stop him now if we fought again."

Palmer is hoping to find a debut flyweight fight within the next month, and is looking for sponsorship to help his pro career get off the ground.

In the meantime, he will get his first taste of in-ring pro action this Saturday in Wales when he takes on former ABA national champion Lee Selby in an exhibition fight.

"It won't be a competitive fight because I will weigh in at 8st 2lb and he is 8st 13lbs," Palmer added.

"It's more about getting a feel for the pro game. It will be more of a sparring session with three two-minute rounds, but it's on the undercard of a show up there and will be in front of a few hundred people."

For more information about sponsorship, contact Palmer on 07833 942720.

■ BACK: Robert Palmer.

Palmer's back in town

■ BACK WITH A BANG: England boxer Aaron Seldon bears the scars of his war with returning Robert Palmer (above) while Lee Slade gets down to work against Allen O'Callaghan

BOXING

By CHRIS ROGERS
crogers@tc-dm.co.uk

A THREE-YEAR spell in the boxing wilderness didn't stop Robert Palmer making an explosive ring return at Barnstaple ABC's big dinner show on Saturday night.

A disillusioned Palmer - considered one of the town's brightest boxing prospects a few years ago - had not donned the gloves since his heartbreaking NACYP final defeat in December 2004.

But he was a surprise addition to the Barnstaple Hotel card, and took great delight in showing the home crowd just what they'd been missing with an impressive unanimous triumph over England international Aaron Seldon.

A sharp Palmer showed little sign of any ring rust . . . in fact, while his casual hands-down style may not be to everybody's liking, it did demonstrate a high level of confidence.

Exeter fighter Seldon didn't take the bait and refused to rush in and strike, so Palmer's dominance only continued to increase - especially after landing a couple of cracking lefts in a solid second round.

By the third, Seldon looked a beaten man and, when he chewed on a rasping combination of Palmer punches in his own corner, the referee had no choice but to step in and give him a standing count.

It was no shock, then, to see the Barum boxer's arm raised courtesy of a 23-14, 21-7, 15-8 verdict.

Perhaps even more apt was the choice of music as the crowd waited for the decision - Thin Lizzy's classic *The Boys Are Back In Town* was blaring over the PA system.

It was true, they certainly were . . . not only was Palmer returning, but the show also marked the long-awaited ring return of another Barum boy.

Lee Slade climbed back into the squared circle to take on Kingswood ABC's Allen O'Callaghan, but sadly it wasn't to be the same fairytale outcome.

There was little to separate the two men in a stiff opening couple of rounds, and Slade landed a couple of great shots in the final moments of the third, but it wasn't enough to prevent a narrow 17-11, 13-12, 6-10 majority defeat.

In fact, it was a pretty bad night for the red corner as, going into the final bout, Palmer had been the only Barnstaple boxer to produce a positive result.

What better way to stop a losing run, though, than to send Lithuanian powerhouse Valantin Bumbul into combat?

The crowd favourite didn't disappoint and claimed the win needed to send the fans home happy, but it certainly wasn't as comfy as some of his previous whirlwind displays.

Mayflower ABC's Neil Herbert was a game opponent, and a frustrated Bumbul looked distinctly unhappy at the end of the second round after being troubled by some fierce left jabs.

He stepped up a gear in the third, though, and Herbert's golden curly locks were shaken by a couple of huge right hands.

And his committed performance was good enough to get an 18-16, 21-17, 18-20 majority nod from the judges at ringside.

Earlier, the cursed red corner had already started getting the blues after show opener Billy Hammett was beaten by Kingswood's Gary Coles, and Barum clubmate Dale Palmer went down to Exeter's Joe Pilkington.

Debutant Phil Whitley then suffered a unanimous loss to Kingswood's Scott Bateman, before Brooke Hawkins was unable to celebrate his recent NACYP Southern success against Tom Gardner.

After a frenetic opening exchange, the pace of the fight slowed down somewhat as Portland foe Gardner began looking pragmatically for a way through Hawkins' defence.

He got through a couple of times, and was able to shake off a ferocious square left shot in the closing stages of the third to take a tight majority decision.

Tommy Hull was awarded the fight of the night accolade for his ring-war with Synwell ABC's Mitchell Lever, but that was scant consolation as he came out on the wrong end of the judges' unanimous verdict.

Stewart Wrenn was given the task of starting off the second half of the evening with a Barum win but, given that he had scrambled out of his sick bed to fight, a reversal in home fortunes didn't seem likely.

And so it proved when the referee stepped in to stop the bout after just 25 seconds when it became clear Wrenn was struggling to breathe well enough.

The red defeats continued as Byryn Haywood lost unanimously to tough Truro man Adam Tanner and heavyweight Craig Lavercombe went down by majority to Portsmouth University's Simon Easter.

Darren Hull also made a brave bid to halt the run, but he was forced onto the back foot in another narrow majority defeat at the hands of Pompey pugilist Mick O'Sullivan.

■ ENTERTAINING: Tommy Hull tangles with Mitchell Lever in the fight of the night, but it was the Synwell ABC boxer who emerged victorious. Rob Tibbles 0802-10_09

Rookies show fighting skills

■ VALIANT DEFEAT: Tom Allum (red) showed great spirit in his defeat by Oliver Hall Green from Apollo.
Picture: Jo Tibbles 0906-117-15

■ DEBUT BOUT: Jake Coates (red) in his debut bout defeated Jay Warren from Carls Boxing.
Picture: Jo Tibbles 0906-117-08

■ EARLY EXIT: Andy Stevens (red) loses to Jamie Harrison. He went crashing out in the second round.
Picture: Jo Tibbles 0906-117-19

382

By MARK JENKIN
mjenkin@c-dm.co.uk

A STRING of new boxing talents took to the ring for the first time at Barnstaple ABC's Rugby Club Show.

And judging by the excitement on offer, the host club can look forward to seeing their rookies develop in the coming years.

While Bideford's Tommy Langford provided a fitting finale with his silky skills, further down the bill it was all about the will to win.

Debuts don't come much more explosive than Jake Coates' rip-roaring introduction against Jay Warren of Carl's Boxing Club.

For a fight featuring two lads testing themselves on the big stage for the first time, the standard was superb.

The bout had just about everything. Not even a delay for some emergency repairs to the ropes, could ruin a pulsating clash.

Coates came back from a standing count in the first round before responding with real heart.

It didn't look good for the home prospect when Warren came out firing in the first, gaining control with stiff, two-handed assaults.

But Coates cleverly switched his attack downstairs, seizing the momentum in round two with a succession of wincing rights to his rival's ribs.

When Warren was slammed into the ropes at the start of the third, the visitor required a standing count, but it was the ring that needed running repairs.

One of the ropes came loose, delaying the action for 10 minutes and giving Warren, and the fans, a valuable chance to catch their breath.

The delay didn't affect either boxers' concentration though. If anything, it added to the drama and tension.

Coates came back to finish the job, as the crowd roared their approval at the judges' majority verdict.

Another Barum newcomer, Tom Altum, showed similar spirit in the next bout against Apollo's Oliver Hall-Green, a constant danger with his powerful left leads.

Despite losing unanimously, Altum can be proud of his efforts, standing strong and being prepared to trade with the tough Torquay opponent.

Split decisions also went in favour of Barum boys Brook Hawkins, Keir McKinnon and Joe Ogijewicz.

Hawkins showed real maturity to out-point Finchley's Mark Osbourne after his fellow ABA quarter-finalist made a pacy start.

Swiping left hooks from the Londoner proved a real menace before Hawkins got in close, doing his best work on the inside.

The home favourite picked it up in the second round, feigning and landing with single shots, and the clever movement continued in the third with Hawkins dropping his shoulder to score at close quarters.

Having lost to Watchet's Cole Nixon at Barnstaple's Chivenor show in April, McKinnon was determined to put the record straight.

He succeeded with a real hustle-and-bustle display, convincing the judges in the tightest of contests.

While the visitor was an early threat with his raking right hooks, McKinnon steamed forward with solid left jabs, impressing with his relentless work ethic.

Ogijewicz, known affectionately to the home fans as Joe Ogi, added to his growing reputation with another tidy display against Launceston's Marley Seal.

One year on from his all-action victory over Jake Foley of Finchley, Bideford's Jake Langdon repeated the trick.

This time it was Langdon's composure and concentration that stood out in a desperately close bout.

Connecting with a flashing overhand right at the end of the second round, he kept up the good work in the third workmanship behind a tight defence and getting through with hurtful single shots.

Both boxers were praised by the referee for their performances.

The clash between Barnstaple's Billy Hammett and John Kerrigan of Romford was shaping up to be an intriguing tussle — when it ended in anti-climax.

Hammett went over on his ankle at the end of the first round, forcing the referee to call an early halt to proceedings.

Until then the pair had put up a decent show in a well-matched bout. Hammett will hope for better luck in a re-match at Romford when the new season gets underway.

There was also an early exit for Andy Stevens who was sent crashing to the canvas by Jamie Harrison of Carl's Boxing Club midway through the second round.

Harrison had already caught his rival with a punishing body shot in the opening round forcing him to drop to one knee.

And the visitor started the second as he did the first, plastering his rival with punches.

Caught by a glancing blow on the chin, Stevens stumbled on to his back and was left staring up at the ring lights.

In the battle of the big guys, Apollo's Harry Armstrong outpointed Barum's Aiden Hobbs over three tough rounds.

Hobbs went bulldozing in early, connecting with a couple of sturdy lefts before his rival got on top as the tempo simmered down.

A powerful final round from Armstrong saw him landing the majority of the meaty shots for a unanimous victory.

Rudi Davies found herself against an opponent with real pedigree in the evening's only female contest.

Finchley's Lucy Murphy, daughter of three-times ABA champ Shaun Murphy, won by a first-round stoppage.

Meanwhile, Barnstaple's Harry Sugars and Kai Avery of Tivvy/South Molton both missed out by unanimous decisions. Further down the bill, Barum youngster Alfie Bond and Jack Harper of National Smeltings honed their skills in a kid gloves contest.

Results: Alfie Bond (Barnstaple) v Jack Harper (National Smeltings), skills bout; Kai Avery (Tivvy/South Molton) lost to Connor Betteridge (Golden Ring), U; Jack Featherston (Portsmouth Stacey) lost to Lewis Hughes (Romford), U; George Gibbons (Exmouth) lost to Robert Andrews (Golden Ring), R1 stoppage; Billy Pickingham (Southend) lost to Tyrone Trixter-Hinckes (Starminster Newton), U; Michael Battlingal (Portsmouth Stacey) beat Jack Sawyer (Romford), R1 stoppage; Josh McAbe (Launceston) beat Jack Chynworth (Pilgrims), U; Harry Sugars (Barnstaple) lost to Bradley Barclay (Romford), U; Rudi Davies (Barnstaple) beat Lucy Murphy (Finchley) R1 stoppage; Joe Ogijewicz (Barnstaple) beat Marley Seal (Launceston), M; Keir McKinnon (Barnstaple) beat Cole Nixon (Watchet), M; Jake Langdon (Bideford) beat Jake Foley (Finchley), M; Billy Hammett (Barnstaple) lost to John Kerrigan (Romford) R1 stoppage; Brook Hawkins (Barnstaple) beat Mark Osbourne (Finchley), M; Aidan Hobbs (Barnstaple) lost to Harry Armstrong (Apollo), U; Josh Williams (Launceston) beat Ben Memish (Pilgrims), U; Jake Coates (Barnstaple) beat Jay Warren (Carl's Boxing Club), M; Tom Altum (Barnstaple) lost Oliver Hall-Green (Apollo), U; Tobin Foote (Devonport) lost to Adam Banister (Paignton), U; Andy Stevens (Barnstaple) lost to Jamie Harrison (Carl's Boxing Club), R2 stoppage; Tommy Langford (Bideford) beat Liam Power (Paignton), U.

25-6-2009.

BARNSTAPLE and BIDEFORD ABC

BOXERS

■ SWINGING: Troy Elworthy (right) takes on Archie Nash.

Thursday October 29, 2015 **The Journal**

■ FIGHTING BACK: Barnstaple boxer Connor Woods tries to get off the ropes against Lewis Coles.

PLENTY of YOUNG TALENT

COMING THROUGH!

BARNSTAPLE PANNIER MARKET BOXING SHOW.

BARNSTAPLE and BIDEFORD BOXING CLUBS.

387

■ **ON THE BACK FOOT:** Tom Allum, of Barnstaple ABC, misses with a left in his narrow defeat to Pilgrims boxer Mike Dann at the Pannier Market on Sunday afternoon. Pictures: Mike Southon. To order this photograph call 0844 4060 262 and quote Ref: BNMS20110619F-022_C

■ **LOCAL RIVALS:** Swain (left) and Hatch. Ref: BNMS20110619F-007_C

■ **PATIENT:** Billy Hammett (left). Ref: BNMS20110619F-029_C

BARNSTAPLE ABC

Results

Red corner 1st: Alfie King (Bideford) v James Hill-Perdin (Bideford) skills bout, Alfie Bond (Barnstaple) lost to Louis Down (Chard), Otis Llewelyn (Barnstaple) beat Josh Hallem (Gloucester), Liam Laird (Barnstaple) beat Jordan Letts (Solihull), Fen Everest (Barnstaple) lost to Billy Harley (Oakmead), Charlie Burbidge (Barnstaple) lost to Liam Houlahan (Paignton), Kai Avery (Barnstaple) lost to Ricky Dymond (Bideford) U, Alex Jones (Tiverton) beat Callum James (Sydenham) M, Jack Gabriel (Barnstaple) lost to Jack Brierley (Paignton) RSC 2nd round, Marcus Yeo (Sydenham) lost to Lee Owen (Watchet) U, Henry Swain (Barnstaple) beat Jake Hatch (Bideford) M, Tom Allum (Barnstaple) lost to Mike Dann (Pilgrims) U, Billy Hammett (Barnstaple) beat Jack Green (Pilgrims) M.

BARNSTAPLE ABC

BEN GREENSMITH

MARK SIMPSON, CONNOR WOODS, MICHAEL 'MITCH' WARBURTON.

Waiting for the SCORE CARDS!

Crowd-pleaser John makes his followers happy

By DAVE PEDLER

JOHN SABIN is a crowd-pleaser . . . and he pleased a big one in Barnstaple's Ex-Service & Social Club on Saturday night.

The man from Brunei - backed by a cacophonous crowd of supporters from South Molton - was making his Barnstaple Boxing Club debut.

And, after three rounds of eccentric action against Mayflower's Pearce Davies he gave the fans what they wanted - a home win.

Sabin's basic tactic was to stalk his opponent around the ring until he got the chance to unleash what they used to call a "roundhouse right".

And he did it often enough and effectively enough to get the verdict on all three judges' cards.

Brian Birchmore was Barum's other debut man but he lost a unanimous verdict to Julian Bray of Bideford.

Southpaw Bray's straight right and solid left hook won the day quite comfortably but he could never quell the spirit of a courageous opponent who never took a backward step no matter how many times he was hit.

Gary Turner used a big height and reach advantage to good effect to stop a bloodied but brave J. Willey of Exeter in the 3rd round.

Compact

And Jimmy Briggs was the host club's other winner with a compact, busy and confident display to outpoint D. Abbott of Phoenix.

His club-mates Dan Davies and Joe Stanley, though, both faded in the final round to suffer unanimous defeats at the hands of B. Wakeham of Apollo and C. Calloway of Camborne respectively.

Three Bideford boxers provided the other local interest on the bill with Tommy Langford given another chance to display his talent.

He got hit rather too often for comfort by A. Crowe of Mayflower but, for the most part, once again looked a very good prospect as he won a majority decision in what was judged the best bout of the night.

Club-mate Sam Stevens also won the vote of two judges to beat fellow novice C. Ellis of Camborne but a more tentative Joe Grimley lost his first bout on all three cards to S. Cross of Sturminster.

■ The next boxing action in North Devon is the Bideford club show at the Pannier Market on April 13.

JOHN SABIN

JOHN pictured after his EXCITING BOUT with BIDEFORD'S JOHN VAN EMMENIS.

BARNSTAPLE ABC

BARNSTAPLE ABC

393

BARNSTAPLE ABC

BARNSTAPLE ABC

Sweet revenge for Benny Boy

BEN CHAPPELL dined out on the sweet taste of revenge on Saturday night.

Two months after his Golden Belt semi-final loss to Bexley's Joe McCully, Chappell got even by winning the big rematch at Barnstaple ABC's show.

You can only feel sympathy for the judges scoring a battle between these two pint-sized predators.

The first contest came down to a single punch, and this one was equally close.

In fact, one judge marked an 18-12 win for Golden Belt winner McCully, but Benny Boy got the nod from the other two.

It was fought at a breakneck pace from first bell to last, and Chappell kept the Bexley boy on his toes with excellent combinations.

He was given a 21-15 win on the second card, and took the decision 14-13 on the third.

Chappell's Barum clubmate Nico Faassen also caught the eye with another superb display – this time beating Sydenham ABC's Karl Hawkins unanimously to be named as boxer of the night.

Faassen used his height to full advantage, teasing Hawkins with some tasty left jabs in round one before backing them up with some good-looking rights.

And two cracking right hooks in particular, both midway through the third, made sure the Sydenham man was done and dusted.

Joey Kerner also gave the vociferous home crowd value for money – and sent them home happy.

Kerner closed the Ex-Servicemen's Club show by seeing off Camborne's Adam Williams in one minute.

Williams made a cautious start, but it soon became clear he was not going to be able to cope when the first of Kerner's rights sneaked through his guard and wobbled him.

Soon after, his face absorbed another rocket and the referee stepped it for the standing count.

Williams' dazed look was enough to convince the ref he had had enough, and Kerner's arm was raised.

The evening ended as it had begun . . . with local success.

Following an entertaining kid gloves curtain-raiser with Barum youngsters Reece Haywood and Billy Hammett, Jake Langden got the ball rolling with a majority win over Pilgrims' Nico Blight.

Langden's best moments came in the opening minute of four cracking unanswered blows.

The Plymouth fighter finally came up with some testing offence of his own in the third – one right appeared to trouble Langden, but it was too late to make any massive alteration on the cards.

Ben Hunter also claimed a majority win against Bexley's James Hales.

The home boxer struggled to cope with his lofty opponent's left jabs in the early going, but gradually found his feet.

He just edged round two, and came out all guns blazing in the third to seal the win.

Barum's Eddie Shiels battled Minehead's Danny Wilson in a skills contest to bring the first half of the evening's card to a close.

And after the interval, it started badly for the local clubs with three losses.

Tommy Hull had to absorb a few wincing blows from Camborne's Luke Rosevear and

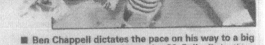

■ Ben Chappell dictates the pace on his way to a big win over Golden Belt champ Joe McCully. Order this picture at www.ndjphotos.com ref: 060212964

lost unanimously, as did Tommy Herd against Bexley's Joe Kingswell.

Herd's nose kept in regular contact with Kingswell's left jab, and he was unable to turn the tables.

Bideford's lone representative, Nick Bower, then lost unanimously to Kingswell's club mate Rob Stacey.

This one was fairly close, and Bower ended well, but he was unable to change the judges' minds.

CHRIS ROGERS

■ Tommy Herd takes one in the face during his loss to Bexley's Joe Kingswell. Order this picture at

Barum pack ready for action in Rugby Club Show

Thursday June 11, 2009

The Journal

■ HOME FAVOURITES: All Barnstaple ABC's carded fighters have bouts lined up at Pottington Road.

■ FLOORED: Ultra-distance runner Vicky Skelton with Valentin Bumbul.

BOXING

BARNSTAPLE Amateur Boxing Club are gearing up to host a huge summer event.

On June 20, the club's popular Rugby Club Show returns, featuring a whopping bill of 25 bouts at Pottington Road.

All Barum's carded boxers have contests lined up and England international Tommy Langford is also expected to appear in the Saturday night spectacular.

Langford, of Hall Green ABC, may be joined by his brother, Jack, and fellow Bideford ABC favourites Richard Grigg and Ray Penfold.

The meeting between Barum's Brook Hawkins and fellow junior ABA quarter-finalist Mark Osborne, of Finchley, promises to be an entertaining contest.

Boxers from Ilfracombe and South Molton will add to the local interest, while prospects from as far away as Romford, Cwmbran and Southampton will add to the action.

Two Barnstaple boxers, Harry Sugars and Keir McKinnon, prepared for the show with bouts in Wiltshire at the weekend.

McKinnon left no doubt against Jack Williamson, dominating all three rounds at Malmesbury Football Club.

Non-stop attacks forced his opponent on to the back foot, achieving a unanimous verdict for his fifth win from six in an impressive season.

Sugars boxed Charlie Ferris in a high-paced contest between evenly-matched rivals. The Barnstaple boy missed out by a mere one-point majority.

Fans are advised to book early for the Rugby Club Show. Doors open at 4pm with tickets costing £10 and £5 for under-14s accompanied by an adult. Children under six go free.

Tickets are available from the Corner House, Barnstaple Boxing Club or by calling Sarah Simpson on 01271 345638.

● Strength, stamina and determination are vital ingredients for any successful boxer or athlete.

The two sports came together when Vicky Skelton visited Combe Martin ABC to pass on some top advice.

The ultra-distance runner, rated number one 24-hour racer for Great Britain and the Commonwealth, gave a talk on roadwork training.

Skelton, head coach for North Devon Road Runners, gave the boxers a plan on how to focus running training toward their sport.

After impressing the boxers, parents and coaches with her knowledge, she then stepped into the ring for some quick boxing tips.

ABA coach Tim Pike provided the advice before a brief sparring session with England's Senior Novice Heavyweight finalist Valentin Bumbul.

Club members passed on their best wishes to Skelton as she prepares to represent England at the Commonwealth Ultra Distance Championships in the Lake District in September.

To find out more about training at Combe Martin ABC, contact Lloyd Chappell on 07792 129933.

Edwards gets verdict in the high-speed highlight

BOXING

By MARK JENKIN

mjenkin@c-dm.co.uk

THE FEROCIOUS tussle between Steve Edwards and Lloyd Roberts lit up Barnstaple ABC's boxing show.

Eager to impress, two hungry young boxers provided the high-speed highlight at the Chivenor marine base on Saturday night.

And it was the energetic Edwards who led the entertainment, shading the contest for a popular hometown victory.

Setting the tempo with pacy, two-handed attacks, he held firm against the rapid replies of the Yeovil visitor.

Although Roberts got through on the inside to land a powerful right at the end of the first round, Edwards was going nowhere.

His blurring left-right combinations wobbled Roberts on to the ropes early in the second as the home support got behind their man.

By the end of the third, Edwards had earned the judges' approval, but both lads accepted applause from an appreciative crowd.

A few last-minute cancellations meant the show was reduced to just 10 bouts, but there was still some decent displays from the North Devon contingent.

At the top of the bill, Jimmy Randall had to be patient to see off the threat of Devonport's Aidie Campbell.

Content to box defensively and swipe forward on the counter-attack, Campbell proved difficult to hit.

While the home favourite tried to force the issue with his right jab, by the end of the third it was a tough bout to call.

In the end, Randall took a split decision with one of the judges giving him the nod for showing better style.

Another boxer prepared to go the distance was fast-improving Barum junior Joe Ogijewicz. His commitment to the cause was evident even before he stepped into the ring.

After visiting family in Po-

■ SETTING THE PACE: Steve Edwards prepares to land another blow on Lloyd Roberts. 0904-174_11

land, Ogi only arrived back in England in the afternoon but was determined not to miss out.

Facing Devonport's Connor Webb, he stood strong in a tight bout, getting through with occasional rights to land a majority verdict.

Not that all the marginal decisions went the way of the North Devon lads.

Bideford's Richard Grigg could feel a little hard done by after missing out by majority against Sam Fletcher.

Never allowing the tempo to drop, Grigg kept the pressure on with left-right combinations, particularly in the second round.

But the equally energetic Devonport boxer was always a threat with his flashing right hook, getting the nod from two of the judges.

Keir McKinnon's three-bout winning streak may have ended, but the Barum newcomer will have learned a lot

from his majority defeat against the more experienced Cole Nixon.

Both pressure fighters who like to pile forward, the bout got untidy as they grappled for control.

The Watchet visitor landed the cleaner shots to take the honours, while McKinnon was named Barnstaple's best boxer of the night by guest of honour Glen Adair, the club's only ABA champion.

Aiden Hobbs is also improving, although not at a quick enough rate to trouble Berinsfield's Joe Joyce.

Hobbs was stopped in the second round when the pair met the previous week, but this time he held out until the third before the referee intervened.

With an obvious reach advantage, Joyce landed some dangerous rights from distance while Hobbs held out bravely before his resistance finally ended.

Chris Collins found life

equally tough against Bideford's Ray Penfold, retiring at the end of the second round, worn down by his opponent's relentless work-rate.

There was disappointment for Barum juniors Harry Sügars and Dan Jury, both beaten despite promising displays.

Sügars lost against Golden Ring's Jack Terrell while Jury missed out in his first bout, outscored by Tiverton's Dan Broom.

Results: Harry Sügars (Barnstaple) lost to Jack Terrell (Golden Ring) M 15-11, 7-10, 7-14; Dan Jury (Barnstaple) lost to Dan Broom (Tiverton) U 10-21, 8-22, 7-16; Ray Penfold (Bideford) beat Chris Collins (Berinsfield) R2 retired; Jack Knapton (Tiverton) lost to Liam Simpson (Portland) M 8-9, 12-5, 9-12; Joe Ogijewicz (Barnstaple) beat Connor Webb (Devonport) M 10-4, 15-9, 10-12; Aiden Hobbs (Barnstaple) lost to Joe Joyce (Berinsfield) R3 stoppage; Steve Edwards (Barnstaple) beat Lloyd Roberts (Yeovil) M 16-20, 22-11, 20-12; Keir McKinnon (Barnstaple) lost to Cole Nixon (Watchet) M 8-10, 10-9, 20-12; Richard Grigg (Bideford) lost to Sam Fletcher (Devonport) M 18-11, 14-8, 12-13; Jimmy Randall (Barnstaple) beat Aidie Campbell (Devonport) M 10-17, 12-8, 9-9.

NORTH DEVON JOURNAL Sport

Thursday June 14, 2012

First women's boxing bout makes North Devon history

BARNSTAPLE ABC

PAST AND FUTURE: This picture captures boxing fans watching the bout between Becky McMillan, of Plympton, and Zoe Young, of the Navy, at Barnstaple Pannier Market.

It is believed to be the first women's amateur bout to be staged at a venue steeped in North Devon boxing history.

Women's boxing is a fast growing sport and this summer, for the first time, it will be included at the Olympic Games.

McMillan gained a unanimous win in one of 21 contests at the show hosted by Barnstaple ABC on Sunday afternoon.

Tom's composed performance

■ ON TARGET: Liam Laird lands a punch on Jake Demmery.   Picture: Mike Southon. To order call 0844 4060 269 and quote Ref: BNMS201206100-030_C

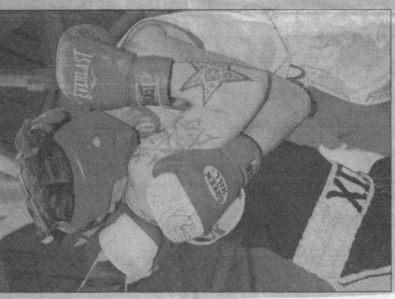

■ CLINCH: Nicco Faaassen (right) grapples with Robin Collins.   Picture: Mike Southon. To order call 0844 4060 269 and quote Ref: BNMS201206100-005_C

By MARK JENKIN
mjenkin@c-dm.co.uk

DEDICATION and desire helped Tom Allum, of Barnstaple Amateur Boxing Club, complete the first half of a sporting double on Sunday.

Topping the bill at Barnstaple Pannier Market, he rounded off a fine afternoon for the host club with a rousing win against Joe Smith, of the Tavern club.

Now Allum hopes those attributes will help him go the distance over 26.2 miles of hills in the North Devon AONB Marathon next week.

There were not too many ups and downs for the home favourite during a composed three-round performance against the visitor from Somerset.

Urged by his corner not to become embroiled in a scrap, Allum was wise to stick with a measured approach, dictating with the jab and keeping his guard held high.

And the loudest cheer of the day echoed around the historic venue when the majority verdict was announced in his favour.

The following day, Allum was due to complete a 13-mile training run in preparation for his first marathon.

Fitness was a vital factor for many of the young boxers as so many bouts were simply too close to call.

Split decisions were the order of the day with no fewer that 14 of the 19 competitive fights dividing the judges' opinions.

Persistence paid off for Liam Laird in a real hustle-and-bustle contest against Downend's Jake Demmery which had the crowd barking their approval.

Both lads had success with flurries of punches in the first two rounds and Laird seized the initiative in the third with a jarring left to leave Demmery briefly dazed and confused.

Although the Bristol boxer regained his composure, Laird maintained the work-rate to win it 17-14, 17-13, 11-12.

For Kai Avery it was a case of "no pain no gain" with a gutsy win over Fabian Peterkin, despite a wrist injury in the second half of the fight.

Avery is nicknamed Arshavin at Barnstaple after the Russian footballer but unlike the one-time Arsenal player, you can always guarantee 100 per cent effort from the Barum boxer.

Maintaining a tight guard and throwing fast combinations, he dictated the pace against the dangerous counter-puncher from Weymouth.

Avery was clearly in some discomfort ahead of the final round but adrenalin and aggression were enough to see him through.

While most of the Barum boys had been training hard in the gym, Nico Faassen spent the build-up to the show topping up his sun tan on holiday in Turkey.

And the relaxed approach did him no harm at all in clash of styles against Rob Collins, of the Tavern club.

The long left jab of Faassen and the swiping combinations of Collins made for an intriguing encounter which was shaded once again by the hosts.

The meeting between Harry Sugars, of Barnstaple, and Rhys Geisheimer, of Barry East End, was always going to be a boxing match rather than a brawl.

Two technicians bided their time and patiently tried to break down each other's defensive guards.

More often it was Sugars doing the pressing and showing why he made the England ABA semi-finals this season yet Geisheimer, the Welsh ABA champion, did enough for the majority win.

Joe Freeman is improving all the time and his hand speed was the key to victory over Downend's Morgan Hart in a high-tempo clash.

Like Freeman, Patrick Morton is a Barnstaple prospect enjoying a promising introduction to the sport.

He was well matched against Jake Burnard, of Pilgrims, with only a handful of points separating two slight and speedy youngsters after three rounds.

Jordan Jones could not hide his delight after winning a painstakingly tight Devon-versus-Cornwall clash for the host club.

William Jeffries, of St Ives, missed out on a scorecard which read 10-9, 13-12, 4-5 in favour of the Barum boy.

That one was also impossible to call and it was a similar story as Mitch Turner traded hefty blows with Wallace Atwell, of Weston-super-Mare.

Strong and stocky, the pair were prepared to plant their feet and plough forward in a crowd-pleasing slugfest.

The referee congratulated them for an excellent encounter which finished level on points as Atwell got the nod from two of the three judges.

Rob Squires battled gamely against Morgan Burgess, of Llanharan, but the Welsh visitor, with reach advantage, always had the edge.

A bumper afternoon of boxing started for Barnstaple with Bailey Murphy showing his skills in a kid gloves bout against James Stockwell, of Blandford.

North Devon's final boxing show of the season will be hosted by Combe Martin ABC at Combe Martin Village Hall on June 23.

For Allum, attention now turns to the marathon when he will be running to raise money for North Devon Hospice.

Joining him to represent Barnstaple ABC over the marathon or half marathon are Liz Gayton, Claire Meech, Mandi Yeo, Adam Buckeridge, Jacqui Pearcey, Kate Simpson, Jenny Stone and Joyce Mulholland.

On Sunday they raised the sum of £159.59 with an auction and collection. Boxing fans can support their marathon effort at www.justgiving.com/north-devonboxingclubs.

16-6-2012.

Barnstaple Amateur Boxing Club Presents

BARNSTAPLE BOXING

★ ★ ★

The Barnstaple Pannier Market
Sunday 2nd June 2013
Doors open 1pm - Boxing Starts 2.30pm

Ticket price £10.00 per ticket

Tickets to be bought in advance at £10.00. Contact: Mark Simpson 07749 231121

Tickets can also be picked up from the
Barnstaple Amateur Boxing Club or The Corner House.

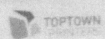 TOPTOWN PRINTERS   Printed by: Toptown Printers T: 01271 371271   E: enquiries@toptown.co.uk

Design by: RWCS E: robwrey@rwcs.co.uk

■ SETTING OUT THEIR STALL: Barnstaple Pannier Market makes for an impressive venue as Jordan Jones (left) takes on Shirkhan Armedi. Picture: Paula Davies. Ref: BNP020130602C-006_C

Elworthy proves he is multi talented

By LIAM CURTIS
liam@northdevonjournal.co.uk

WHEN Flynn Elworthy stepped out of the ring on Saturday night you might have expected the teenage boxer to have a headache.

Yet it wasn't the six minutes of pounding gloves giving Elworthy grief but the realisation he has more than one sport craving his attention.

The 15-year-old was crowned Western Counties junior champion as he dispatched Jake Carr at Barnstaple ABC's show despite undergoing an intense rugby trial earlier in the day.

Elworthy completed a training session with Exeter Chiefs U15 before racing back for his

● DAISY Burdett took to the ring for the first time and was edged out on a unanimous decision against Chantelle Whiting, of Mayflower ABC. The 13-year-old was bombarded with head shots in the early stages and forced into an eight count before fighting back in the bravest display of the night.
Daisy hopes her exploits will spur more girls into joining her at Barnstaple ABC as she dreams of a regular sparring partner.
"I am the only girl at the boxing club and I really want more to join," she said.
"Boxing is really energetic and I love giving it my all in the ring, it's really fun.
"You do get hit a lot but it never hurts very much and you are always friends at the end."

championship bout – all without the knowledge his coach Mark Simpson.

"Flynn was the highlight of the night by miles, he was awesome," said Simpson.

"He had lost to the other lad twice but it was a complete turnaround and Flynn won when it mattered.

"I didn't realise he played rugby earlier in the day until he boxed. Hopefully he can continue to balance both because he's a brilliant boxer."

Elworthy was pitted against a strong and powerful opponent from Arena Boxing Club in Bournemouth who came tearing out of the blocks in the opening round.

The home boxer remained composed and intelligent with his shots, picking off a series of well-executed jabs before ducking and diving from the outside in the second round to attack Carr's head in a bruising manner.

In the final round both boxers looked drained as a relentless tempo took its toll but Elworthy shone through as he forced an eight count towards the final bell and won on a split decision.

A national junior championship semi-final bout awaits Elworthy on March 21 providing rugby doesn't get in the way.

"I'm going to be really nervous in the next round but I want to get to the final," said Elworthy who plays rugby for Barnstaple where his brother, Matt Gohl, is in the first team.

"I was pretty tired coming into the fight from the Chiefs academy day but it was worth it.

"I prefer my rugby because

I've progressed further in it and one day I want to play professionally."

In Barnstaple ABC's other Western Counties match-up, Nick Forrest narrowly lost to Ben Benham, of Blandford ABC, by technical knockout.

Bragging rights went Bideford ABC's way in the evening's club bouts.

Kye Cook claimed victory over Barnstaple's Troy Elworthy. Both boxers displayed a high level of technical ability before Cook's reach and sweeping footwork took a unanimous decision.

When Barnstaple's Liam Laird and Bideford's Ben Owen matched up, two contrasting styles smashed against each other.

Owen rushed into clumsy shots in the opening round as Laird worked patiently behind his jab and took the middle of the ring. But Owen's sheer power saw him get back into the fight with thumping body shots evening up the score.

In the final round Laird maintained his dynamite left and right combinations but it was Owen was able to dash

away from danger with sharp head movements and take the win on a split decision.

Beth Warne, of Devonport ABC, and Elizabeth Bools, of Trowbridge, sparked the show into life in only the third bout.

The junior female contest was electric from the opening bell. Warne's towering presence took her to a unanimous decision in the final round.

Results – cadets: Jake Hooper (Barnstaple ABC) lost to Terry Price (Weston-super-Mare) TKO. Jack Silk (Lympstone) bt Bailey Phillips (Yeovil) U. **Juniors:** Beth Warne (Devonport) bt Elizabeth Bools (Trowbridge) U, Daisy Burdett (Barnstaple ABC) lost to Chantelle Whiting (Mayflower) U, Ryan Hoar (Bodmin) bt Tynan Gleed (Emeralds) TKO, Troy Elworthy (Barnstaple ABC) lost to Kye Cook (Bideford ABC) U, Callum Smith (Trowbridge) bt Thomas Tovey (Downend) U, Michael Cash (Yate) lost to Brad Ingram (Gloucester) U, Nick Forrest (Barnstaple ABC) lost to Ben Benham (Blandford) TKO, Samuel Vallis (Horseshoe) lost to Owen Pirret (Downend) U, Flynn Elworthy (Barnstaple ABC) bt Jake Carr (Arena) S. **Men's open elite:** Liam Laird (Barnstaple ABC) lost to Ben Owen (Bideford ABC) S.

Sweet success for Sugars as he takes title

HARRY Sugars claimed the Western Counties Middleweight title as he topped the bill at the Barnstaple Pannier Market Show.

Almost four hours of boxing had built up to Sugars' showdown with Jake Toogood from Paddy Johns ABC, and the Barum boxer showed tremendous resilience to win on a split decision having fallen behind in the opening round.

A fast-moving Toogood danced between stances and probed at Sugars with a swagger of over confidence as showboating was brought into play.

But the Paddy Johns boxer had all the right skills to match this and when the first three minutes were up it was Sugars who was clearly off the pace.

"I didn't know if I had won it to be honest, it was close," said Sugars.

"Normally my fitness pulls me through but it wasn't really there as I have only boxed one other time this year, and that was last week.

"Luckily the crowd cheered me on and with them behind me I found the extra strength to come back in the final round."

Sugars had racked up a few more points in the second round with a more aggressive approach although his opponent was still able to pick off points on the counter.

It was at the bell of the final three minutes where Sugars saw red as he forced Toogood into the corner, battering his body with blows and chucking any sign of showboating out of the ring.

"The showboating's not for me but each to their own," said Sugars.

"I'm a little more old school in my approach but at the end of the day it's about whatever works for you."

The show had kicked off in style with an early, and only, Barnstaple v Bideford bout on the cards where the home show's Jake Hooper walked away the victor.

But Bideford regained their voice when Lewis McKenzie put Yeovil ABC's Liam Marchant to the sword with a brave and bruising performance and the laid-back Ben Owen later took centre stage.

The Biddy boxer controlled his fight throughout with only lapses of concentration causing him grief.

But before he could get bored of his own bout, which he so often does, Owen exploded with pace and accuracy to secure a unanimous win.

Ilfracombe's Dan Goulding put in a tough shift against Steve Priest from Launceston before he fell short and Liam Laird was unable to end a terrific season on a high.

"It's disappointing to lose at home and on the last show," said Laird.

"But it's been a great season and I've only lost three times.

"I knew I hadn't given the fight enough but with a shoulder injury it was always going to be difficult."

Results

School boys: Webber Ellison (Priorswood) L-unan D Nash (King Alfred's), Louis Sik (Lympstone) W-unan Freddie Wright (Bideford), Connor Woods (Barnstaple) L-split Lewis Coles (St Ives Bay), Reece Mitchell (Yeovil) L-tko Callum Cunningham (Bideford), Jake Hooper (Barnstaple) W-unan Bailey Radcliffe (Bideford), Joel Garrett (Avalon) W-unan Tyler Barber (Bude), Troy Elworthy (Barnstaple) W-split Archie Nash (Portland).

Junior: Jed Davies (Barnstaple) W-unan Alan Barney (Blandford), Nic Forrest 9Barnstaple) L-unan Josh Cunningham (Devonport), Lewis Ademi (Downed) W-tko Tommy Stone (King Alfred's), Tony Burdett (Barnstaple) L-unan Eithan Liffle (Wachet).

Senior: Liam Marchant (Yeovil) L-unan Lewis McKenzie (Bideford), Jordan Jones L-unan Lewis Shaw (Lympstone), Dan Goulding (Ilfracombe) L-unan Steve Priest (Launceston), Ryan Hibbard (Devonport) L-unan Ben Owen (Bideford).

Elite: Liam Laird (Barnstaple) L-unan Dead Dodge (Yeovil).

Western Counties Middleweight title: Harry Sugars (Barnstaple) W-unan Jake Toogood (Paddy Johns).

BARNSTAPLE ABC

SAM ADAIR and brother GLENN present Trophies.

Former BARNSTAPLE BOXER, PETER MALLET at a BARNSTAPLE
PANNIER MARKET SHOW, DB.

Squires fights back after being floored

The Journal   Thursday February 26, 2015

BOXING

By LIAM CURTIS
liam@northdevonjournal.co.uk

ROBBIE Squires bounced back from his first competitive knockdown to claim the heavyweight title at the England Boxing Youth Championships.

The Barnstaple ABC boxer was both the youngest and lightest fighter on the night at 81kg but blitzed his way to the final over three days of competition.

Having overcome George Muncher from Leeds Tigers and Romford's Tim Olla in the semi-final, Squires was ready to face Cory Clarke, of Warley ABC, in Sunday's showdown.

Moments after the first bell he was forced to the deck by a big right hook and his fight already looked over.

"Everything went white and all I remember thinking is, 'I have to get back up and recover'," said Squires. "It was strange and the first time I've ever been knocked down.

"But I never wanted to back down or quit, it just took me a minute to get my head right."

Squires rose to his feet following an eight count before fighting back with added force and taking his opponent by surprise.

In the second round a flurry of speedy shots did further damage before Squires went on to win a unanimous decision.

Coach Mark Simpson was proud of his boxer's resilience in the final, although he had his doubts after the knockdown.

"Rob was hit with a huge right bomb at the start and was dropped like a stone, it looked like it was all over but he showed great resilience and determination to get back on to his feet," said Simpson

Squires's motivation for success stems from losing in the same final last year and the growing likelihood he will box for England.

"Everyone who wins a national title gets to join an England assessment day so I have that to look forward to on March 7," said Squires.

"With a bit of luck I could be representing my country at the Three Nations competition which will be amazing."

Although Squires is taking a well-deserved break, fellow Barnstaple ABC boxers Mitch Turner, Flynn Elworthy and Nic Forrest will all be in action in the Western Counties junior finals on Saturday at Barnstaple Rugby Club, along with a host of club bouts.

Doors open at 4pm and tickets (£10) are available from the Corner House, the gym or Mark Simpson on 07749 231121.

■ HEAVYWEIGHT CHAMPION: Barnstaple's Robbie Squires.

Webber wins

BOXING

EBONY WEBBER is gaining a reputation for her fast work in the boxing ring.

After winning by first-round stoppage on her debut for Torrington Police ABC last month, she repeated the trick in Exmouth on Saturday night.

Home boxer Marni Martinez found the power and variety too much in a frantic opening.

Martinez tried to work in close but was soon tagged by her opponent's right hand and required a standing count. Webber went straight on the attack again and when Martinez had her legs buckled by a hook-uppercut, the referee stopped the fight.

On Sunday, Torrington's Cheryl Cottle-Hunkin and 10-year-old Molly Munro attended the Western Counties training squad at Puritan ABC.

407

Squires shows his champion quality

BOXING

ROBBIE Squires returned to the ring in emphatic style as he kick-started his season with a unanimous victory against Louis Phillips.

The England youth heavyweight champion, from Barnstaple ABC, showed his class in the 85kg fight in Solihull.

He landed some big shots in the first round and then took control over Phillips, a junior champion and England representative, with devastating lefts and his trademark short right hook.

It left the judges in no doubt after three rounds.

Barnstaple's Jacob Hooper was narrowly defeated on a split decision by Solihull's Josh McCabe in a nip-and-tuck fight.

Mark Simpson, coach of Barnstaple ABC, said: "It was a barnstorming contest with Jacob coming on stronger in the final round right up to the bell.

"There has to be a winner in amateur boxing and McCabe got the nod on a split with the referee congratulating both boxers for their efforts."

Hooper has a chance for immediate revenge in his club's show at Petroc on Saturday. Squires is also set to feature on the bill.

Tickets are on sale at the gym and Corner House. Doors open at 7pm and boxing starts at 8pm. Find Barnstaple ABC on Facebook for more details.

It was too little too late as Bideford ABC's Alex Dovell lost a split decision to Dave Lewis.

The Minehead ABC boxer pulled ahead in the early stages at Exmouth Pavilions, landing several right hands, while Dovell missed with the jab in a scrappy opener.

It was a tighter affair in the second round as the Bideford man used his footwork to score at range, while Lewis's only success came in tight brawling when he managed to smother Dovell.

In the final round, Dovell came into his own, catching Lewis with some straight combinations. But it was not to be, as Lewis secured the victory on a split decision.

The pair will meet in a rematch at Durrant House Hotel, Northam, on November 20.

■ EMPHATIC: Robbie Squires has his arm raised in victory.

Judges left in no doubt by Squires on return

By JONNY BONELL
jonny.bonell@northdevonjournal.co.uk

TALENTED boxer Robbie Squires insisted there is more to come despite a unanimous victory against Kieron Williams.

Barnstaple ABC's England youth heavyweight champion performed in a home show for the first time in more than two years when he got in the ring at Petroc for the top of the bill clash on Saturday night.

Squires lost to Williams last year in a junior final, but showed his class throughout the fight to leave the judges in no doubt.

"It is nice to get a bit of revenge on him," said Squires, who described the atmosphere as incredible.

"It was good but there is a lot more to come from me.

"Hopefully I can work my way back up to that England standard again."

After an even first round, Squires took control in the second with a big left hand before showing his speed with a left and right combination which shook Williams.

The third round continued in the same vein as Squires's trademark short right hook caused his opponent all sorts of problems.

● THE CROWD created a noisy atmosphere at the first boxing show at Petroc in five years. Barnstaple youngsters had been roared on by home fans throughout, but the noise was cranked up a notch as the show reached its final few bouts.
Ben Stone, Harry Sugars and – in particular – Robbie Squires had to focus solely on their opponents as the spectators' cheers echoed around the college sports hall.
Each Barnstaple jab was met with a roar of encouragement and, when results were announced, an almost deafening noise filled the venue.

"It was a very tough fight," said Squires.

"He is a very good fighter and opponent.

"We have both been on England training together and I have known him for a while, so it was tough and really hard work."

Also on the bill was Barnstaple's Ben Stone, who impressed in his unanimous win over Bideford's Alex Dovell.

From the moment Stone connected with a big right early in the first, the result was never in doubt. He showed a range of shots as Dovell struggled to deal with his pace and power.

A right and left combination from Stone forced the referee to make a standing count in the third round as he continued to dominate.

Harry Sugars battled hard to come through a tough encounter with Lewis Scott, of Sydenham, to win on a split decision.

It was an even fight throughout as they both showed strong defensive work, but Sugars did enough to edge his man.

Mark Simpson, coach of Barnstaple ABC, hailed all the fighters who took part the show.

"Overall I am very pleased with the event and the excellent performances throughout," said Simpson. "It was brilliant and they all did really well.

"I am delighted for Rob (Squires) as well as he is becoming what he should be and what we know he can be."

Jed Davies was also victorious for Barnstaple as he overcame Arena Boxing's Liam Anderson on a split decision.

Liam Laird, Tony Burdett, Jack Hooper, Troy Elworthy, Connor Woods and Daisy Burdett gave good accounts of themselves but just came up short in the judges' decision.

Youngster Dylan Willis also showed his potential in a skills bout.

■ TRIUMPHANT: Jed Davies has his arm raised in victory by the referee. Ref: BNMS20151024E-029_C

■ BOBBING AND WEAVING: Jed Davies, of Barnstaple ABC, sways out of the way of a shot from Liam Anderson during his club's show at Petroc. Ref: BNMS20151024E-026_C

Rob gets warmed up for title defence

■ Rob Squires (right) lost a tight points decision to Luis Williams.

Picture: SUBMITTED

North Devon Gazette | Wednesday, December 9, 2015

BOXING

Barnstaple Amateur Boxing Club's youth heavyweight champion Rob Squires travelled up to Leamington Spar to take on national champion Luis Williams.

The Cleary's ABC fighter was a true test for England youth representative Squires.

The tough Midlander ultimately shaded it, winning on a split decision from the judges.

Despite the judges plumping for Williams, Squires showed plenty of skill and determination and large sections of the crowd felt he was worthy of the victory over the home boxer.

It was a thrilling bout, and an ideal warm-up for Squires ahead of his first title defence in January.

■ MIGHTY FLYNN: Barnstaple ABC's Flynn Elworthy after winning his fight against Jake Carr.

411

Thursday June 11, 2015   **The Journal**

BOXING Barnstaple show

Sporting family gets another win under its belt

■ **SUCCESS:** Troy Elworthy takes on Archie Nash from Portland in a schoolboys' bout. Picture: Rob Tibbles. To order this photograph call 0844 4060 269 and quote Ref: BNRT20150607C-015_C

BARNSTAPLE'S Pannier Market show benchmarked another sporting success for the Elworthy family.

Having raced to the show from the Pollyfield Centre BMX tournament, East-the-Water, Rebecca Gohl arrived in the nick of time to see her son Troy Elworthy in action.

The junior boxer overcame Portland's Archie Nash with a split decision in a repeat bout of his Western Counties Schoolboy final, which he lost.

"It was very nerve-wracking before I went in the ring but I'm so happy to get a win over him," said Troy.

Troy rattled off solid head shots in the opening round as his opponent struggled to break through a compact guard.

Both boxers continued to perfect their jab in the second but it was Troy who took the centre of the ring and despite being tagged with a few late uppercuts, he had done enough damage to secure the win.

For mum Rebecca however, who also spent the year watching elder son Flynn box his way to a Western Counties title while completing a successful trial with Exeter Chiefs U15 rugby team, it was an exhausting process.

"Troy told me he was nervous before the fight and I said, well now you know how I feel," said Rebecca.

"I can get very animated on the side and it's scary watching, exhausting.

"I don't like to think about the endless amounts of travelling we do either.

"Who knows how much money we spend on petrol money? But it's all worth it in the end."

Another son, Matt Gohl, plays rugby for Barnstaple RFC.

Jones' return is a step in the right direction

By JAMES JEFFREY

EVERYONE knows a boxer's confidence is paramount to success in the ring.

Eye-bursting staring contests at weigh-in and trash talk behind the scenes may not be part of the amateur boxing scene but there is a lot that can throw a fighter's confidence.

For Barnstaple ABC's Jordan Jones it was the return to box on his club's final show of the year, having fought just once in over a year, after suffering from an infected lymph node.

The 19-year-old lost on a unanimous decision to Lympstone ABC's Lewis Shaw, but against a boxer with a record of 7-7 it was a step in the right direction to fully reloading his weapon of confidence.

"These bouts in front of my home crowd mean a lot to me. I've been back at training since March, getting my diet right and working hard on my fitness," said Jones.

"I was really nervous as I knew it was going to be a tough fight."

Jones came out strong, working his opponent's body well and weaving his way out of several combos before fitness took its toll.

Nevertheless, the young boxer was pleased to have gone the full four rounds having been stopped after three last time out.

"My fitness is still letting me down," said Jones.

"That's the most important thing about my sport and it builds up over time. I've only had two and a half months back in so I can't expect too much.

"Shaw was a really strong opponent. The first and second I came out confidently and felt good, my fatigue started to get to me early in the third and by the fourth I was really tired."

■ RETURN: Jordan Jones (in red) back in the ring to take on Lewis Shaw, from Lympstone. Picture: Feb Tisdale. To order this photograph call 0844 4060 269 and quote Ref: BNRT2010060'7C-035_C

413

JIMMY ISAAC, RONNIE ISAAC, BARNSTAPLE ABC SPONSOR, DB.

JIMMY ISAAC, ROBBIE SQUIRES, RONNIE ISAAC.

MARK SIMPSON with ENGLISH CHAMPION ROBBIE SQUIRES.

Mark's dedication to BARNSTAPLE ABC for over 20 years has guaranteed the CLUB'S existence and brought it through many troubled times.

CONTINUED
IN
PART 2

Made in the USA
Charleston, SC
07 February 2017